RUDOLF STEINER

Leitsätze

Leading Thoughts

RUDOLF STEINER

Leitsätze
Leading Thoughts

Zweisprachige Ausgabe
Bilingual Edition

VERLAG DES ITA WEGMAN INSTITUTS
STEINERBOOKS
UNIVERS ENCICLOPEDIC

Herausgegeben vom
Ita Wegman Institut für
anthroposophische Grundlagenforschung/
Allgemeine Anthroposophische Sektion (Goetheanum)

Edited by the Ita Wegman Institute for Basic Research into Anthroposophy/General Anthroposophical Section of the School for Spiritual Science (Goetheanum)

Texte Rudolf Steiners gemäß GA 26 (Rudolf Steiner Verlag)
Text by Rudolf Steiner according to GA 26

Translation by George and Mary Adams
with revisions by Thomas O'Keefe

Gesamtgestaltung: Walter Schneider, www.schneiderdesign.net

Druck: Offizin Scheufele, Stuttgart

ISBN Verlag des Ita Wegman Instituts: 978-3-906947-89-1

ISBN SteinerBooks: 978-1-62148-383-0

ISBN Univers Enciclopedic: 978-606-096-520-6

Inhalt

Im Inhaltsverzeichnis und in den Überschriften des Buches beziehen sich die Daten in Klammern auf das Erstveröffentlichungsdatum der Texte in der Wochenschrift *Das Goetheanum*. Die Daten ohne Klammern wurden von Rudolf Steiner angegeben und beziehen sich auf sein Entstehungsdatum (und nicht auf das Erscheinungsdatum) (vgl. GA 26).

Contents

In the Table of Contents and in the running heads throughout this book, the dates in parentheses refer to the first date of publication of the texts in the weekly journal *Das Goetheanum*. Dates without parentheses were given by Rudolf Steiner and refer to his date of writing (and not to the date of publication) (cf. GA 26).

Vorwort

Erstmals werden in dieser Sonder-Ausgabe zum 100. Geburtstag der *Leitsätze* die Texte Rudolf Steiners zusammen mit einer englischen Übersetzung publiziert. Dabei folgen wir bei den deutschen Originaltexten der letzten Auflage der Gesamtausgabe (GA 26) , unter Beibehaltung der dort vorgenommenen fortlaufenden Nummerierung der *Leitsätze*, und haben uns für die englische Übersetzung von George und Mary Adams entschieden, die speziell für diese Neupublikation von Thomas O'Keefe überarbeitet worden ist. Aufgenommen wurde zusätzlich der Text Rudolf Steiners im «Nachrichtenblatt» vom 2. März 1924, der bisher nur in GA 260a und in der Ausgabe «Briefe an die Mitglieder» enthalten war, jedoch mit den *Leitsätzen* Nr. 6 und 7 in engem Zusammenhang steht.

Die *Leitsätze* erschienen ab dem 17. Februar 1924 im internen Nachrichtenblatt «Was in der Anthroposophischen Gesellschaft vorgeht»; sie standen, mit drei Sternchen (von Rudolf Steiner) abgegrenzt, jeweils am Ende seiner Aufsätze «An die Mitglieder!», die sich mit Fragen der Weiterentwicklung der Anthroposophischen Gesellschaft und der Anthroposophie-Rezeption nach der Weihnachtstagung beschäftigten oder auf Veranstaltungen zurückblickten. Anfänglich nur sehr

Foreword

In this special edition marking the centennial of the *Leading Thoughts*, Rudolf Steiner's texts are being published together with an English translation for the first time. We have followed the format of the German original texts in the latest edition of the collected works (GA 26) and have opted for the English translation by George and Mary Adams, which has been specially revised for this new publication by Thomas O'Keefe. We have also included Rudolf Steiner's text from the "Nachrichtenblatt" (Newsletter) of March 2, 1924, which was previously only included in the first section of GA 260a as well as in the German offprint *Briefe an die Mitglieder* ("Letters to the Members" – published in English under the title *The Life, Nature, and Cultivation of Anthroposophy*), but which is closely related to *Leading Thoughts* 6 and 7.

The *Leading Thoughts* appeared in the internal newsletter "What Is Happening in the Anthroposophical Society" from February 17, 1924 and on; they were marked with three asterisks (by Rudolf Steiner) at the end of his essays "To the Members!", which dealt with questions regarding the further development of the Anthroposophical Society and the reception of Anthroposophy after the Christmas Conference, or looked back upon events. Initially he only very rarely added the words

selten, ab Oktober 1924, in der Zeit seines Krankenlagers, regelmäßig führten seine Ausführungen «An die Mitglieder!» zu den *Leitsätzen* hin. Die Überschrift «Anthroposophische *Leitsätze* als Anregungen vom Goetheanum ausgegeben» bzw. «Weitere *Leitsätze*, die für die Anthroposophische Gesellschaft vom Goetheanum ausgesendet (oder: ‹ausgeben›) werden» stellte Rudolf Steiner bis zuletzt den *Leitsätzen* voran; bis zu seiner «Weihnachtsbetrachtung: Das Logos-Mysterium» beendete er seine Manuskripte, die in säuberlicher Handschrift mit nur wenigen Korrekturen verfasst wurden, mit dem Satz «Fortsetzung in nächster Nummer». Die Intentionen, die Rudolf Steiner mit der Niederschrift und der internen Publikation der *Leitsätze* verband, werden in der nachfolgenden Einleitung geschildert. Die Darstellung basiert auf den Ausführungen des siebten Bandes meiner Werkbiografie.[1]

Diese zweisprachige Sonderausgabe ist ein Projekt der Allgemeinen Anthroposophischen Sektion am Goetheanum. Zugutekommen soll sie der Anthroposophischen Gesellschaft in der Welt und ihren Arbeitsgruppen sowie allen Menschen, die sich mit der anthroposophischen Geisteswissenschaft befassen. Sergej O. Prokofieff (1954–2014) waren solche zweisprachigen

1 Vgl. Peter Selg: *Rudolf Steiner 1861 – 1925. Lebens- und Werkgeschichte. Band 7: Die Freie Hochschule für Geisteswissenschaft und das Lebensende 1924 – 1925*. Arlesheim 2017.

"To the Members!" above the *Leading Thoughts*, but from October 1924 and on, when he was ill, he did so regularly. The heading "Further *Leading Thoughts* issued by the Goetheanum for the Anthroposophical Society" preceded the *Leading Thoughts* until the very end; up until his "Christmas Consideration: The Mystery of the Logos," he concluded his manuscripts, which were written in neat handwriting with only a few corrections, with the sentence "To be continued in the next issue." The intentions that Rudolf Steiner had for the writing and internal publication of the *Leading Thoughts* are described in the following Introduction. The account is based on the information in the seventh volume of my work biography.[1]

This special bilingual edition is a project of the General Anthroposophical Section at the Goetheanum. It is intended to benefit the Anthroposophical Society in the world and its working groups, as well as all people involved in anthroposophical spiritual science. Sergei O. Prokofieff (1954 – 2014) was particularly interested in such bilingual editions of Rudolf

1 See Peter Selg: *Rudolf Steiner, Life and Work. Vol. 7 (1924 – 1925): The Anthroposophical Society and the School for Spiritual Science.* Great Barrington, MA: SteinerBooks, 2019.

Ausgaben von Schriftwerken Rudolf Steiners ein besonderes Anliegen, und wir besprachen noch in der letzten Zeit seines Lebens die besonderen Möglichkeiten, die mit ihnen verbunden sind: Eine präzise Parallelübersetzung ins Englische macht es für viele Leser möglich, Rudolf Steiner auch in seiner Originalsprache zu studieren und damit weniger abhängig von einer notwendigerweise interpretierenden Übersetzung zu sein.

Mein Dank für das Zustandekommen der Edition gilt in erster Linie *Thomas O'Keefe*, mit dem ich – zusammen mit *Constanza Kaliks*, *Andrea De la Cruz* und *Nicolas Criblez* (Allgemeine Anthroposophische Sektion) – das Vorhaben seit Langem bewegt habe und der die Durchsicht und behutsame Überarbeitung der Übersetzung von George und Mary Adams leistete. Sodann danke ich *Michael Davis*, der die Arbeit in ihrer Anfangsphase finanziell unterstützte und so den Beginn des Projekts ermöglichte, sowie *Robert McKay*, der Gelder für die Druckkosten sammelte. Weiter danke ich *Nana Badenberg*, die mir im Rudolf Steiner Archiv Dornach wie schon so oft in der Durchsicht der Textunterlagen behilflich war.

Allgemeine Anthroposophische Sektion — Peter Selg
Goetheanum. Dornach
Ita Wegman Institut, Arlesheim
November 2024

Steiner's writings, and during the last period of his life we discussed the special possibilities associated with them: A precise parallel translation into English makes it possible for many readers to also study Rudolf Steiner in his original language and thus to be less dependent on a necessarily interpretive translation.

My thanks for the realization of the edition go first and foremost to *Thomas O'Keefe*, with whom I – together with *Constanza Kaliks*, *Andrea De la Cruz*, and *Nicolas Criblez* (General Anthroposophical Section) – have been working on the project for a long time and who reviewed and carefully revised the translation by George and Mary Adams. I would also like to thank *Michael Davis*, who supported the work financially in its initial phase and thus made the start of the project possible, as well as *Robert McKay*, who gathered funds for the printing costs. I would also like to thank *Nana Badenberg*, who, as so often before, helped me in the Rudolf Steiner Archive in Dornach in reviewing the text documents.

General Anthroposophical Section Peter Selg
Goetheanum. Dornach
Ita Wegman Institute, Arlesheim
November 2024

Einleitung: Zur Entstehung und der Aufgabe der *Leitsätze* in ihrem Zusammenhang mit der Anthroposophischen Gesellschaft

(Peter Selg)

Seine sogenannten *Leitsätze* und die mit ihnen verbundenen Aufsätze schrieb Rudolf Steiner von Februar 1924 bis Ende März 1925, d.h. bis zu seinem Tod. Sie sind sein letztes, vermächtnishaftes schriftliches Werk und in gewisser Weise die Krönung seiner lebenslangen Bemühung, die neue anthroposophische Geisteswissenschaft unter Einschluss ihrer erkenntnismethodischen Fundierung ideell darzustellen.

Obwohl in ihnen die Kulmination seines schriftstellerischen Werkes, auch in der Präzision der Formulierungen, zu finden ist, verfasste Rudolf Steiner die *Leitsatz*-Betrachtungen nicht als Buch, sondern in Form von Aufsätzen für die Mitglieder der Anthroposophischen Gesellschaft. Sie wurden – jeweils mit dem Titel «An die Mitglieder!» – im sogenannten «Nachrichtenblatt», dem gesellschaftsinternen Teil der Wochenschrift «Das Goetheanum» publiziert und gehören zu dem grundlegenden Neuanfang und gesellschaftlichen Aufbruch, den Rudolf Steiner mit der Weihnachtstagung 1923/24 – und der Neubegrünung der Anthroposophischen Gesellschaft und

Introduction: On the Origin and Task of the *Leading Thoughts* in Their Relation to the Anthroposophical Society

(Peter Selg)

Rudolf Steiner wrote his so-called *Leading Thoughts* and the essays associated with them from February 1924 until the end of March 1925, that is, until his death. They constitute his final, legacy-like written work and, in a way, the culmination of his lifelong endeavor to present anthroposophical spiritual science, including its epistemological foundation.

Although they embody the culmination of his literary work, even down to the precision of the formulations, Rudolf Steiner did not write the *Leading Thought* considerations as a book but in the form of essays for the members of the Anthroposophical Society. They were published – each with the title "To the Members!" – in the so-called "Nachrichtenblatt," the Society's internal section of the weekly journal *Das Goetheanum*, and they constitute part of the fundamental new beginning and social awakening that Rudolf Steiner attempted with the Christmas Conference of 1923/24 and the re-founding of the Anthroposophical Society and its School of Spiritual

ihrer Freien Hochschule für Geisteswissenschaft – versuchte.[2] Er erwartete von den Mitgliedern der Gesellschaft von nun an «Fleiß», «Hingabe» und «Mut» zur «Führung der anthroposophischen Angelegenheiten»,[3] d.h. zu «kräftigem, heilkräftigem Wirken in der Welt».[4] Eine wirkliche «Gesinnungsgesellschaft»[5] sollte entstehen, deren Sein oder Nichtsein im Verständnis Steiners mit der Umsetzung (oder Nicht-Umsetzung) der Weihnachtstagungsintentionen unmittelbar verbunden war. Er setze «für die Gesellschaft gewissermaßen letzte Hoffnungen auf die Weihnachtszusammenkunft», schrieb er an Marie Steiner-von Sivers im Dezember 1923,[6] vor der Zusammenkunft, und sagte auf der Tagung selbst: «Nur wenn wir in dieser Art die anthroposophische Bewegung in uns selbst zu unserer tiefsten Herzensangelegenheit machen können, wird die Anthroposophische Gesellschaft bestehen. Wenn wir das

2 Vgl. Peter Selg: *Rudolf Steiner 1861 – 1925. Lebens- und Werkgeschichte. Band 7: Die Freie Hochschule für Geisteswissenschaft und das Lebensende 1924 – 1925*, S. 1803ff.

3 Rudolf Steiner: *Die Weltgeschichte in anthroposophischer Beleuchtung und als Grundlage der Erkenntnis des Menschengeistes*. GA 233. Dornach [5]1991, S. 157.

4 Ebd., S. 162.

5 Rudolf Steiner: *Die Weihnachtstagung zur Begründung der Allgemeinen Anthroposophischen Gesellschaft 1923/24*. GA 260. Dornach [5]1994, S. 48.

6 Rudolf Steiner/Marie Steiner-von Sivers: *Briefwechsel und Dokumente 1901 – 1925*. GA 262. Dornach [2]2002, S. 361.

Science.[2] From then on, he expected the members of the Society to show "hard work," "devotion," and "courage to carry on the affairs of Anthroposophy"[3] – that is, "to do work in the world that is strong in healing."[4] A true "Society of attitudes"[5] was to emerge, whose existence or non-existence, in Steiner's understanding, was directly linked to the implementation (or non-implementation) of the intentions of the Christmas Conference. In December 1923, before the meeting, he wrote to Marie Steiner-von Sivers that "in a certain sense my *last* hope for the Society lies in this Christmas meeting,"[6] and said at the meeting itself: "The Anthroposophical Society will endure only if within ourselves we make of the Anthroposophical Movement the profoundest concern of our hearts. If we

2 See Peter Selg: *Rudolf Steiner, Life and Work. Vol. 7 (1924 – 1925): The Anthroposophical Society and the School for Spiritual Science*; Ch. 11.

3 Rudolf Steiner: *The Christmas Conference for the Foundation of the General Anthroposophical Society 1923/1924*. GA 260. Hudson, NY: Anthroposophic Press, 1990 (reprinted 2020); lecture of January 1, 1924; p. 268.

4 Ibid., p. 273.

5 Ibid., "Rudolf Steiner's Opening Lecture and Reading of the Statutes" on December 24, 1923 at 11:15am; p. 57.

6 Rudolf Steiner and Marie Steiner von Sivers: *Correspondence and Documents, 1901–1925*. GA 262. London/New York: Rudolf Steiner Press/Anthroposophic Press, 1988; section II, p. 187.

nicht können, wird sie nicht bestehen.»[7] Aus dem spirituellen Grundstein der Anthroposophischen Gesellschaft sollte, so Steiner, «das Gebäude errichtet werden, dessen einzelne Steine sein werden die Arbeiten, die in allen unseren Gruppen nun von den Einzelnen draußen in der weiten Welt geleistet werden.»[8] Am Ende der Tagung und im Rückblick auf die Zerstörung des ersten Goetheanum-Baues sagte er:

> Und so möge denn unser Schmerz so gewendet werden, dass aus ihm eine kräftige, leuchtende Anthroposophische Gesellschaft durch Ihre Arbeit, meine lieben Freunde, entstehe.[9]

Für eine «kräftige, leuchtende»,[10] das heißt spirituell aktive und in der Zivilisation arbeitende Anthroposophische Gesellschaft setzte sich Rudolf Steiner noch einmal mit letzter Kraft ein – und auch die Sinnhaftigkeit (oder Sinnlosigkeit) eines

7 Rudolf Steiner: *Die Weihnachtstagung zur Begründung der Allgemeinen Anthroposophischen Gesellschaft 1923/24*. GA 260, S. 36.
8 Rudolf Steiner: *Die Weltgeschichte in anthroposophischer Beleuchtung und als Grundlage der Erkenntnis des Menschengeistes*. GA 233, S. 158.
9 Rudolf Steiner: *Die Weihnachtstagung zur Begründung der Allgemeinen Anthroposophischen Gesellschaft 1923/24*. GA 260, S. 281.
10 Ebd.

fail, the Society will not endure."[7] Upon the spiritual Foundation Stone of the Anthroposophical Society, said Steiner, "shall be erected the building whose individual stones will be the work achieved in all our groups by the individuals outside in the wide world."[8] At the end of the meeting and looking back on the destruction of the first Goetheanum building, he said:

> So let us transform our pain so that out of it may arise a strong and shining Anthroposophical Society by dint, my dear friends, of your work.[9]

With his last strength, Rudolf Steiner once again committed himself to a "strong and shining,"[10] i.e. spiritually active, Anthroposophical Society working in civilization – and the meaningfulness (or meaninglessness) of a possible second

7 Rudolf Steiner: *The Christmas Conference for the Foundation of the General Anthroposophical Society 1923/1924*. GA 260; proceedings of December 24, 1923, 11:15am; p. 46.
8 Ibid., lecture of January 1, 1924; p. 269.
9 Ibid., p. 270.
10 Ibid.

eventuellen zweiten Baus war für ihn mit dem Gelingen (oder Nicht-Gelingen) dieses Gesellschaftsprojektes, dieser gesellschaftlichen Herausforderung verbunden:

> Wenn das Goetheanum neu ersteht, so wird es nur dann eine Wahrheit sein, wenn die Anthroposophische Gesellschaft überall ein lebendiger Zeuge seiner Wahrheit wird sein wollen.[11]

Die Anthroposophische Gesellschaft sollte in Zukunft ein lebendiges Zeugnis von der Wahrheit des Goetheanum sein, sonst war alles vergeblich und sinnlos. Dafür aber, so machte Steiner deutlich, müsse ein «neues anthroposophisches Leben»[12] in die Anthroposophische Gesellschaft einziehen, in ihr geradezu entfacht werden. Aber wodurch?

Es ist bekannt, dass Rudolf Steiner die mehr als 12 000 Mitgliedskarten der neugegründeten Gesellschaft in den Monaten Januar bis März 1924 eigenhändig unterschrieb, durchschnittlich ca. 130 Karten am Tag. «Es ist eine menschliche Beziehung, allerdings zunächst winzigen Inhaltes, aber es ist eine menschliche Beziehung», sagte er,[13] die Notwendigkeit

11 Rudolf Steiner: *Die Konstitution der Allgemeinen Anthroposophischen Gesellschaft und der Freien Hochschule für Geisteswissenschaft. Der Wiederaufbau des Goetheanum.* GA 260a. Dornach [2]1987, S. 43.

12 Ebd.

13 Ebd., S. 383.

building was also, for him, linked with the success (or failure) of this social project, this social challenge:

> The Goetheanum, when rebuilt, will only be a thing of truth if the Anthroposophical Society everywhere will bear this living witness to its truth.[11]

The Anthroposophical Society was to be a living testimony to the truth of the Goetheanum in the future – otherwise, everything would be in vain and pointless. But in order for this to happen, Steiner clarified, a "new anthroposophical life"[12] would need to enter the Anthroposophical Society and be kindled within it. But by what means?

It is known that Rudolf Steiner personally signed the more than 12,000 membership cards of the newly founded Society in the months from January to March 1924 – on average, about 130 cards per day. "It is a human relationship, albeit initially one of modest content, but still it is a human relationship," he

11 Rudolf Steiner: *The Life, Nature, and Cultivation of Anthroposophy*. GA 260a. London: The Anthroposophical Society in Great Britain, 1963/1976; letter of January 27, 1924 ("To the Members – II: The Right Relationship of the Society to Anthroposophy"); p. 17.

12 Ibid., p. 18.

der persönlichen Unterschrift begründend, obwohl ihm der ganze Vorgang viel Zeit kostete. Er begab sich in diese Gesellschaft, übernahm in personam ihren Vorsitz – und er tat nach der Weihnachtstagung alles, den Mitgliedern die Wichtigkeit der Anthroposophischen Gesellschaft noch einmal nahezubringen, mithin ein Bewusstsein ihres Wesens zu ermöglichen.[14] Ab Mitte Februar 1924 begann er, seine Vorträge über das Karma der Anthroposophischen Bewegung und Gesellschaft zu halten; ab Juli 1924 erreichten diese Vorträge nach systematischer Vorbereitung ihr von Anfang an intendiertes Zentrum – und handelten von der Anthroposophischen Gesellschaft als einer michaelischen Schicksalsgemeinschaft. Es ging Rudolf Steiner um das «Erwachen am Seelisch-Geistigen des Anderen»[15] in der gemeinsamen Hinwendung zum Wesen «Anthroposophia»,[16] um das zu entwickelnde «Gefühl […] für das Leben der Anthroposophie in Menschenseelen»[17] und um ein Bewusstsein von der

14 Vgl. hierzu auch Peter Selg: *Die Weltgesellschaft und ihre Hochschule.* Dornach 2023.

15 Rudolf Steiner: *Anthroposophische Gemeinschaftsbildung (1923).* GA 257. Dornach [4]1989, S. 116.

16 Vgl. hierzu u. a. Sergej O. Prokofieff: *Die himmlische Sophia und das Wesen Anthroposophia.* Dornach 1995.

17 Rudolf Steiner: *Die Konstitution der Allgemeinen Anthroposophischen Gesellschaft und der Freien Hochschule für Geisteswissenschaft. Der Wiederaufbau des Goetheanum.* GA 260a, S. 119.

said,[13] justifying the necessity of the personal signature, although the whole process cost him a lot of time. He went to this Society, took over its presidency in person – and after the Christmas Conference he did everything he could to make the members aware of the importance of the Anthroposophical Society once again, i.e. to enable an awareness of its being.[14] From mid-February 1924, he began to give his lectures on the karma of the Anthroposophical Movement and Society; from July 1924, after systematic preparation, these lectures reached the core theme that was intended from the beginning: dealing with the Anthroposophical Society as a Michaelic destiny-community. Rudolf Steiner was concerned with the process of "awakening in the encounter with the soul-spiritual element of our fellow human beings"[15] in the common turning toward the being of "Anthroposophia,"[16] with developing a "feeling

13 Rudolf Steiner: *Die Konstitution der Allgemeinen Anthroposophischen Gesellschaft und der Freien Hochschule für Geisteswissenschaft* [The Constitution of the Anthroposophical Society and the School of Spiritual Science]. GA 260a. Dornach 1987; elaborations of September 5, 1924; p. 383 (not available in English).

14 On this theme, see also Peter Selg: *The Anthroposophical World Society and Its School for Spiritual Science*. Hudson, NY: SteinerBooks, 2024.

15 Rudolf Steiner: *Awakening to Community*. GA 257. Spring Valley, NY: Anthroposophic Press, 1975; lecture of February 27, 1923; p. 97.

16 On this theme, see, among others, Sergei O. Prokofieff: *The Heavenly Sophia and the Being Anthroposophia.* Forest Row, UK: Temple Lodge, 2006.

Bedeutung dieses «Lebens» in menschheitlicher Dimension – «dass es uns gelingen möge, zusammenzuarbeiten, zusammenzuarbeiten so, dass wir fühlen: Was jeder Einzelne getan hat in der Arbeit, ist getan für ein großes Ganzes, das geistig die Menschheit tragen soll».[18]

Bereits knapp zwei Wochen nach dem Ende der Weihnachtstagung, am 13. Januar 1924, erschien erstmals das interne Nachrichtenblatt «Was in der anthroposophischen Gesellschaft vorgeht» mit Rudolf Steiners Aufsatz: «Die Bildung der Allgemeinen Anthroposophischen Gesellschaft durch die Weihnachtstagung 1923». Jede der folgenden Nummern dieser Beilage der Wochenschrift begann Rudolf Steiner dann mit einem Aufsatz «An die Mitglieder!», in dem er sich zu prinzipiellen Fragen und Zielen der Gesellschaft äußerte, aber auch über die von ihm unternommenen Aktivitäten und gehaltenen Kurse informierte. Er betonte, dass es darum gehe, «die gesamte Mitgliedschaft zu einem gemeinsamen Bewusstsein von dem Wesen der Anthroposophischen Gesellschaft zu erheben»:

18 Ebd., S. 493.

[...] for the life of Anthroposophy in human souls"[17] and with an awareness of the significance of this "life" in a human dimension – "that we may succeed in working together, working together in such a way that we feel: What each individual has done in the work is done for a great whole that is to carry humanity spiritually."[18]

Just two weeks after the end of the Christmas Conference, on January 13, 1924, the internal newsletter "What Is Happening in the Anthroposophical Society" appeared for the first time with Rudolf Steiner's essay: "The Foundation of the General Anthroposophical Society at the Christmas Conference of 1923." Rudolf Steiner then began each of the following issues of this supplement to the weekly journal with an essay entitled "To the Members!", in which he commented on fundamental questions and aims of the Society, but also provided information about the activities he had undertaken and the courses he had held. He emphasized that the aim was to "raise the entire membership to a common awareness of the nature of the Anthroposophical Society":

17 Rudolf Steiner: *The Constitution of the School of Spiritual Science*. GA 260a. London: The Anthroposophical Society in Great Britain, 1964/1980; lecture of January 30, 1924; p. 30.

18 Rudolf Steiner: *Die Konstitution* (op. cit.). GA 260a; lecture of May 25, 1924 in Paris; p. 493 (not available in English).

> Es muss in der Zukunft ein einheitlicher Geist, ein realer einheitlicher Geist in die ganze anthroposophische Bewegung hineinkommen.[19]

Die «Isoliertheit» der einzelnen Arbeitsgruppen müsse überwunden werden – und zwar durch eine gezielte, gemeinschaftliche Aktivität; die Anthroposophische Gesellschaft sollte endlich zu einem «lebendig-geistigen Organismus» werden,[20] ein Organismus von Menschen, die zusammen ein «gemeinsames Geistesziel» verfolgen.[21] Worin dieses «Geistesziel» – im großen Zusammenhang der «Michael-Bewegung» – bestand, beschrieb Rudolf Steiner in den Karma-Vorträgen ab Juli 1924 vor einem weltgeschichtlichen Horizont.

In seinen – unter dem Titel «Briefe an die Mitglieder» – in der GA im Rahmen des Bandes 260a, aber auch in einer Sonderausgabe erschienenen Texten hob Steiner nach der Weihnachtstagung immer wieder die Bedeutung einer Bemühung um den geistigen Kern der Anthroposophie für die Neuausrichtung der Anthroposophischen Gesellschaft hervor. Wenn es die Aufgabe der Anthroposophischen Gesellschaft ist, die

19 Ebd., S. 323.
20 Ebd., S. 173.
21 Ebd., S. 119.

> In the future, a unified spirit, a real unified spirit must enter the whole Anthroposophical Movement.[19]

The "isolation" of the individual working groups had to be overcome – through a focused communal activity; the Anthroposophical Society should finally become a "living spiritual organism,"[20] an organism of human beings who together pursue a "common spiritual aim."[21] In the Karma Lectures from July 1924 and on, Rudolf Steiner described what this "spiritual aim" consists of – in the larger context of the "Michael Movement" – against a world-historical horizon.

In his texts published under the title "Letters to the Members" – contained in the Collected Works as part of volume 260a but also gathered in a special offprint after the Christmas Conference (in English: *The Life, Nature, and Cultivation of Anthroposophy*) – Steiner repeatedly emphasized the importance of striving for the spiritual core of Anthroposophy in

19 Ibid., elaborations of June 22, 1924 in Dornach; p. 323.

20 Ibid., elaborations of January 28, 1924 in Zurich; p. 173.

21 Rudolf Steiner: *The Constitution of the School of Spiritual Science*. GA 260a; lecture of January 30, 1924; p. 29f.

moderne Geisteswissenschaft «suchenden Seelen» auffindbar werden zu lassen, so muss diese Gesellschaft zuallererst «als Gesellschaft selbst das rechte Verhältnis zur Anthroposophie finden».[22] Das war nach Steiners mehr als zwei Jahrzehnte langem Wirken für einen intensiven und effektiven Sozialorganismus noch immer nicht der Fall. Die Weihnachtstagung und die mit ihr verbundene Neugründung der Gesellschaft sollten die Wende herbeiführen. Die neue Gesellschaft sollte Anthroposophie in sich «lebendig» machen – und das Leben der Anthroposophie suchenden Seelen zugänglich machen, entgegen der Gefahr einer «Gewöhnung» an das Vorhandensein der Anthroposophie. Ein neues Erwachen für die Spiritualität der anthroposophischen Geisteswissenschaft und ihre weltgeschichtliche Aufgabe tat Not; im März 1924 sagte Rudolf Steiner in geradezu persönlicher Wendung:

> Ich möchte schon sagen: Es fielen mir mehrere Steine vom Herzen, wenn ich die Gewissheit erringen könnte, dass bei einer genügend großen Anzahl von Mitgliedern dieses Bewusstsein bestünde, wie wichtig im allgemeinen geistigen Kulturgange heute Anthroposophie ist, und

22 Ebd., S. 41.

order to enable the reorientation of the Anthroposophical Society. If it is the task of the Anthroposophical Society to make modern spiritual science accessible to "searching souls," then it is of the highest priority that this Society must "itself, as a Society, find its true relationship to Anthroposophy."[22] After more than two decades of Steiner's work for an intensive and effective social organism, this was still not the case. The Christmas Conference and the re-founding of the Society associated with it were intended to bring about the turning point. The new Society was to make Anthroposophy "alive" within itself – and make the life of Anthroposophy accessible to the souls seeking it, thereby countering the risk of becoming "habituated" to the existence of Anthroposophy. A new awakening to the spirituality of anthroposophical spiritual science and its world-historical task was needed; in March 1924, Rudolf Steiner said, in an almost personal turn:

> I would like to say that several stones would fall from my heart if I could gain the certainty that a sufficiently large number of members are aware of how important Anthroposophy is today in the general spiritual-cultural process –

22 Rudolf Steiner: *The Life, Nature, and Cultivation of Anthroposophy.* GA 260a; letter of January 27, 1924 ("To the Members – II: The Right Relationship of the Society to Anthroposophy"); p. 15.

> wenn dieses Bewusstsein nur in der Intensität bestände, im guten Sinne, im zustimmenden Sinne, wie es bei den Gegnern im Anti-Sinne, sagen wir, besteht. Das ist wirklich etwas, was dringend zu wünschen wäre.[23]

Mit diesem «Bewusstsein» von der Bedeutung der Anthroposophie aber war die Kenntnis ihrer Inhalte notwendig verbunden, ihre Kenntnis und Verinnerlichung. Der «esoterische Impuls» der Weihnachtstagung bestand keineswegs nur in Mantren, sondern in einer neuen oder anderen Art, mit der Anthroposophie und ihren Inhalten umzugehen, nicht im Sinne eines gelehrten Wissens, sondern vielmehr existenziell, unter Beteiligung des Herzens, dem Organ des «Grundsteins» und des «wahren Ichs». «Esoterik beruht auf dem [...] Verinnerlichen in der Mitteilung von Wahrheiten. Man sollte in dieser Verinnerlichung etwas von dem Impuls sehen, den die Weihnachtstagung in die Anthroposophische Gesellschaft hat bringen wollen.»[24] Anthroposophie, so betonte Rudolf Steiner in seinen Aufsätzen, wurde nicht nur als ein «geisteswissenschaftliches Erkenntnissystem» begründet, sondern sollte von Anfang an «etwas Lebendiges in den Herzen vieler

23 Ebd., S. 446. 24 Ebd., S. 74f.

> and if this awareness would only exist to the same degree of intensity in the good sense, in the approving sense, as it exists among the opponents in the anti-sense, let us say. That is really something that would be urgently desirable.[23]

However, this "awareness" of the importance of Anthroposophy was necessarily linked to knowledge of its content, to understanding and internalizing it. The "esoteric impulse" of the Christmas Conference consisted not only in mantras, but in a new or different way of dealing with Anthroposophy and its content – not in the sense of learned knowledge, but rather existentially, involving the heart, the organ of the "Foundation Stone" and the "true self." "Esotericism depends on [...] deepening in the communication of truths; in this deepening, one should see something of the impulse that the Christmas Conference wanted to bring into the Anthroposophical Society."[24] Anthroposophy, Rudolf Steiner emphasized in his essays, was not only founded as a "spiritual-scientific system of

23 Rudolf Steiner: *Die Konstitution* (op. cit.). GA 260a; proceedings of March 14, 1924 in Dornach; p. 446 (not available in English).
24 Rudolf Steiner: *The Life, Nature, and Cultivation of Anthroposophy*. GA 260a; letter of May 25, 1924 ("To the Members – XIV: What Is the Tone Which Should Prevail in the Group Meetings?"), p. 49.

Menschen» sein.[25] Anthroposophie berge in sich Leben, «aus dem Geiste fließendes Leben»; ihr «Grundzug» sei geradezu «Leben».[26] Sie trete «unter Menschen» in der «Urform» der «Idee» auf – «und das erste Tor, an das sie sich bei Menschen wendet, ist die Einsicht».[27] Das ihr eigene Leben aber muss immer wieder neu aus und an ihr entfacht werden, d. h., es muss im Einzelnen und in der Gemeinschaft in der Beschäftigung mit den geisteswissenschaftlichen Inhalten neu erstehen. Anthroposophie ist keine «Sache für Bibliotheken» – und auch die von ihr handelnden Bücher müssen «im Lesen lebendig werden».[28] Rudolf Steiner sprach nach der Weihnachtstagung von der Entstellung, ja, sogar von der «Tötung» der Anthroposophie durch ihre rein intellektuelle Aufnahme, ohne Beteiligung des menschlichen Herzens, und beschrieb, was stattdessen Not tut: die «Ehrfurcht vor dem geistigen Leben» und der «Grundton der Liebe» im Umgang mit der Anthroposophie als einem lebendigen Wesen. «Diesen Ton hört die Menschenseele aus dem Gesprochenen mit feiner Empfindlichkeit heraus. Und er bildet im höchsten Grade einen Vermittler des Verständnisses.»[29] Nur so könne die Anthroposophie in ihrer Gesellschaft und – von dieser Gesellschaft ausstrahlend – in der Öffentlichkeit leben, denn: «Wo

25 Ebd., S. 39. 26 Ebd., S. 41. 27 Ebd. 28 Ebd.
29 Ebd., S. 62.

knowledge," but was intended from the beginning to be "a thing of life in many human hearts."[25] Anthroposophy contained life within it, "life flowing from the spirit"; its "fundamental character" is "life."[26] It appeared "among human beings" in the "basic form" of the "idea" – "and the first door at which it knocks is that of insight."[27] But its own life must always be kindled anew from and in it – i.e., it must arise anew in the individual and in the community through engagement with the content of spiritual science. Anthroposophy is not, in its nature, "of the library shelf" – and the books dealing with it must "come to life in the human being as he reads."[28] After the Christmas Conference, Rudolf Steiner spoke of the distortion, even the "killing" of Anthroposophy through its purely intellectual reception without the involvement of the human heart, and described what was needed instead: "reverence for the spiritual life" and the "fundamental tone of human love" in dealing with Anthroposophy as a living being. "The human soul has a fine sensitivity in being able to perceive this tone in what is spoken; and this in the very highest degree becomes a medium of understanding."[29] Only in this

25 Ibid., letter of January 20, 1924 ("To the Members – I"), p. 12.

26 Ibid., letter of January 27, 1924 ("To the Members – II: The Right Relationship of the Society to Anthroposophy"), p. 15.

27 Ibid. 28 Ibid., p. 16.

29 Ibid., letter of March 16, 1924 ("To the Members – IX: Individual Formulation of Anthroposophical Truths"), p. 37.

diese Ehrfurcht fehlt, da ist in dem Besprechen anthroposophischer Wahrheiten keine Kraft.»[30]

Im Januar 1924 begann Rudolf Steiner in Dornach einen Vortragskurs, den er als «eine Art von Einführung in die Anthroposophie selbst» bezeichnete – und der zugleich eine Anleitung dazu bilden sollte, «wie man Anthroposophie vor der Welt heute vertreten kann».[31] Er wollte die Anthroposophie aus ihren «Fundamenten» entwickeln und zeigen, wie von nun an «der Ton sein soll in der Anthroposophie».[32] Auch machte er einmal mehr deutlich, wie zeitgemäß die Anthroposophie ist, welche intensiven Fragen in den Seelen der Menschen der Gegenwart leben – Fragen, die nach dem Wesen des Menschen und seiner geistigen Heimat gerichtet sind, ohne jedoch eine Antwort zu finden:

30 Ebd., S. 63. 31 Ebd., S. 169. 32 Ebd., S. 596.

way can Anthroposophy live in its Society and – radiating from this Society – live in public, for: "Where such reverence is absent, there is no power in the discussion of anthroposophical truths."[30]

In January 1924, Rudolf Steiner began a lecture course in Dornach which he described as "a kind of introduction to Anthroposophy itself" – and which was at the same time intended as a guide to "how one can represent Anthroposophy in the world today."[31] He wanted to develop Anthroposophy from its "foundations" and show the way in which, from now on, "the tone should be when it comes to Anthroposophy."[32] He also made it clear once again how contemporary Anthroposophy is, what intense questions live in the souls of human beings today – questions that are directed toward the essential nature of the human being and his spiritual home but without finding an answer:

30 Ibid., letter of March 23, 1924 ("To the Members – X: On How to Present Anthroposophical Truths"), p. 37.

31 Rudolf Steiner: *Die Konstitution* (op. cit.). GA 260a; p. 169 (not available in English).

32 Rudolf Steiner: *Anthroposophy and the Inner Life: An Esoteric Introduction* (previously published under the title *Anthroposophy: An Introduction*). GA 234. Forest Row, UK: Rudolf Steiner Press, 2013; lecture of January 27, 1924; p. 51.

Man sieht, dass die Menschen heute in ihrem Unterbewusstsein schwere Fragen haben, Fragen, die nicht einmal in klare Gedanken gebracht werden können, geschweige denn durch dasjenige, was in der zivilisierten Welt vorhanden ist, eine Antwort finden können. Aber vorhanden sind diese Fragen. Und sie sind tief vorhanden bei einer großen Anzahl von Menschen. Sie sind eigentlich vorhanden bei allen wirklich denkenden Menschen der Gegenwart. [...] Die bange, die große Zweifelsfrage steht [vor dem Menschen in der Gegenwart] da: Wo ist die Welt, der ich angehöre? – Und je mehr die menschliche Zivilisation vorgeschritten ist, je mehr die Menschen intensiv denken gelernt haben, desto mehr ist diese Frage eine bange Frage geworden. Und sie sitzt heute in den Tiefen der Gemüter. Die Menschen teilen sich, insofern sie der zivilisierten Welt angehören, eigentlich nur in zwei Klassen in Bezug auf diese Frage. Die einen drängen sie hinunter, würgen sie hinunter, bringen sie sich nicht zur Klarheit, aber leiden darunter als unter einer furchtbaren Sehnsucht, dieses Menschenrätsel zu lösen; die anderen betäuben sich gegenüber

In their subconscious life, the men and women of today harbor earnest questions. They cannot even express these in clear thoughts, much less find answers in what the civilized world can offer; but these questions are there, and a large number of people feel them deeply. In fact, these questions are present today in all who really think. [...] The great riddle, the anxious doubt confronts [the human being of the present]: Where is the world to which I belong? The more human civilization has advanced and people have learned to think intensively, the more anxiously have they felt this question. It is deep-seated in human hearts today, and divides the civilized world into two classes. There are those who repress this question, smother it, do not bring it to clarity within themselves. But they suffer from it nevertheless, as from a terrible longing to solve this riddle of the human being. Others deaden themselves in face of this question, numbing themselves with all sorts of things in outer life. But in so deadening themselves, they kill within themselves the secure feeling of their own being. Emptiness comes over

> dieser Frage, reden sich allerlei Dinge aus dem äußeren Dasein vor, um sich zu betäuben. Und indem sie sich betäuben, tilgen sie in sich selber das feste Gefühl des eigenen Seins aus. Nichtigkeit befällt ihre Seele. Und dieses Gefühl der Nichtigkeit sitzt heute im Unterbewussten unzähliger Menschen.[33]

Die anthroposophische Menschen- und Welterkenntnis eröffne jedoch, so Rudolf Steiner weiter, einen methodischen Schulungs- und Erkenntnisweg, und auf diesem Weg konkrete Perspektiven zur Beantwortung der Frage nach dem wahren Wesen des Menschen; sie, die Anthroposophie, habe «durch die Stimme des menschlichen Herzens» eine «gewaltige Aufgabe» in der Gegenwart, ja, sie sei in sich selbst «nichts anderes als Menschensehnsucht der Gegenwart».[34] Dadurch aber konfiguriere sich die Aufgabenstellung der Anthroposophischen Gesellschaft: durch ein wirkliches Leben mit der anthroposophischen Geisteswissenschaft und ihren Ideenbildungen die Anthroposophie zugänglich zu machen, in ihrer ganzen Bedeutung. «Die Anthroposophische Gesellschaft muss den Weg

33 Rudolf Steiner: *Anthroposophie – Eine Zusammenfassung nach einundzwanzig Jahren. Zugleich eine Anleitung zu ihrer Vertretung vor der Welt.* GA 234. Dornach [7]2009, S. 17f.

34 Ebd., S. 25f.

> their souls. This feeling of emptiness is present in the subconsciousness of countless human beings today.[33]

According to Rudolf Steiner, however, anthroposophical knowledge of the human being and the world opens up a methodical path of training and knowledge – and, on this path, opens concrete perspectives for answering the question of the true nature of the human being. Anthroposophy, "from the voice of the human heart itself," receives its "mighty task" in the present; indeed, it is in itself "nothing other than what humanity is longing for today."[34] This, however, configures the task of the Anthroposophical Society: to make Anthroposophy accessible in all its significance through a real life with anthroposophical spiritual science and its formation of ideas. "The Anthroposophical Society [. . .] must find the way to let the hearts of human beings speak from out of their deepest longings."[35] In January 1924, Rudolf Steiner wrote in the "Nachrichtenblatt":

33 Ibid., lecture of January 19, 1924; pp. 14 – 18.

34 Ibid., p. 25. 35 Ibid.

finden, die Herzen der Menschen aus ihren tiefsten Sehnsuchten heraus sprechen zu lassen.»[35] Im Januar 1924 schrieb Rudolf Steiner im Nachrichtenblatt:

> Wir leben ja heute in einer Zeit, in der im Grunde genommen Anthroposophie dann für unzählige Menschen auf der Erde eine brennende Frage werden müsste, wenn einmal es der Anthroposophischen Gesellschaft gelänge, wirklich so zu arbeiten, dass die Bedürfnisse der Menschen an dem, was ihnen als Anthroposophie entgegentritt, Feuer fangen könnten.[36]

Um dieses bewirken und so «arbeiten» zu können, aber müsse, so führte Rudolf Steiner aus, die Anthroposophische Gesellschaft das zuvor genannte «rechte Verhältnis zur Anthroposophie» finden. Viele von Rudolf Steiners Texten des Nachrichtenblatts, die später unter dem Titel «Briefe an die Mitglieder!» herausgegeben wurden, handeln von den inneren Wegen zu diesem «rechten Verhältnis», der einführende Kurs im Januar 1924 dagegen von den anthroposophischen

35 Ebd.

36 Rudolf Steiner: *Die Konstitution der Allgemeinen Anthroposophischen Gesellschaft und der Freien Hochschule für Geisteswissenschaft. Der Wiederaufbau des Goetheanum.* GA 260a, S. 104.

> We are living in a time when Anthroposophy would become a burning question for countless human beings on the earth – if only the Anthroposophical Society succeeded in working in such a way that people's real needs could "catch fire" by what is presented to them as Anthroposophy.[36]

In order to achieve this and to be able to "work" in this way, however, Rudolf Steiner explained that the Anthroposophical Society had to find the aforementioned "right relationship to Anthroposophy." Many of Rudolf Steiner's texts in the "Nachrichtenblatt," which were later published under the title "Letters to the Members!" (*The Life, Nature, and Cultivation of Anthroposophy*), deal with the inner paths to this "right relationship," while the introductory course in January 1924 deals with the anthroposophical content

36 Rudolf Steiner: *The Constitution of the School of Spiritual Science.* GA 260a; lecture of January 18, 1924; p. 14.

Inhalten selbst, vom neuen Menschen- und Kosmosverständnis.

Den letzten Gesichtspunkt griffen auch jene *Leitsätze* und *Leitsatz*-Aufsätze auf, die Rudolf Steiner im internen Nachrichtenblatt der Wochenschrift ab der zweiten Februarhälfte 1924 erscheinen ließ. Im Paragraph 2 der Weihnachtstagungsstatuten hatte er formuliert:

> Den Grundstock dieser Gesellschaft bilden die in der Weihnachtszeit 1923 am Goetheanum in Dornach versammelten Persönlichkeiten, sowohl die Einzelnen wie auch die Gruppen, die sich vertreten ließen. Sie sind von der Anschauung durchdrungen, dass es gegenwärtig eine wirkliche Wissenschaft von der geistigen Welt schon gibt und dass der heutigen Zivilisation die Pflege einer solchen Wissenschaft fehlt. Die Anthroposophische Gesellschaft soll diese Pflege zu ihrer Aufgabe haben.[37]

37 Ebd., S. 30.

itself, with the new understanding of humanity and the cosmos.

The latter point of view was also taken up in the *Leading Thoughts* and essays that Rudolf Steiner published in the internal newsletter of the weekly journal from the second half of February 1924. In paragraph 2 of the Christmas Conference statutes, he had formulated:

> The persons gathered at the Goetheanum in Dornach at Christmas 1923, both the individuals and the groups represented, form the nucleus of the Society. They are convinced that there exists in our time a genuine science of the spiritual world and that the civilization of today is lacking the cultivation of such a science. This cultivation is to be the task of the Anthroposophical Society.[37]

37 Rudolf Steiner: *The Christmas Conference for the Foundation of the General Anthroposophical Society 1923/1924*. GA 260; proceedings of December 24, 1923, 11:15am; p. 57.

Nach einem Ergänzungswunsch von Seiten Carl Ungers war dieser Paragraph am 27. Dezember 1923 mit leicht verändertem Wortlaut von der Versammlung verabschiedet worden: «Sie [die Mitglieder der Anthroposophischen Gesellschaft] sind von der Anschauung durchdrungen, dass es gegenwärtig eine wirkliche, seit Jahren erarbeitete und in wichtigen Teilen veröffentlichte Wissenschaft von der geistigen Welt schon gibt.»[38]

Eine Wegleitung durch die «in wichtigen Teilen [bereits] veröffentlichte Wissenschaft» der Anthroposophie sollten die *Leitsätze* und die ihnen vorausgehenden Betrachtungen nunmehr eröffnen. «Es geht nicht an, dass viele Mitglieder, die jahrelang in der Gesellschaft sind, in den Zweigversammlungen nichts zu hören bekommen über Dinge, von denen bestimmte Erkenntnisse in der vorhandenen Literatur vorliegen», schrieb Rudolf Steiner nunmehr sehr deutlich,[39] und unterstrich, dass es für die Anthroposophische Gesellschaft darum gehe, «die vorhandene Literatur allmählich wirklich zum geistigen Eigentum der Mitgliedschaft zu machen».[40] «Ich habe vor, in der Zukunft in jeder Nummer [des

38 Rudolf Steiner: *Die Weihnachtstagung zur Begründung der Allgemeinen Anthroposophischen Gesellschaft 1923/24.* GA 260, S. 118/120.

39 Rudolf Steiner: *Die Konstitution der Allgemeinen Anthroposophischen Gesellschaft und der Freien Hochschule für Geisteswissenschaft. Der Wiederaufbau des Goetheanum.* GA 260a, S. 68.

40 Ebd.

Following a request for an addition from Carl Unger, this paragraph was adopted by the assembly on December 27, 1923 with slightly different wording: "They [the members of the Anthroposophical Society] are convinced that there exists in our time a genuine science of the spiritual world elaborated for years past, and in important particulars already published."[38]

The *Leading Thoughts* and the considerations that preceded them were now intended to provide guidance through the "science" of Anthroposophy that, "in important particulars," has "already [been] published." "It is not right that many members who have been for years in the Society hear nothing in the branch meetings of matters concerning which definite knowledge has been given in the literature," Rudolf Steiner now wrote very clearly,[39] and emphasized that the Anthroposophical Society was concerned with "gradually making the anthroposophical literature the spiritual property of all the members."[40] "Going forward, I intend to include short aphorisms in each issue [of the Newsletter] that briefly summarize important aspects of life, so that such

38 Ibid., proceedings of December 27, 1923, 10am; pp. 122/124.

39 Rudolf Steiner: *The Life, Nature, and Cultivation of Anthroposophy.* GA 260a; letter of April 6, 1924 ("To the Members – XII: Concerning Group Meetings"); p. 42f.

40 Ibid., p. 42.

Nachrichtenblattes] kleine, kurze Aphorismen zu bringen, welche wichtige Lebensinhalte kurz zusammenfassen, sodass man solche Aphorismen wird verwenden können in den Zweigen oder bei anderen Gelegenheiten», führte Steiner noch vor der Publikation seiner ersten *Leitsätze* in einem Zürcher Vortrag aus.[41] Allerdings ging es ihm nicht nur um seine in der Vergangenheit gehaltenen und in Schriftform vorliegenden anthroposophischen Kurse sowie um seine Bücher und die in ihnen veröffentlichten Forschungsergebnisse, sondern auch um seine aktuellen Arbeiten und Darstellungen. Das «lebendige Wirken des Goetheanum» und damit auch die laufenden geisteswissenschaftlichen Lehrkurse sollten mit Hilfe der *Leitsatz*-Betrachtungen den weiter entfernt wohnenden Mitgliedern der Allgemeinen Anthroposophischen Gesellschaft zugänglich werden, um das Goetheanum zu jenem «Mittelpunkt» der anthroposophischen Arbeit und spirituellen Gemeinschaft werden zu lassen, von dem in der Weihnachtstagung die Rede war. «Es wäre ja gewiss wünschenswerter, wenn jede Woche sogleich die Vorträge, die in Dornach gehalten werden, in allen Richtungen an die einzelnen Zweige gebracht werden könnten», schrieb Steiner;[42] da dies aber nicht geschah, wollte er die Zusammenfassung seiner wichtigsten Aussagen mit den *Leitsätzen* kommunizieren,

41 Ebd., S. 174. 42 Ebd., S. 84.

aphorisms can be used in the branches or on other occasions," Steiner explained in a lecture in Zurich even before the publication of his first *Leading Thoughts*.[41] However, he was not only concerned with the anthroposophical courses he had given in the past and which were available in written form, nor with his books and the research results published in them, but also with his current work and presentations. The "living work of the Goetheanum," and thus also the ongoing spiritual-scientific courses, were to be made accessible to the more distant members of the General Anthroposophical Society with the help of the *Leading Thought* considerations, in order to make the Goetheanum into the "center" of anthroposophical work and spiritual community that was described at the Christmas Conference. "It would without doubt be more desirable for the lectures given in Dornach to be carried at once in all directions to the individual branches," Steiner wrote;[42] but since this was not possible, he wanted to communicate a summary of his most important statements by means of the *Leading Thoughts* in a systematic-

41 Rudolf Steiner: *Die Konstitution* (op. cit.). GA 260a; elaborations of January 28, 1924 in Zurich; p. 174 (not available in English).

42 Rudolf Steiner: *The Life, Nature, and Cultivation of Anthroposophy*. GA 260a; letter of August 10, 1924 ("To the Members – XVIII: How the Leading Thoughts Are to Be Used"); p. 59. (Also printed in the present volume: *Anthroposophical Leading Thoughts*, GA 26.)

in einem systematisch-methodischem Aufbau, d. h. in der Integration in ein großes Ganzes. Auf diese Weise sollte es den Arbeitsgruppen der Anthroposophischen Gesellschaft in Zukunft möglich sein, mit Hilfe der *Leitsätze* die Themen anzuschlagen, die in den Treffen behandelt und vertieft werden konnten – in freier Anknüpfung an die *Leitsätze* und unter Berücksichtigung der vorhandenen «anthroposophischen Bücher- und Zyklenliteratur», in deren «Zusammenlesen», d. h. im synoptischen Einbezug der bereits vorhandenen Darstellungen zu einem gewissen Themenzusammenhang. In Stuttgarter Lehrerkonferenzen und in einer Zusammenkunft mit jungen Ärzten sagte Rudolf Steiner: «Für den Menschen finden Sie fast alles irgendwie in meinen Zyklen zerstreut. Es ist fast alles irgendwo gesagt.»[43] «Und heute liegt schon die Möglichkeit vor, dass dasjenige, was in einer kurzen Skizze angedeutet ist, durch viele Einzelheiten, die in Zyklen und Schriften von mir vorliegen, ausgebaut werde. Das ist nur zum geringsten Teil bis jetzt geschehen ...»[44]

Beginnen sollte nun in der Arbeitsgemeinschaft der neu gegründeten Anthroposophischen Gesellschaft der Prozess

43 Rudolf Steiner: *Konferenzen mit den Lehrern der Freien Waldorfschule 1919 – 1921.* GA 300a. Dornach [1]1975, S. 106.

44 Rudolf Steiner: *Meditative Betrachtungen und Anleitungen zur Vertiefung der Heilkunst. Vorträge für Ärzte und Medizinstudierende.* GA 316. Dornach [5]2009, S. 58.

methodical structure, i.e. by integrating them into a large whole. In this way, it should be possible in the future for the working groups of the Anthroposophical Society to be empowered with the help of the *Leading Thoughts* to address the topics that could be dealt with and deepened in the meetings – and to do so in free connection with the *Leading Thoughts* and taking into account the existing "anthroposophical books and lecture-cycle literature" in their "reading together," i.e. in the synoptic inclusion of the already existing presentations on a given thematic context. In the Stuttgart teachers' conferences and in a meeting with young doctors, Rudolf Steiner said: "Concerning human beings, you will find nearly everything somewhere in my lecture cycles. Almost everything is said somewhere."[43] "It is possible to expand what has been briefly outlined here by means of the numerous details that can be found in my lecture-cycles and writings. Not much has yet been done to that effect ..."[44]

The working community of the newly founded

43 Rudolf Steiner: *Faculty Meetings with Rudolf Steiner, 1919 – 1922, Vol. 1*. GA 300a. Hudson, NY: Anthroposophic Press, 1998; discussion of September 26, 1919.

44 Rudolf Steiner: *Understanding Healing: Meditative Reflections on Deepening Medicine through Spiritual Science* (previously published under the title *Course for Young Doctors*). GA 316. Forest Row, UK: Rudolf Steiner Press, 2013; lecture of January 5, 1924.

einer Aufarbeitung der gesamten Anthroposophie, ohne die die Gesellschaft und ihre «Freie Hochschule für Geisteswissenschaft», so Steiner, kein Fundament, keine Arbeitsgrundlagen und keine Daseinsberechtigung haben. Die Anthroposophie sollte zum «geistigen Eigentum» der Mitglieder werden, allerdings nicht als Kopfwissen, sondern durchdacht, «durchfühlt» und in den Willen aufgenommen. Dadurch würde, so Rudolf Steiner, die Anthroposophische Gesellschaft zu einer esoterischen Gemeinschaft werden können:

> Man sollte nicht glauben: Den Inhalt der Vorträge höre ich an; die Erkenntnis der geistigen Welt eigne ich mir durch Meditation an. So wird man nie im wahren Sinne weiterkommen. Beides muss in der Seele zusammenwirken. Und das Fortdenken und Fortfühlen des anthroposophischen Inhaltes ist auch Seelenübung. Man lebt sich in die geistige Welt schauend hinein, wenn man so, wie es hier gesagt ist, mit diesem Inhalt verfährt.[45]

45 Rudolf Steiner: *Anthroposophische Leitsätze. Der Erkenntnisweg der Anthroposophie – Das Michael-Mysterium*. GA 26. Dornach [10]1998, S. 56.

Anthroposophical Society was now to begin the process of working through Anthroposophy as a whole, without which, according to Steiner, the Society and its "School of Spiritual Science" would have no foundation, no working basis, and no right to exist. Anthroposophy was to become the "spiritual property" of the members, although not as mere head knowledge, but thought through, "felt through," and absorbed into the will. According to Rudolf Steiner, this would enable the Anthroposophical Society to become an esoteric community:

> One should not think: "I listen to the content of the lectures; I prepare myself for knowledge of the spiritual world separately by means of meditation." One will never come further in the true sense in this way. Both must work together in the soul. And the further-thinking and further-feeling of anthroposophical content is also an exercise of the soul. One gradually comes to live *seeingly* into the spiritual world if one proceeds with the content in the manner described.[45]

45 Rudolf Steiner: *Anthroposophical Leitsätze / Anthroposophical Leading Thoughts*. GA 26. Arlesheim: Ita Wegman Institute, 2024 (the present volume); letter of August 10, 1924: "How the Leading Thoughts Are to Be Used." (Also printed in *The Life, Nature, and Cultivation of Anthroposophy*, GA 260a; p. 60f.)

Mit den *Leitsätzen* und der durch sie ermöglichten geistigen Arbeit hoffte Rudolf Steiner, die Allgemeine Anthroposophische Gesellschaft aus einem «Chaos verschiedener Gruppen» zu einer spirituellen Arbeitsgemeinschaft und objektiven Realität formen zu können. Er betonte in diesem Zusammenhang auch, die Zweige der Gesellschaft könnten und dürften nicht länger der Schauplatz einzelner Persönlichkeiten sein, die für sich ein persönliches Podium und Auditorium suchten, sondern müssten endlich der Anthroposophie und ihrer Verbreitung in der Welt dienen: «Es kann doch eben nicht *so* sein, dass das Vorhandensein der Anthroposophischen Gesellschaft von dieser oder jener Persönlichkeit nur als Gelegenheit benützt wird, um *das* zu sagen, was man aus dieser oder jener Absicht heraus persönlich sagen will, sondern die Gesellschaft muss die Pflegestätte dessen sein, *was Anthroposophie* ist. Alles andere kann ja auch außerhalb ihres Rahmens gepflegt werden. *Sie* kann nicht dafür da sein.»[46] Es gehe um die Schaffung einer «Gesellschaft mit einem geistigen Inhalt», nicht jedoch um Beliebigkeit und Eigensinn. Führende Persönlichkeiten der Gesellschaft sollten in Zukunft anhand des «geistigen Eigentums» der Anthroposophie «produktiv» werden – und damit dem Gesamten dienen.

46 Ebd., S. 12f.

With the *Leading Thoughts* and the spiritual work they made possible, Rudolf Steiner hoped to be able to shape the General Anthroposophical Society from a "chaos of different groups" into a spiritual working community and objective reality. In this context, he also emphasized that the branches of the Society could and should no longer be the arena of individual personalities seeking a personal platform and auditorium for themselves, but should finally serve Anthroposophy and its dissemination in the world: "It cannot be allowed that the existence of the Anthroposophical Society is merely made use of by this or that individual as an opportunity to say what he personally wishes to say with this or that intention. Rather, the Society must be the place where true *Anthroposophy* is cultivated. Everything else can, after all, be pursued outside its framework. The Society is not there for such matters."[46] The aim was to create a "Society with a spiritual content," not arbitrariness and stubbornness. From now on, leading figures in the Society should become "productive" on the basis of the "spiritual property" of Anthroposophy – and thus serve the whole.

46 Ibid., letter of February 17, 1924, titled: "Anthroposophical Leading Thoughts." (Also printed in *The Life, Nature, and Cultivation of Anthroposophy*, GA 260a, p. 25f.)

Es war ein Versuch eines intensiven Neuanfangs nach der Weihnachtstagung – nicht nur die Texte «An die Mitglieder» erschienen wöchentlich, sondern auch die Karmavorträge und Klassenstunden hielt Rudolf Steiner seit Mitte Februar 1924 regelmäßig. Es war der entschiedene Versuch einer spirituellen Gemeinschaftsbildung durch die Schaffung eines gesteigerten und in gewisser Hinsicht «einheitlichen» Bewusstseins – für die Anthroposophische Gesellschaft, aber auch für die in und mit ihr arbeitenden beruflichen Gemeinschaften, für die Sektionen der Hochschule.

Die *Leitsätze* waren in gewisser Weise eine Fortsetzung des Vortragskurses vom Januar 1924 über die «Fundamente» der Anthroposophie – und ihre Niederschrift begann Rudolf Steiner im Februar mit Darstellungen zur anthroposophischen Menschenkunde. An den Anfang stellte er Sätze, die mit dem Eröffnungsvortrag des Januar-Kurses «Anthroposophie. Eine Einführung» zusammenklangen:

> Anthroposophie ist ein Erkenntnisweg, der das Geistige im Menschenwesen zum Geistigen im Weltenall führen möchte. Sie tritt im Menschen als Herzens- und Gefühlsbedürfnis auf. Sie muss ihre Rechtfertigung dadurch finden, dass sie diesem Bedürfnisse Befriedigung gewähren kann. Anerkennen kann Anthroposophie nur

It was an attempt at an intensive new beginning after the Christmas Conference – not only did the texts "To the Members" appear weekly, but Rudolf Steiner also gave the Karma Lectures and Class Lessons regularly from mid-February 1924 and on. It was a determined attempt at spiritual community-building through the creation of a heightened and, in a certain sense, "unified" consciousness – for the Anthroposophical Society, but also for the professional communities working in and with it, i.e. for the Sections of the School.

The *Leading Thoughts* were in a sense a continuation of the January 1924 lecture course on the "foundations" of Anthroposophy – and Rudolf Steiner began writing them down in February with descriptions of anthroposophical anthropology. He began with sentences that resonated with the opening lecture of the January course, *Anthroposophy: An Introduction*:

> Anthroposophy is a path of knowledge that would guide the spiritual in the human being to the spiritual in the universe. It arises in the human being as a need of the heart and of the life of feeling. It must find its justification by virtue of its ability to fulfill these needs. Only he can acknowledge Anthroposophy who finds in it

> derjenige, der in ihr findet, was er aus seinem Gemüte heraus suchen muss. Anthroposophen können daher nur Menschen sein, die gewisse Fragen über das Wesen des Menschen und die Welt so als Lebensnotwendigkeit empfinden, wie man Hunger und Durst empfindet.[47]

Rudolf Steiners *Leitsatz*-Aufsätze behandelten ab dem Februar 1924 die anthroposophische Menschenkunde und die menschlichen Wesensglieder, die nachtodliche Entwicklung des Menschen und die übersinnlichen Erkenntnisstufen. Ab Mitte Juli 1924 mündeten sie in die Schicksalsthematik ein («Etwas vom Geist-Verstehen und Schicksals-Erleben»); Ende Juli schrieb Rudolf Steiner dann erstmals über die Karma- und Hierarchienlehre im Zusammenhang der *Leitsätze*. Sein fundamentaler Aufsatz «Im Anbruch des Michael-Zeitalters» erschien im Nachrichtenblatt Mitte August 1924 und wurde zwei Wochen später mit der Studie «Die menschliche Seelenverfassung vor dem Anbruch des Michael-Zeitalters» fortgesetzt, die am 31. August 1924, wenige Tage vor Steiners Rückkehr nach Dornach und dem Beginn der letzten Septemberkurse, erschien. Bereits mit diesen beiden Michael-Aufsätzen begann etwas Neues im Kontext

47 Ebd., S. 14.

> what, out of his heart and soul, he must seek. Hence, only they can be anthroposophists who feel certain questions about the essential nature of the human being and the world as a need of life, just as one feels hunger and thirst.[47]

From February 1924, Rudolf Steiner's *Leading Thought* essays dealt with the anthroposophical study of the human being and the various human sheaths or members, the development of the human being after death, and the supersensible stages of knowledge. From mid-July 1924, they led into the theme of destiny ("Understanding of the Spirit; Conscious Experience of Destiny"); at the end of July, Rudolf Steiner then wrote for the first time about the teachings of karma and the hierarchies in the context of the *Leading Thoughts*. His fundamental essay "At the Dawn of the Michael Age" appeared in the "Nachrichtenblatt" in mid-August 1924 and was continued two weeks later with the study "The Condition of the Human Soul before the Dawn of the Michael Age," which appeared on August 31, 1924, a few days before Steiner's return to Dornach and the beginning of the last September courses. These two Michael essays already marked the beginning of

47 Ibid., Leading Thought no. 1.

der *Leitsätze*, im Inhalt und Stil der Darstellung. Ohne Zweifel ging es Rudolf Steiner darum, die Thematik seiner zentralen Karma-Vorträge vom Juli 1924 (in Dornach und Arnheim) in konzentrierter Schriftform den Mitgliedern der Allgemeinen Anthroposophischen Gesellschaft zukommen zu lassen. Er schrieb über die Schicksale der – ursprünglich kosmischen und von Michael «verwalteten» – Intelligenz, die sich bewusstseinsgeschichtlich immer mehr dem Menschen einverwandelte und zur «persönlich-individuellen Intelligenz»,[48] zum seelischen Eigentum wurde. Zugleich verfolgte Steiner den Weg Michaels selbst, der dem «Strom des intellektuellen Lebens nachgezogen war»[49] – und den Weg der «Michaeldiener» und der «Michaelgemeinschaft» von Menschen, die in Michaels Sinne leben und wirken.

Im September 1924, während der letzten Kurse in Dornach, musste sich Rudolf Steiner auf kurze, menschenkundlich orientierte *Leitsatz*-Formulierungen beschränken und schrieb im Nachrichtenblatt stattdessen ausführlich über die Inhalte und Ziele seiner Ausführungen über Sprachgestaltung und Dramatische Kunst, sodann, Ende September (mit Erscheinungsdatum vom 5. Oktober), über seinen Apokalypse-Kurs für die Priesterschaft. Mit der Ausgabe der Wochenschrift vom 12. Oktober 1924 nahm er dann seine großen Michael-Studien

48 Ebd., S. 59. 49 Ebd., S. 61.

something new in the context of the *Leading Thoughts* in terms of their content and style of presentation. There is no doubt that Rudolf Steiner's intention was to provide the members of the General Anthroposophical Society with a concentrated written version of his central Karma Lectures of July 1924 (held in Dornach and Arnhem). He wrote about the fate of the intelligence – originally cosmic and "ruled" by Michael – which was increasingly assimilated into the human being throughout the history of consciousness, eventually becoming "personal-individual intelligence,"[48] the property of the soul. At the same time, Steiner followed the path of Michael himself, who had "followed the stream of intellectual life"[49] – and the path of the "Michael servants" and the "Michael community" of human beings who live and work in Michael's spirit.

In September 1924, during the last courses in Dornach, Rudolf Steiner had to confine himself to short, anthropologically oriented formulations of *Leading Thoughts* and instead wrote at length in the "Nachrichtenblatt" about the content and aims of his explanations on speech formation and dramatic art – and then, at the end of September (with a publication date of October 5), about his Apocalypse course for the priesthood. With the October 12, 1924 issue of the

48 Ibid., "At the Dawn of the Michael Age."

49 Ibid.

vom August 1924 wieder auf – und führte die Folge langer Aufsätze über nahezu sechs Monate, bis zu seinem Tod am 30. März 1925, in grandioser Weise fort. All diese Texte verfasste er nun von seinem Krankenlager im Atelier des Schreinerei-Gebäudes, wohin er am 1. Oktober 1924 gezogen war; die *Leitsätze* und *Leitsatz*-Betrachtungen bildeten ab dann das letzte Wirkensorgan Rudolf Steiners nach dem krankheitsbedingten Abbruch seiner Vortragstätigkeit, was bei ihrer Lektüre zu beachten ist. Sie handeln von Michaels Kampf mit Ahriman um die menschliche Intelligenz, von Christus- und Antichristkräften, von der Zukunft der Erde, des Menschen und des Kosmos.[50] Als die letzten beiden *Leitsatz*-Betrachtungen am 5. und 12. April 1925 erschienen, lebte Rudolf Steiner nicht mehr. Dem Schlusssatz des letzten Aufsatzes «Von der Natur zur Unter-Natur»: «Und gerade durch das erkennende Aufnehmen derjenigen Geistigkeit, zu der die ahrimanischen Mächte keinen Zutritt haben, wird der Mensch gestärkt, um *in der Welt* Ahriman gegenüberzutreten», hatte Rudolf

50 Vgl. zu den *Leitsatz*-Aufsätzen und -motiven in Rudolf Steiners letzter Lebenszeit in seinem Atelier: Peter Selg: *Rudolf Steiner 1861 – 1925. Lebens- und Werkgeschichte. Band 7: Die Freie Hochschule für Geisteswissenschaft und das Lebensende 1924 – 1925.* Arlesheim 2017, S. 2038ff. Die Beschreibung der letzten Lebenszeit und Leitsatzarbeit findet sich auch in der zweisprachigen Ausgabe: Peter Selg: *Rudolf Steiners Atelier. Die letzte Lebenszeit. The Final Years.* Arlesheim 2019.

"Wochenschrift" (Weekly Newsletter), he then resumed his great Michael studies of August 1924 – and continued the series of long essays for almost six months, in sublime fashion, until his death on March 30, 1925. He wrote all these texts from his sickbed in the studio of the carpentry building, to which he had moved on October 1, 1924; from then on, the *Leading Thoughts* and the *Leading Thought* considerations formed Rudolf Steiner's final organ of work after the cessation of his lecturing activities due to illness, which should be borne in mind when reading them. They deal with Michael's battle with Ahriman for human intelligence, with the forces of Christ and Antichrist, and with the future of the earth, the human being, and the cosmos.[50] Rudolf Steiner was no longer alive when the last two *Leading Thought* considerations were published on April 5 and 12, 1925. In the final sentence of his last essay "From Nature to Sub-Nature" – "It is precisely through the knowing reception of this spirituality to which the ahrimanic powers have no access that the human being is

50 See the essays and motifs related to the Leading Thoughts in Rudolf Steiner's last years in his studio: Peter Selg: *Rudolf Steiner, Life and Work. Vol. 7 (1924 – 1925): The Anthroposophical Society and the School for Spiritual Science.* SteinerBooks, 2019; Ch. 12. The description of the last period of his life and the work on the *Leading Thoughts* can also be found in the bilingual edition: Peter Selg: *Rudolf Steiners Atelier: Die letzte Lebenszeit/The Final Years.* Arlesheim 2019.

Steiner in einer letzten Manuskriptkorrektur noch das Wort *erkennend* eingefügt («das *erkennende* Aufnehmen»)[51] – eine abschließende Ergänzung und Verdeutlichung der Signatur seiner Lebensarbeit sowie seiner Hoffnung auf die Rezeption der Anthroposophie im 20. Jahrhundert und in den nachfolgenden Zeiten.

51 Vgl. Rudolf Steiner Archiv, Dornach.

strengthened to confront Ahriman *within the world*" – Rudolf Steiner had, in a final manuscript correction, added the word *knowing* ("the *knowing* reception")[51] – a concluding expansion and clarification of the signature of his life's work as well as his hope for the reception of Anthroposophy in the twentieth century and beyond.

51 See the Rudolf Steiner Archive, Dornach. *Ed. note:* The German word in question is *erkennende* (lit. "recognizing").

Anthroposophische *Leitsätze*

Man soll an dieser Stelle in der Zukunft eine Art anthroposophischer *Leitsätze* finden. Sie sind so aufzufassen, dass sie Ratschläge enthalten über die Richtung, welche die Vorträge und Besprechungen in den einzelnen Gruppen der Gesellschaft durch die führenden Mitglieder nehmen können. Es wird dabei nur an eine Anregung gedacht, die vom Goetheanum aus der gesamten Gesellschaft gegeben werden möchte. Die Selbstständigkeit im Wirken der einzelnen führenden Mitglieder soll damit nicht angetastet werden. Es ist gut, wenn die Gesellschaft sich so entfaltet, dass in völlig freier Art in den einzelnen Gruppen zur Geltung kommt, was die führenden Mitglieder zu sagen haben. Dadurch wird das Leben der Gesellschaft bereichert und in sich mannigfaltig gestaltet werden.

Aber es sollte ein einheitliches Bewusstsein in der Gesellschaft entstehen können. Das kann geschehen, wenn man von den Anregungen, die an den einzelnen Orten gegeben werden, überall weiß. Deshalb werden hier in kurzen Sätzen solche Darstellungen zusammengefasst werden, die von mir am Goetheanum für die Gesellschaft in Vorträgen gegeben werden. Ich denke mir, dass dann von denjenigen Persönlichkeiten, die in den Gruppen (Zweigen) Vorträge halten oder die

Anthroposophical *Leading Thoughts*

In the future, one will find in these pages something in the nature of anthroposophical *Leading Thoughts* or principles. These may be taken to contain advice on the direction that leading members can give to the lectures and discussions in the various groups. It is but a stimulus and suggestion which the Goetheanum would like to give to the whole Society. The independence of individual leading members in their work is in no way to be interfered with. It is good if the Society unfolds such that, in an entirely free manner, there comes to expression in the individual groups what the leading members have to say. Through this, the life of the Society will be enriched and made manifold.

But it should also be possible for a unity of consciousness to arise in the whole Society. This can happen if the initiative and ideas that emerge at different places become known everywhere. Thus in these columns will be summarized in short paragraphs the descriptions and lines of thought given by me in my lectures to the Society at the Goetheanum. I could imagine that those who hold lectures or conduct the discussions in the groups or branches will make use of what are here

Besprechungen leiten, dabei das Gegebene als Richtlinien genommen werde, um in freier Art daran anzuknüpfen. Es kann dadurch zu einer einheitlichen Gestaltung im Wirken der Gesellschaft etwas beigetragen werden, ohne dass an einen Zwang in irgendeiner Art gedacht wird.

Fruchtbar für die ganze Gesellschaft kann die Sache werden, wenn der Vorgang auch die entsprechende Gegenliebe findet, wenn die führenden Mitglieder über Inhalt und Art ihrer Vorträge und Anregungen auch den Vorstand am Goetheanum unterrichten. Wir werden dadurch erst aus einem Chaos verschiedener Gruppen zu einer Gesellschaft mit einem geistigen Inhalt.

Die Leitlinien, die hier gegeben werden, sollen gewissermaßen Themen anschlagen. Man wird dann in der anthroposophischen Bücher- und Zyklenliteratur an den verschiedensten Stellen die Anhaltspunkte finden, um das im Thema Angeschlagene so auszugestalten, dass es den Inhalt der Gruppenbesprechungen bilden kann.

Auch dann, wenn neue Ideen von den leitenden Mitgliedern in den einzelnen Gruppen zutage treten, können sie ja an dasjenige angeknüpft werden, was in der geschilderten Art vom Goetheanum aus als ein Rahmen für das geistige Wirken der Gesellschaft angeregt werden soll.

Es ist ganz gewiss eine Wahrheit, gegen die nicht gesündigt werden darf, dass geistiges Wirken *nur* aus der freien Entfaltung

given as guidelines in the sense of freely connecting with or building upon them in what they have to say. This will contribute to the unity and organic wholeness of the work of the Society, without there being any question of constraint.

This idea can become fruitful for the whole Society if the process also finds the appropriate response – if the leading members also inform the Executive at the Goetheanum of the content and nature of their own lectures and suggestions. Only then will we grow, from a chaos of separate groups, into a Society with a spiritual content.

The guidelines given here are meant to open up subjects for study and discussion. Points of contact with them will be found in countless places in the anthroposophical books and lecture courses, so that the subjects thus opened up can be enlarged upon and the discussions in the groups centered around them.

When new ideas emerge among leading members in the various groups, these too can be brought into connection with the suggestions that will be sent out from the Goetheanum. An open framework will thus be provided for all the spiritual activity in the Society.

It is a very clear truth – which must not be sinned against – that spiritual activity can *only* thrive by means of free unfolding

der wirkenden Persönlichkeiten hervorgehen kann. Allein, es braucht dagegen nicht gesündigt zu werden, wenn in rechter Art innerhalb der Gesellschaft der eine mit dem anderen im Einklang handelt. Wenn das nicht sein könnte, so müsste die Zugehörigkeit des Einzelnen oder der Gruppen zur Gesellschaft immer etwas Äußerliches bleiben. Diese Zugehörigkeit soll aber etwas sein, das man als *Innerliches* empfindet.

Es kann doch eben nicht *so* sein, dass das Vorhandensein der Anthroposophischen Gesellschaft von dieser oder jener Persönlichkeit nur als Gelegenheit benutzt wird, um *das* zu sagen, was man aus dieser oder jener Absicht heraus persönlich sagen will, sondern die Gesellschaft muss die Pflegestätte dessen sein, *was Anthroposophie ist.* Alles andere kann ja auch außerhalb ihres Rahmens gepflegt werden. *Sie* kann nicht dafür da sein.

Es ist in den letzten Jahren nicht zum Vorteil der Gesellschaft gewesen, dass in sie einzelne Mitglieder ihre Eigenwünsche hineingetragen haben, bloß weil sie mit deren Vergrößerung für diese Eigenwünsche ein Wirkungsfeld zu finden glaubten. Man kann sagen: Warum ist dem nicht in der gebührenden Art entgegengetreten worden? – Wäre das geschehen, so würde heute überall die Meinung zu hören sein: Ja, wenn man damals die Anregungen von dieser oder jener Seite aufgenommen hätte, wo wären wir gegenwärtig? Nun, man hat vieles aufgenommen, was kläglich gescheitert ist, was uns zurückgeworfen hat.

on the part of the active personalities. But there is no need to sin against this truth when one group or member within the Society acts in proper harmony with the other. If such cooperation were impossible, the attachment of individuals or groups to the Society would always remain a purely external thing – whereas it should in fact be felt as an *inner reality*.

It cannot be allowed that the existence of the Anthroposophical Society is merely made use of by this or that individual as an opportunity to say what he personally wishes to say with this or that intention. Rather, the Society must be the center of cultivation of *what Anthroposophy is*. Everything else can, after all, be pursued outside its framework. The Society is not there for such matters.

It has not helped us that in the last few years, individual members have brought into the Society their own personal wishes simply because they thought that as the Society grew, it would become a suitable sphere of action for them. It may be said: Why was this not met and counteracted with the proper firmness? If that had been done, then the opinion would be heard on all sides: "Oh, if only the initiative that arose in this or that quarter had been followed up at the time, how much farther we would be today!" Well, many things were followed up which pitifully failed and only resulted in throwing us back.

Aber nun ist es genug. Die Probe auf das Exempel, das einzelne Experimentatoren in der Gesellschaft geben wollten, ist gemacht. Man braucht dergleichen nicht ins Endlose zu wiederholen. Der Vorstand am Goetheanum soll ein Körper sein, der Anthroposophie pflegen will, und die Gesellschaft sollte eine Verbindung von Menschen sein, die sich mit ihm über ihre Pflege der Anthroposophie lebendig verständigen wollen.

Man soll nicht denken, dass, was angestrebt werden soll, von heute auf morgen erreicht werden kann. Man wird Zeit brauchen. Und es wird Geduld nötig sein. Wenn geglaubt wird, in ein paar Wochen könne verwirklicht da sein, was in den Absichten der Weihnachtstagung liegt, so wird das wieder von Schaden sein.

But now it is enough. The demonstrations that individual experimenters in the Society wished to provide are done with. Such things need not be repeated endlessly. The Executive at the Goetheanum is to be a body which intends to cultivate Anthroposophy itself; and the Society should be an association of human beings who have the same object and are ready to enter into a living understanding with the Executive in the pursuit of it.

One should not think that what is to be striven for can be attained from one day to the next. Time will be needed, and patience too. If it were to be believed that what lay in the intentions of the Christmas Conference could be brought into existence in a few weeks' time, this again would be harmful.

Leitsätze Nr. 1 bis 3

1. Anthroposophie ist ein Erkenntnisweg, der das Geistige im Menschenwesen zum Geistigen im Weltenall führen möchte. Sie tritt im Menschen als Herzens- und Gefühlsbedürfnis auf. Sie muss ihre Rechtfertigung dadurch finden, dass sie diesem Bedürfnisse Befriedigung gewähren kann. Anerkennen kann Anthroposophie nur derjenige, der in ihr findet, was er aus seinem Gemüte heraus suchen muss. Anthroposophen können daher nur Menschen sein, die gewisse Fragen über das Wesen des Menschen und die Welt so als Lebensnotwendigkeit empfinden, wie man Hunger und Durst empfindet.

2. Anthroposophie vermittelt Erkenntnisse, die auf geistige Art gewonnen werden. Sie tut dies aber nur deswegen, weil das tägliche Leben und die auf Sinneswahrnehmung und Verstandestätigkeit gegründete Wissenschaft an eine Grenze des Lebensweges führen, an der das seelische Menschendasein ersterben müsste, wenn es diese Grenze nicht überschreiten könnte. Dieses tägliche Leben und diese Wissenschaft führen nicht so zur Grenze, dass an dieser stehengeblieben werden muss, sondern es eröffnet sich an dieser Grenze der Sinnesanschauung durch die menschliche Seele selbst der Ausblick in die geistige Welt.

Leading Thoughts 1 to 3

1. Anthroposophy is a path of knowledge that would guide the spiritual in the human being to the spiritual in the universe. It arises in the human being as a need of the heart and of the life of feeling. It must find its justification by virtue of its ability to fulfill these needs. Only he can acknowledge Anthroposophy who finds in it what, out of his heart and soul, he must seek. Hence, only they can be anthroposophists who feel certain questions about the essential nature of the human being and the world as a need of life, just as one feels hunger and thirst.

2. Anthroposophy communicates knowledge that is achieved in a spiritual way. Yet it does so only because daily life and the science founded on sense perception and intellectual activity lead to a boundary in the course of life, and the human being's soul existence must perish if it could not cross over this boundary. This daily life and this science do not lead to this boundary in such a way that one must stop at it; rather, at this boundary of sensory perception there opens up, through the human soul itself, the view into the spiritual world.

3. Es gibt Menschen, die glauben, mit den Grenzen der Sinnesanschauung seien auch die Grenzen *aller* Einsicht gegeben. Würden diese aufmerksam darauf sein, *wie* sie sich dieser Grenzen bewusst werden, so würden sie auch in diesem Bewusstsein die Fähigkeiten entdecken, die Grenzen zu überschreiten. Der Fisch schwimmt an die Grenze des Wassers; er muss zurück, weil ihm die physischen Organe fehlen, um außer dem Wasser zu leben. Der Mensch kommt an die Grenze der Sinnesanschauung; er kann erkennen, dass ihm auf dem Wege dahin die Seelenkräfte geworden sind, um seelisch in dem Elemente zu leben, das nicht von der Sinnesanschauung umspannt wird.

3. There are those who believe that with the boundaries of sensory perception, the boundaries of *all* insight are also given. Yet if they were attentive to *how* they are able to become conscious of this boundary, they would also discover in this consciousness the capacities needed to cross the boundary. The fish swims to the limits of the water; it must turn back because it lacks the physical organs that would enable it to live outside of the water. The human being reaches the boundaries of sensory perception; he can come to know that on the path to this experience, powers of soul have arisen in him that enable him to live, with his soul, in that element not encompassed by sensory perception.

Leitsätze Nr. 4 und 5

4. Der Mensch braucht zur Sicherheit in seinem Fühlen, zur kraftvollen Entfaltung seines Willens eine Erkenntnis der geistigen Welt. Denn er kann die Größe, Schönheit, Weisheit der natürlichen Welt im größten Umfange empfinden: *Diese* gibt ihm keine Antwort auf die Frage nach seinem eigenen Wesen. Dieses eigene Wesen hält die Stoffe und Kräfte der natürlichen Welt so lange in der lebend-regsamen Menschengestalt zusammen, bis der Mensch durch die Pforte des Todes schreitet. Dann übernimmt die Natur diese Gestalt. Sie kann dieselbe nicht zusammenhalten, sondern nur auseinandertreiben. Die große, schöne, weisheitsvolle Natur gibt wohl Antwort auf die Frage, wie wird die Menschengestalt aufgelöst, nicht aber, wie wird sie zusammengehalten. Kein theoretischer Einwand kann *diese* Frage aus der empfindenden Menschenseele, wenn diese sich nicht selbst betäuben will, auslöschen. *Ihr* Vorhandensein muss die Sehnsucht nach geistigen Wegen der Welterkenntnis unablässig in jeder Menschenseele, die wirklich wach ist, regsam erhalten.

5. Der Mensch braucht zur inneren Ruhe die Selbst-Erkenntnis im Geiste. Er findet sich selbst in seinem

Leading Thoughts 4 and 5

4. For certainty in his life of feeling and for the strong unfolding of his will, the human being needs knowledge of the spiritual world. For even if he is able to experience to their fullest extent the majesty, beauty, and wisdom of the natural world, *this* experience gives him no answer to the question posed by his own being. His own being holds together the substances and forces of the natural world in the living human form only until he crosses the threshold of death. Then nature takes over this form: It cannot hold this form together, but can only disintegrate it. Great, beautiful, and wisdom-filled nature does indeed answer the question as to how the human form is dissolved, but not as to how it is held together. No theoretical objection can extinguish *this* question from the feeling soul, so long as one does not want to benumb oneself. The presence of *this question* must unceasingly keep alive – in every human soul that is truly awake – the longing for spiritual paths of world knowledge.

5. For inner tranquility, the human being needs self-knowledge in the spirit. He finds himself in his thinking,

Denken, Fühlen und Wollen. Er sieht, wie Denken, Fühlen und Wollen von dem natürlichen Menschenwesen abhängig sind. Sie müssen in ihren Entfaltungen der Gesundheit, Krankheit, Kräftigung und Schädigung des Körpers folgen. Jeder Schlaf löscht sie aus. Die gewöhnliche Lebenserfahrung weist die denkbar größte Abhängigkeit des menschlichen Geist-Erlebens vom Körper-Dasein auf. Da erwacht in dem Menschen das Bewusstsein, dass in dieser gewöhnlichen Lebenserfahrung die Selbst-Erkenntnis verloren gegangen sein könne. Es entsteht zunächst die bange Frage: Ob es eine über die gewöhnliche Lebenserfahrung hinausgehende Selbst-Erkenntnis und damit die Gewissheit über ein wahres Selbst geben könne? Anthroposophie will auf der Grundlage sicherer Geist-Erfahrung die Antwort auf diese Frage geben. Sie stützt sich dabei nicht auf ein Meinen oder Glauben, sondern auf ein Erleben im Geiste, das in seiner Wesenheit so sicher ist wie das Erleben im Körper.

feeling, and willing. He sees how thinking, feeling, and willing are dependent on the natural human being. In their unfolding development, they must follow the health, illness, strengthening, and damaging of the body. Every instance of sleep extinguishes them. The experience of ordinary life shows that human spirit-experience stands in the greatest imaginable dependence on one's bodily existence. There awakens in the human being the consciousness that, in the midst of this ordinary life-experience, self-knowledge can be lost. There arises then the anxious question as to whether there could be a form of self-knowledge that extends beyond the realm of ordinary life-experience, and whether, through this, the certainty of a true self can emerge. On the foundation of reliable spiritual experience, Anthroposophy wishes to give an answer to this question. In doing so, it supports itself not on opinion or belief, but on an experience in the spirit which in its essential nature is as certain as the experience in the body.

An die Mitglieder!

In meinen Vorträgen für die Anthroposophische Gesellschaft, die ich gegenwärtig am Goetheanum halte, suche ich, die Grundfragen des menschlichen Seelenlebens zur Darstellung zu bringen. In den fünf *Leitsätzen*, die bisher in diesem Mitteilungsblatte enthalten waren, ist der Gesichtspunkt gekennzeichnet, von dem aus die Darstellung gegeben wird. Ich wollte der Grundforderung eines anthroposophischen Vortrages entsprechen. Der Zuhörer soll die Empfindung haben, dass Anthroposophie von dem spricht, was er bei voller Selbstbesinnung als ureigene Angelegenheit seiner Seele empfindet. Kann man für eine solche Darstellung die rechte Art finden, dann wird sich unter den Mitgliedern das Bewusstsein entwickeln: *In der Anthroposophischen Gesellschaft wird der Mensch wirklich verstanden.*

Man trifft damit auf dasjenige, was für die Menschen, die Mitglieder werden, der treibende Impuls ist. Sie wollen eine Stätte finden, an der Menschenverständnis seine rechte Pflege findet.

Man ist eigentlich schon auf dem Wege zur Anerkennung des Geisteswesens der Welt, wenn man ernstlich Menschenverständnis sucht. Denn man wird in diesem Suchen gewahr, dass die Naturerkenntnis in Bezug auf den Menschen keine Aufschlüsse gibt, sondern nur Fragen erzeugt.

To the Members!

In the lectures to the Anthroposophical Society which I am now giving at the Goetheanum, I am seeking to give expression to the root-questions of the inner life of the human being. The underlying point of view has been indicated in the first five *Leading Thoughts* published in the newsletter. My aim has been to meet the fundamental requirement of an anthroposophical lecture. The listener must feel that Anthroposophy is speaking of what he, when he holds counsel with himself most deeply, realizes as essential concern of his soul. If one can thus find the right way of representing Anthroposophy, there will arise among the members the feeling that *in the Anthroposophical Society the human being is truly understood.*

And this is the fundamental impulse in those who become members. They want to find a place where the understanding of the human being is duly cultivated.

When one earnestly seeks to understand the human being, one is indeed already on the way to recognition of the spiritual being of the world. For one is made aware that, as to the human being himself, knowledge of nature affords no insights but only gives rise to questions.

In den anthroposophischen Darstellungen kommt nur Verwirrung zustande, wenn man die Seele von der Liebe zur Natur hinwegführen will. Nicht in der Geringschätzung dessen, was die Natur den Menschen offenbart, kann der Ausgangspunkt der anthroposophischen Betrachtung liegen. Naturverachtung, Abkehr von der Wahrheit, die in den Erscheinungen des Lebens und der Welt dem Menschen entgegenstrahlt, von der Schönheit, die in diesen Erscheinungen waltet, von den Aufgaben, die sie dem Menschenstreben stellen, kann nur zu einem Zerrbilde vom Geisteswesen führen.

Ein solches Zerrbild wird immer einen persönlichen Charakter haben. Es wird, auch wenn es nicht bloß aus Träumen gewoben ist, doch wie das Träumen erlebt werden. Wenn der Mensch im wachen Dasein mit Menschen lebt, dann muss sein Streben auf Verständigung über *Gemeinsames* ausgehen. Was der eine behauptet, muss Bedeutung für den anderen haben; was der eine erarbeitet, muss für den anderen einen gewissen Wert haben. Die Menschen, die mit einander leben, müssen das Gefühl haben, dass sie in einer gemeinsamen Welt sind. Wenn der Mensch in seinen Träumen webt, dann löst er sich aus dieser gemeinsamen Welt heraus. Ein anderer Mensch in seiner unmittelbaren Nähe kann ganz andere Träume haben. Im Wachen haben die Menschen eine gemeinsame Welt; im Träumen hat ein jeder sein eigene.

Anthroposophie sollte nicht aus dem Wachen in das

If in anthroposophical presentations one tends to lead the soul away from love of nature, confusion alone is the result. The true starting point of anthroposophical considerations cannot lie in the belittling of what nature reveals to the human being. To despise nature, to turn away from the truth which flows to the human being from the phenomena of life and the world, or from the beauty that pervades them and the tasks they offer to the human being's will: this frame of mind can at most produce a caricature of the spirit.

Such a caricature will always have a personal element. Even if it is not composed of dreams, it will be experienced in a dreaming way. In waking life, the human being lives with others, and his effort must be for mutual understanding on that which is common. What one person states must have some meaning for the other; what one achieves by his work must have a certain value for the other. Those who live with one another must have the feeling that they are in a common world. But when a person is living in his own dreams, he detaches himself from the common world of human beings. The dreams of another – even his nearest neighbor – may be utterly different from his. In waking life, people have a world in common; in dreaming, each person has his own.

Anthroposophy should lead from waking life, not to a

Träumen, sondern in ein stärkeres Erwachen hineinführen. Im alltäglichen Leben ist zwar Gemeinsamkeit vorhanden, aber diese wird doch in engen Grenzen erlebt. Man ist da in ein Stück Dasein hineingebannt; man trägt die Sehnsucht nach dem *vollen* Leben nur im Herzen. Man fühlt, die Gemeinsamkeit des menschlichen Erlebens geht weiter als der Umkreis des alltäglichen Lebens. Und wie man von der Erde weg zur Sonne blicken muss, wenn man die allem Irdischen gemeinsame Quelle des Lichtes gewahr werden will, so muss man von der Sinnenwelt hinweg zum Geistesinhalt sich wenden, wenn man finden will, was aus dem echt Menschlichen heraus die Seele zur befriedigenden Menschengemeinschaft, zum vollen Erleben dieser Gemeinschaft führen kann.

Da ist es denn leicht möglich, dass man sich vom Leben abwendet, statt in einem intensiveren Maße in dasselbe einzutreten.

Und dieser Gefahr unterliegt der Naturverächter. Er wird in die Einsamkeit der Seele hineingetrieben, für die das natürliche Träumen ein Vorbild ist. Für menschliche Wahrheit, die zugleich Weltwahrheit ist, entwickelt man am besten den Sinn, wenn man diesen heranerzieht an derjenigen Wahrheit, die aus der Natur der Menschenseele entgegenleuchtet. Wer aber *Naturwahrheit* mit offenem, freiem Sinn in sich erlebt, der wird durch sie zur Geisteswahrheit hingeführt. Wer sich von der *Schönheit*, *Größe* und *Erhabenheit* der Natur durchdringt, in

dreaming, but to a more intense awakening. In everyday life, community is indeed present, but it is confined within narrow limits. One is banished to a certain fragment of existence, and only in one's heart does one bear the longing for *full* life. One feels that the true community of human life extends beyond the confines of the everyday. One looks away from the earth to the sun when one would see the source of light common to all earthly things. So too must one turn away from the world of the senses to the reality of the spirit to find the true sources of humanity, where the soul can experience the fullness of community it needs.

Here it may easily happen that one turns away from life instead of entering it more fully and more strongly.

The person who despises nature has fallen victim to this danger. He is driven into that isolation of the soul of which ordinary dreaming is a good example. The best way to develop one's sense of human truth, which is at the same time world truth, is to educate this sense in light of the truth immanent in nature that shines forth to the human soul. The *truths of nature*, experienced with a free and open mind, lead one already toward the truths of the spirit. For one who fills himself with the *beauty*, *greatness*, and *majesty* of nature, this becomes a

dem werden diese zur Quelle der Geistempfindung. Und wer sein Herz der stummen Naturgebärde öffnet, die jenseits von Gut und Böse in ewiger Unschuld sich offenbart, dem erschließt sich der Blick für die geistige Welt, die in die stumme Gebärde das lebendige Wort tönen lässt, das den Unterschied von Gut und Böse offenbart.

Geistanschauung, die durch die Liebe zur Naturanschauung hindurchgegangen ist, bereichert das Leben um die wahren Schätze der Seele; Geistesträumen, das im Widerspruch mit der Naturanschauung sich entwickelt, verarmt das Menschenherz.

Wer Anthroposophie im tiefsten Wesen durchdringt, wird, was in diesen Sätzen angedeutet ist, als den Gesichtspunkt empfinden, von dem in den anthroposophischen Darstellungen ausgegangen werden muss. Man wird durch solche Ausgangspunkte dasjenige berühren, von dem ein jedes Mitglied der Anthroposophischen Gesellschaft sich sagt: Darin liegt, was den wahren Grund meines Eintrittes in die Gesellschaft gebildet hat.

Bei den Mitgliedern, die in der Gesellschaft tätig sein wollen, wird es nicht genügen, dass sie von dem hier Angedeuteten theoretisch überzeugt sind. Es wird das rechte Leben in ihre Überzeugung erst kommen, wenn sie ein warmes Interesse für alles entfalten, was in der Gesellschaft vorgeht. Durch das Erfahren dessen, was von den Persönlichkeiten, die in der

source of feeling for the spirit. And for one who opens his heart to the silent gesture of nature revealing her eternal innocence beyond all good and evil, his eyes are opened to the spiritual world, from whence – into the silent gesture – the living Word sounds forth, revealing the difference between good and evil.

Spirit-seeing, brought up in the loving perception of nature, brings to life the true riches of the soul. Spiritual dreaming, elaborated in contradiction to true knowledge of nature, can but impoverish the human heart.

If one penetrates Anthroposophy in its deepest being, one will feel the point of view here indicated to be the one from which all anthroposophical descriptions should take their start. Through such a point of departure, one will come into living touch with the reality, of which every member will say, "Therein lies the true reason why I entered the Anthroposophical Society."

It will not be enough, for the members who wish to be active in the Anthroposophical Society, to be theoretically convinced of this. Real life will only enter their conviction when they unfold a warm interest in all that goes on in the Society. As they learn of what is being thought and done by active individuals in the Society, they will receive the warmth they need

Gesellschaft sind, erdacht und erlebt wird, werden sie die Wärme empfangen, die sie für ihre Arbeit in der Gesellschaft brauchen. Man muss viel Interesse für die anderen Menschen haben, wenn man ihnen auf anthroposophische Art gegenübertreten will. Das Studium dessen, was in «der Gesellschaft vorgeht», muss die Unterlage für das Wirken in der Gesellschaft werden. Gerade diejenigen Mitglieder brauchen dieses Studium, die in der Gesellschaft tätig sein wollen.

for their own work in it. One must be filled with interest in other human beings in order to meet them in an anthroposophical way. The study of what "is happening in the Society" must become the basis for our work within the Society. Those above all who wish to be active members will stand in need of this.

Leitsätze Nr. 6 und 7

6. Wenn man den Blick auf die leblose Natur wendet, so findet man eine Welt, die sich in gesetzmäßigen Zusammenhängen offenbart. Man sucht nach diesen Zusammenhängen und findet sie als den Inhalt der Naturgesetze. Man findet aber auch, dass durch diese Gesetze die leblose Natur sich mit der Erde zu einem Ganzen zusammenschließt. Man kann dann von diesem Erdenzusammenhang, der in allem Leblosen waltet, zu der Anschauung der lebendigen Pflanzenwelt übergehen. Man sieht, wie die außerirdische Welt aus den Weiten des Raumes die Kräfte hereinsendet, welche das Lebendige aus dem Schoße des Leblosen hervorholen. Man wird in dem Lebendigen das Wesenhafte gewahr, das sich dem bloß irdischen Zusammenhange entreißt und sich zum Offenbarer dessen macht, was aus den Weiten des Weltenraumes auf die Erde herunterwirkt. In der unscheinbarsten Pflanze wird man die Wesenheit des außerirdischen Lichtes gewahr, wie im Auge den leuchtenden Gegenstand, der vor diesem steht. In diesem Aufstieg der Betrachtung kann man den Unterschied des Irdisch-Physischen schauen, das im Leblosen waltet, und des Außerirdisch-Ätherischen, das im Lebendigen kraftet.

Leading Thoughts 6 and 7

6. When one turns his gaze to lifeless nature, one finds a world that reveals itself in lawful relationships. One searches in these relationships and finds them to be the content of the laws of nature. One also finds, however, that through these laws lifeless nature forms itself into one whole with the earth. One can then proceed from this earthly interrelationship, which holds sway in all that is lifeless, to a consideration of the living plant-world. One sees how, from out of the wide expanse of space, the universe beyond this world sends in the forces which bring forth the living from the womb of the lifeless. In the living, one becomes aware of the essential being of what wrests itself from the mere earthly interrelations and makes itself into the revealer of that which, from out of the wide expanses of cosmic space, works down upon the earth. In the most modest plant, one becomes aware of the being of the light from beyond this world, just as the eye becomes aware of the luminous object standing before it. In ascending to this level in our consideration, one can see the difference between the earthly-physical that holds sway in what is lifeless, and the etheric from beyond this world that is the power in what is living.

7. Man findet den Menschen mit seinem außerseelischen und außergeistigen Wesen in diese Welt des Irdischen und Außerirdischen hineingestellt. Sofern er in das Irdische, das das Leblose umspannt, hineingestellt ist, trägt er seinen *physischen Körper* an sich; sofern er in sich diejenigen Kräfte entwickelt, welche das Lebendige aus den Weltenweiten in das Irdische hereinzieht, hat er einen *ätherischen* oder Lebensleib. Diesen Gegensatz zwischen dem Irdischen und Ätherischen hat die Erkenntnisrichtung der neueren Zeit ganz unberücksichtigt gelassen. Sie hat gerade aus diesem Grunde über das Ätherische die unmöglichsten Anschauungen entwickelt. Die Furcht davor, sich in das Fantastische zu verlieren, hat davon abgehalten, von diesem Gegensatz zu sprechen. Ohne ein solches Sprechen kommt man aber zu keiner Einsicht in Mensch und Welt.

Leitsätze Nr. 8 bis 10

8. Man kann die Wesenheit des Menschen betrachten, insoferne diese aus seinem physischen und seinem ätherischen Leib sich ergibt. Man wird finden, dass alle Erscheinungen am Menschen, die von dieser Seite ausgehen, nicht zum Bewusstsein führen, sondern im

7. One finds the human being, with his transcendent being of soul and spirit, placed into this world of the earthly and of what is beyond this world. Insofar as he is placed into the earthly element that encompasses what is lifeless, he carries with him his *physical body*; insofar as he develops within himself those forces that the living element draws into the earthly realm from out of cosmic expanses, he has an *etheric*- or life-body. The trends of modern thought have entirely left out of consideration this contrast between the earthly and the etheric. For this very reason, they have developed the most untenable notions of the etheric. The fear of losing oneself in the fantastic has discouraged one from speaking of this contrast. Without speaking of such matters, however, one will fail to arrive at any insight into the human being and the world.

Leading Thoughts 8 to 10

8. One can observe the nature of the human being insofar as this nature comes to expression in his physical and etheric body. One will find that all the phenomena of the human being's life which proceed from this aspect of his nature do not lead to consciousness, but remain in

Unbewussten verbleiben. Das Bewusstsein wird nicht erhellt, sondern verdunkelt, wenn die Tätigkeit des physischen und des Ätherleibes erhöht wird. Ohnmachtszustände kann man als Ergebnis einer solchen Erhöhung erkennen. Durch die Verfolgung einer solchen Urteilsorientierung gelangt man dazu, anzuerkennen, dass in die Organisation des Menschen – und auch des Tieres – etwas eingreift, das mit dem Physischen und Ätherischen *nicht* von der gleichen Art ist. Es ist *nicht* wirksam, wenn das Physische und Ätherische aus seinen Kräften heraus tätig sind, sondern wenn diese *aufhören*, auf ihre Art wirksam zu sein. Man kommt so zum Begriffe des Astralleibes.

9. Die *Wirklichkeit* dieses Astralleibes wird gefunden, wenn man durch die Meditation von dem Denken, das durch die Sinne von außen angeregt wird, zu einem innerlichen Anschauen fortschreitet. Man muss dazu das von außen angeregte Denken innerlich ergreifen und es in der Seele als solches, ohne seine Beziehung auf die Außenwelt, intensiv *erleben*; und dann durch die Seelenstärke, die man in solchem Ergreifen und Erleben sich angeeignet hat, gewahr werden, dass es innere Wahrnehmungsorgane gibt, die ein Geistiges *schauen* da, wo in Tier und Menschen der physische und der ätherische

the unconscious realm. Consciousness is not brightened, but rather darkened when the activity of the physical and etheric body is increased. One can recognize states of faintness or unconsciousness as the result of such increased activity. In pursuing such an orientation of judgment, one is led to acknowledge that into the human organization – and also that of the animal – something enters in that is *not* of the same nature as the physical and etheric. This new element *does not* come into activity when the physical and the etheric are active from out of their own forces, but only when the latter *cease to be active* in their own way. Thus one arrives at the concept of the astral body.

9. The *reality* of this astral body is found when, through meditation, one progresses from a thinking that is stimulated from outside through the senses to an inner seeing. For this, one must inwardly take hold of a thinking stimulated from outside and *experience* it intensely in the soul, in-itself, apart from its relation to the external world; and then, through the strength of soul gained in such taking-hold and experiencing, one must become aware that there are inner organs of perception that *see* a spiritual element precisely there where, in the animal and in the human being, the physical and etheric bodies

Leib in ihren Schranken gehalten werden, damit Bewusstsein entstehe.

10. Das Bewusstsein entsteht *nicht* durch ein Fortführen derjenigen Tätigkeit, die aus dem physischen und dem Ätherleib als Ergebnis kommt, sondern diese beiden Leiber müssen mit ihrer Tätigkeit auf den Nullpunkt kommen, ja, noch unter denselben, damit «Platz entstehe» für das Walten des Bewusstseins. Sie sind nicht die Hervorbringer des Bewusstseins, sondern sie geben nur den Boden ab, auf dem der Geist stehen muss, um innerhalb des Erdenlebens Bewusstsein hervorzubringen. Wie der Mensch auf der Erde einen Boden braucht, auf dem er stehen kann, so braucht das Geistige innerhalb des Irdischen die materielle Grundlage, auf der es sich entfalten kann. Und so wie im Weltenraum der Planet den Boden nicht braucht, um seinen Ort zu behaupten, so braucht der Geist, dessen Anschauung nicht durch die Sinne auf das Materielle, sondern durch die Eigenkraft auf das Geistige gerichtet ist, *nicht* diese materielle Grundlage, um seine bewusste Tätigkeit in sich rege zu machen.

are kept within their bounds so that consciousness may arise.

10. Consciousness, therefore, *does not* arise by a further enhancement of activities which proceed from the physical and etheric bodies. On the contrary, these two bodies, with their activities, must be reduced to zero – indeed even below zero – to "make space" for the working of consciousness. They do not generate consciousness; they only furnish the ground on which the spirit must stand in order to bring forth consciousness within the earthly life. Just as on earth the human being needs the ground on which to stand, so does the spiritual within the earthly realm need a material foundation through which it may unfold itself. And just as a planet in the cosmic spaces does not require any ground beneath it in order to assert its place, so too the spirit, when it looks not through the senses into the material but through its own strength into the spiritual, needs *no* material foundation to call its conscious activity to life.

Leitsätze Nr. 11 bis 13

11. Das Selbstbewusstsein, das im «Ich» sich zusammenfasst, steigt aus dem Bewusstsein auf. Dieses entsteht, wenn das Geistige in den Menschen dadurch eintritt, dass die Kräfte des physischen und des ätherischen Leibes diese abbauen. Im Abbau dieser Leiber wird der Boden geschaffen, auf dem das Bewusstsein sein Leben entfaltet. Dem Abbau muss aber, wenn die Organisation nicht zerstört werden soll, ein Wiederaufbau folgen. So wird, wenn für ein Erleben des Bewusstseins ein Abbau erfolgt ist, genau das Abgebaute wieder aufgebaut werden. In der Wahrnehmung dieses Aufbaues liegt das Erleben des Selbstbewusstseins. Man kann in innerer Anschauung diesen Vorgang verfolgen. Man kann empfinden, wie das Bewusste in das Selbstbewusste dadurch übergeführt wird, dass man *aus sich* ein Nachbild des bloß Bewussten schafft. Das bloß Bewusste hat sein Bild in dem durch den Abbau gewissermaßen Leer-Gewordenen des Organismus. Es ist in das Selbstbewusstsein eingezogen, wenn die Leerheit von innen wieder erfüllt worden ist. Das Wesenhafte, das zu dieser Erfüllung fähig ist, wird als «Ich» erlebt.

Leading Thoughts 11 to 13

11. Self-consciousness, which concentrates itself in the 'I', emerges out of consciousness. Self-consciousness arises when the forces of the physical and etheric bodies break down these bodies, thus making way for the spiritual to enter into the human being. For through this breaking down is provided the ground on which consciousness can unfold its life. However, if the organism is not to be destroyed, the breaking down must be followed by a rebuilding. Thus, when a process of breaking down has taken place for an experience of consciousness, precisely that which has been broken down will be built up again. The experience of self-consciousness lies in the perception of this upbuilding process. This process can be followed with inner vision. One can feel how the conscious is led over into the self-conscious by the human being's activity of creating *out of himself* a reproduction of the merely conscious. The merely conscious has its image in the emptiness, as it were, produced within the organism by the breaking-down process. It passes into self-consciousness when the emptiness has been fulfilled again from within. The essential being that is capable of this "fulfillment" is experienced as 'I'.

12. Die Wirklichkeit des «Ich» wird gefunden, wenn man die innere Anschauung, durch die der Astralleib erkennend ergriffen wird, dadurch weiter fortbildet, dass man das erlebte Denken in der Meditation mit dem Willen durchdringt. Man hat sich diesem Denken zuerst willenlos hingegeben. Man hat es dadurch dazu gebracht, dass ein Geistiges in dieses Denken eintritt, wie die Farbe bei der sinnlichen Wahrnehmung in das Auge, der Ton in das Ohr eintritt. Hat man sich in die Lage gebracht, dasjenige, das man auf diese Art, durch passive Hingabe, im Bewusstsein verlebendigt hat, durch einen Willensakt nachzubilden, so tritt in diesen Willensakt die Wahrnehmung des eigenen «Ich» ein.

13. Man kann auf dem Wege der Meditation zu der Gestalt, in der das «Ich» im gewöhnlichen Bewusstsein auftritt, drei weitere Formen finden:

1. In dem Bewusstsein, das den Ätherleib erfasst, erscheint das «Ich» als Bild, das aber zugleich tätige Wesenheit ist und als solche dem Menschen Gestalt, Wachstum, Bildekräfte verleiht.
2. In dem Bewusstsein, das den Astralleib erfasst, offenbart sich das «Ich» als Glied einer geistigen Welt, von der es seine Kräfte erhält.
3. In dem Bewusstsein, das eben als das zuletzt zu

12. The reality of the 'I' is found when the inner vision whereby the astral body is known and taken hold of, is carried a stage further: The thinking which has become alive in meditation must now be permeated by the will. To begin with, one simply gave oneself up to this new thinking without active will. One thereby enabled spiritual realities to enter into this thinking life, even as in outer sense-perception color enters the eye, or sound the ear. If one brings oneself to the point of reproducing by an act of will what one had previously called to life in one's consciousness by a more passive devotion, then there enters into this act of will the perception of one's own 'I'.

13. On the path of meditation one can discover, in addition to the form in which the 'I' occurs in ordinary consciousness, three further forms:

1. In the consciousness which takes hold of the etheric body, the 'I' appears in image-form; yet the image is at the same time active being, and as such it gives the human being structure and figure, growth, and the formative forces that create his body.
2. In the consciousness which takes hold of the astral body, the 'I' is manifested as a member of a spiritual world from which it receives its forces.

erringende angeführt worden ist, zeigt sich das «Ich» als eine von der geistigen Umwelt relativ unabhängige, selbstständige geistige Wesenheit.

Leitsätze Nr. 14 bis 16

14. Die zweite Gestalt des «Ich», die in der Darstellung des dritten *Leitsatzes* angedeutet worden ist, tritt als «Bild» dieses Ich auf. Durch das Gewahrwerden dieses Bildcharakters wird auch ein Licht geworfen auf die Gedankenwesenheit, in der das «Ich» vor dem gewöhnlichen Bewusstsein erscheint. Man sucht durch allerlei Betrachtungen in dem gewöhnlichen Bewusstsein das «wahre Ich». Doch eine ernstliche Einsicht in die Erlebnisse dieses Bewusstseins zeigt, dass man in demselben dieses «wahre Ich» nicht finden kann; sondern dass da nur der gedankenhafte Abglanz, der weniger als ein Bild ist, aufzutreten vermag. Man wird von der Wahrheit dieses Tatbestandes erst recht erfasst, wenn man fortschreitet zu dem «Ich» als Bild, das in dem Ätherleibe lebt. Und dadurch wird man erst richtig zu dem *Suchen* des Ich als der wahren Wesenheit des Menschen angeregt.

3. In the consciousness just indicated, as the last to be achieved, the 'I' reveals itself as a self-contained spiritual being – relatively independent of the surrounding spiritual world.

Leading Thoughts 14 to 16

14. The second form of the 'I' – the first of the three forms indicated in the last section – appears as an "image" of the 'I'. Through becoming aware of this image-character, a light is also thrown on the quality of thought in which the 'I' appears before ordinary consciousness. With all manner of reflections, human beings have sought within this consciousness for the "true I." Yet an earnest insight into the experiences of the ordinary consciousness will suffice to show that the "true I" cannot be found therein. Only a thought-like reflection is able to appear there, even less than an image. The truth of this seizes one all the more when one progresses to the 'I' as image, which lives in the etheric body. And only through this is one stimulated to *search* for the 'I', for the true human being.

15. Die Einsicht in die Gestalt, in der das «Ich» im Astralleibe lebt, führt zu einer rechten Empfindung von dem Verhältnisse des Menschen zu der geistigen Welt. Diese Ich-Gestalt ist für das gewöhnliche Erleben in die dunklen Tiefen des Unbewussten getaucht. In diesen Tiefen tritt der Mensch mit der geistigen Weltwesenheit durch Inspiration in Verbindung. Nur ein ganz schwacher gefühlsmäßiger Abglanz von dieser in den Seelentiefen waltenden Inspiration aus den Weiten der geistigen Welt steht vor dem gewöhnlichen Bewusstsein.

16. Die dritte Gestalt des «Ich» gibt die Einsicht in die selbstständige Wesenheit des Menschen innerhalb einer geistigen Welt. Sie regt die Empfindung davon an, dass der Mensch mit seiner irdisch-sinnlichen Natur nur als die Offenbarung dessen vor sich selber steht, was er in Wirklichkeit ist. Damit ist der Ausgangspunkt wahrer Selbsterkenntnis gegeben. Denn jenes Selbst, das den Menschen in seiner Wahrheit gestaltet, wird sich der Erkenntnis erst offenbaren, wenn er vom Gedanken des Ich zu dessen Bilde, von dem Bilde zu den schöpfenden Kräften dieses Bildes und von da zu den geistigen Trägern dieser Kräfte fortschreitet.

15. Insight into the form in which the 'I' lives in the astral body leads to a right feeling of the relation of the human being to the spiritual world. For ordinary consciousness, this form of the 'I' is sunken in the dark depths of the unconscious. In these depths, the human being enters into connection with the spiritual world-being through inspiration. Ordinary consciousness experiences only a very faint feeling-echo of this inspiration from the wide expanse of the spiritual world, which holds sway in depths of the soul.

16. It is the third form of the 'I' which gives insight into the autonomous existence of the human being within a spiritual world. It stimulates the feeling for how, with his earthly-sensory nature, the human being stands before himself as a mere outer manifestation of what he really is. Here lies the starting-point of true self-knowledge. For the self which fashions the human being in his true nature is revealed to him in knowledge only when he progresses from the thought of the 'I' to its image, from the image to the creative forces of the image, and from there to the spiritual bearers of these forces.

Leitsätze Nr. 17 bis 19

17. Der Mensch ist ein Wesen, das in der Mitte zwischen zwei Weltgebieten sein Leben entfaltet. Er ist mit seiner Leibes-Entwickelung in eine «untere Welt» eingegliedert; er bildet mit seiner Seelen-Wesenheit eine «mittlere Welt», und er strebt mit seinen Geisteskräften nach einer «oberen Welt» hin. Seine Leibes-Entwickelung hat er von dem, was ihm die Natur gegeben hat; seine Seelen-Wesenheit trägt er als seinen eigenen Anteil in sich; die Geisteskräfte findet er in sich als die Gaben, die ihn über sich selbst hinausführen zur Anteilnahme an einer göttlichen Welt.

18. Der Geist ist in diesen drei Weltgebieten schaffend. Die Natur ist nicht geistlos. Man verliert erkennend auch die Natur, wenn man in ihr den Geist nicht gewahr wird. Aber man wird allerdings innerhalb des Naturdaseins den Geist wie schlafend finden. So wie aber der Schlaf im Menschenleben seine Aufgabe hat und das «Ich» eine gewisse Zeit schlafen muss, um zu einer anderen recht wach zu sein, so muss der Weltengeist an der «Natur-Stelle» schlafen, um an einer anderen recht wach zu sein.

Leading Thoughts 17 to 19

17. The human being is a being who unfolds his life in the middle-realm, between two regions of the world. With his bodily development he is a member of a "lower world"; with his soul-nature he himself constitutes a "middle world"; and with his faculties of spirit he is ever striving toward an "upper world." He owes his bodily development to all that nature has given him; he bears the being of his soul within him as his own portion; and he finds in himself the forces of the spirit, as the gifts that lead him out beyond himself to participate in a divine world.

18. The spirit creates in these three regions of the world. Nature is not void of spirit. One loses even one's understanding for nature if one does not become aware of the spirit within her. Nevertheless, in nature's existence one finds the spirit asleep, as it were. Yet just as sleep has its task in human life – as the 'I' must be asleep for some time in order to be the more awake at another – so must the world-spirit be asleep in the "realm of nature," in order to be truly awake elsewhere.

19. Der Welt gegenüber ist die Menschenseele ein träumendes Wesen, wenn sie nicht auf den Geist achtet, der in ihr wirkt. Dieser weckt die im eigenen Innern webenden Seelenträume zur Anteilnahme an der Welt, aus welcher des Menschen wahres Wesen stammt. Wie sich der Träumende vor der physischen Umwelt verschließt und in das eigene Wesen einspinnt, so müsste die Seele ihren Zusammenhang mit dem Geiste der Welt verlieren, aus dem sie stammt, wenn sie die Weckrufe des Geistes in sich selbst nicht hören wollte.

Leitsätze Nr. 20 bis 22

20. Es gehört zur rechten Entfaltung des Seelenlebens im Menschen, dass er sich innerhalb seines Wesens des Wirkens aus dem Geiste vollbewusst werde. Viele Bekenner der neueren naturwissenschaftlichen Weltanschauung sind in dieser Richtung so stark in einem Vorurteile befangen, dass sie sagen, die allgemeine Ursächlichkeit ist in allen Welterscheinungen das Herrschende. Wenn der Mensch glaubt, er könne aus Eigenem die Ursache von etwas sein, so kann das nur eine Illusion bilden. Die neuere Natur-Erkenntnis will in allem treu der Beobachtung und Erfahrung folgen.

19. In relation to the world, the human soul is like a dreaming being if it does not pay heed to the spirit at work within it. The spirit awakens the dreams of the soul from their weaving in the inner life, to active participation in that world where the human being's true being has its origin. As the dreamer shuts himself off from the surrounding physical world and entwines himself into himself, so would the soul lose connection with the spirit of the world from which it has its source if it turned a deaf ear to the awakening calls of the spirit within itself.

Leading Thoughts 20 to 22

20. It belongs to the right unfolding of the soul life in the human being that he becomes fully conscious within his being of the working out of the spirit. Many adherents of the modern scientific world-conception have a very strong prejudice in this respect. They say that a universal causality is dominant in all phenomena of the world; and that if the human being believes that he himself, out of his own resources, can be the cause of anything, it is a mere illusion on his part. The modern science of nature wishes to follow observation and experience faithfully in all things, but in its prejudice about the hidden

Durch dieses Vorurteil von der verborgenen Ursächlichkeit der eigenen menschlichen Antriebe sündigt sie gegen diesen ihren Grundsatz. Denn das freie Wirken aus dem Innern des menschlichen Wesens ist ein ganz elementares Ergebnis der menschlichen Selbstbeobachtung. Man darf es nicht wegleugnen, sondern muss es mit der Einsicht in die allgemeine Verursachung innerhalb der Naturordnung in Einklang bringen.

21. Die Nicht-Anerkennung dieses Antriebes aus dem Geiste heraus im Innern des menschlichen Wesens ist das größte Hindernis für die Erlangung einer Einsicht in die geistige Welt. Denn Einordnung des eigenen Wesens in den Naturzusammenhang bedeutet Ablenkung des Seelenblickes von diesem Wesen. Man kann aber in die geistige Welt nicht eindringen, wenn man den Geist nicht zuerst da erfasst, wo er ganz unmittelbar gegeben ist: in der unbefangenen Selbstbeobachtung.

22. Die Selbstbeobachtung bildet den Anfang der Geistbeobachtung. Und sie kann deshalb den rechten Anfang bilden, weil der Mensch bei wahrer Besinnung nicht bei ihr stehen bleiben kann, sondern von ihr fortschreiten muss zu weiterem geistigen Weltinhalt. Wie der menschliche Körper verkümmert, wenn er nicht physische

causality of the human being's inner sources of action it sins against its own principle. For the free and active working out of the inner resources of the human being is an entirely elementary experience of self-observation. It cannot be argued away; rather, one must bring it into harmony with the insight about universal causation within the order of nature.

21. Non-recognition of this impulse of the spirit that works in the inner life of the human being is the greatest hindrance to the attainment of an insight into the spiritual world. For to consider one's own being as a mere part of the order of nature is in reality to divert the soul's attention from this being. Nor can one penetrate into the spiritual world unless one first takes hold of the spirit where it is immediately given, namely in clear and open-minded self-observation.

22. Self-observation is the first beginning in the observation of the spirit. It can indeed be the right beginning, for through true contemplation, the human being cannot possibly stop short at it, but is bound to progress to the further spiritual content of the world. As the human body becomes stunted when bereft of physical

Nahrung erhält, so wird der im rechten Sinne sich selbst beobachtende Mensch sein Selbst in Verkümmerung empfinden, wenn er nicht sieht, wie in dieses Selbst die Kräfte einer außer ihm tätigen geistigen Welt hineinwirken.

Leitsätze Nr. 23 bis 25

23. Der Mensch betritt, indem er durch die Todespforte geht, die geistige Welt, indem er von sich abfallen fühlt alles, was er durch die Sinne des Leibes und durch das Gehirn während des Erdenlebens an Eindrücken und an Seeleninhalten erworben hat. Sein Bewusstsein hat dann in einem umfassenden Tableau in Bildern vor sich, was an Lebensinhalt während des Erdenwandels in Form von bildlosen Gedanken in das Gedächtnis gebracht werden konnte oder was zwar für das Erdenbewusstsein unbemerkt geblieben ist, doch aber einen unterbewussten Eindruck auf die Seele gemacht hat. Diese Bilder verblassen nach wenig Tagen bis zum Entschwinden. Wenn sie sich ganz verloren haben, so weiß der Mensch, dass er auch seinen Ätherleib abgelegt hat, in dem er den Träger dieser Bilder erkennen kann.

nourishment, so will the human being who rightly observes himself feel that his self is becoming stunted if he does not see working into it the forces from a creative spiritual world outside him.

Leading Thoughts 23 to 25

23. In passing through the gate of death, the human being enters the spiritual world and feels falling away from him all the impressions and content of soul which he acquired during earthly life through the bodily senses and the brain. His consciousness then has before it in an all-embracing image-tableau the whole content of life which, during his earthly wanderings, entered as imageless thoughts into his memory, or which – remaining unnoticed by the earthly consciousness – nevertheless made a subconscious impression on his soul. After a very few days, these images grow faint and fade away. When they have altogether vanished, he knows that he has laid aside his etheric body too; for in the etheric body he can recognize the bearer of these images.

24. Der Mensch hat nach der Ablegung des Ätherleibes noch den Astralleib und das Ich als die ihm verbleibenden Glieder. Solange der Erstere an ihm ist, lässt dieser von dem Bewusstsein alles das erleben, was während des Erdenlebens den unbewussten Inhalt der im Schlafe ruhenden Seele gebildet hat. In diesem Inhalt sind die Urteile enthalten, welche die Geistwesen einer höheren Welt während der Schlafzeiten dem Astralleib einprägen, die aber dem Erdenbewusstsein sich verbergen. Der Mensch lebt sein Erdenleben noch einmal durch, doch so, dass sein Seeleninhalt jetzt die Beurteilung seines Tuns und Denkens vom Gesichtspunkte der Geisteswelt aus ist. Das Durchleben geschieht rückläufig: erst die letzte Nacht, dann die zweitletzte und so weiter.

25. Die nach dem Durchgang durch die Todespforte im Astralleibe erlebte Lebensbeurteilung dauert so lange, wie die Zeit betragen hat, die während des Erdenlebens von dem Schlafe eingenommen war.

24. Having laid aside the etheric body, the human being has the astral body and the 'I' as the members of his being still remaining to him. The astral body, so long as it is with him, brings to his consciousness all that during earthly life was the unconscious content of the soul when at rest in sleep. This content includes the judgments impressed upon the astral body by spirit-beings of a higher world during the periods of sleep – judgments which remain concealed from earthly consciousness. The human being now lives through his earthly life a second time, yet in such a way that the content of his soul is now the judgment of his thought and action from the standpoint of the world of spirit. He lives it through in backward order: first the last night, then the last but one, and so on.

25. This judgment of his life, which the human being experiences in the astral body after passing through the gate of death, lasts as long as the sum-total of the time he spent during his earthly life in sleep.

Leitsätze Nr. 26 bis 28

26. Erst nach Ablegung des Astralleibes, nach der vollendeten Lebensbeurteilung, tritt der Mensch in die geistige Welt ein. In dieser steht er zu Wesenheiten rein geistiger Art in einer solchen Beziehung wie auf der Erde zu den Wesenheiten und Vorgängen der Naturreiche. Es wird im geistigen Erleben dann alles, was im Erdenleben Außenwelt war, zur Innenwelt. Der Mensch nimmt dann nicht bloß diese Außenwelt wahr, sondern er erlebt sie in ihrer Geistigkeit, die ihm auf Erden verborgen war, als seine Innenwelt.

27. Der Mensch, wie er auf Erden ist, wird im Geistgebiet Außenwelt. Man schaut auf diesen Menschen, wie man auf Erden auf Sterne, Wolken, Berge, Flüsse schaut. Und *diese* Außenwelt ist nicht weniger inhaltreich, wie die Erscheinung des Kosmos dem irdischen Leben erscheint.

28. Die im Geistgebiet vom Geiste des Menschen erbildeten *Kräfte* wirken in der Gestaltung des Erdenmenschen fort, so wie die im physischen Menschen vollbrachten *Taten* in dem Leben nach dem Tode als Seeleninhalt fortwirken.

Leading Thoughts 26 to 28

26. Only when the astral body has been laid aside – when the judgment of his life is over – does the human being enter the spiritual world. There he stands in relation to beings of a purely spiritual character in the same way as, on earth, he did to the beings and processes of the realms of nature. In spiritual experience, everything that was his outer world on earth now becomes his inner world. He no longer merely perceives it, but now experiences it in its spiritual aspect – which was hidden from him while on earth – as the content of his own inner world.

27. In the spirit-realm, the human being as he is on earth becomes an outer world. One gazes upon these human beings, just as on earth one gazes upon the stars and clouds, the mountains and rivers. And *this* outer world is no less rich in content than the manifestation of the cosmos as it appears in earthly life.

28. The *forces* begotten by the human spirit in the spirit-realm work on in the fashioning of the earthly human being, just as the *deeds* accomplished in the physical work on as content of the soul in the life after death.

Leitsätze Nr. 29 bis 31

29. In der entwickelten imaginativen Erkenntnis wirkt, was im Innern des Menschen seelisch-geistig lebt und in seinem Leben am physischen Leib gestaltet und auf dessen Grundlage das Menschendasein in der physischen Welt entfaltet. Dem sich im Stoffwechsel immer wieder erneuernden physischen Leib steht da die in ihrem Wesen von der Geburt (bzw. Empfängnis) bis zum Tode *dauernd* sich entfaltende innere Menschenwesenheit gegenüber, dem physischen Raumesleib ein Zeitenleib.

30. In der inspirierten Erkenntnis lebt im Bilde, was das Menschenwesen in der Zeit zwischen dem Tode und einer neuen Geburt innerhalb einer geistigen Umgebung erfährt. Da ist anschaulich, was der Mensch ohne seinen physischen und Ätherleib, durch die er das irdische Dasein durchmacht, seinem Wesen nach im Weltenzusammenhange ist.

31. In der intuitiven Erkenntnis kommt das Herüberwirken früherer Erdenleben in das gegenwärtige zum Bewusstsein. Diese früheren Erdenleben haben in ihrer

Leading Thoughts 29 to 31

29. In what is developed as imaginative cognition, there works what lives soul-spiritually in the human being's inner life as well as that which fashions his life in the physical body and upon whose foundation human existence unfolds in the physical world. Over against the physical body – the substances of which are renewed ever again through the process of metabolism – there is the inner nature of the human being, unfolding itself *continuously* from birth (or conception) until death; over against the physical spatial-body, there is a time-body.

30. In inspirative cognition, there lives, in image-form, what the human being experiences in a spiritual environment in the time between death and a new birth. What the human being is in his own cosmically-connected essential nature – without the physical and etheric bodies by means of which he undergoes his earthly life – is here made visible.

31. In intuitive cognition, there comes to consciousness the working-over of former earthly lives into the present. These former lives have, in their further development,

Weiterentwickelung die Zusammenhänge abgestreift, in denen sie mit der physischen Welt gestanden haben. Sie sind zum rein geistigen Wesenskern des Menschen geworden und wirken als solcher im gegenwärtigen Leben. Sie sind dadurch auch Gegenstand der Erkenntnis, die als die Entfaltung der imaginierenden und inspirierten sich ergibt.

Leitsätze Nr. 32 bis 34

32. In dem Haupte des Menschen ist die physische Organisation ein Abdruck der geistigen Individualität. Physischer und ätherischer Teil des Hauptes stehen als abgeschlossene Bilder des Geistigen, und *neben* ihnen in selbstständiger seelisch-geistiger Wesenheit stehen der astralische und der Ichteil. Man hat es daher im Haupte des Menschen mit einer Nebeneinanderentwickelung des relativ selbstständigen Physischen und Ätherischen einerseits, des Astralischen und der Ich-Organisation andererseits zu tun.

33. In dem Gliedmaßen-Stoffwechselteil des Menschen sind die vier Glieder der Menschenwesenheit innig miteinander verbunden. Ich-Organisation und astralischer

been divested of their erstwhile connections with the physical world. They have become the purely spiritual core-being of the human being and, as such, continue to work in his present life. In this way, they too are an object of knowledge – of that knowledge which presents itself as the further unfolding of the imaginative and inspirative elements.

Leading Thoughts 32 to 34

32. In the human head, the physical organization is an "imprint" of the spiritual individuality. The physical and etheric parts of the head stand out as complete and self-contained images of the spiritual; *beside* them, in independent soul-spiritual being, there stand the astral and 'I'-components. Thus, in the human head one has to do with a side-by-side development of the relatively independent physical and etheric on the one hand, and of the astral and 'I'-organization on the other.

33. In the limb and metabolic part of the human being, the four members of the human being are intimately bound up with one another. The 'I'-organization and astral

Leib sind nicht neben dem physischen und ätherischen Teil. Sie sind *in* diesen; sie beleben sie, wirken in ihrem Wachstum, in ihrer Bewegungsfähigkeit und so weiter. Dadurch aber ist der Gliedmaßen-Stoffwechselteil wie ein Keim, der sich weiter entwickeln will, der fortwährend darnach strebt, Haupt zu werden, und der fortwährend davon während des Erdenlebens des Menschen zurückgehalten wird.

34. Die rhythmische Organisation steht in der Mitte. Hier verbinden sich Ich-Organisation und Astralleib abwechselnd mit dem physischen und ätherischen Teil und lösen sich wieder von diesen. Atmung und Blutzirkulation sind der physische Abdruck dieser Vereinigung und Loslösung. Der Einatmungsvorgang bildet die Verbindung ab; der Ausatmungsvorgang die Loslösung. Die Vorgänge im Arterienblut stellen die Verbindung dar; die Vorgänge im Venenblute die Loslösung.

Leitsätze Nr. 35 bis 37

35. Man versteht das physische Menschenwesen nur, wenn man es als *Bild* des Geistig-Seelischen betrachtet. Für sich genommen bleibt der physische Körper

body are not *there beside* the physical and etheric parts. They are *within* them, vitalizing them, working in their growth, in their faculty of movement, and so forth. Through this very fact, the limb and metabolic part of the human being is like a germinal seed, wishing to further develop itself, striving continually to become a "head," and – during the earthly life of the human being – continually held back from achieving this.

34. The rhythmic organization stands in the middle. Here the 'I'-organization and astral body alternately unite with, and loosen themselves from, the physical and etheric part. The breathing rhythm and the circulation of the blood are the physical imprint of this alternating union and loosening. The inbreathing process portrays the connection; the outbreathing the loosening. The processes in the arterial blood represent the connection; those in the venous blood the loosening.

Leading Thoughts 35 to 37

35. One understands the physical nature of the human being only if one regards it as an *image* of the spiritual-soul element. Taken by itself, the human physical body is

des Menschen unverständlich. Aber er ist in seinen verschiedenen Gliedern in verschiedener Art Bild des Geistig-Seelischen. Das Haupt ist dessen vollkommenstes, abgeschlossenes Sinnesbild. Alles, was dem Stoffwechsel- und Gliedmaßensystem angehört, ist wie ein Bild, das noch nicht seine Endformen angenommen hat, sondern an dem erst gearbeitet wird. Alles, was zur rhythmischen Organisation des Menschen gehört, steht in Bezug auf das Verhältnis des Geistig-Seelischen zum Körperlichen zwischen diesen Gegensätzen.

36. Wer von diesem geistigen Gesichtspunkte aus das menschliche Haupt betrachtet, hat an dieser Betrachtung eine Hilfe zum Verständnisse geistiger Imaginationen; denn in den Formen des Hauptes sind imaginative Formen gewissermaßen bis zur physischen Dichte geronnen.

37. In derselben Art kann man an der Betrachtung des rhythmischen Teiles der Menschenorganisation eine Hilfe haben für das Verständnis von Inspirationen. Der physische Anblick der Lebensrhythmen trägt im Sinnesbilde den Charakter des Inspirierten. Im Stoffwechsel- und Gliedmaßensystem hat man, wenn man diese in

unintelligible. But it is an image of the spiritual-soul element in different ways in its various members. And of the body, the head is the most perfect and complete sense-perceptible image of the spiritual-soul element. All that pertains to the system of the metabolism and limbs is like an image that has not yet assumed its finished form, but is still being worked out. All that belongs to the human rhythmic organization, as regards the relation of the spiritual-soul element to the body, stands in an intermediate position between these aforementioned poles.

36. The person who contemplates the human head from this spiritual point of view will find in it a help to his understanding of spiritual imaginations. For in the forms of the head, imaginative forms are as it were coagulated to the point of physical density.

37. In the same way, in contemplating the rhythmic part of the human organization, one will find a help in understanding inspirations. The physical appearance of the life-rhythms bears, in a sense-perceptible image, the character of inspiration. In the system of the metabolism and limbs – if one observes it in full action, in the

voller Aktion, in der Entfaltung ihrer notwendigen oder möglichen Verrichtungen betrachtet, ein sinnlich-übersinnliches Bild des rein übersinnlichen Intuitiven.

exercise of its necessary or possible functions – one has a sensory-suprasensory image of pure suprasensory intuitions.

Zu den vorangegangenen *Leitsätzen* über die Bildnatur des Menschen

Es kommt viel darauf an, dass durch die Anthroposophie begriffen werde, wie die Vorstellungen, die der Mensch im Anblicke der äußeren Natur gewinnt, vor der Menschenbetrachtung Halt machen müssen. Gegen diese Forderung sündigt die Denkungsart, die durch die geistige Entwickelung der letzten Jahrhunderte in die Menschengemüter eingezogen ist. Durch sie gewöhnt man sich, Naturgesetze zu denken; und durch diese Naturgesetze erklärt man sich die Naturerscheinungen, die man mit den Sinnen wahrnimmt. Man sieht nun nach dem menschlichen Organismus hin und betrachtet auch diesen so, wie wenn seine Einrichtung begriffen werden könnte, wenn man die Naturgesetze auf ihn anwendet.

Das ist nun gerade so, als ob man das Bild, das ein Maler geschaffen hat, betrachtete nach der Substanz der Farben, nach der Kraft, mit der die Farben an der Leinwand haften, nach der Art, wie sich diese Farben auf die Leinwand streichen lassen, und nach ähnlichen Gesichtspunkten. Aber mit alledem trifft man nicht, was sich in dem Bilde offenbart. In dieser Offenbarung, die durch das Bild da ist, leben ganz

On the Preceding *Leading Thoughts* on the Image-Nature of the Human Being

Much depends on it being understood, through Anthroposophy, how the representations one gains by looking upon outer nature must stop short at the observation of the human being. The way of thinking that has entered the minds and souls of human beings during the spiritual development of the last few centuries sins against this requirement. Through this way of thinking, one has grown accustomed to thinking out the laws of nature and to explaining by means of them the phenomena perceived by the senses. One then turns one's attention to the human organism, and thinks that it too can be explained through bringing the laws of nature to bear upon it.

Now this would be just as if, in considering a picture that a painter had created, one were to take into account only the substance of the colors, their power of adhering to the canvas, the way in which these colors were applied, and similar such observations. But such a way of regarding the picture does not reveal what is contained within it. Quite other laws are active in the revelation contained in the picture than

andere Gesetzmäßigkeiten als diejenigen, die aus den angegebenen Gesichtspunkten gewonnen werden können.

Es kommt nun darauf an, sich darüber klar zu werden, dass sich auch in der menschlichen Wesenheit etwas offenbart, das von den Gesichtspunkten, von denen aus die Gesetze der äußeren Natur gewonnen werden, nicht zu ergreifen ist. Hat man diese Vorstellung in der rechten Art sich zu eigen gemacht, dann wird man in der Lage sein, den Menschen *als Bild* zu begreifen. Ein Mineral ist in diesem Sinne nicht Bild. Es offenbart nur dasjenige, was unmittelbar die Sinne wahrnehmen können.

Beim Bilde richtet sich die Anschauung gewissermaßen durch das sinnlich Angeschaute *hindurch* auf einen Inhalt, der im Geiste erfasst wird. Und so ist es auch bei der Betrachtung des Menschenwesens. Erfasst man dieses in rechter Art mit den Naturgesetzen, so fühlt man sich im Vorstellen dieser Naturgesetze nicht dem wirklichen Menschen nahe, sondern nur demjenigen, durch das sich dieser wirkliche Mensch offenbart.

Man muss es im Geiste erleben, dass man mit den Naturgesetzen so vor dem Menschen steht, wie man vor einem Bilde stünde, wenn man nur wüsste, da ist Blau, da ist Rot, und man nicht imstande wäre, in einer inneren Seelentätigkeit das Blau und Rot auf etwas zu beziehen, das sich durch diese Farben offenbart.

those which can be perceived by considering such points as these.

It is a matter of realizing that also in the human being something is revealed which cannot be grasped from the perspective won from the laws of outer nature. If anyone has once thoroughly made this representation his own in the right way, then he will be in a position to understand the human being *as an image*. A mineral is not an image in this sense. It is a revelation of only what is already directly evident to the senses.

To a certain extent, when approaching an image it is a matter of looking *through* what the senses perceive to its spiritual content. And so it is likewise in the case of observing the human being. If one truly understands the human being in light of the laws of nature, then one feels, in forming inner representations of these laws, unable to approach the true human being but only that through which the true human being reveals himself.

One must experience spiritually that when one regards a human being only from the point of view of the laws of nature, it is as if one stands before an image seeing only "blue" and "red," and is quite unable, through inner soul-activity, to relate the blue and red to what reveals itself through these colors.

Man muss eben eine andere Empfindung haben, wenn man mit den Naturgesetzen einem Mineralischen, und eine andere, wenn man dem Menschen gegenübersteht. Beim Mineralischen ist es für die geistige Auffassung so, als wenn man das Wahrgenommene unmittelbar ertastete; beim Menschen ist es so, als ob man ihm mit den Naturgesetzen so ferne stünde, wie man einem Bilde ferne steht, das man nicht mit Seelenaugen anblickt, sondern nur betastet.

Hat man erst in der Anschauung des Menschen begriffen, dass dieser *Bild* von etwas ist, dann wird man in der rechten Seelenstimmung auch zu dem fortschreiten, was sich in diesem Bilde darstellt.

Und im Menschen offenbart sich die Bildnatur nicht auf eine eindeutige Weise. Ein Sinnesorgan ist in seinem Wesen am wenigsten Bild, am meisten eine Art Offenbarung seiner selbst, wie das Mineral. Man kann gerade an die Sinnesorgane mit den Naturgesetzen am nächsten heran. Man betrachte nur die wundervolle Einrichtung des menschlichen Auges. Man erfasst durch Naturgesetze *annähernd* diese Einrichtung. Und bei den anderen Sinnesorganen ist es ähnlich, wenn auch die Sache nicht so offen zutage tritt wie beim Auge. Es kommt dies daher, dass die Sinnesorgane in ihrer Bildung eine gewisse Abgeschlossenheit zeigen. Sie sind als *fertige* Bildungen dem Organismus eingegliedert, und als solche vermitteln sie die Wahrnehmungen der Außenwelt.

When viewing things from the standpoint of the laws of nature, one must perceive the mineral in one way and the human being in another. In the case of the mineral, for the spiritual understanding it is as if one is in direct relation with what is perceived by touching; but in the case of the human being, it is as if one can only come as near to him through the laws of nature as to an image which one does not see clearly with the eye of the soul but only by touching.

When one has once gained the perception that the human being is an *image* of something, one shall be in the right mood of soul to progress to what comes to manifestation through this image.

The image-like nature of the human being does not manifest in one way only. A sense organ is, in its nature, least of all an image and primarily a kind of revelation of itself, like the mineral. It is precisely the sense organs that one can approach most closely by means of the laws of nature. One need only contemplate the wonderful arrangement of the eye. Through the laws of nature, one can grasp *something that approximates* this arrangement. It is the same with the other organs, though it is often not as clearly evident as with the eye. This is because the sense organs, in their formation, show a certain completion. They are arranged in the organism as *complete* formations, and as such they assist in the perception of the outer world.

So aber ist es nicht mit den rhythmischen Vorgängen, die sich im Organismus abspielen. Sie stellen sich nicht als etwas Fertiges dar. In ihnen vollzieht sich ein fortwährendes Entstehen und Vergehen des Organismus. Wären die Sinnesorgane so wie das rhythmische System, so würde der Mensch die Außenwelt in der Art wahrnehmen, dass diese in einem fortwährenden Werden sich befände.

Die Sinnesorgane stellen sich dar wie ein Bild, das an der Wand hängt. Das rhythmische System steht vor uns wie das Geschehen, das sich entfaltet, wenn Leinwand und Maler im Entstehen des Bildes von uns betrachtet werden. Das Bild ist noch nicht da; aber es ist immer mehr da. In dieser Betrachtung hat man es nur mit einem *Entstehen* zu tun. Was entstanden ist, bleibt zunächst bestehen. In der Betrachtung des menschlichen rhythmischen Systems schließt sich das Vergehen, der Abbau, sogleich an das Entstehen, an den Aufbau an. Im rhythmischen System offenbart sich ein *werdendes* Bild.

Die Tätigkeit, welche die Seele verrichtet, indem sie sich einem ihr Gegenüberstehenden wahrnehmend hingibt, das fertiges Bild ist, kann als *Imagination* bezeichnet werden. Das Erleben, das entfaltet werden muss, um ein werdendes Bild zu erfassen, ist dem gegenüber *Inspiration*.

Noch anders liegt die Sache, wenn man das Stoffwechsel- und das Bewegungssystem des menschlichen Organismus

But it is otherwise with the rhythmic processes that play out in the organism. They do not represent something complete. Within them the organism arises and fades away continuously. If the sense organs were so constituted as the rhythmic system, then the human being would perceive the outer world in a state of perpetual becoming.

The sense organs present themselves like a picture that hangs on the wall. The rhythmic system is like the scene that unfolds itself if canvas and painter are envisioned by us at the conception of the picture. The picture is not yet there, but it comes more and more into being. In considering the rhythmic system, one has to do with a *perpetual process of becoming*. What has come into existence remains for a time in existence. But in this consideration one finds the process of becoming, the up-building process, followed directly and without a gap by the passing out of existence, the breaking-down process. In the rhythmic system there appears a picture *in becoming*.

The activity which the soul carries out in conscious devotion to what is brought before it as finished picture may be designated *imagination*. On the other hand, the experience that must be unfolded in order to comprehend a picture coming into existence is *inspiration*.

But the situation is different again when one contemplates the metabolic and limb system of the human organism. Here

betrachtet. Da ist es, als ob man vor der noch ganz leeren Leinwand, den Farbentöpfen und dem noch nicht malenden Künstler stünde. Will man dem Stoffwechsel- und dem Gliedmaßensystem gegenüber zum Begreifen kommen, so muss man ein Wahrnehmen entwickeln, das mit dem Wahrnehmen dessen, was die Sinne erfassen, nicht mehr zu tun hat als der Anblick von Farbentöpfen, leerer Leinwand und Maler mit dem, was später als Bild des Malers vor unsere Augen tritt. Und die Tätigkeit, in der die Seele rein geistig den Menschen aus dem Stoffwechsel und aus seinen Bewegungen heraus erlebt, ist so, wie wenn man im Anblicke vom Maler, leerer Leinwand und Farbentöpfen das später gemalte Bild erlebte. Dem Stoffwechsel- und Gliedmaßensystem gegenüber muss in der Seele die *Intuition* walten, wenn es zum Begreifen kommen soll.

Es ist nötig, dass die tätig wirkenden Mitglieder der Anthroposophischen Gesellschaft in solcher Art auf die Wesenheit hindeuten, die dem anthroposophischen Betrachten zugrunde liegt. Denn nicht nur soll eingesehen werden, was durch Anthroposophie an Erkenntnisinhalt gewonnen wird, sondern auch, wie man zum Erleben dieses Erkenntnisinhaltes gelangt.

Von dem hier Dargestellten wird der Weg der Betrachtung zu den folgenden *Leitsätzen* hinüberführen.

it is as if one stands before an entirely empty canvas, unused paints, and the painter who has not yet begun to paint. To get a perception of the metabolic and limb system, one must develop a form of perception that has as little connection with what is perceived by the senses as the empty canvas, unused paints, and artist have with what later stands before our eyes as the artist's picture. And this activity, in which the soul achieves a purely spiritual experience of the human being out of his metabolism and movements, is as when, upon seeing the painter, the empty canvas, and the unused paints, one experiences the yet-to-be-painted picture. In order to understand the metabolic and limb system, the power of *intuition* must hold sway in the soul.

It is necessary that the active members of the Anthroposophical Society should concentrate in this way on the essential and fundamental nature of anthroposophical consideration. For it is not only a matter of the knowledge-content gained, but also of how one comes to an experience of this knowledge-content.

From what has here been presented, our consideration leads to the following *Leading Thoughts*.

Leitsätze Nr. 38 bis 40

38. Ist man dazu gelangt, in der durch die vorigen *Leitsätze* angedeuteten Richtung den Menschen in seiner *Bildnatur* und in der dadurch sich offenbarenden Geistigkeit zu betrachten, so steht man davor, in der geistigen Welt, in der man den Menschen als Geistwesen waltend schaut, auch die seelisch-moralischen Gesetze in ihrer Wirklichkeit *mit*zuschauen. Denn die moralische Weltordnung stellt sich dann als das irdische Abbild einer zur geistigen Welt gehörigen Ordnung dar. Und physische und moralische Weltordnung gliedern sich zur Einheit zusammen.

39. Aus dem Menschen wirkt der *Wille*. Der steht den an der Außenwelt gewonnenen Naturgesetzen ganz fremd gegenüber. Das Wesen der Sinnesorgane ist noch an seiner Ähnlichkeit gegenüber den äußeren Naturgegenständen zu erkennen. In ihrer Tätigkeit kann sich der Wille noch nicht entfalten. Das Wesen, das sich im rhythmischen System des Menschen offenbart, ist allem Äußeren schon unähnlicher. In dieses System kann der Wille schon bis zu einem gewissen Grade eingreifen. Aber es ist dieses System im Entstehen und Vergehen begriffen. An diese ist der Wille noch gebunden.

Leading Thoughts 38 to 40

38. It has been shown how the human being is to be regarded in his *image-nature* and in the spirituality which thereby reveals itself. Once this perception is attained, then, in the spiritual world, where one sees the human being living and moving as a spirit-being, one is also at the point of seeing-*with* the reality of the moral laws of the soul. For the moral world-order is then revealed as the earthly image of an order belonging to the spiritual world. And the physical and the moral world-order merge into a unity.

39. From out of the human being, there works the human *will*. This will confronts the laws of nature derived from the external world as something altogether foreign to their being. The nature of the sense organs can still be acknowledged by virtue of their likeness to the objects of external nature. In the activity of these organs, the will is not yet able to unfold itself. The nature that manifests itself in the human rhythmic system is already far less akin to any external thing. Into this system the will can already work to some extent. But the rhythmic system is in a constant process of coming-into-being and fading away, and the will is still bound to this process.

40. Im Stoffwechsel- und Gliedmaßensystem offenbart sich ein Wesen zwar durch die Stoffe und die Vorgänge an den Stoffen, aber diese Stoffe und diese Vorgänge haben mit ihm nichts weiter zu tun als der Maler und seine Mittel mit dem fertigen Bilde. In dieses Wesen kann daher der Wille unmittelbar eingreifen. Erfasst man hinter der in Naturgesetzen lebenden Menschenorganisation die im Geistigen webende Menschenwesenheit, so hat man in *dieser* ein Gebiet, in dem man das Wirken des Willens gewahr werden kann. Gegenüber dem Sinnesgebiete bleibt der menschliche Wille ein Wort ohne allen Inhalt. Und wer ihn in diesem Gebiete erfassen will, der verlässt im Erkennen das wahre Wesen des Willens und setzt etwas anderes an dessen Stelle.

Leitsätze Nr. 41 bis 43

41. Durch den dritten *Leitsatz* der vorigen Gruppe wird auf das Wesen des *menschlichen Willens* hingewiesen. Erst wenn man dieses Wesen gewahr geworden ist, steht man mit seinem Begreifen in einer Weltsphäre darinnen, in der das Schicksal (Karma) wirkt. Solange man nur die Gesetzmäßigkeit erblickt, die im Zusammenhange der

40. In the system of metabolism and limbs, there is a being which manifests itself in material substances and in the processes they undergo; yet the substances and processes are actually no closer to this being than are the artist and his materials to the finished picture. In this being, therefore, the will is able to enter in and work directly. If, behind the human organization that lives in the laws of nature, one grasps the human being that weaves in the spiritual, then *here* one has a realm in which one can become aware of the working of the will. With regard to the sensory realm, the human will remains a word empty of all content. And one who wishes to comprehend it within this realm leaves behind, in the knowledge process, the true being of the will and sets something else in its place.

Leading Thoughts 41 to 43

41. In the third of the last *Leading Thoughts*, the being of the *human will* was indicated. Only when one brings this being to realization does one enter with understanding into a sphere of the world where destiny (karma) works. As long as one perceives only the lawfulness which holds sway in the relations among the things and facts of

Naturdinge und Naturtatsachen herrscht, bleibt man dem ganz fern, das im Schicksal gesetzmäßig wirkt.

42. In einem solchen Erfassen der Gesetzmäßigkeit im Schicksal offenbart sich auch, dass sich dieses durch den Gang des einzelnen physischen Erdenlebens nicht zum Dasein bringen kann. Solange der Mensch in demselben physischen Leibe lebt, kann er den moralischen Inhalt seines Willens nur so zur Wirklichkeit werden lassen, wie es dieser physische Leib innerhalb der physischen Welt gestattet. Erst, wenn der Mensch durch die Todespforte in die Geistessphäre eingezogen ist, kann die Geistwesenheit des Willens zur vollen Wirklichkeit gelangen. Da wird das Gute in seinen ihm entsprechenden Ergebnissen, das Schlechte in den seinigen, zunächst zur geistigen Verwirklichung kommen.

43. In dieser geistigen Verwirklichung gestaltet sich der Mensch selber zwischen dem Tode und einer neuen Geburt; er wird *wesenhaft* ein Abbild dessen, was er im Erdenleben *getan* hat. Aus diesem seinem Wesenhaften heraus gestaltet er dann beim Wieder-Betreten der Erde sein physisches Leben. Das Geistige, das im Schicksal waltet, kann im Physischen nur seine Verwirklichung finden, wenn seine entsprechende Verursachung *vor* dieser Verwirklichung sich

nature, one remains completely distant from the lawfulness which works in human destiny.

42. In such an understanding of the lawfulness in destiny, it is revealed at the same time that destiny cannot come into existence in the course of a single physical life on earth. So long as a person inhabits the same physical body, he can realize the moral content of his will only in the way that this particular physical body, within the physical world, allows. Only when he has passed through the gate of death into the sphere of the spirit can the spirit-nature of the will come to full effect. Then the good in its corresponding results, and likewise the bad in its results, will each come to an initial spiritual realization.

43. In this spiritual realization, the human being fashions and forms himself between death and a new birth; he becomes *in essential being* an image of what he *did* during his earthly life. And out of this essential being of his, he forms his physical life on his subsequent return to earth. The spiritual that works and weaves in destiny can only find realization in the physical if its corresponding cause were to withdraw, *before* this realization, back into the

in das geistige Gebiet zurückgezogen hat. Denn aus dem Geistigen *heraus*, nicht in der Folge der physischen Erscheinungen gestaltet sich, was sich als schicksalsgemäß auslebt.

Leitsätze Nr. 44 bis 46

44. Ein Übergang zu der geisteswissenschaftlichen Betrachtung der Schicksalsfrage sollte dadurch herbeigeführt werden, dass man an Beispielen aus dem Erleben einzelner Menschen den Gang des Schicksalsmäßigen in seiner Bedeutung für den Lebenslauf erörtert; zum Beispiel wie ein Jugenderlebnis, das ganz sicher nicht in voller Freiheit durch eine Persönlichkeit herbeigeführt ist, das ganze spätere Leben zu einem großen Teile gestalten kann.

45. Es sollte die Bedeutung der Tatsache, dass im physischen Lebenslaufe zwischen Geburt und Tod der Gute unglücklich im Außenleben, der Böse wenigstens scheinbar glücklich werden kann, geschildert werden. Beispiele in Bildern sind für die Erörterung wichtiger als theoretische Erklärungen, weil sie die geisteswissenschaftliche Betrachtung besser vorbereiten.

spiritual realm. For what comes to formation in life by way of destiny takes shape not within the sequence of physical phenomena, but proceeds *out of the spiritual.*

Leading Thoughts 44 to 46

44. A transition should be made to a spiritual-scientific consideration of the question of destiny by taking examples from the life and experience of individual human beings, showing how the forces of destiny express their meaning for the whole course of human life. It may be shown, for instance, how an experience that a person undergoes in his youth, which he certainly could not have brought upon himself entirely of his own free will, may nonetheless to a large extent give shape to the whole of his later life.

45. The significance should be described of the fact that in the physical course of life between birth and death the good may become unhappy in their outer life, and the wicked at any rate apparently happy. In expounding these things, pictures of individual cases carry more weight than theoretical explanations; they are a far better preparation for the spiritual-scientific consideration of the subject.

46. Es sollte an Schicksalsfällen, die in das Dasein des Menschen so eintreten, dass man ihre Bedingungen im jeweilig gegenwärtigen Erdenleben nicht finden kann, gezeigt werden, wie gegenüber solchen Schicksalsfällen schon rein die verstandesgemäße Lebensansicht auf früheres Erleben hindeutet. Es muss natürlich aus der Art der Darstellung klar sein, dass mit solchen Darstellungen nichts Verbindliches behauptet, sondern nur etwas gesagt werden soll, das die Gedanken nach der geisteswissenschaftlichen Betrachtung der Schicksalsfrage hin orientiert.

Leitsätze Nr. 47 bis 49

47. Was in der Schicksalsgestaltung des Menschen liegt, das tritt nur zum allerkleinsten Teile in das gewöhnliche Bewusstsein ein, sondern es waltet zumeist im Unbewussten. Aber gerade durch die Enthüllung des Schicksalsgemäßen wird ersichtlich, wie Unbewusstes zum Bewusstsein gebracht werden kann. Es haben eben diejenigen durchaus Unrecht, die von dem zeitweilig Unbewussten so sprechen, als ob es absolut im Gebiete des Unbekannten bleiben müsste und so eine Erkenntnisgrenze darstellte. Mit jedem Stück, das sich von seinem

46. Events of destiny should be cited which enter into the life of the human being in such a way that their determining conditions cannot possibly be found in his present life. Faced with such happenings, a purely reasonable view of life already points in the direction of former lives on earth. It must of course be made clear by the very way in which these things are described that no dogmatic or binding statement is implied. The purpose of such examples is simply to orient one's thoughts toward a spiritual-scientific consideration of the question of destiny.

Leading Thoughts 47 to 49

47. Of all that is latent in the forming of the human being's destiny, only the very smallest part enters everyday consciousness; it mostly holds sway in the unconscious. But it is precisely through the unveiling of destiny that it becomes apparent how the unconscious can be brought to consciousness. They are completely wrong who speak of what is, for the time being, the unconscious as though it must remain absolutely in the realm of the unknown and thus constitutes a barrier of knowledge. With every fragment of his destiny that is unveiled to him, the

Schicksale dem Menschen enthüllt, hebt er ein vorher Unbewusstes in das Gebiet des Bewusstseins herauf.

48. Durch ein solches Heraufheben wird man gewahr, wie innerhalb des Lebens zwischen Geburt und Tod das Schicksalsgemäße *nicht* gewoben wird; man wird dadurch gerade an der Schicksalsfrage auf die Betrachtung des Lebens zwischen Tod und neuer Geburt gewiesen.

49. In dem Besprechen dieses Hinausweisens des menschlichen Erlebens aus sich selbst an der Schicksalsfrage wird man ein wahres Gefühl entwickeln können für das Verhältnis des Sinnlichen und des Geistigen. Wer das Schicksal im Menschenwesen waltend schaut, der steht schon im Geistigen darinnen. Denn die Schicksalszusammenhänge haben gar nichts Naturhaftes an sich.

Leitsätze Nr. 50 bis 52

50. Es ist von ganz besonderer Wichtigkeit, darauf hinzuweisen, wie die Betrachtung des geschichtlichen Lebens der Menschheit dadurch belebt wird, dass man zeigt, es sind die Menschenseelen selbst, welche die Ergebnisse

human being lifts into the realm of consciousness something that was hitherto unconscious.

48. In such a lifting of destiny into consciousness, one becomes aware of how matters of destiny are *not* woven within the life between birth and death. One is thereby led, in regard to questions of destiny, to a consideration of life between death and a new birth.

49. Conscious human experience is thus impelled by the question of destiny to look beyond itself. Moreover, as one dwells upon this fact, one will develop a true feeling for the relation between the natural and the spiritual. Whoever beholds the living sway of destiny within the human being stands already in the midst of the spiritual. For the inner connections of destiny have nothing of the character of outer nature.

Leading Thoughts 50 to 52

50. It is of special importance to point out how the consideration of the life of humanity as revealed through history is enlivened when one shows that it is the souls of human beings themselves, passing from epoch to epoch

der einen Geschichtsepoche in die andere hinübertragen, indem sie in ihren wiederholten Erdenleben von Epoche zu Epoche wandeln.

51. Man wird leicht gegen eine solche Betrachtung einwenden, dass sie der Geschichte das Elementarische und Naive nimmt; aber man tut damit unrecht. Sie vertieft vielmehr die Anschauung des Geschichtlichen, das sie bis in das Innerste der Menschenwesenheit hinein verfolgt. Geschichte wird dadurch reicher und konkreter, nicht ärmer und abstrakter. Man muss nur in der Darstellung Herz und Sinn für die lebende Menschenseele entwickeln, in die man dadurch tief hineinschaut.

52. Es sollen die Epochen im Leben zwischen Tod und neuer Geburt mit Beziehung auf die Karmabildung behandelt werden.

Das «Wie» dieser Behandlung der Karmabildung soll den Inhalt der weiteren *Leitsätze* bilden.

in their repeated lives on earth, who carry over the results of one historical age into another.

51. It may easily be objected that such a line of thought robs history of its naive and elemental force. But this would not be correct. On the contrary, a view of historical life is deepened when it can be traced thus into the human being's innermost being. History becomes more real and more abundant, not poorer and more abstract. In describing these things one must, however, unfold heart and sense for the living soul of the human being, into which one gazes deeply along these lines of thought.

52. The epochs in the life between death and a new birth should be treated in relation to the forming of karma. The "how" of this treatment of karma-formation will comprise the content of the further *Leading Thoughts*.

Leitsätze Nr. 53 bis 55

53. Die Entfaltung des Menschenlebens zwischen Tod und neuer Geburt geschieht in aufeinanderfolgenden Stufen. Während weniger Tage unmittelbar nach dem Durchgang durch die Todespforte wird in *Bildern* das vorangegangene Erdenleben überschaut. Dieses Überschauen zeigt zugleich die Ablösung des Trägers dieses Lebens von der menschlichen Seelen-Geist-Wesenheit.

54. In einer Zeit, die ungefähr ein Drittel des eben vollendeten Erdenlebens umfasst, wird in Geisteserlebnissen, welche die Seele hat, die Wirkung erfahren, welche im Sinne einer ethisch gerechten Weltordnung das vorangegangene Erdenleben haben muss. Es wird während dieses Erlebens die Absicht erzeugt, das nächste Erdenleben zum Ausgleich der vorangegangenen so zu gestalten, wie es diesem Erleben entspricht.

55. Eine lang dauernde, rein geistige Daseinsepoche folgt, in der die Menschenseele mit anderen mit ihr karmisch verbundenen Menschenseelen und mit Wesenheiten der höheren Hierarchien das kommende Erdenleben im Sinne des Karma gestaltet.

Leading Thoughts 53 to 55

53. The unfolding of the human being's life between death and a new birth takes place in successive stages. For a few days after passing through the gate of death, the whole of the past earthly life is seen in *images*. This experience reveals at the same time the gradual severance of the carrier of the past life from the human soul-spirit-being.

54. In a time that comprises about a third of the past earthly life, the soul discovers in spiritual experiences the effect which this life must have in accordance with an ethically just world-order. During this experience, the intention is engendered to shape the next earthly life as a balance to the past in a way corresponding to this experience.

55. There follows a long, purely spiritual epoch of existence, during which the human soul – along with other human souls karmically connected with it and with the beings of the higher hierarchies – fashions the next life on earth in the sense of karma.

Leitsätze Nr. 56 bis 58

56. Die Daseinsepoche zwischen Tod und neuer Geburt, in der das Karma des Menschen gestaltet wird, kann nur aufgrund der Ergebnisse geistiger Forschung dargestellt werden. Aber es ist immer im Bewusstsein zu halten, dass diese Darstellung der Vernunft einleuchtend ist. Diese braucht nur das Wesen der Sinneswirklichkeit unbefangen zu betrachten, dann wird sie gewahr, dass dieses ebenso auf ein Geistiges hinweist wie die Form eines Leichnams auf das ihm einwohnende Leben.

57. Die Ergebnisse der Geisteswissenschaft zeigen, dass der Mensch zwischen Tod und Geburt ebenso Geistesreichen angehört, wie er zwischen Geburt und Tod den drei Reichen der Natur, dem mineralischen, pflanzlichen und tierischen angehört.

58. Das mineralische Reich ist in der augenblicklichen Gestaltung des Menschen zu erkennen, das pflanzliche ist als Ätherleib die Grundlage seines Werdens und Wachsens, das tierische als Astralleib der Impuls für Empfindungs- und Willensentfaltung. Die Krönung des bewussten Empfindungs- und Willenslebens im *selbstbewussten*

Leading Thoughts 56 to 58

56. The epoch of existence between death and a new birth, during which human karma is formed, can be described only on the basis of the results of spiritual research. But it must always be borne in mind that such a description appeals to the faculty of reason. One need only consider with open mind the nature of the world of the senses, and one will become aware that it points to a spiritual reality – as the form of a corpse points to the life that dwelt within it.

57. The results of the science of the spirit show that between death and birth the human being belongs to spirit-realms, just as he belongs between birth and death to the three realms of nature: the mineral, the plant, and the animal.

58. The mineral realm is recognizable in the form of the human being at any given moment; the plant realm, as the etheric body, is the basis of his growth, his becoming; the animal realm, as the astral body, is the impulse for his unfolding of sensation and volition. The crowning of the conscious life of sensation and volition in the

Geistesleben macht den Zusammenhang des Menschen mit der Geisteswelt unmittelbar anschaulich.

Leitsätze Nr. 59 bis 61

59. Eine unbefangene Betrachtung des Denkens zeigt, dass die Gedanken des gewöhnlichen Bewusstseins kein eigenes Dasein haben, dass sie nur wie Spiegelbilder von etwas auftreten. Aber der Mensch fühlt sich als *lebendig* in den Gedanken. Die *Gedanken* leben nicht; *er aber* lebt *in* den Gedanken. Dieses Leben urständet in Geist-Wesen, die man (im Sinne meiner *Geheimwissenschaft*) als die der dritten Hierarchie, als eines Geist-Reiches, ansprechen kann.

60. Die Ausdehnung dieser unbefangenen Betrachtung auf das Fühlen zeigt, dass die Gefühle aus dem Organismus aufsteigen, dass sie aber nicht von diesem erzeugt sein können. Denn ihr Leben trägt ein vom Organismus unabhängiges Wesen in sich. Der Mensch kann sich mit seinem Organismus in der Naturwelt fühlen. Er wird aber gerade dann, wenn er dies sich selbst verstehend tut, sich mit seiner Gefühlswelt in

self-conscious spiritual life makes the connection of the human being with the spiritual world straightaway apparent.

Leading Thoughts 59 to 61

59. An impartial consideration of thinking shows that the thoughts of ordinary consciousness have no existence of their own, but arise only as the reflected images of something. The human being, however, feels himself to be *alive* in his thoughts. The *thoughts* are not alive, *but he himself* lives *in* the thoughts. This life has its origins in spirit-beings whom one may describe (in the sense of my book *Occult Science*) as the beings of the third hierarchy – a realm of the spirit.

60. Extended to the life of feeling, the same impartial consideration shows that the feelings, though they arise out of the body, cannot have been engendered by it. For the life within the feelings bears a character independent of the bodily organism. With his bodily nature the human being can feel himself to be within the world of nature. Yet it is just in realizing this with true self-understanding that he will feel that with his world of feeling he is

einem geistigen Reiche fühlen. Das ist dasjenige der zweiten Hierarchie.

61. Als Willenswesen wendet sich der Mensch nicht an seinen Organismus, sondern an die Außenwelt. Er fragt nicht, wenn er gehen will, was empfinde ich in meinen Füßen, sondern, was ist dort draußen für ein Ziel, zu dem ich kommen will. Er vergisst seinen Organismus, indem er will. In seinem Willen gehört er *seiner* Natur nicht an. Er gehört da dem Geist-Reich der ersten Hierarchie an.

in a spiritual realm. This is the realm of the second hierarchy.

61. As a being of will, the human being's attention is directed not to his own bodily nature but to the outer world. When he wants to walk, he does not ask, "What do I feel in my feet?" but "What is the goal out there which I want to reach?" In willing, the human being forgets his body. In his will he belongs, not to *his own* nature, but to the spirit-realm of the first hierarchy.

Etwas vom Geist-Verstehen und Schicksals-Erleben

In die Mitteilungen und Betrachtungen, die an dieser Stelle an die Mitglieder gerichtet werden, soll diesmal einiges einfließen, das geeignet sein kann, den Gedanken über die *Leitsätze* eine weitere Richtung zu geben.

Das Verständnis des anthroposophischen Erkennens kann gefördert werden, wenn die menschliche Seele immer wieder auf das Verhältnis von Mensch und Welt hingelenkt wird.

Richtet der Mensch die Aufmerksamkeit auf die Welt, in die er hineingeboren wird und aus der er herausstirbt, so hat er zunächst die Fülle seiner Sinneseindrücke um sich. Er macht sich Gedanken über diese Sinnes-Eindrücke.

Indem er dieses sich zum Bewusstsein bringt: «Ich mache mir Gedanken über das, was mir meine Sinne als Welt offenbaren», kann er schon mit der Selbstbetrachtung einsetzen. Er kann sich sagen: In meinen Gedanken lebe «ich». Die Welt gibt mir Veranlassung, in Gedanken *mich* zu erleben. Ich finde mich in meinen Gedanken, indem ich die Welt betrachte.

So fortfahrend im Nachsinnen verliert der Mensch die Welt aus dem Bewusstsein; und das Ich tritt in dieses ein. Er hört auf, die Welt vorzustellen; er fängt an, das Selbst zu erleben.

On Understanding of the Spirit and the Experience of Destiny

At this point, something will be given in the communications addressed to members in these columns which may serve to provide a further orientation to our considerations of the weekly *Leading Thoughts.*

The understanding of anthroposophical recognition can be furthered if the existing relation between the human being and the world is constantly brought before the human soul.

When the human being turns his attention to the world into which he is born and out of which he dies, he is surrounded in the first place by the fullness of his sense impressions. He forms thoughts about these sense impressions.

In bringing to his consciousness: "I form thoughts about what my senses reveal to me as the world," he has already come to the point where he can contemplate himself. He can say to himself: In my thoughts "I" live. The world gives me the opportunity of experiencing *myself* in thoughts. I find myself in my thoughts when I contemplate the world.

And continuing to reflect in this way, he ceases to be conscious of the world; he becomes conscious of the 'I'. He ceases to have the world before him; he begins to experience the self.

Wird umgekehrt die Aufmerksamkeit auf das Innere gerichtet, in dem die Welt sich spiegelt, so tauchen im Bewusstsein die Lebensschicksalsereignisse auf, in denen das menschliche Selbst von dem Zeitpunkte an, bis zu dem man sich zurückerinnert, dahingeflossen ist. Man erlebt das eigene Dasein in der Folge dieser Schicksals-Erlebnisse.

Indem man sich dieses zum Bewusstsein bringt: «Ich habe mit meinem Selbst ein Schicksal erlebt», kann man mit der Weltbetrachtung einsetzen. Man kann sich sagen: In meinem Schicksal war ich nicht allein; da hat die Welt in mein Erleben eingegriffen. Ich habe dieses oder jenes *gewollt*; in mein Wollen ist die Welt hereingeflutet. Ich finde die Welt in meinem Wollen, indem ich dieses Wollen selbstbetrachtend erlebe.

So fortfahrend, sich in das eigene Selbst einlebend, verliert der Mensch das Selbst aus dem Bewusstsein; die Welt tritt in dieses ein. Er hört auf, das Selbst zu erleben; er fängt an, die Welt im Erfühlen gewahr zu werden.

Ich denke hinaus in die Welt; da finde ich mich; ich versenke mich in mich selbst, da finde ich die Welt. Wenn der Mensch *dieses* stark genug empfindet, steht er in den Welt- und Menschenrätseln drinnen.

Denn fühlen: Man müht sich im Denken ab, um die Welt zu ergreifen, und man steckt in diesem Denken doch nur selbst darinnen, das gibt das erste Welträtsel auf.

Vom Schicksal in seinem Selbst sich geformt fühlen und in

Were the experience to be reversed, and were the attention to be directed to the inner life in which the world is mirrored, then those life-destiny events emerge into consciousness into which our human self has flowed from the point of time to which our memory reaches back. In the results of these destiny-events, a human being experiences his own inner being.

Insofar as a person brings to consciousness: "I with my own self have experienced an event of destiny," he can enter into a consideration of the world. He can say to himself: I was not alone in my destiny; the world played a part in my experience. I *willed* this or that; the world streamed into my will. I find the world in my will insofar as I experience this will in self-contemplation.

In continuing to live into his own self in this way, the human being ceases to be conscious of the self; he becomes conscious of the world. He ceases to experience himself; he begins to become aware of the world in feeling.

"I send my thoughts out into the world; there I find myself. I sink into myself; there I find the world." If a person experiences *this* strongly enough, then he stands in the midst of the great riddles of the world and of the human being.

For to have the feeling: "One labors in thinking to understand the world, and in the end there is but oneself in this thinking" – this gives rise to the first world-riddle.

And to feel that one's own self is formed through destiny, yet

diesem Formen das Fluten des Weltgeschehens empfinden; das drängt zum zweiten Welträtsel hin.

In dem Erleben dieses Welt- und Menschenrätsels erkeimt die Seelenverfassung, in der der Mensch der Anthroposophie so begegnen kann, dass er in seinem Innern von ihr einen Eindruck erhält, der seine Aufmerksamkeit erregt.

Denn Anthroposophie macht nun dieses geltend: Es gibt ein geistiges Erleben, das nicht im Denken die Welt verliert. Man kann auch im Denken noch *leben*. Sie gibt im Meditieren ein inneres Erleben an, in dem man nicht denkend die Sinneswelt verliert, sondern die Geistwelt gewinnt. Statt in das Ich einzudringen, in dem man die Sinnnen-Welt versinken fühlt, dringt man in die Geist-Welt ein, in der man das Ich erfestigt fühlt.

Anthroposophie zeigt im Weiteren: Es gibt ein Erleben des Schicksals, in dem man nicht das Selbst verliert. Man kann auch im Schicksal noch sich selbst als *wirksam erleben*. Sie gibt in dem unegoistischen Betrachten des Menschenschicksals ein Erleben an, in dem man nicht nur das eigene Dasein, sondern die Welt lieben lernt. Statt in die Welt hineinzustarren, die in Glück und Unglück das Ich auf ihren Wellen trägt, findet man das Ich, das wollend das eigene Schicksal gestaltet. Statt an die Welt zu stoßen, an der das Ich zerschellt, dringt man in das Selbst ein, das sich mit dem Weltgeschehen verbunden fühlt.

Das Schicksal des Menschen wird ihm von der Welt bereitet,

to perceive in this process the onward flow of the world-course – this urges us toward the second world-riddle.

In the experience of these riddles of the human being and the world, there germinates the state of soul in which a person can so encounter Anthroposophy that he receives from it, in his inner being, an impression that rouses his attention.

For Anthroposophy asserts that there is a spiritual experience which does not lose the world when thinking. One can also *live* in thought. Anthroposophy tells of a meditative inner experience in which one does not lose the sensory world when thinking, but gains the spiritual world. Instead of penetrating into the 'I' in which the sensory world is felt to disappear, one penetrates into the spiritual world in which the 'I' feels strengthened.

Anthroposophy shows, further, that there is an experience of destiny in which one does not lose the self. In destiny, too, one can still *feel oneself to be active*. Anthroposophy points out, in the impartial, unegoistic observation of human destiny, an experience in which one learns to love the world and not only one's own existence. Instead of staring into the world which carries the 'I' on the waves of fortune and misfortune, one finds the 'I' which shapes its own destiny voluntarily. Instead of striking against the world on which the 'I' is dashed to pieces, one penetrates into the self, which feels itself united with the course of world-events.

The human being's destiny comes to him from the world

die ihm seine Sinne offenbaren. Findet er die eigene Wirksamkeit in dem Schicksalswalten, so steigt ihm sein Selbst wesenhaft nicht nur aus dem eigenen Innern, sondern es steigt ihm aus der Sinneswelt auf.

Kann man auch nur leise empfinden, wie im Selbst die Welt als Geistiges erscheint und wie in der Sinneswelt das Selbst sich als wirksam erweist, so ist man schon im sicheren Verstehen der Anthroposophie darinnen.

Denn man wird dann einen Sinn dafür entwickeln, dass in der Anthroposophie die Geist-Welt beschrieben werden darf, die vom Selbst erfasst wird. Und dieser Sinn wird auch Verständnis dafür entwickeln, dass in der Sinneswelt das Selbst auch noch anders als durch Versenken in das Innere gefunden werden kann. Anthroposophie findet das Selbst, indem sie zeigt, wie aus der Sinneswelt für den Menschen nicht nur sinnliche Wahrnehmungen sich offenbaren, sondern auch die Nachwirkungen aus seinem vorirdischen Dasein und aus den vorigen Erdenleben.

Der Mensch kann nun in die Welt der Sinne hinausblicken und sagen: Da ist ja nicht nur Farbe, Ton, Wärme; da wirken auch die Erlebnisse der Seelen, die diese Seelen vor ihrem gegenwärtigen Erdendasein durchgemacht haben. Und er kann in sich hineinblicken und sagen: Da ist nicht nur mein Ich, da offenbart sich eine geistige Welt.

In einem solchen Verständnisse kann der von den Welt- und

that is revealed to him by his senses. If he finds his own activity in the working of his destiny, then his self rises up before him in its essential nature not only out of his inner being but out of the sensory world too.

If a person is able to feel, even faintly, how in the self the world appears as a spiritual element, and likewise how the self proves to be working in the outer sensory world, then he already stands within a sound understanding of Anthroposophy.

For he will then develop a sense for the fact that in Anthroposophy it is possible to describe the spiritual world which the self can comprehend. And this will enable him to understand that in the sensory world the self can also be found – in a different way than by diving within. Anthroposophy finds the self insofar as it shows how the sensory world reveals to the human being not only sense perceptions but also the aftereffects of his life before birth and his former earthly lives.

The human being can now gaze upon the world perceptible to his senses and say: It contains not only color, sound, and warmth; in it are also active the experiences passed through by souls before their present earthly life. And he can look into himself and say: I find there not only my 'I', but also a spiritual world reveals itself.

In an understanding of this kind, a person who is moved by

Menschenrätseln berührte Mensch sich mit dem Eingeweihten zusammenfinden, der, nach seinen Einsichten, von der äußeren Sinneswelt so reden muss, als ob aus derselben nicht nur sinnliche Wahrnehmungen sich kundgäben, sondern die Eindrücke von dem, was Menschenseelen im vorirdischen Dasein und in verflossenen Erdenleben gewirkt haben; und der von der inneren Selbst-Welt aussagen muss, dass sie Geistzusammenhänge offenbart, so eindrucks- und wirkungsvoll, wie die Wahrnehmungen der Sinneswelt sind.

Bewusst sollten sich die tätig sein wollenden Mitglieder zu Vermittlern dessen machen, was die fragende Menschenseele als Welt- und Menschenrätsel fühlt, mit dem, was die Eingeweihten-Erkenntnis zu sagen hat, wenn sie aus Menschen-Schicksalen eine vergangene Welt heraufholt, und wenn sie aus seelischer Erkraftung die Wahrnehmung einer Geist-Welt erschließt.

So kann im Arbeiten der tätig sein wollenden Mitglieder die Anthroposophische Gesellschaft zu einer echten Vorschule der Eingeweihten-Schule werden. Auf dieses wollte die Weihnachtstagung kräftig hinweisen; und wer diese Tagung richtig versteht, wird mit diesem Hinweisen fortfahren, bis ein genügendes Verständnis dafür der Gesellschaft wieder neue Aufgaben bringen kann.

Aus diesen Hinweisen mögen denn die im Folgenden zu gebenden *Leitsätze* erfließen.

the great cosmic and human riddles can meet on a common ground with the initiate. In accordance with his insight, the initiate is obliged to speak of the outer world of the senses as manifesting not only sense perceptions but also the impressions of what human souls have done in their life before birth and in past earthly lives; and he has to say of the world of the inner self that it reveals spiritual interconnections which are just as impressive and effective as the perceptions of the sensory world.

Those who wish to be active members should consciously make themselves mediators between what the questioning human soul feels as the problems of the human being and the world, and what the knowledge of the initiates has to say when it draws forth a past world out of the destiny of human beings and when, by strengthening the soul, it opens up the perception of a spiritual world.

In this way, through the work of the members who wish to be active, the Anthroposophical Society may become a true preparatory school for the School of Initiates. It was the intention of the Christmas Conference to strongly indicate this; and one who truly understands this conference will continue forward with these indications until sufficient understanding of them can bring the Society renewed tasks and possibilities.

May the following *Leading Thoughts*, therefore, proceed out of these indications.

Leitsätze Nr. 62 bis 65

62. Die Sinneswelt trägt in den Sinneswahrnehmungen nur einen Teil des Wesens an die Oberfläche, das sie in ihren Wellentiefen birgt. Bei eindringlicher geistgemäßer Beobachtung zeigt sie, dass in diesen Tiefen die Nachwirkungen dessen sind, was Menschenseelen noch in lang vergangenen Zeiten gewirkt haben.

63. Die menschliche Innenwelt offenbart dem gewöhnlichen Selbstbetrachten nur einen Teil dessen, in dem sie darinnen steht. Bei erstarktem Erleben zeigt sie, dass sie in einer geistlebendigen Wirklichkeit steht.

64. In dem Schicksal des Menschen offenbart sich nicht bloß die Wirksamkeit einer Außenwelt, sondern auch diejenige des eigenen Selbst.

65. In den menschlichen Seelen-Erlebnissen offenbart sich nicht bloß ein Selbst, sondern auch eine Geistwelt, die das Selbst in geistmäßiger Erkenntnis mit der eigenen Wesenheit verbunden wissen kann.

Leading Thoughts 62 to 65

62. In sense perceptions, the world of the senses carries to the surface only a portion of the being that lies concealed in the depths of its waves beneath. Penetrative spiritual observation reveals within these depths the aftereffects of what was done by human souls in ages long past.

63. To ordinary self-observation, the inner world of the human being reveals only a portion of that in the midst of which it stands. Intensified experience in consciousness shows that this inner world dwells within a living spiritual reality.

64. The destiny of the human being reveals the workings not only of an external world, but also the workings of one's own self.

65. The experiences of the human soul reveal not only a self but also a world of spirit which the self can know, in spiritual cognition, to be united with its own being.

Leitsätze Nr. 66 bis 68

66. Die Wesenheiten der dritten Hierarchie offenbaren sich in dem Leben, das im menschlichen Denken als Geist-Hintergrund zur Entfaltung gelangt. Dieses Leben verbirgt sich in der menschlichen Denktätigkeit. Wirkten sie in dieser als Eigensein fort, so könnte der Mensch nicht zur Freiheit gelangen. Wo kosmische Denktätigkeit aufhört, beginnt menschliche Denktätigkeit.

67. Die Wesenheiten der zweiten Hierarchie offenbaren sich in einem außermenschlichen Seelischen, das dem menschlichen Fühlen als kosmisch-seelisches Geschehen verborgen ist. Dieses Kosmisch-Seelische schafft im Hintergrunde des menschlichen Fühlens. Es gestaltet das Menschlich-Wesenhafte zum Gefühls-Organismus, bevor in diesem selbst das Fühlen leben kann.

68. Die Wesenheiten der ersten Hierarchie offenbaren sich in einem außermenschlichen Geistschaffen, das dem menschlichen Wollen als kosmisch-geistige Wesenswelt innewohnt. Dieses Kosmisch-Geistige erlebt sich selbst schaffend, indem der Mensch will. Es gestaltet den Zusammenhang des Menschlich-Wesenhaften mit

Leading Thoughts 66 to 68

66. The beings of the third hierarchy reveal themselves in the life which is unfolded as a spiritual background in human thinking. This life is concealed in the human activity of thought. If it worked on as its own being in human thought, the human being would not be able to attain to freedom. Where cosmic thought-activity ceases, human thought-activity begins.

67. The beings of the second hierarchy manifest themselves in a soul element beyond the human realm – a world of cosmic-soul occurrences, hidden from human feeling. This cosmic-soul element is ever creative in the background of human feeling. It forms the essential nature of the human being into a feeling-organism; only then can feeling itself first be brought to life within him.

68. The beings of the first hierarchy manifest themselves in a form of spiritual creating from beyond the human realm, which indwells human willing as a cosmic-spiritual world of Being. This cosmic-spiritual element experiences itself in creative action when the human being wills. It first forms the interconnection of the human

der außermenschlichen Welt, bevor der Mensch durch seinen Willens-Organismus zum frei wollenden Wesen wird.

being's essential nature with the world beyond the human realm; only then does the human being himself become, through his organism of will, a freely willing being.

Geistige Weltbereiche und menschliche Selbsterkenntnis

Die *Leitsätze*, die in diesen Wochen vom Goetheanum aus den Mitgliedern der Anthroposophischen Gesellschaft gesandt worden sind, lenken den Seelenblick zu den Wesenheiten der geistigen Reiche hin, mit denen nach oben der Mensch ebenso zusammenhängt wie nach unten hin mit den Naturreichen.

Eine wahre Selbsterkenntnis des Menschen kann die Führerin werden zu diesen geistigen Reichen. Und wenn nach solcher Selbsterkenntnis mit rechtem Sinne gestrebt wird, so wird sich in ihr das Verständnis für dasjenige erschließen, was die Anthroposophie aus dem Einblick in das Leben der geistigen Welt an Erkenntnissen vermittelt. Man muss nur die Selbsterkenntnis im wirklichen Sinne, nicht in dem eines bloßen Hineinstarrens in das «Innere» üben.

Bei einer solchen wirklichen Selbst-Erkenntnis findet man zunächst, was in der *Erinnerung* lebt. In Gedanken-Bildern ruft man die Schatten dessen in das Bewusstsein herauf, in dem man in vergangener Zeit mit unmittelbarem lebendigen Erfahren darinnen gestanden hat. Wer einen Schatten sieht, wird aus einem inneren Drang heraus im Denken nach dem Gegenstande

Spiritual Realms and Human Self-Knowledge

Through the *Leading Thoughts* which have been sent out from the Goetheanum during the past weeks to members of the Anthroposophical Society, the soul has been directed to the beings of the spiritual realms with whom the human being is connected from above just as, from below, he is connected with the realms of nature.

True self-knowledge may become the guide through which the human being finds his way into these spiritual realms. And when such self-knowledge is striven for in the right way, the understanding will be awakened for what Anthroposophy is able to make known through its insight into the life of the spiritual world. But self-knowledge must be practiced in the true sense, not as a mere gazing into one's "inner being."

By means of such a true practice of self-knowledge, one arrives in the first place at what lives in *memory*. In thought-images one calls forth into consciousness the shadows of what, in the past, one had stood in the midst of as a direct and living experience. Anyone seeing a shadow will, out of an inner impulse of thought, be guided to the object which threw the

hingelenkt, der den Schatten wirft. Wer eine Erinnerung in sich trägt, kann in solch unmittelbarer Art nicht den Seelenblick nach dem Erlebnisse hinlenken, das in der Erinnerung nachwirkt. Wenn er sich aber wirklich auf sein eigenes Sein besinnt, so wird er sich sagen müssen: Er selbst sei, seiner seelischen Wesenheit nach, dasjenige, was die Erlebnisse aus ihm gemacht haben, die in der Erinnerung ihre Schatten werfen. Im Bewusstsein treten die Erinnerungsschatten auf, im Seelensein *leuchtet*, was in der Erinnerung *schattet*. Toter Schatten west in der Erinnerung; lebendiges Sein west in der Seele, in der die Erinnerung wirkt.

Man muss sich dieses Verhältnis der Erinnerung zum wirklichen Seelenleben nur klarmachen; und man wird in diesem Streben nach Klarheit im Selbst-Erkennen empfinden, wie man auf dem Wege nach der geistigen Welt ist.

Durch die Erinnerung sieht man auf das Geistige der eigenen Seele. Für das gewöhnliche Bewusstsein kommt dieses Sehen nicht zu einem wirklichen Ergreifen dessen, wonach der Blick gerichtet ist. Man schaut nach etwas hin; aber der Blick begegnet keiner Wirklichkeit. Anthroposophie weist aus der imaginativen Erkenntnis auf diese Wirklichkeit hin. Sie verweist von dem Schattenden auf das Leuchtende. Sie tut dies, indem sie von dem *Ätherleibe* des Menschen spricht. Sie zeigt, wie in den Gedanken-Schatten-Bildern der physische Leib wirkt; wie aber in dem Leuchtenden der Ätherleib *lebt*.

shadow. Anyone who bears a memory within himself cannot in this direct way turn the eye of his soul to the experience which lives on in the memory. But when he truly reflects on his own nature, he will be obliged to say to himself that he himself, in his soul-being, is the result of what his experiences have made of him – those experiences which now throw their shadows into the memory. The memory-shadows emerge onto the stage of consciousness; in the soul there *shines forth* what in the memory appears as *shadow*. Dead shadows work in the memory; living being works in the soul, in which the memory works.

It is only necessary that this relationship of the memory to the actual soul-life should be made clear; and in this striving for clarity in self-knowledge, one will then experience that one is on the path to the spiritual world.

Through memory, the human being sees the spiritual element of his own soul. But in the ordinary state of consciousness, this seeing does not arrive at a real grasp of what the inner gaze is directed to. One looks in the direction of something; but one's gaze meets with no reality. Out of imaginative knowledge, Anthroposophy shows the way to this reality. Anthroposophy points from the shadow to that which is luminous. It does this in that it speaks of the human *etheric body*. It shows how the physical body is active in the thought-shadow images, but likewise how in the luminous element the etheric body *lives*.

Mit dem physischen Leibe ist der Mensch in der sinnlichen Welt; mit dem Ätherleibe ist er in der Ätherwelt. In der sinnlichen Welt hat er eine Umgebung; er hat eine solche auch in der Ätherwelt. Die Anthroposophie spricht von dieser Umgebung als von der ersten verborgenen Welt, in der sich der Mensch befindet. Es ist das Reich der *dritten Hierarchie*.

Man nähere sich nun in derselben Art, wie man so an die Erinnerung herangetreten ist, der *Sprache*. Sie quillt aus dem Inneren des Menschen hervor wie die Erinnerung. In ihr verbindet sich der Mensch mit einem Sein, wie er sich in der Erinnerung mit seinen eigenen Erlebnissen verbindet. Im Worte lebt auch ein Schattendes. Dieses ist kräftiger als das Schattende der Erinnerungsgedanken. Indem der Mensch seine Erlebnisse in der Erinnerung innerlich abschattet, ist er mit seinem eigenen verborgenen Selbst bei dem ganzen Vorgange selbst wirksam. Er ist dabei, indem das Leuchtende den Schatten wirft.

In der Sprache ist auch ein Schattenwerfen. Worte sind Schatten. Was leuchtet da? Kräftigeres leuchtet, weil Worte kräftigere Schatten sind als Erinnerungsgedanken. Was im menschlichen Selbst Erinnerungen im Laufe eines Erdenlebens schaffen kann, kann nicht die Worte schaffen. Sie muss der Mensch im Zusammenhange mit anderen Menschen lernen. Ein tiefer in ihm liegendes Wesen als das in der Erinnerung Schattende muss sich daran beteiligen. Anthroposophie

With the physical body, the human being dwells in the sensory world; with the etheric body he dwells in the etheric world. In the sensory world he is surrounded by an environment; in the etheric world he likewise has such an environment. Anthroposophy speaks of this latter environment as the first of the hidden worlds in which the human being finds himself. It is the realm of the *third hierarchy*.

One can find the right approach to *speech* in the same way that one has considered memory. It issues forth from the innermost being of the human being just as does the memory. In speech, the human being connects himself with a state of being, just as in memory he unites himself with his own experiences. In words, too, there lives a shadowy element. This is deeper than the shadow-nature of the memory-thoughts. When the human being inwardly casts the shadow of his experiences as his memories, his own hidden self is active in the whole process. He is present in that the luminous casts the shadow.

In speech there is also a process of shadow-casting. The words are the shadows. What is it in this case that shines? Something stronger shines, because words are stronger shadows than are the thoughts of memory. The element in the human self which in the course of an earthly life can produce memories, cannot create words. Words must be learned in connection with other human beings. A being which lies deeper in the human being than that which casts the shadow

spricht da aus der inspirierten Erkenntnis heraus vom Astralleib, wie sie der Erinnerung gegenüber vom Ätherleib spricht. Zu dem physischen und Ätherleib tritt der Astralleib als ein drittes Glied der menschlichen Wesenheit.

Aber auch dieses dritte Glied hat eine Welt-Umgebung. Es ist diejenige der *zweiten Hierarchie*. In der menschlichen Sprache ist ein Schattenbild dieser zweiten Hierarchie gegeben. Der Mensch lebt innerhalb des Bereiches dieser Hierarchie mit seinem Astralleibe.

Man kann weiter gehen. An dem Sprechen ist der Mensch mit einem Teile seines Wesens beteiligt. Er bringt im Sprechen sein Inneres in Bewegung. Wovon dieses Innere umschlossen wird, das bleibt im Sprechen selbst in Ruhe. Die Bewegung des Sprechens entringt sich diesem ruhig bleibenden Menschenwesen. Aber der ganze Mensch kommt in Bewegung, wenn er in Regsamkeit bringt, was gliedmaßenartig an ihm ist. In dieser Bewegung ist der Mensch nicht minder ausdrucksvoll wie in der Erinnerung und in der Sprache. Die Erinnerung drückt die Erlebnisse aus; die Sprache hat ihr Wesen eben darinnen, dass sie Ausdruck von etwas ist. So auch drückt der in seinem ganzen Wesen bewegte Mensch ein «Etwas» aus.

Was so ausgedrückt wird, weist die Anthroposophie als ein weiteres Glied der menschlichen Wesenheit auf. Sie spricht aus der intuitiven Erkenntnis heraus von dem «wahren Selbst»

of memory must take part in this word-learning process. Here Anthroposophy speaks from inspirative knowledge of the astral body, just as with memory it speaks of the etheric body. The astral body emerges to join the physical and etheric bodies as a third element of the human being.

This third part, too, is surrounded by a cosmic environment. It is that of the *second hierarchy*. In human language one is given a shadow-image of this second hierarchy. The human being lives within the province of this hierarchy by means of his astral body.

One may go still further. In speech, a person is engaged with a part of his being. In speaking, he brings his inner being into motion. That which surrounds this inner being remains at rest in the activity of speaking. The movement of speech wrings itself loose from the human being while he remains at rest. But the whole human being comes into movement when he brings into activity all that belongs to his limbs. In such movement the human being is no less full of expression than in memory and language. Memory itself brings experiences to direct expression; the nature of language consists in its being the expression of something else. In the same way, the person whose whole being is in motion brings to expression a "something."

Anthroposophy points out that this "something" is another member of the human being. From intuitive knowledge, Anthroposophy speaks of the "true self" or "I." This

oder dem «Ich». Auch für dieses findet sie eine Welt-Umgebung. Es ist diejenige der *ersten Hierarchie.*

Indem der Mensch an seine Erinnerungsgedanken herantritt, begegnet ihm ein erstes Übersinnliches, sein eigenes Ätherwesen. Anthroposophie weist ihm die entsprechende Welt-Umgebung auf. Indem sich der Mensch als Sprechenden erfasst, begegnet ihm sein Astralwesen. Das wird nicht mehr in dem erfasst, was nur innerlich wie die Erinnerung wirkt. Es wird von der Inspiration geschaut als dasjenige, was in dem Sprechen aus dem Geistigen heraus einen physischen Vorgang gestaltet. Sprechen ist ein physischer Vorgang. Ihm liegt das Schaffen aus dem Bereiche der zweiten Hierarchie zugrunde.

In dem ganzen bewegten Menschen ist ein intensiveres physisches Wirken vorhanden als im Sprechen. Nicht etwas am Menschen wird gestaltet; der ganze Mensch wird gestaltet. Da wirkt die erste Hierarchie in dem in Gestaltung webenden Physischen.

So kann wirkliche Selbst-Erkenntnis des Menschenwesens geübt werden. Aber der Mensch erfasst dabei nicht das eigene Selbst allein. Stufenweise erfasst er seine Glieder: den physischen Leib, den Ätherleib, den Astralleib, das Selbst. Aber indem er diese erfasst, kommt er auch stufenweise an höhere Welten heran, die wie die drei Naturreiche, das tierische, das pflanzliche, das mineralische, als drei geistige Reiche zu der Gesamtwelt gehören, in der sich sein Wesen entfaltet.

too, it finds, has a cosmic environment. It is that of the *first hierarchy*.

When the human being approaches the thoughts in his memory, he meets with the first suprasensory element – his own etheric being. Anthroposophy points out to him the cosmic environment corresponding to it. When the human being comprehends himself as one who speaks, he meets his astral being. This is no longer comprehended in that which only acts inwardly, like memory. It is seen by inspiration as that which, in the act of speaking, shapes a physical process out of the spiritual. Speaking is a physical process. At its foundation lies an activity which proceeds from the sphere of the second hierarchy.

When the whole human being is in motion, there is a more intense physical action than in speech. It is not merely that a part of him is molded; the whole human being is given shape. In the physical element that lives and weaves in form, the first hierarchy is active.

Thus can true self-knowledge be cultivated. But in doing so, the human being does not grasp his own self alone. Step by step he comprehends the members of his being: the physical body, the etheric body, the astral body, and the self. And by comprehending these he also reaches up, step by step, to higher worlds which like the three realms of nature – the animal, plant, and mineral realms – belong, as the three spiritual realms, to the world-whole in which his being unfolds.

Leitsätze Nr. 69 bis 71

69. Die dritte Hierarchie offenbart sich als ein rein Geistig-Seelisches. Sie webt in dem, was der Mensch auf seelische Art ganz innerlich erlebt. Weder im Ätherischen noch im Physischen könnten Vorgänge entstehen, wenn nur diese Hierarchie wirkte. Seelisches könnte allein da sein.

70. Die zweite Hierarchie offenbart sich als ein Geistig-Seelisches, das im Ätherischen wirkt. Alles Ätherische ist Offenbarung der zweiten Hierarchie. Sie offenbart sich aber nicht unmittelbar im Physischen. Ihre Stärke reicht nur bis zu den ätherischen Vorgängen. Es würde nur Seelisches und Ätherisches bestehen, wenn nur dritte und zweite Hierarchie wirkten.

71. Die stärkste, erste Hierarchie offenbart sich als das im Physischen geistig Wirksame. Sie gestaltet die physische Welt zum Kosmos. Die dritte und zweite Hierarchie sind dabei die dienenden Wesenheiten.

Leading Thoughts 69 to 71

69. The third hierarchy reveals itself as a pure spiritual-soul element. It lives and weaves in everything of a soul nature that the human being experiences deep in his inner life. Neither in the etheric nor in the physical could any processes arise if this hierarchy alone were active. All that would exist is the soul-life alone.

70. The second hierarchy reveals itself as a spiritual-soul element that works in the etheric. All that is etheric is a revelation of the second hierarchy. This hierarchy, however, does not reveal itself directly in the physical; its power extends only to etheric processes. Only soul-life and the etheric element could exist if the third and second hierarchies alone were active.

71. The strongest, first hierarchy reveals itself as the spiritually active principle within the physical element. It forms the physical world into a cosmos. The third and second hierarchies are the beings who serve it in this activity.

Leitsätze Nr. 72 bis 75

72. Sobald man an die höheren Glieder der menschlichen Wesenheit, den ätherischen, astralischen Leib und die Ich-Organisation, herantritt, ist man genötigt, das Verhältnis des Menschen zu den Wesen der geistigen Reiche zu suchen. Nur die physische Leibesorganisation kann von den drei physischen Naturreichen aus beleuchtet werden.

73. Im Ätherleibe gliedert sich dem Menschenwesen die Intelligenz des Kosmos ein. Dass dies geschehen kann, setzt die Tätigkeit von Welt-Wesen voraus, die in ihrem Zusammenwirken den menschlichen Ätherleib so gestalten wie die physischen Kräfte den physischen.

74. Im Astralleibe prägt die geistige Welt dem Menschenwesen die moralischen Impulse ein. Dass diese in der menschlichen Organisation sich darleben können, ist von der Tätigkeit solcher Wesen abhängig, die das Geistige nicht nur denken, sondern wesenhaft gestalten können.

75. In der Ich-Organisation erlebt der Mensch im physischen

Leading Thoughts 72 to 75

72. As soon as one approaches the higher members of the human being – the etheric, the astral body, and the 'I'-organization – one is obliged to seek for the human being's relation to the beings of the spiritual realms. It is only the physical body's organization that can be illumined by reference to the three physical realms of nature.

73. In the etheric body, the intelligence of the cosmos becomes embodied in the human being. That this can happen requires the activity of cosmic beings who, in their working together, shape the human etheric body just as the physical forces shape the physical.

74. In the astral body, the spiritual world implants the impulses of morality into the human being. That these impulses can show forth their life in the human being's organization, depends on the activity of beings who are able not only to think the spiritual, but to shape it in its essential nature.

75. In the 'I'-organization, the human being experiences

Leib sich selbst als Geist. Dass dies geschehen kann, ist die Tätigkeit von Wesen notwendig, die selbst als geistige in der physischen Welt leben.

himself in the physical body as a spirit. That this can happen requires the activity of beings who themselves are of a spiritual nature and who live in the physical world.

Wie die *Leitsätze* anzuwenden sind

In den *Leitsätzen*, die vom Goetheanum ausgegeben werden, soll die Anregung für die tätig sein wollenden Mitglieder gegeben sein, den Inhalt des anthroposophischen Wirkens einheitlich zu gestalten. Man wird finden, wenn man an diese Sätze jede Woche herantritt, dass sie eine Anleitung dazu geben, sich in den vorhandenen Stoff der Zyklen zu vertiefen und diesen in einer gewissen Anordnung in den Zweigversammlungen vorzubringen.

Es wäre ja gewiss wünschenswerter, wenn jede Woche sogleich die Vorträge, die in Dornach gehalten werden, in allen Richtungen an die einzelnen Zweige gebracht werden könnten. Allein man sollte auch bedenken, welch komplizierte technische Einrichtungen dazu nötig sind. Es wird gewiss von Seite des Vorstandes am Goetheanum nach dieser Richtung alles Mögliche angestrebt und noch getan werden. Aber man muss mit den vorhandenen Möglichkeiten rechnen. Die Absichten, die auf der Weihnachtstagung geäußert worden sind, werden verwirklicht werden. Aber wir brauchen Zeit.

Vorläufig sind diejenigen Zweige im Vorteil, welche Mitglieder in sich haben, die das Goetheanum besuchen, da die Vorträge hören und deren Inhalt in den Zweigversammlungen

How the *Leading Thoughts* Are to Be Used

In the *Leading Thoughts* given out from the Goetheanum, the members who want to take an active part should get an enlivening impulse enabling them to bring unity and wholeness into all anthroposophical activity. They will find in them, as they receive them week by week, guidance for deepening their understanding of the material that is already at hand in the lecture-courses, and for putting it forward in the branch meetings with a certain composition.

It would without doubt be more desirable for the lectures given in Dornach to be carried at once in all directions to the individual branches. But one has to remember what complicated technical arrangements this would necessitate. The members of the Executive Council at the Goetheanum are making every possible effort in this direction, and still more will be done in the future. But one must reckon with the existing possibilities. The aims that found expression at the Christmas Conference will be realized. But we need time.

For the time being, those branches that have members who are able to visit the Goetheanum, hear the lectures, and then bring back their substance to the branch meetings, have an

vorbringen können. Und es sollte von den Zweigen erkannt werden, dass die Entsendung solcher Mitglieder an das Goetheanum eine Wohltat ist. Aber man sollte auch nicht die Arbeit, die in der Anthroposophischen Gesellschaft schon geleistet ist und die in den gedruckten Zyklen und Vorträgen vorliegt, allzu sehr unterschätzen. Wer diese Zyklen vornimmt, sich nach den Titeln erinnert, welcher Stoff in diesem oder jenem enthalten ist, und dann an die *Leitsätze* herantritt, der wird finden, dass er in dem einen Zyklus das eine und in dem anderen ein anderes findet, das den *Leitsatz* weiter ausführt. Aus dem Zusammenlesen dessen, was in den einzelnen Zyklen getrennt steht, können die Gesichtspunkte gefunden werden, von denen aus in Anlehnung an die *Leitsätze* gesprochen werden kann.

Wir wirken in der Anthroposophischen Gesellschaft wie rechte Verschwender, wenn wir die gedruckten Zyklen ganz unbenutzt lassen und immer nur «das Neueste» vom Goetheanum empfangen wollen. Es ist doch auch leicht begreiflich, dass allmählich jede Möglichkeit, die Zyklen zu drucken, aufhören müsste, wenn diese nicht ausgiebig benutzt würden.

Es kommt noch ein anderer Gesichtspunkt in Frage. Bei der Verbreitung des Inhaltes der Anthroposophie ist Gewissenhaftigkeit und Verantwortlichkeitsgefühl in allererster Linie notwendig. Man muss das, was über die geistige Welt gesagt wird, in eine Form bringen, dass die Bilder der geistigen

advantage. And branches should recognize that the sending of members to the Goetheanum in this way is a benefit. On the other hand, however, the work that has already been achieved within the Anthroposophical Society and that is embodied in the printed courses and lectures, should not be undervalued. Whoever takes up these courses and calls to mind from the titles what is contained in this one and in that, and then turns to the *Leading Thoughts*, will find that he meets with one thing in one course, another in another, which serve to explain the *Leading Thoughts* more fully. By reading together passages that are found separated in different courses, one will discover the right points of view for what can be elaborated in accord with the *Leading Thoughts*.

We in the Anthroposophical Society are wasting opportunities all the time if we leave the printed courses quite untouched and only want always to receive "the latest" from the Goetheanum. And it will readily be understood that all possibility of printing the courses would gradually cease if they were not widely made use of.

Another point of view also comes into consideration. In spreading the content of Anthroposophy, conscientiousness and a feeling of responsibility are necessary above all else. What is said about the spiritual world must be brought into such a form that what is given as images of spiritual facts and

Tatsachen und Wesenheiten, die gegeben werden, nicht Missverständnissen ausgesetzt werden. Wer am Goetheanum einen Vortrag hört, kann einen unmittelbaren Eindruck haben. Wenn er dessen Inhalt wiedergibt, so kann bei ihm dieser Eindruck nachklingen, und er ist imstande, die Dinge so zu formulieren, dass sie richtig verstanden werden können. Wird aber ein Zweiter, Dritter der Vermittler, so wird die Wahrscheinlichkeit immer größer, dass sich Ungenauigkeiten einschleichen. Alle diese Dinge sollten bedacht werden.

Und ein weiterer Gesichtspunkt ist ja wohl der allerwichtigste. Es handelt sich ja nicht darum, dass der anthroposophische Inhalt nur äußerlich angehört oder gelesen werde, sondern dass er in das lebendige Seelenwesen aufgenommen werde. Im Fortdenken und Fortfühlen des Aufgenommenen liegt ein Wesentliches. Das aber soll mit Bezug auf die schon vorliegenden gedruckten Zyklen gerade durch die *Leitsätze* angeregt werden. Wird dieser Gesichtspunkt zu wenig berücksichtigt, so wird es fortdauernd daran fehlen, dass das Wesen der Anthroposophie durch die Anthroposophische Gesellschaft sich offenbaren könne. Man sagt nur mit scheinbarem Recht: Was nützt es mir, noch so viel von geistigen Welten zu hören, wenn ich nicht selbst in solche Welten hineinschauen kann. Man berücksichtigt dabei nicht, dass dieses Hineinschauen gefördert wird, wenn über die Verarbeitung des anthroposophischen Inhaltes so gedacht wird, wie es hier angedeutet

beings is not exposed to misunderstanding. Anyone who hears a lecture at the Goetheanum will receive an immediate and direct impression. When he conveys the content of what he heard, this impression can echo within him, thereby enabling him to formulate this content in such a way that it can be rightly understood. But if it is repeated second- or third-hand, the possibility of elements of imprecision creeping in becomes greater and greater. All these things should be considered.

The following point of view is, however, certainly the most important. The point is not that anthroposophical content should simply be outwardly listened to or read, but that it should be taken into the living soul-being. Something of the most essential significance lies in the further-thinking and the further-feeling of what is thus taken in. And the *Leading Thoughts* should serve to encourage this activity with regard to the courses already printed and in circulation. If this perspective is not sufficiently considered, then there will be a lack of manifestation of the essence of Anthroposophy through the Anthroposophical Society. People say, though only with apparent justice: "What use is it to me to hear all these things about the spiritual worlds if I cannot look into those worlds for myself?" One who speaks thus does not realize that the capacity for such independent vision is fostered when the working out of anthroposophical ideas is thought of in the manner

ist. Die Vorträge am Goetheanum sind so gehalten, dass ihr Inhalt lebendig und frei in den Gemütern der Zuhörer fortwirken kann. Und so ist auch der Inhalt der Zyklen. Da ist kein totes Material zur bloßen äußeren Mitteilung; da ist Stoff, der unter verschiedene Gesichtspunkte gerückt das Schauen in geistige Welten anregt. Man sollte nicht glauben: Den Inhalt der Vorträge höre ich an; die Erkenntnis der geistigen Welt eigne ich mir durch Meditation an. So wird man nie im wahren Sinne weiterkommen. Beides muss in der Seele zusammenwirken. Und das Fortdenken und Fortfühlen des anthroposophischen Inhaltes ist auch Seelenübung. Man lebt sich in die geistige Welt *schauend* hinein, wenn man so, wie es hier gesagt ist, mit diesem Inhalt verfährt.

Es wird eben doch in der Anthroposophischen Gesellschaft viel zu wenig darauf gesehen, dass Anthroposophie nicht graue Theorie, sondern wahres Leben sein soll. Wahres Leben, das ist ihr Wesen; und wird sie zur grauen Theorie *gemacht*, dann ist sie oft gar nicht eine *bessere*, sondern eine *schlechtere* Theorie als andere. Aber sie wird eben erst Theorie, wenn man sie dazu *macht*, wenn man sie tötet. Das wird noch viel zu wenig gesehen, dass Anthroposophie nicht nur eine andere Weltanschauung ist als andere, sondern dass sie auch *anders aufgenommen werden muss*. Man erkennt und erlebt ihr Wesen erst in dieser anderen Art des Aufnehmens.

indicated above. The lectures at the Goetheanum are given in such a way that their content can live on and work freely in the minds of the listeners. The same applies also to the content of the courses. These contain no dead material to be imparted externally; rather they contain substance which, when engaged with from various perspectives, enlivens the capacity for vision into spiritual worlds. One should not think: "I listen to the content of the lectures; I prepare myself for knowledge of the spiritual world separately by means of meditation." One will never come further in the true sense in this way. Both must work together in the soul. And the further-thinking and further-feeling of anthroposophical content is also an exercise of the soul. One gradually comes to live *seeingly* into the spiritual world if one proceeds with the content in the manner described.

Far too little consideration is given in the Anthroposophical Society to the fact that Anthroposophy should not be grey theory but true life. True life – that is its nature and being; and if it is *made into* an abstract theory, then it is often not at all a better but a *worse* theory than others. But it becomes theory only when one *makes* it such, when one kills it. It is still far too little realized that Anthroposophy is not only a conception of the world, different from others, but that *it must also be received differently*. One first comes to know and experience its nature and being only by means of this different way of receiving.

Das Goetheanum sollte als der *notwendige* Mittelpunkt des anthroposophischen Arbeitens und Wirkens angesehen werden; aber man sollte nicht aus dem Auge verlieren, dass in den Zweigen der anthroposophische Stoff, der erarbeitet worden ist, auch zur Geltung komme. Was am Goetheanum *gewirkt* wird, das kann im vollen lebendigen Sinne die ganze Anthroposophische Gesellschaft *nach und nach* haben, wenn möglichst viele Mitglieder aus dem Leben der Zweige heraus an das Goetheanum selbst herankommen und, soviel ihnen möglich ist, an *seinem* lebendigen Wirken teilnehmen. Das alles aber muss mit Innerlichkeit gestaltet werden; mit dem äußerlichen «Mitteilen» des Inhaltes von jeder Woche geht es nicht. Der Vorstand am Goetheanum wird Zeit brauchen und bei den Mitgliedern Verständnis finden müssen. Dann *wird* er im Sinne der Weihnachtstagung wirken können.

The Goetheanum should be looked upon as the *necessary* center of anthroposophical work and activity, but one ought not to lose sight of the fact that the anthroposophical material which has been worked out should also be made use of in the branches. What is *worked out* at the Goetheanum can be obtained *gradually* by the whole Anthroposophical Society in a full and living sense when as many members as possible come from the life of the branches to the Goetheanum itself and participate as much as possible in *its* living work. But all this must be formed with inwardness; the mere "reporting" of the content of the lectures each week is useless. The Executive Council at the Goetheanum will need time and understanding from the members. Then the Council *will* be able to work in the sense of the Christmas Conference.

Leitsätze Nr. 76 bis 78

76. Will man eine Vorstellung der ersten Hierarchie (Seraphim, Cherubim und Throne) hervorrufen, so wird man darnach suchen müssen, Bilder zu gestalten, in denen Geistiges (nur übersinnlich Schaubares) in den Formen sich wirkend offenbart, die in der Sinnenwelt zur Erscheinung kommen. Geistiges in sinnenfälliger Bildlichkeit muss Inhalt der Gedanken über die erste Hierarchie sein.

77. Will man eine Vorstellung der zweiten Hierarchie (Kyriotetes, Dynameis, Exusiai) hervorrufen, so wird man darnach suchen müssen, Bilder zu gestalten, in denen Geistiges nicht in sinnenfälligen Formen, sondern auf rein geistige Art sich offenbart. Geistiges in nicht sinnenfälliger, sondern rein geistiger Bildlichkeit muss der Inhalt der Gedanken über die zweite Hierarchie sein.

78. Will man eine Vorstellung der dritten Hierarchie (Archai, Archangeloi, Angeloi) hervorrufen, so wird man darnach suchen müssen, Bilder zu gestalten, in denen Geistiges nicht in sinnenfälligen Formen, aber auch nicht auf rein geistige Art, sondern so sich offenbart, wie Denken, Fühlen und Wollen in der menschlichen Seele

Leading Thoughts 76 to 78

76. To call forth a representation of the first hierarchy (Seraphim, Cherubim, and Thrones), one must try to form images in which the spiritual (that which can be beheld only supersensibly) reveals its working in forms that come to manifestation in the world of sense. The spiritual in sense-perceptible imagery: this must be the content of our thoughts about the first hierarchy.

77. To call forth a representation of the second hierarchy (Kyriotetes, Dynamis, Exusiai), one must try to form images in which the spiritual reveals itself not in sense-perceptible forms, but in a purely spiritual way. The spiritual not in sense-perceptible but in purely spiritual imagery: this must be the content of our thoughts about the second hierarchy.

78. To call forth a representation of the third hierarchy (Archai, Archangeloi, Angeloi), one must try to form images in which the spiritual reveals itself not in sense-perceptible forms, yet also not in a purely spiritual way, but in the way in which thinking, feeling, and willing come to life in the human soul. The spiritual in soulful

sich darleben. Geistiges in seelenhafter Bildlichkeit muss der Inhalt der Gedanken über eine dritte Hierarchie sein.

imagery: this must be the content of our thoughts about the third hierarchy.

Im Anbruch des Michael-Zeitalters

Bis zum neunten Jahrhundert nach dem Mysterium von Golgatha stand der Mensch anders zu seinen Gedanken als später. Er hatte nicht die Empfindung, dass er die in seiner Seele lebenden Gedanken selbst hervorbringe. Er betrachtete sie als Eingebungen einer geistigen Welt. Auch wenn er über das Gedanken hatte, was er mit seinen Sinnen wahrnahm, waren ihm die Gedanken Offenbarungen des Göttlichen, das aus den Sinnesdingen zu ihm sprach.

Wer geistige Schauungen hat, begreift diese Empfindung. Denn, wenn ein geistig Wirkliches sich der Seele mitteilt, so hat man niemals das Gefühl, da ist die geistige Wahrnehmung, und man formt selber den Gedanken, um die Wahrnehmung zu begreifen; sondern man *schaut* den Gedanken, der in der Wahrnehmung enthalten und mit ihr gegeben ist, so objektiv wie sie selbst.

Mit dem neunten Jahrhundert – selbstverständlich sind solche Angaben so zu nehmen, dass sie eine mittlere Zeitangabe bilden; der Übergang geschieht ganz allmählich – leuchtete in den Menschenseelen die persönlich-individuelle Intelligenz auf. Der Mensch bekam das Gefühl: *Ich bilde* die Gedanken. Und dieses Bilden der Gedanken wurde das Überragende im

At the Dawn of the Michael Age

Up until the ninth century after the Mystery of Golgotha, the human being stood differently in a relation to his thoughts than he did in later times. He did not have the feeling that he himself brought forth the thoughts that lived in his soul. He regarded them as gifts prompted by a spiritual world. And when he had thoughts about what he perceived with his senses, even these thoughts were to him revelations of the divine that spoke to him from the things of the senses.

Whoever has achieved spiritual vision will understand this experience. For when something that is real in the spiritual sense communicates itself to the soul, one never has the feeling: "There is the spiritual perception, and I myself am developing the thought with which to understand it." Rather, one *sees* the thought which the perception contains – and which is given with it – as objectively as the perception itself.

When dates are given in this connection, they are to be taken only as a rough indication of the period; the transition takes place quite gradually. In this sense, one may say that the ninth century saw the lighting-up, in human souls, of the personal-individual intelligence. The human being began to have the feeling: "*I form* my thoughts." And this forming of thoughts

Seelenleben, sodass die Denkenden das Wesen der Menschenseele im intelligenten Verhalten sahen. Vorher hatte man von der Seele eine imaginative Vorstellung. Man sah ihr Wesen nicht im Gedanken-Bilden, sondern in ihrem Teilhaben an dem geistigen Inhalt der Welt. Die übersinnlichen geistigen Wesen dachte man denkend; und sie wirken in den Menschen hinein; sie denken auch in ihn hinein. Was so von der übersinnlichen geistigen Welt im Menschen lebt, das empfand man als Seele.

Sobald man in die geistige Welt mit seiner Anschauung hinaufdringt, kommt man an konkrete geistige Wesensmächte heran. In alten Lehren hat man die Macht, aus der die Gedanken der Dinge erfließen, mit dem Namen *Michael* bezeichnet. Der Name kann beibehalten werden. Dann kann man sagen: Die Menschen empfingen einst von Michael die Gedanken. Michael verwaltete die kosmische Intelligenz. Vom neunten Jahrhundert an verspürten die Menschen nicht mehr, dass ihnen Michael die Gedanken inspiriert. Sie waren seiner Herrschaft entfallen; sie fielen aus der geistigen Welt in die individuellen Menschenseelen.

Innerhalb der Menschheit wurde nunmehr das Gedankenleben ausgebildet. Man war zunächst unsicher, was man an den Gedanken hatte. Diese Unsicherheit lebte in den scholastischen Lehren. Die Scholastiker zerfielen in Realisten und

came to be of paramount importance to the soul's life, so that thinkers saw the very being of the soul in the experience of intelligence. In earlier times, human beings had had an imaginative representation of the soul. One saw its being not in the formation of thoughts, but in its partaking in the spiritual content of the world. The suprasensory spiritual beings were conceived as thinking; they were thought to extend their influence into the human being, even thinking into him. That element of the suprasensory spiritual world which lives in the human being – this one felt as the soul.

As soon as the spiritual world is penetrated with inner seeing, one meets with concrete spiritual beings. In ancient teachings, the power from whom the thoughts in things proceed was designated by the name *Michael.* This name can still be applied. Then one can say: The human being once received thoughts from Michael. Michael held sway over the cosmic intelligence. But from the ninth century onwards, human beings no longer felt that Michael was inspiring the thoughts into them. The thoughts had fallen away from Michael's dominion; they had fallen out of the spiritual world into the individualized human souls.

Henceforth it was within humanity that the life of thought was evolved. To begin with, human beings were uncertain as to what it was they had in their thoughts. This uncertainty found very real expression in the Scholastic teachings. The

Nominalisten. Die Realisten – deren Führer Thomas von Aquino und die ihm Nahestehenden waren – fühlten noch die alte Zusammengehörigkeit von Gedanke und Ding. Sie sahen daher in den Gedanken ein Wirkliches, das in den Dingen lebt. Die Gedanken des Menschen sahen sie als etwas an, das als Wirklichkeit aus den Dingen in die Seele hinüberfließt. – Die Nominalisten fühlten stark den Tatbestand, dass die Seele ihre Gedanken bildet. Sie empfanden die Gedanken nur als Subjektives, das in der Seele lebt und das mit den Dingen nichts zu tun hat. Sie meinten: Die Gedanken seien nur vom Menschen gebildete Namen für die Dinge. (Man sprach nicht von «Gedanken», sondern von «Universalien»; aber das kommt für das Prinzipielle der Anschauung nicht in Betracht, da Gedanken ja immer etwas Universelles im Verhältnis zu den einzelnen Dingen haben.)

Man kann sagen: Die Realisten wollten Michael die Treue bewahren; auch da die Gedanken aus *seinem* Bereich in den der Menschen gefallen waren, wollten sie als Denker dem Michael dienen als dem Fürsten der Intelligenz des Kosmos. – Die Nominalisten vollzogen in ihrem unbewussten Seelenteil den Abfall von Michael. Sie betrachteten nicht Michael, sondern den Menschen als den Eigentümer der Gedanken.

Der Nominalismus gewann an Verbreitung und Einfluss. Das konnte so fortgehen bis in das letzte Drittel des neunzehnten Jahrhunderts. In diesem Zeitalter empfanden diejenigen

Schoolmen were divided into Nominalists and Realists. The Realists, led by St. Thomas Aquinas and those who stood near to him, still felt the ancient togetherness of thought and thing. Hence they saw in the thoughts a reality living in the things. They regarded human thoughts as a reality which flows over from the things themselves into the human soul. – The Nominalists felt very strongly the fact that the soul forms its own thoughts. They felt that the thoughts were merely something that existed subjectively in the soul and had nothing to do with the things themselves. They were of the opinion that thoughts are only names that human beings form for things. (They did not speak of "thoughts" but of "universals"; but that does not come into consideration for the principle of this perspective, for thoughts indeed always contain something universal as compared with the particular things.)

One may say that the Realists wished to remain faithful to Michael; even though the thoughts had fallen from *his* sphere into that of the human being, they wished, as thinkers, to serve Michael as the lord of the intelligence of the cosmos. – The Nominalists, in the unconscious part of their soul, took leave of Michael. They did not consider Michael to be the owner of the thoughts, but the human being himself.

Nominalism spread abroad and increased in influence up to the last third of the nineteenth century. In this period, those human beings who were able to perceive and understand the

Menschen, die sich auf die Wahrnehmung der geistigen Geschehnisse innerhalb des Weltalls verstehen, dass Michael dem Strom des intellektuellen Lebens nachgezogen war. Er sucht nach einer neuen Metamorphose seiner kosmischen Aufgabe. Er ließ vorher von der geistigen Außenwelt her die Gedanken in die Seelen der Menschen strömen; vom letzten Drittel des neunzehnten Jahrhunderts an will er *in* den Menschenseelen leben, in denen die Gedanken gebildet werden. Vorher sahen die Michael verwandten Menschen Michael im Geistbereich seine Tätigkeit entfalten; jetzt erkennen sie, dass sie Michael im Herzen wohnen lassen sollen; jetzt weihen sie ihm ihr gedankengetragenes geistiges Leben; jetzt lassen sie sich im freien, individuellen Gedankenleben von Michael darüber belehren, welches die rechten Wege der Seele sind.

Menschen, die im vorangehenden Erdenleben in inspiriertem Gedankenwesen gestanden haben, also Michaeldiener waren, fühlten sich, am Ende des neunzehnten Jahrhunderts wieder ins Erdenleben gekommen, zu solcher freiwilligen Michaelgemeinschaft gedrängt. Sie betrachteten ihren alten Gedankeninspirator nunmehr als den Weiser im höheren Gedankenwesen.

Wer auf solche Dinge zu achten versteht, der konnte wissen, welch ein Umschwung im letzten Drittel des neunzehnten Jahrhunderts sich mit Bezug auf das Gedankenleben der Menschen vollzogen hat. Vorher konnte der Mensch nur fühlen,

spiritual events within the universe felt that Michael had followed the stream of intellectual life. He seeks for a new metamorphosis of his cosmic task. Formerly he allowed the thoughts to stream from the spiritual outer world into the souls of human beings; since the last third of the nineteenth century, he wishes to live *in* the human souls in which the thoughts are formed. In earlier times, those human beings who were related to Michael saw him develop his activity in the spiritual sphere; they now know that they should let Michael dwell in their hearts; they now dedicate to him their thought-borne spiritual life; they now allow themselves, in their free and individual life of thought, to be taught by Michael as to the right paths of soul.

When those who in their former earthly life received their thoughts by inspiration – i.e., who were servants of Michael – had returned to earthly life at the close of the nineteenth century, they felt urged toward this voluntary Michael-community. They now looked upon their former thought-inspirer as their guide in the higher being of thoughts.

One who understands how to observe such things knows what a great change took place in the last third of the nineteenth century with respect to the life of human thought. Before that time, the human being could only feel how

wie aus seinem Wesen heraus die Gedanken sich formten; von dem angedeuteten Zeitabschnitt an kann er sich über sein Wesen erheben; er kann den Sinn ins Geistige lenken; da tritt ihm Michael entgegen, und der erweist sich als altverwandt mit allem Gedankenweben. Der befreit die Gedanken aus dem Bereich des Kopfes; er macht ihnen den Weg zum Herzen frei; er löst die Begeisterung aus dem Gemüte los, sodass der Mensch in seelischer Hingabe leben kann an alles, was sich im *Gedankenlicht* erfahren lässt. Das Michaelzeitalter ist angebrochen. Die Herzen beginnen, Gedanken zu haben; die Begeisterung entströmt nicht mehr bloß mystischem Dunkel, sondern gedankengetragener Seelenklarheit. Dies verstehen, heißt, Michael in sein Gemüt aufnehmen. Gedanken, die heute nach dem Erfassen des Geistigen trachten, müssen Herzen entstammen, die für Michael als den feurigen Gedankenfürsten des Weltalls schlagen.

thoughts formed themselves in his own being; from the time indicated he is able to raise himself above his own being; he can turn his awareness to the spiritual; there Michael meets him, revealing his ancient kinship with all that is interwoven with thought. Michael liberates thought from the sphere of the head; he clears the way for it to the heart; he enkindles enthusiasm in the inner soul, so that the human being can live in soul-imbued devotion for all that can be experienced *in the light of thought*. The Age of Michael has dawned. Hearts begin to have thoughts; enthusiasm streams no longer from mystical obscurity, but from thought-borne soul-clarity. To understand this means to receive Michael into one's soul. Thoughts which at the present time strive to grasp the spiritual must originate in hearts which beat for Michael as the fiery thought-lord of the universe.

Leitsätze Nr. 79 bis 81

79. An die dritte Hierarchie (Archai, Archangeloi, Angeloi) kann man geistig herantreten, wenn man Denken, Fühlen und Wollen so kennen lernt, dass man in ihnen das in der Seele wirkende Geistige gewahr wird. Das Denken stellt zunächst nur *Bilder*, nicht ein Wirkliches in die Welt. Das Fühlen webt in diesem Bildhaften; es spricht für ein Wirkliches im Menschen, kann es aber nicht ausleben. Das Wollen entfaltet eine Wirklichkeit, die den Leib voraussetzt, aber an seiner Gestaltung nicht bewusst mitwirkt. Das Wesenhafte, das im Denken lebt, um den Leib zur Grundlage dieses Denkens zu machen, das Wesenhafte, das im Fühlen lebt, um den Leib zum Mit-Erleber einer Wirklichkeit zu machen, das Wesenhafte, das im Wollen lebt, um an seiner Gestaltung bewusst mitzuwirken, ist in der dritten Hierarchie lebendig.

80. An die zweite Hierarchie (Exusiai, Dynameis, Kyriotetes) kann man geistig herantreten, wenn man die Naturtatsachen als Erscheinungen eines in ihnen *lebenden* Geistigen erschaut. Die zweite Hierarchie hat dann die Natur zu ihrem Aufenthalt, um in ihr an den Seelen zu wirken.

Leading Thoughts 79 to 81

79. One can spiritually approach the third hierarchy (Archai, Archangeloi, Angeloi) when one learns to know thinking, feeling, and willing in such a way as to perceive in them the spiritual element working in the soul. Thinking, to begin with, does not place an effective reality into the world but only *images*. Feeling lives and moves in this realm of images; it bears witness to the presence of a reality in the human being, but cannot live it or express it outwardly. Willing unfolds a reality which presupposes the existence of the body but does not consciously assist in its formation. The essential being that lives in thinking in order to make the body the foundation of this thinking; the essential being that lives in feeling in order to enable the body to share in the experience of a reality; the essential being that lives in willing in order consciously to assist in the body's formation – all of this lives in the third hierarchy.

80. One can spiritually approach the second hierarchy (Exusiai, Dynamis, Kyriotetes) by awakening to see the facts of nature as the manifestation of the spiritual element *living* within them. The second hierarchy then has nature for its dwelling-place, in order from there to work upon human souls.

81. An die erste Hierarchie (Seraphim, Cherubim, Throne) kann man geistig herantreten, wenn man die im Natur- und Menschenreich vorhandenen Tatsachen als die Taten (Schöpfungen) eines in ihnen wirkenden Geistigen erschaut. Die erste Hierarchie hat dann das Natur- und Menschenreich zu ihrer Wirkung, in der sie sich entfaltet.

Leitsätze Nr. 82 bis 84

82. Der Mensch blickt zu den Sternenwelten auf; was sich da den Sinnen darbietet, sind nur die äußeren Offenbarungen derjenigen Geistwesenheiten und ihrer Taten, von denen in den vorigen Betrachtungen als den Wesen der geistigen Reiche (Hierarchien) gesprochen worden ist.

83. Die Erde ist der Schauplatz der drei Naturreiche und des Menschenreiches, insofern diese den äußeren Sinnenschein von der Tätigkeit geistiger Wesenheiten offenbaren.

84. Die Kräfte, welche in die irdischen Naturreiche und in das Menschenreich von Seiten geistiger Wesen

81. One can spiritually approach the first hierarchy (Seraphim, Cherubim, Thrones) by awakening to see the facts that confront one in the realm of nature and of humanity as the deeds (creations) of a spiritual element working within them. The first hierarchy then has the realm of nature and of humanity as the arena of its working, wherein it unfolds itself.

Leading Thoughts 82 to 84

82. The human being looks upward to the world of stars; what is there presented to his senses is but the outer revelation of those spirit-beings – and their deeds – who were spoken of as the beings of the spiritual realms or hierarchies.

83. The earth is the venue of the three realms of nature and of the human realm, inasmuch as these make manifest the outward and sensory glory of the activity of spiritual beings.

84. The forces working from spiritual beings into the earthly realms of nature and into the human realm

hineinwirken, enthüllen sich dem Menschengeiste durch die wahre, die geistgemäße Erkenntnis der Gestirnwelten.

reveal themselves to the human spirit through the true, the spiritual knowledge of the starry worlds.

Die menschliche Seelenverfassung vor dem Anbruch des Michael-Zeitalters

Heute soll eine Betrachtung hier eingefügt werden, die sich an die Ideen «Im Anbruch des Michael-Zeitalters» anschließt. Dieses Michael-Zeitalter ist in der Entwickelung der Menschheit heraufgekommen nach dem Vorherrschen der intellektuellen Gedankenbildung auf der einen Seite und der auf die äußere Sinnenwelt – die physische Welt – gerichteten menschlichen Anschauungsweise auf der anderen.

Die Gedankenbildung ist in ihrer eigenen Wesenheit *nicht* eine Entwickelung nach dem Materialistischen hin. Dasjenige, was in älteren Zeitaltern wie inspiriert an den Menschen herantrat, die Ideenwelt, wurde in der Zeit, die der Michael-Epoche voranging, Eigentum der menschlichen Seele. Diese empfängt nicht mehr die Ideen «von oben» aus dem geistigen Inhalt des Kosmos; sie holt sie aktiv aus der eigenen Geistigkeit des Menschen herauf. Damit ist der Mensch erst reif geworden, sich auf die eigene geistige Wesenheit zu besinnen. Vorher drang er bis zu dieser Tiefe des eigenen Wesens nicht vor. Er sah in sich gewissermaßen den Tropfen, der aus dem Meere der kosmischen Geistigkeit sich für das Erdenleben

The Condition of the Human Soul before the Dawn of the Michael Age

Today there will be added some further considerations in line with the ideas given in "At the Dawn of the Michael Age." The Michael Age has taken its rise in humanity's development at a time that follows, on the one hand, the predominance of the intellectual forming of thoughts, and on the other hand, the turning of human perception and vision to the outer world of the senses, to the physical world.

The forming of thoughts, in its own nature, is *not* a development in the direction of materialism. That which in bygone times came to the human being as something inspired into him – namely, the world of ideas – became, in the time preceding the Michael epoch, the property of the human soul. The soul no longer receives the ideas "from above" out of the spiritual content of the cosmos: It now actively draws them forth out of the human being's own spirituality. With this development, the human being first becomes mature enough for reflection upon his own spiritual being. Hitherto he did not penetrate this deeply into his own nature. In a sense, he saw his own being as a drop from the sea of cosmic spirituality – a

abgetrennt hat, um sich nach demselben wieder mit ihm zu vereinigen.

Es ist die im Menschen stattfindende Gedankenbildung ein Fortschritt in der menschlichen Selbsterkenntnis. Im Übersinnlichen angeschaut, stellt sich die Sache so dar: Die geistigen Mächte, die man mit dem Michael-Namen bezeichnen kann, verwalteten im geistigen Kosmos die Ideen. Der Mensch erlebte diese Ideen, indem er mit seiner Seele an dem Leben der Michael-Welt teilnahm. Dieses Erleben ist nun sein eigenes geworden. Dadurch ist eine zeitweilige Trennung des Menschen von der Michael-Welt eingetreten. Mit den inspirierten Gedanken der Vorzeit empfing der Mensch zugleich die geistigen Weltinhalte. Indem diese Inspiration aufhörte und der Mensch in eigener Tätigkeit die Gedanken bildet, ist er auf die Anschauung der Sinne verwiesen, um für diese Gedanken einen Inhalt zu haben. So musste der Mensch zunächst die errungene eigene Geistigkeit mit materiellem Inhalt erfüllen. Er fiel in die materialistische Anschauung in dem Zeitalter, das sein eigenes geistiges Wesen auf eine Stufe brachte, die höher ist als die vorangehenden.

Das kann leicht verkannt werden; man kann den «Fall» in den Materialismus nur allein beachten, und dann über ihn traurig sein. Aber während das *Anschauen* dieses Zeitalters sich auf die äußere physische Welt beschränken musste, entfaltete sich im Innern der Seele eine *gereinigte, in sich selbst bestehende*

drop that has separated off for the time of this earthly life, to reunite when the earthly life is over.

The thought-forming that takes place in the human being marks an advance in human self-knowledge. Viewed from the suprasensory, it appears thus: The spiritual powers that one may designate with the name of Michael held rule over the ideas in the spiritual cosmos. The human being experienced these ideas in that he partook with his soul in the life of the Michael-world. This experience has now become his own. And through this, a temporary separation of the human being from the Michael-world has come about. With the inspired thoughts of earlier times, the human being simultaneously received the spiritual world-content. In that this inspiration has ceased and the human being now forms his thoughts out of his own activity, he is referred to the perception of the senses to find a content for these thoughts. Thus was the human being obliged to fill with material content the spirituality that he had won. He fell into the materialistic worldview in the very epoch that brought his own spiritual being a stage higher in development.

This can easily be misunderstood; for example, one could observe solely the "fall" into materialism and be sad about it. However, while the *perception* of this age had to be limited to the external physical world, there was unfolding in the inner realm of the soul a *purified and self-subsisting spirituality* of the

Geistigkeit des Menschen als *Erleben*. Diese Geistigkeit muss nun im Michael-Zeitalter nicht mehr unbewusstes *Erleben* bleiben, sondern sich ihrer Eigenart bewusst werden. Das bedeutet den Eintritt der Michael-Wesenheit in die menschliche Seele. Der Mensch hat eine gewisse Zeit hindurch das eigene Geistige mit dem Materiellen der Natur erfüllt; er soll es wieder mit ureigener Geistigkeit als kosmischen Inhalt erfüllen.

Die Gedankenbildung verlor sich eine Weile an die Materie des Kosmos; sie muss sich in dem kosmischen Geiste wieder finden. In die kalte, abstrakte Gedankenwelt kann Wärme, kann wesenserfüllte Geist-Wirklichkeit eintreten. Das stellt den Anbruch des Michael-Zeitalters dar.

Nur in der Trennung von dem Gedankenwesen der Welt konnte in den Tiefen der menschlichen Seele das Bewusstsein der Freiheit erwachsen. Was von den Höhen kam, musste aus den Tiefen wiedergefunden werden. Deshalb ist die Entwickelung dieses Bewusstseins der Freiheit zunächst mit einer nur auf das Äußere gerichteten Naturerkenntnis verbunden gewesen. Während der Mensch im Innern seinen Geist unbewusst zur Reinheit der Ideen erbildete, waren seine Sinne nach außen nur auf das Materielle gerichtet, das in keiner Weise störend in das eingriff, was zunächst als zarter Keim in der Seele aufleuchtete.

Aber es kann in die Anschauung des äußeren Materiellen

human being as *experience*. And now in the Age of Michael this spirituality must no longer remain as unconscious *experience*, it must become conscious of its own unique nature. This signifies the entry of the Michael-being into the human soul. For a certain length of time the human being has filled his own spiritual element with the material aspect of nature; he must once again fill it with a spirituality of his very own, as cosmic content.

Thought-forming was lost for a time in the material element of the cosmos; it must discover itself again in the cosmic spirit. Into the cold, abstract world of thought can enter warmth, can enter an essential reality of spirit. This represents the dawn of the Michael Age.

Only through this separation from the thought-being of the world could the consciousness of freedom develop in the depths of the human soul. What came from the heights had to be found again in the depths. For this reason the development of the consciousness of freedom was connected first of all with knowledge of nature directed only to the external. While inwardly the human being was unconsciously developing his spirit by means of his striving for purity in ideas, outwardly his senses were directed solely to the material; but this did not in any way have a disturbing influence on what, as delicate germinal seed, was beginning to light up in the soul.

But in the vision of the outer material world, the experience

das Erleben des Geistigen und damit die geistige *Anschauung* in neuer Art wieder einziehen. Was im Zeichen des Materialismus an Naturerkenntnis gewonnen worden ist, kann in geistgemäßer Art im inneren Seelenleben erfasst werden. Michael, der «von oben» gesprochen hat, kann «aus dem Innern», wo er seinen neuen Wohnsitz aufschlagen wird, gehört werden. Mehr imaginativ gesprochen, kann dies so ausgedrückt werden: Das Sonnenhafte, das der Mensch durch lange Zeiten nur aus dem Kosmos in sich aufnahm, wird im Innern der Seele leuchtend werden. Der Mensch wird von einer «inneren Sonne» sprechen lernen. Er wird sich deshalb in seinem Leben zwischen Geburt und Tod nicht weniger als Erdenwesen wissen; aber er wird das auf der Erde wandelnde eigene Wesen als *sonnengeführt* erkennen. Er wird als Wahrheit empfinden lernen, dass ihn im Innern eine Wesenheit in ein Licht stellt, das zwar auf das Erdendasein leuchtet, aber nicht in diesem entzündet wird. Im Anbruche des Michael-Zeitalters mag es noch scheinen, als ob dies alles der Menschheit recht ferne liegen könne; doch es ist «im Geiste» nahe; es muss nur «gesehen» werden. Von dieser Tatsache, dass die Ideen des Menschen nicht nur «denkend» bleiben, sondern im Denken «sehend» werden, hängt unermesslich viel ab.

of the spiritual – and with it the capacity of spiritual *vision* – can re-enter in a new way. What has been won as the knowledge of nature under the sign of materialism can be comprehended in the inner soul-life in a spiritual way. Michael, who had once spoken "from above," can now be heard "from within," where he will establish his new dwelling. Speaking more imaginatively, this may be expressed as follows: The sun-nature, which for long periods of time the human being could only take into himself from the cosmos, will become luminous within the inner being of the soul. The human being will learn to speak of an "inner sun." He will not thereby lose any certainty in knowing himself, during his life between birth and death, to be a being of the earth; but he will come to recognize that his own being, as it wanders the earth, is *led by the sun*. He will learn to feel as a truth that, in his inner nature, a being places him into a light which indeed shines upon earthly existence, but which is not enkindled within it. In the dawn of the Michael Age it may still seem as if all this were very far removed from humanity; but in fact it is near "in spirit"; it must only be "seen." Immeasurably much depends upon the realization of this fact – that human ideas do not merely remain "thinking," but in thought become "seeing."

Leitsätze Nr. 85 bis 87

85. Im wachen Tagesbewusstsein erlebt sich im gegenwärtigen Weltenalter zunächst der Mensch. Dieses Erleben verhüllt ihm, dass innerhalb der Wachheit die dritte Hierarchie in seinem Erleben gegenwärtig ist.

86. Im Traumbewusstsein erlebt der Mensch in chaotischer Art das eigene Wesen mit dem Geistwesen der Welt unharmonisch vereinigt. Stellt sich dem Traumbewusstsein das Imaginative als dessen anderer Pol gegenüber, so wird der Mensch gewahr, dass die zweite Hierarchie in seinem Erleben gegenwärtig ist.

87. Im traumlosen Schlafbewusstsein erlebt der Mensch ohne eigene Bewusstheit das eigene Wesen mit dem Geistwesen der Welt vereinigt. Stellt sich dem Schlafbewusstsein das Inspirierte als dessen anderer Pol gegenüber, so wird der Mensch gewahr, dass die erste Hierarchie in seinem Erleben gegenwärtig ist.

Leading Thoughts 85 to 87

85. It is in waking day-consciousness that the human being experiences himself, to begin with, during the present cosmic age. This experience veils from him the fact that in this waking state the third hierarchy is present in his experience.

86. In dream-consciousness the human being experiences, in a chaotic way, his own being unharmoniously united with the spirit-being of the world. When the imaginative is realized as the other pole of dream-consciousness, the human being becomes aware that the second hierarchy is present in his experience.

87. In dreamless sleep-consciousness the human being experiences, without his own consciousness, his own being united with the spirit-being of the world. When the inspirative is realized as the other pole of dreamless sleep-consciousness, the human being becomes aware that the first hierarchy is present in his experience.

Aphorismen

(Aus einem am 24. August [1924] in London gehaltenen Mitgliedervortrag)

Das menschliche Bewusstsein entwickelt im gegenwärtigen Weltstadium seiner Entwickelung drei Formen, das wachende, das träumende und das traumlos schlafende Bewusstsein.

Das wachende erlebt die sinnenfällige Außenwelt, bildet über diese Ideen und kann aus diesen Ideen heraus solche gestalten, welche eine rein geistige Welt abbilden. Das träumende Bewusstsein entwickelt Bilder, welche die Außenwelt umformen, zum Beispiel an die in das Bett scheinende Sonne das Traumerlebnis einer Feuersbrunst mit vielen Einzelheiten knüpfen. Oder es stellt die menschliche Innenwelt in symbolischen Bildern vor die Seele, zum Beispiel das stark pochende Herz im Bild eines überheizten Ofens. Auch die Erinnerungen leben umgestaltet im Traumbewusstsein auf. Dazu kommen Inhalte solcher Bilder, die nicht der Sinneswelt entnommen sind, sondern der geistigen, die aber nicht die Möglichkeit bieten, in die geistige Welt erkennend einzudringen, weil ihr Dämmersein nicht ganz in das Wachbewusstsein sich heben lässt und weil, was in dieses herüberspielt, nicht wahrhaft ergriffen werden kann.

Aphorisms

(From a lecture to members given in London on 24 August [1924])

In the present world-stage of its development, human consciousness unfolds three forms: the waking, the dreaming, and the dreamless-sleep consciousness.

The waking consciousness experiences the outer world through the senses, forms ideas about it, and out of those ideas it can create something in the likeness of a purely spiritual world. The dreaming consciousness develops images in which the outer world is transformed, as, for instance, when the sunshine on the bed is experienced in dream as a conflagration in all its details. Or a human being's own inner world may appear before him in symbolic images – for instance, the throbbing heart may appear in the image of an over-heated oven. Memories likewise reappear in a transformed manner in dream consciousness. In addition one has the inner content of these images, stemming not from the sensory world but from the spiritual. But this content does not provide the possibility of penetrating with understanding into the spiritual world, because its twilight character does not allow itself to be completely raised into waking consciousness, and because what thus plays over into waking consciousness from the spiritual cannot be truly grasped.

Es ist aber möglich, von der Traumwelt unmittelbar im Erwachen so viel zu erfassen, dass man gewahr wird, wie sie der unvollkommene Abdruck eines geistigen Erlebens ist, das den Schlaf erfüllt, aber dem Wachbewusstsein sich zum weitaus größten Teile entzieht. Es ist nur nötig, um das zu durchschauen, den Augenblick des Erwachens so zu gestalten, dass dieses nicht mit einem Schlage die Außenwelt vor die Seele zaubert, sondern dass die Seele, ohne noch nach außen zu schauen, sich dem innen Erlebten hingegeben fühlt.

Das traumlose Schlafbewusstsein lässt die Seele Erlebnisse durchmachen, die in der Erinnerung nur als unterschiedsloses Einerlei der Zeit-Erfüllung erscheinen. Man wird von diesen Erlebnissen so lange als von etwas gar nicht Vorhandenem sprechen können, solange man nicht durch geisteswissenschaftliche Forschung in sie eindringt. Geschieht dies aber, entwickelt man auf die in der anthroposophischen Literatur gegebene Art das imaginierte und inspirierte Bewusstsein, dann treten aus der Finsternis des Schlafes die Bilder und die Inspirationen von Erlebnissen früheren Erdendaseins hervor. Und dann kann man auch den Inhalt des Traumbewusstseins überschauen. Er besteht in einem vom Wachbewusstsein nicht zu ergreifenden Inhalt, der in diejenige Welt verweist, in welcher der Mensch zwischen zwei Erdenleben als unverkörperte Seele verweilt.

Lernt man kennen, was für die gegenwärtige Weltenphase

But it is possible in the moment of waking to grasp so much of the dream world as to become aware that it is the imperfect imprint of a spiritual experience which has filled the time of sleep but which for the most part evades the waking consciousness. In order to comprehend this reality, it is only necessary to shape the moment of waking in such a way that the outer world is not conjured all at once before the soul, but that the soul, without as yet regarding the outer world, feels itself surrendered to what has been experienced within.

In dreamless sleep-consciousness, the soul passes through experiences which appear in memory as nothing more than an indifferent period of time between falling asleep and waking. One will speak of these experiences as non-existent so long as one has not found the way into them through spiritual-scientific investigation. But if this takes place, if the imaginative and inspirative consciousness described in anthroposophical literature are developed, then out of the darkness of sleep the images and inspirations belonging to the experience of previous lives on earth make their appearance. It then also becomes possible to have an overview of the content of dream consciousness. This consists in a content not graspable by waking consciousness – a content which refers to the world in which the human being dwells as a disembodied soul between two earthly lives.

If one learns to know what is hidden behind the dream- and

das Traum- und das Schlafbewusstsein verbergen, dann wird der Weg eröffnet auf die Entwickelungsformen des menschlichen Bewusstseins in der Vorwelt. Man kann dazu allerdings nicht durch die äußere Forschung gelangen. Denn die erhaltenen äußeren Zeugnisse bringen nur Nachwirkungen von vorgeschichtlichen Erlebnissen des menschlichen Bewusstseins. Die anthroposophische Literatur bringt Aufschlüsse darüber, wie man durch geistige Forschung zur Anschauung von solchen Erlebnissen gelangen kann.

In der alten Zeit Ägyptens findet diese Forschung ein Traumbewusstsein, das dem Wachbewusstsein viel näher steht, als das jetzt beim Menschen der Fall ist. Die Traumerlebnisse strahlten erinnerungsgemäß in das Wachbewusstsein herüber; und dieses lieferte nicht bloß die in scharf konturierte Gedanken zu fassenden Sinneseindrücke, sondern verbunden mit diesen das Geistige, das in der Sinneswelt wirkt. Dadurch stand der Mensch mit seinem Bewusstsein instinktiv in der Welt darinnen, die er bei seiner Erdenverkörperung verlassen hat und die er wieder betreten wird, wenn er durch die Todespforte geschritten sein wird.

Die erhaltenen Schrift-Denkmäler und anderes geben dem, der unbefangen in ihren Inhalt eindringt, deutliche Nachbilder eines solchen Bewusstseins, das einer Zeit angehört, aus der äußere Denkmäler nicht vorhanden sind.

sleep-consciousness in the present phase of world-development, then the way is open to the developing forms of human consciousness in ages past. One cannot, however, arrive at this understanding by means of outer investigation; for evidence received from the outer world shows only the aftereffects of the experiences of human consciousness in prehistoric times. Anthroposophical literature gives insights as to how, by means of spiritual research, one may attain to the vision of such experiences.

In ancient Egyptian times, this research finds a dream-state-consciousness which was much closer in nature to their waking state of consciousness than is the case for human beings of the present day. The dream experiences passed into the waking state of consciousness in a memory-like way, and these experiences gave not merely the sense impressions to be grasped in sharply outlined thoughts, but, connected with these, the spiritual element that works in the world of the senses. Thus, with his consciousness the human being stood instinctively within that world which he had left when he incarnated on earth, and which he will re-enter upon passing through the gate of death.

To those who enter impartially into their content, written records inherited from ancient times provide clear evidence of a consciousness of this kind, belonging to an age of which no outer written records exist.

Das Schlafbewusstsein der ägyptischen Urzeit enthielt Träume der geistigen Welt in einer ähnlichen Art, wie das gegenwärtige Träume aus der physischen Welt enthält.

Bei anderen Völkern findet man aber noch ein anderes Bewusstsein. Der Schlaf strahlte seine Erlebnisse in das Wachen herüber, und zwar so, dass in diesem Herüberstrahlen eine Anschauung der wiederholten Erdenleben instinktiv vorhanden war. Die Traditionen von der Erkenntnis der wiederholten Erdenleben durch die Urmenschen entstammen diesen Bewusstseinsformen.

Man findet, was in alten Zeiten an Traumbewusstsein dämmerhaft instinktiv vorhanden war, in der entwickelten imaginativen Erkenntnis wieder. Nur ist es bei dieser vollbewusst wie das Wachleben.

Und man wird durch die inspirierte Erkenntnis ebenso die vorzeitliche instinktive Einsicht gewahr, die noch etwas von den wiederholten Erdenleben sah. Auf diese Verwandlung der menschlichen Bewusstseinsformen geht die heutige Menschheitsgeschichte nicht ein. Sie möchte gerne glauben, dass im Wesentlichen die gegenwärtigen Bewusstseinsformen immer vorhanden waren, solange es eine Erdenmenschheit gibt.

Und was doch auf solche anderen Bewusstseinsformen hinweist, die Mythen und Märchen, möchte man als den Ausfluss der dichtenden Fantasie des Urmenschen ansehen.

In ancient Egyptian times, the sleep-consciousness contained dreams of the spiritual world just as the sleep-consciousness of the present day contains dreams originating from the physical world.

But among other peoples one finds yet another kind of consciousness. The experiences undergone during sleep shone over into waking consciousness in such a way that a vision of repeated earthly lives was instinctively present. The traditions of ancient humanity regarding the knowledge of repeated earthly lives originate from these forms of consciousness.

In what is developed as imaginative cognition, one finds again what, in ancient times, was present in a dim and instinctive way in the state of dream-consciousness. However, in imaginative cognition this content is as fully conscious as our waking life.

And through inspirative cognition, one also becomes aware of the primeval instinctive insight which was still able to perceive something of repeated earthly lives. The modern-day understanding of human history makes no note of this transformation in the forms of human consciousness. It would like to believe that, in essence, the present forms of consciousness have existed as long as there has been an earthly humanity.

And what, in spite of this, does point to other forms of consciousness – the myths and fairy-tales – one would prefer to look upon as the result of the poetic fantasy of ancient human beings.

Leitsätze Nr. 88 bis 90

88. Im wachen Tagesbewusstsein erlebt sich im gegenwärtigen Weltenalter der Mensch als innerhalb der physischen Welt stehend. Dieses Erleben verbirgt ihm, dass innerhalb seiner eigenen Wesenheit die Wirkungen eines Lebens zwischen Tod und Geburt vorhanden sind.

89. Im Traumbewusstsein erlebt der Mensch in chaotischer Art das eigene Wesen mit dem Geisteswesen der Welt unharmonisch vereint. Das Wachbewusstsein kann den eigentlichen Inhalt dieses Traumbewusstseins nicht ergreifen. Es enthüllt sich dem imaginativen und inspirierten Bewusstsein, dass die Geistwelt, die der Mensch zwischen Tod und Geburt durchlebt, an dem Aufbau seines Innenwesens beteiligt ist.

90. Im traumlosen Schlafbewusstsein erlebt der Mensch ohne eigene Bewusstheit das eigene Wesen als durchdrungen mit den Ergebnissen vergangener Erdenleben. Das inspirierte und intuitive Bewusstsein dringt zur Anschauung dieser Ergebnisse vor und sieht das Wirken voriger Erdenleben in dem Schicksalsverlauf (Karma) des gegenwärtigen.

Leading Thoughts 88 to 90

88. In waking day-consciousness the human being experiences himself, during the present world-age, as standing in the midst of the physical world. This experience conceals from him the fact that, within his being, the effects of a life between death and birth are present.

89. In dream-consciousness the human being experiences, in a chaotic way, his own being unharmoniously united with the spiritual being of the world. Waking consciousness cannot grasp the actual content of this dream-consciousness. To imaginative and inspirative consciousness, it is revealed how the world of spirit, in which the human being lives between death and birth, helps to build up his inner being.

90. In dreamless sleep-consciousness the human being experiences, without his own awareness, his own being permeated with the results of past earthly lives. Inspirative and intuitive consciousness penetrate to a clear perception of these results and see the working of former earthly lives in the present-day course of destiny (karma).

Leitsätze Nr. 91 bis 93

91. Der Wille tritt in das gewöhnliche Bewusstsein im heutigen Weltalter nur durch den Gedanken ein. Dieses gewöhnliche Bewusstsein kann aber nur an das sinnlich Wahrnehmbare anknüpfen. Es ergreift auch an dem eigenen Willen nur das, was von diesem in die sinnliche Wahrnehmungswelt eintritt. Der Mensch weiß in diesem Bewusstsein von seinen Willensimpulsen nur durch die vorstellende Beobachtung seiner selbst, wie er von der Außenwelt nur durch Beobachtung weiß.

92. Das Karma, das im Willen wirkt, ist eine ihm aus vorangegangenen Erdenleben anhaftende Eigenschaft. Diese kann daher nicht durch die Vorstellungen des gewöhnlichen Sinnesseins, die nur auf das gegenwärtige Erdenleben hin orientiert sind, erfasst werden.

93. Weil diese Vorstellungen das Karma nicht erfassen können, verweisen sie das ihnen an den menschlichen Willensimpulsen entgegentretende Unverständliche in das mystische Dunkel der Körperkonstitution, während es die Wirkung vorangegangener Erdenleben ist.

Leading Thoughts 91 to 93

91. In the present world-age, the will enters the ordinary consciousness only through thought. But this ordinary consciousness can only take its start from what is sense-perceptible. Even as regards one's own will, the ordinary consciousness is able to grasp only what passes from the will into the world of sense perceptions. The human being has insight into this consciousness of his own will impulses only through observation of himself by means of forming representations, just as he is aware of the outer world only through observation.

92. The karma that works in the will is a characteristic of the will stemming from former lives on earth. This constituent of the will cannot therefore be apprehended with the representations of ordinary sensory existence, which are oriented only to the present earthly life.

93. Because these representations are unable to encompass karma, they attribute what is incomprehensible to them in human will impulses to the mystical darkness of the bodily constitution, whereas in reality it is the working of past earthly lives.

Leitsätze Nr. 94 bis 96

94. Mit dem gewöhnlichen Vorstellungsleben, das durch die Sinne vermittelt wird, steht der Mensch in der physischen Welt. Um diese in sein Bewusstsein aufzunehmen, muss das Karma im Vorstellungsleben schweigen. Der Mensch *vergisst* gewissermaßen als Vorstellender sein Karma.

95. In den Willensoffenbarungen wirkt das Karma. Aber die Wirkung bleibt im Unbewussten. Durch das Erheben dessen, was im Willen unbewusst wirkt, zur Imagination, wird das Karma ergriffen. Man fühlt in sich sein Schicksal.

96. Tritt Inspiration und Intuition in die Imagination ein, dann wird im Willenswirken außer den Impulsen der Gegenwart das Ergebnis voriger Erdenleben wahrnehmbar. Das vergangene Leben erweist sich in dem gegenwärtigen als wirksam.

Leading Thoughts 94 to 96

94. With the ordinary life of representation mediated by the senses, the human being stands in the midst of the physical world. For this world to enter his consciousness, karma must be silent in his life of representation. As a being who forms representations, the human being in a certain sense *forgets* his karma.

95. In the revelations of the will, karma works itself out. But its working remains in the realm of the unconscious. Through lifting into conscious imagination what works unconsciously in the will, karma is grasped. The human being feels his destiny within him.

96. When inspiration and intuition enter imagination, then, in the workings of the will which do not have their source in the impulses of the present, the outcome of former earthly lives becomes perceptible. The past life presents itself in the present as effective reality.

Leitsätze Nr. 97 bis 99

97. Eine gröbere Darstellung darf sagen: In der Seele des Menschen leben *Denken*, *Fühlen* und *Wollen*. Eine feinere muss sagen: Denken enthält immer einen Untergrund von Fühlen und Wollen, Fühlen einen solchen von Denken und Wollen, Wollen einen von Denken und Fühlen. Im Gedankenleben ist nur das Denken, im Gefühlsleben das Fühlen, im Willensleben das Wollen gegenüber den anderen Seeleninhalten vorherrschend.

98. Das Fühlen und Wollen des Gedankenlebens enthalten das karmische Ergebnis voriger Erdenleben. Das Denken und Wollen des Gefühlslebens bestimmen auf karmische Art den Charakter. Das Denken und Fühlen des Willenslebens reißen das gegenwärtige Erdenleben aus dem karmischen Zusammenhange heraus.

99. Im Fühlen und Wollen des Denkens lebt der Mensch sein Karma der Vergangenheit aus; im Denken und Fühlen des Wollens bereitet er das Karma der Zukunft vor.

Leading Thoughts 97 to 99

97. For a rough description, it is possible to say: *Thinking*, *feeling*, and *willing* live in the human soul. A more refined description must say: Thinking always contains a substratum of feeling and willing; feeling a substratum of thinking and willing; willing a substratum of thinking and feeling. In the life of thought, however, thinking predominates; in the life of feeling, feeling predominates; and in the life of will, willing predominates over the other contents of the soul.

98. The feeling and willing of the life of thought contain the karmic outcome of past lives on earth. The thinking and willing of the life of feeling karmically determine a person's character. The thinking and feeling of the life of will tear the present earthly life away from karmic connections.

99. In the feeling and willing of thinking, the human being lives out his karma of the past; in the thinking and feeling of willing he prepares his karma of the future.

Leitsätze Nr. 100 bis 102

100. Die Gedanken haben ihren eigentlichen Sitz im ätherischen Leib des Menschen. Aber da sind sie lebendig-wesenhafte Kräfte. Sie prägen sich dem physischen Leibe ein. Und als solche «eingeprägte Gedanken» haben sie die schattenhafte Art, in der sie das gewöhnliche Bewusstsein kennt.

101. Was in den Gedanken als Fühlen lebt, das kommt vom astralischen Leib, was als Wollen, vom «Ich» her. Im Schlafen erstrahlt der Ätherleib des Menschen durchaus in dessen Gedankenwelt; nur der Mensch nimmt nicht daran teil, weil er das Fühlen der Gedanken mit dem Astralleib, das Wollen derselben mit dem «Ich» aus dem ätherischen und physischen Leib herausgezogen hat.

102. In dem Augenblicke, in dem während des Schlafes der astralische Leib und das Ich das Verhältnis zu den Gedanken des Ätherleibes lösen, gehen sie ein solches zu dem «Karma», zur Anschauung der Geschehnisse durch die wiederholten Erdenleben hindurch ein. Diese Anschauung ist dem gewöhnlichen Bewusstsein versagt; ein übersinnliches Bewusstsein tritt in sie ein.

Leading Thoughts 100 to 102

100. Thoughts have their actual seat in the human etheric body. There, however, they are forces of essential life and being. They imprint themselves upon the physical body. And as "imprinted thoughts" they have the shadowy character by means of which they are known to ordinary consciousness.

101. What lives in thoughts as feeling comes from the astral body, and what lives in thoughts as willing comes from the 'I'. In sleep, the human etheric body thoroughly radiates into this world of thoughts; but the human being himself does not partake in it. – For with the withdrawing of the astral body he takes the feeling of the thoughts, and with the 'I' the willing, out of the etheric and the physical bodies.

102. The moment the astral body and 'I' loosen their connection with the thoughts of the etheric body during sleep, they enter into connection with "karma" – with the beholding of the events of repeated lives on earth. This vision is denied to ordinary consciousness, but a suprasensory consciousness can enter into it.

Der vor-michaelische und der Michaels-Weg

Man wird nicht im rechten Lichte sehen können, wie der Michael-Einschlag in die Menschheitsentwickelung hereindringt, wenn man sich über das Verhältnis der neueren Ideenwelt zur Natur die Vorstellung macht, die heute allgemein üblich ist.

Da denkt man: Draußen ist die Natur mit ihren Vorgängen und Wesen; im Innern, da sind die Ideen. Diese stellen Begriffe von Naturwesen dar oder auch sogenannte Naturgesetze. Es kommt den Denkern dabei vor allem darauf an, zu zeigen, wie man *die* Ideen bildet, die das rechte Verhältnis zu den Naturwesen haben oder die wahre Naturgesetze enthalten.

Man legt dabei wenig Wert darauf, wie diese Ideen zu dem Menschen stehen, der sie hat. Und doch wird man, worauf es ankommt, nur einsehen, wenn man vor allem die Frage aufwirft: Was erlebt der Mensch in den neueren naturwissenschaftlichen Ideen?

Man wird zu einer Antwort auf die folgende Art kommen.

Heute empfindet der Mensch, dass Ideen in ihm durch die Tätigkeit seiner Seele ausgebildet werden. Er hat das Gefühl:

The Pre-Michaelic Era and the Path of Michael

One will be unable to perceive in the right light how the Michael-impulse enters into human development if one shares the representation which is universally accepted today as to the relation of the modern world of ideas to nature.

It is thought: There, outside us, is nature with her processes and being; within us are the ideas. These ideas present concepts about the being of nature, or about what are known as the laws of nature. The thinkers of today are concerned first of all to show how one forms *those* ideas which stand in a rightful relation to the being of nature, or which encompass the true laws of nature.

It is of little importance to such thinkers how these ideas are related to the human being who has them. But in truth one will only gain insight into this matter when the following question is raised: What does the human being experience through the natural-scientific ideas of modern times?

The answer can be arrived at in the following way.

The human being feels today that the ideas are formed within him through the activity of his soul. He has the feeling

Er ist der Ausbildner der Ideen, während nur die Wahrnehmungen von außen an ihn herandringen.

Dieses Gefühl hatte der Mensch nicht immer. Er empfand in älteren Zeiten den Inhalt der Ideen nicht als etwas Selbst-Gemachtes, sondern als etwas durch Eingebung aus der übersinnlichen Welt Erhaltenes.

Dieses Gefühl machte Stufen durch. Und die Stufen hingen davon ab, mit welchem Teil seines Wesens der Mensch das erlebte, was er heute seine Ideen nennt. Heute in dem Zeitalter der Entwickelung der Bewusstseinsseele gilt uneingeschränkt, was in den vorigen *Leitsätzen* steht: «Die Gedanken haben ihren eigentlichen Sitz im ätherischen Leib des Menschen. Aber da sind sie lebendig-wesenhafte Kräfte. Sie prägen sich dem physischen Leibe ein. Und als solche ‹eingeprägte Gedanken› haben sie die schattenhafte Art, in der sie das gewöhnliche Bewusstsein kennt.»

Man kann nun zurückgehen in Zeiten, in denen Gedanken unmittelbar im «Ich» erlebt wurden. Da aber waren sie nicht schattenhaft wie heute; sie waren nicht bloß *lebend*; sie waren *beseelt* und *durchgeistigt*. Das heißt aber: Der Mensch *dachte nicht* Gedanken; sondern er erlebte die Wahrnehmung von konkreten geistigen Wesenheiten.

Man wird ein Bewusstsein, das so zu einer Welt von geistigen Wesenheiten aufsieht, überall in der Vorzeit der Völker finden. Was sich davon geschichtlich erhalten hat, bezeichnet

that he himself forms his ideas, while only the sense perceptions come to him from without.

The human being did not always have this feeling. In times past, he did not feel the content of his ideas as something he had made himself but as something received as a gift from the suprasensory world.

This feeling underwent various stages. And these stages depended on that part of a person's being in which he experienced what today he calls his ideas. Today, in the period of the development of the consciousness soul, what is contained in the *Leading Thoughts* of the last number is wholly true: "Thoughts have their actual seat in the human etheric body. There, however, they are forces of essential life and being. They imprint themselves upon the physical body. And as 'imprinted thoughts' they have the shadowy character by means of which they are known to ordinary consciousness."

Now one can go back to times in which the thoughts were directly experienced in the 'I'. But in those times they were not shadowy as they are today, nor were they merely *living*; they were *ensouled* and *permeated with spirit.* But this means that the human being *did not think* his thoughts; rather, he experienced the perception of concrete spiritual beings.

Everywhere amongst the peoples of antiquity one finds a consciousness that looked up to a world of spiritual beings in this way. What has been preserved to history of this is

man heute als mythenbildendes Bewusstsein und legt ihm keinen besonderen Wert bei für die Erfassung der wirklichen Welt. – Und doch steht der Mensch mit diesem Bewusstsein in *seiner* Welt, in der Welt seines Ursprunges darinnen, während er sich mit dem heutigen Bewusstsein aus dieser *seiner* Welt heraushebt.

Der Mensch ist Geist. Und *seine* Welt ist die der Geister.

Eine nächste Stufe ist diejenige, wo das Gedankliche nicht mehr vom «Ich», sondern von dem astralischen Leibe erlebt wird. Da geht die unmittelbare Geistigkeit für den seelischen Anblick verloren. Das Gedankliche erscheint als ein beseeltes Lebendiges.

Auf der ersten Stufe, dem Erschauen des konkret geistig Wesenhaften, hat der Mensch gar nicht stark das Bedürfnis, das Erschaute an die Welt des Sinnlich-Wahrgenommenen heranzutragen. Die sinnlichen Welterscheinungen offenbaren sich zwar als die Taten des übersinnlich Erschauten; aber eine besondere Wissenschaft von dem auszubilden, was dem «geistigen Blick» unmittelbar anschaulich ist, liegt keine Nötigung vor. Außerdem ist, was als die Welt der Geistwesen erschaut wird, von solcher Fülle, dass darauf vor allem die Aufmerksamkeit ruht.

Anders wird dies bei der zweiten Bewusstseinsetappe. Da verbergen sich die konkreten Geistwesen; ihr Abglanz, als

described today as a myth-creating consciousness and is not considered of much importance for an understanding of the real world. – And yet, with this consciousness the human being stands in *his own* world – in the world of his true origin – whereas with his present consciousness he is lifted out of *his own* world.

The human being is spirit. And *his* world is that of the spiritual beings.

The next stage was one in which the element of thought was experienced no longer by the 'I' but by the astral body. Here the direct spiritual element is lost to the soul's capacity of vision. Thought appears as an ensouled element of life.

At the first stage, that of the vision of the concrete spiritual essence, the human being does not at all feel strongly the necessity of connecting what he sees with the world of what is perceived through the senses. The phenomena perceptible to the senses are seen to be the deeds of what he observes supersensibly, but he feels no need to develop a special science of that which is directly apparent to the "spiritual view." Moreover, what is visible as the world of spirit-beings is so rich that his attention rests upon this world above all else.

It is different at the second stage of consciousness. Here the concrete spiritual beings are hidden; their reflection appears

beseeltes Leben, erscheint. Man beginnt das «Leben der Natur» an dieses «Leben der Seelen» heranzutragen. Man sucht in den Naturwesen und Naturvorgängen die wirksamen Geistwesen und deren Taten. In dem, was später als alchymistisches Suchen auftrat, ist geschichtlich der Niederschlag dieser Bewusstseinsetappe zu sehen.

Wie der Mensch, indem er auf erster Bewusstseinsetappe Geistwesen «dachte», ganz in *seinem* Wesen lebte, so steht er auf dieser zweiten sich und seinem Ursprung noch nahe.

Damit ist aber auf beiden Stufen ausgeschlossen, dass der Mensch im eigentlichen Sinne zu einem inneren eigenen Antrieb für sein Handeln komme.

Geistiges, das von seiner Art ist, handelt in ihm. Was *er* zu tun scheint, ist Offenbarung von Vorgängen, die sich durch Geistwesen abspielen. Was der Mensch tut, ist die sinnlich-physische Erscheinung eines dahinter stehenden wirklichen göttlich-geistigen Geschehens.

Eine dritte Epoche der Bewusstseinsentwickelung bringt die Gedanken, aber als lebendige, im ätherischen Leib zum Bewusstsein.

Als die griechische Zivilisation groß war, lebte sie in diesem Bewusstsein. Wenn der Grieche dachte, so bildete er sich nicht einen Gedanken, durch den er, als mit seinem eigenen Gebilde, die Welt ansah; sondern er fühlte in sich erregt

in the form of an ensouled life. The human being begins to relate the "life of nature" to this "life of souls." In the beings and processes of nature, he seeks the active spirit-beings and their deeds. What later appeared as alchemical striving may be seen historically as the after-effect of this stage of consciousness.

When, at the first stage of consciousness, the human being "thought" the spirit-beings, he lived entirely in *his own* being; and at the second stage, too, he is still quite near to himself and his origin.

But at both stages it is quite impossible for the human being to develop, in the true sense of the word, his own inner impulses of action.

A spiritual element that is of his own nature acts in him. What *he* appears to do is the revelation of processes which come about through spirit-beings. What the human being does is the sensory-physical manifestation of a real divine-spiritual event standing behind it.

A third epoch in the development of consciousness brings thought to consciousness, but as a living element in the etheric body.

When Greek civilization was at its prime, its people lived in this consciousness. When the Greek thought, he did not form thoughts through which, as if via his own creations, he looked upon the world; rather, he felt enkindled within him a life

Leben, das auch draußen in den Dingen und Vorgängen pulsierte.

Da erstand zum ersten Male die Sehnsucht nach Freiheit des eigenen Handelns. Noch nicht wirkliche Freiheit; aber die Sehnsucht darnach.

Der Mensch, der das Regen der Natur in sich selber sich regend empfand, konnte die Sehnsucht ausbilden, die eigene Regsamkeit loszulösen von der als fremd wahrgenommenen Regsamkeit. Aber es wurde immerhin in der äußeren Regsamkeit noch das letzte Ergebnis der wirksamen Geist-Welt empfunden, die gleicher Art mit dem Menschen ist.

Erst als die Gedanken ihre Prägung im physischen Leibe annahmen und sich das Bewusstsein nur auf diese Prägung erstreckte, trat die Möglichkeit der Freiheit ein. Das ist der Zustand, der mit dem fünfzehnten nachchristlichen Jahrhundert gegeben ist.

In der Welt-Entwickelung kommt es nicht darauf an, was für Bedeutung die Ideen der heutigen Naturanschauung zur Natur haben; denn diese Ideen haben ihre Formen nicht deshalb angenommen, um ein bestimmtes Bild der Natur zu liefern, sondern um den Menschen zu einer bestimmten Stufe seiner Entwickelung zu bringen.

Als die Gedanken den physischen Körper ergriffen, war aus ihrem unmittelbaren Inhalte Geist, Seele, Leben getilgt; und der abstrakte Schatten, der am physischen Leibe haftet, ist

which also pulsed through the things and processes of the outer world.

Then there arose, for the first time, the longing for freedom in one's own actions. Not yet true freedom, but the longing for it.

The human being, who felt the life and activity of nature asserting itself in him, could develop the longing to detach his own activity from the activity that he perceived as foreign and outside himself. But after all, this outer activity was still perceived as the final result of the active world of spirit, which is of like nature to the human being himself.

It is only when the thoughts took their imprint into the physical body, and when the consciousness extended only to this imprint, that the possibility of freedom arose. This is the condition that was provided with the fifteenth century AD.

For world development, the important point is not what significance the ideas of the present-day view of nature have with regard to nature; for these ideas have assumed their forms not in order to provide a certain image of nature, but in order to bring the human being to a certain stage in his development.

When the thoughts grasped hold of the physical body, the spirit, soul, and life were excluded from their direct content; and the abstract shadow, attached to the physical body, alone

allein geblieben. Solche Gedanken können *nur* Physisch-Materielles zum Gegenstande ihrer Erkenntnis machen. Denn sie sind selbst nur *wirklich* an dem physisch-materiellen Leibe des Menschen.

Nicht deshalb ist der Materialismus entstanden, weil nur materielle Wesen und Vorgänge in der äußeren Natur wahrzunehmen sind; sondern weil der Mensch in seiner Entwickelung eine Etappe durchzumachen hatte, die ihn zu einem Bewusstsein führte, das zunächst nur materielle Offenbarungen zu schauen fähig ist. Die einseitige Ausgestaltung dieses menschlichen Entwickelungsbedürfnisses ergab die Naturanschauung der neueren Zeit.

Michaels Sendung ist, in der Menschen Äther-Leiber die Kräfte zu bringen, durch die die Gedanken-Schatten wieder *Leben* gewinnen; dann werden sich den belebten Gedanken Seelen und Geister der übersinnlichen Welten neigen; es wird der befreite Mensch mit ihnen leben können, wie ehedem der Mensch mit ihnen lebte, der nur das physische Abbild *ihres* Wirkens war.

remained. Such thoughts can *only* make the physical-material element into the object of their knowledge. For they themselves are only *real* in the physical-material human body.

Materialism did not originate because only material beings and processes could be perceived in external nature, but because the human being had to pass through a stage in his development which would lead him to a consciousness at first only capable of seeing material revelations. The one-sided shaping of this necessity in human development resulted in the modern view of nature.

It is Michael's mission to bring into human etheric bodies the forces through which the thought-shadows may regain *life*. Then the souls and spirits in the suprasensory worlds will incline toward the enlivened thoughts, and the liberated human being will be able to live with them – just as formerly the human being lived with them when he was only the physical image of *their* activity.

Leitsätze Nr. 103 bis 105

103. In der Menschheitsentwickelung steigt das Bewusstsein auf der Leiter der Gedanken-Entfaltung herab. Es gibt eine erste Bewusstseinsetappe: Da erlebt der Mensch die Gedanken im «Ich» als durchgeistigte, beseelte, belebte Wesen. Auf einer zweiten Etappe erlebt der Mensch die Gedanken im astralischen Leib; sie stellen da nur mehr die beseelten und belebten Abbilder der Geistwesen dar. Auf einer dritten Etappe erlebt der Mensch die Gedanken im Äther-Leibe; sie stellen nur eine innere Regsamkeit wie einen Nachklang von Seelenhaftem dar. Auf der vierten, gegenwärtigen Etappe erlebt der Mensch die Gedanken im physischen Leibe; sie stellen tote Schatten des Geistigen dar.

104. In demselben Maße, in dem das Geistig-Seelisch-Lebendige im Menschendenken zurücktritt, lebt des Menschen Eigenwille auf; die Freiheit wird möglich.

105. Es ist Michaels Aufgabe, den Menschen auf den Bahnen des Willens dahin wieder zu führen, woher er gekommen ist, da er auf den Bahnen des Denkens von dem Erleben des Übersinnlichen zu dem des Sinnlichen mit seinem Erdenbewusstsein heruntergestiegen ist.

Leading Thoughts 103 to 105

103. In human development, consciousness descends on the ladder of unfolding thought. There was a first stage of consciousness: in it, the human being experienced the thoughts in the 'I' as spirit-imbued, ensouled, enlivened beings. At a second stage he experienced the thoughts in the astral body; henceforth, they appeared only as the ensouled and enlivened images of spirit-beings. At a third stage he experienced the thoughts in the etheric body; here they manifested only an inner stirring, like an echo of the soul-quality. At the fourth, which is the present stage, the human being experiences the thoughts in the physical body, where they appear as the dead shadows of the spiritual.

104. To the same degree as the living spiritual-soul element in human thought recedes, the human being's own will comes to life. Freedom becomes possible.

105. It is Michael's task to lead the human being back up again on those paths of will down which he had once come when he descended, with his earthly consciousness, on paths of thought from the experience of the suprasensory to the experience of the sensory.

Michaels Aufgabe in der Ahriman-Sphäre

Goetheanum, 10. Oktober 1924

Wenn der Mensch auf seine Entwickelung zurückblickt und dabei die besondere Eigenheit sich zur geistigen Anschauung bringt, die sein Geistesleben seit fünf Jahrhunderten angenommen hat, so *muss* er schon innerhalb des gewöhnlichen Bewusstseins wenigstens ahnend erkennen, dass er seit diesen fünf Jahrhunderten an einem bedeutsamen Wendepunkte der ganzen irdischen Entwickelung der Menschheit steht.

In der letzten Betrachtung habe ich, von *einem* Gesichtspunkte aus, auf diese bedeutsame Wendung hingewiesen. Da kann man hinauf blicken in die Vorzeit der Entwickelung. Man schaut, wie sich im Menschen die Seelenkraft gewandelt hat, die gegenwärtig als die Kraft der Intelligenz tätig ist.

Jetzt erscheinen Gedanken, tote, abstrakte Gedanken im Felde des menschlichen Bewusstseins. Diese Gedanken sind an den physischen Menschenleib gebunden; der Mensch muss sie als die von ihm erzeugten anerkennen.

In der Urzeit schaute der Mensch, wenn er seinen Seelenblick in die Richtung wendete, in der ihm heute die eigenen Gedanken sich offenbaren, göttlich-geistige Wesenheiten. An diese Wesenheiten fand der Mensch sein ganzes Sein, bis zum

Michael's Task in the Sphere of Ahriman

Goetheanum, 10 October 1924

When the human being looks back upon human development and calls up before his spiritual view the special characteristics which human spiritual life has assumed during the last five hundred years, he *must* recognize – even within ordinary consciousness and if but faintly – that since this period the whole of the earthly development of humanity stands at a significant turning point.

In the previous consideration, I referred from *one* point of view to this significant turning point. One looks up from this point into the distant past of development; one sees how the soul-force in the human being that today is active as the force of intelligence has transformed over the course of time.

In the present period, thoughts – dead, abstract thoughts – make their appearance in the field of human consciousness. These thoughts are bound up with the human physical body; the human being is obliged to recognize that they are of his own creation.

In primeval times, when the human being turned his soul in the direction in which today his own thoughts are revealed to him, he saw divine-spiritual beings. He found himself bound to these beings in his whole nature, even down to the physical

physischen Leib, gebunden; er musste *sich* als das Erzeugnis dieser Wesenheiten anerkennen. Aber als solches Erzeugnis nicht nur sein *Sein* anerkennen, sondern auch sein *Tun*. Der Mensch hatte keinen eigenen Willen. Was er tat, war Erscheinung des göttlichen Willens.

Stufenweise, wie dies geschildert wurde, ist es bis zum eigenen Willen gekommen, dessen Zeit vor ungefähr fünf Jahrhunderten eingetreten ist.

Aber die letzte Etappe unterscheidet sich von allen vorangehenden viel stärker als diese untereinander.

Indem die Gedanken an den physischen Leib übergehen, verlieren sie die Lebendigkeit. Sie werden tot; geistig tote Gebilde. Sie waren vorher, indem sie dem Menschen angehörten, noch immer zugleich Organe der göttlich-geistigen Wesenheiten, zu denen der Mensch gehört. Sie *wollten* im Menschen *wesenhaft*. Und dadurch fühlte sich der Mensch durch sie mit der geistigen Welt lebendig verbunden.

Mit den toten Gedanken fühlt er sich abgelöst von der geistigen Welt. Er fühlt sich ganz versetzt in die physische Welt.

Damit aber ist er in die Sphäre der ahrimanischen Geistigkeit versetzt. Diese hat keine starke Macht in den Gebieten, in denen die Wesenheiten der höheren Hierarchien den

body; he was obliged to recognize *himself* as their creation. But he not only owed his *being* to them, he also owed them what he accomplished as *deed*. The human being had no will of his own. What he did was an expression of divine will.

In stages, as has been described, the human being gradually attained to a will of his own at a period which dawned about five hundred years ago.

But this last stage distinguished itself very starkly from all those preceding it – far more so than any of them from one another.

When the thoughts pass over into the physical body, they lose their living quality. They become deadened – spiritually deadened forms. Previously, though the thoughts belonged to the human being, they were simultaneously organs of the divine-spiritual beings to whom the human being belonged. They *willed* in the human being *as living essence*. And through them the human being felt himself to be in living union with the spiritual world.

With the dead thoughts he feels himself detached from the spiritual world. He feels himself entirely displaced into the physical world.

But with this, he is now transposed into the sphere of ahrimanic spirituality. The ahrimanic spirituality, however, has no great power in those regions in which the beings of the higher

Menschen so in *ihrer* Sphäre halten, dass sie entweder, wie in Urzeiten, selbst im Menschen wirken oder, wie später, durch ihren beseelten oder lebendigen Abglanz. Solange dieses ins Menschenwirken hereingehende Wirken übersinnlicher Wesenheiten besteht, das heißt bis etwa zum fünfzehnten Jahrhundert, haben *innerhalb der Menschheitsentwickelung* die ahrimanischen Mächte nur eine – man möchte sagen – leise anklingende Macht.

Was die persische Weltanschauung von dem Wirken Ahrimans schildert, ist damit nicht im Widerspruche. Denn diese Weltanschauung meint nicht ein Wirken Ahrimans innerhalb der menschlichen Seelen-Entfaltung, sondern ein solches in einer an die menschliche Seelenwelt unmittelbar angrenzenden Welt. Ahrimans Weben spielt da wohl herüber aus einer benachbarten Geistwelt in die menschliche Seelenwelt, aber es greift nicht unmittelbar ein.

Dieses unmittelbare Eingreifen ist eben erst in der Zeitspanne möglich geworden, die vor etwa fünf Jahrhunderten begonnen hat.

So steht der Mensch am Ende einer Entwickelungsströmung, innerhalb welcher sein Wesen aus solcher göttlicher Geistigkeit geworden ist, die zuletzt *für sich* in der abstrakten Intelligenz-Wesenheit des Menschen *erstirbt*.

Der Mensch ist nicht in den Sphären verblieben, in denen er als in dieser göttlichen Geistigkeit seinen Ursprung hat.

hierarchies so retained the human being in *their own* sphere that these beings either, as in primeval times, themselves worked directly into human beings, or, as was the case later on, worked in them through their ensouled or enlivened reflection. As long as this working of suprasensory beings in the deeds of human beings continued – that is, until about the fifteenth century – the ahrimanic powers had *within the development of humanity* only a faintly echoing power, if one may express it so.

What the Persian worldview communicates of Ahriman's activity is not in contradiction with this statement. For that worldview conceives of a working of Ahriman not within the human soul-unfolding, but in a soul-world directly bordering on the world of the human soul. Ahriman's weaving, as there described, does indeed play into the world of the human soul from a neighboring world of spirit, but it does not directly interfere.

This direct interference has only become possible in the period of time which began about five hundred years ago.

Thus the human being stands at the end of a stream of development within which his being has developed out of a divine spirituality that finally *dies to itself* in the abstract being of human intelligence.

The human being has not remained in those spheres of divine spirituality in which he has his origin.

Was vor fünf Jahrhunderten für das Bewusstsein des Menschen begonnen hat, es hatte sich für einen weiteren Umfang seiner Gesamtwesenheit schon vollzogen zur Zeit, als das Mysterium von Golgatha in die irdische Erscheinung getreten ist. Da war es, dass unwahrnehmbar für das damals bei den meisten Menschen vorhandene Bewusstsein, allmählich die Menschheitsentwickelung aus einer Welt, in der Ahriman wenig, in eine solche hineinglitt, in der er viel Macht hat. Dieses Gleiten in eine andere Weltschichte erreichte ihre Vollendung eben im fünfzehnten Jahrhundert.

Ahrimans Einfluss auf den Menschen in dieser Weltschichte ist deshalb möglich und kann verheerend wirken, weil in dieser Schichte das dem Menschen verwandte Götterwirken *erstorben* ist. Aber der Mensch konnte zur Entfaltung des freien Willens gar nicht auf eine andere Art kommen als dadurch, dass er sich in eine Sphäre begab, in der die vom Urbeginn mit ihm verbundenen göttlich-geistigen Wesen nicht lebendig waren.

Kosmisch angesehen liegt in dem Wesen dieser menschlichen Entwickelung das Sonnen-Mysterium. Mit dem, was der Mensch bis zu dem bedeutsamen Wendepunkte seiner Entwickelung in der Sonne wahrnehmen konnte, waren die göttlich-geistigen Wesenheiten seines Ursprungs verbunden. *Diese* haben sich von der Sonne losgelöst und auf dieser nur ihr Erstorbenes zurückgelassen, sodass der Mensch in seine

What began five hundred years ago for human consciousness specifically, had already taken place for the wider sphere of humanity's entire being at the time when the Mystery of Golgotha took place in earthly manifestation. It was then that, imperceptibly to the consciousness of the majority of human beings at that time, human development gradually glided out of a world in which Ahriman has little power, into one in which his power is great. This gliding into a different stratum of the world reached its fulfillment in the fifteenth century.

Ahriman's influence upon the human being in this stratum of the world is possible and can act so devastatingly because in this stratum the activity of the gods in connection with the human being has *died*. But the human being could not develop free will in any other way than by entering a sphere in which the divine-spiritual beings connected with him from the very beginning would now cease to be livingly active.

Considered cosmically, the Sun-Mystery lies in the nature of this human development. The divine-spiritual beings of the human being's origin were connected with that which – up to that important turning-point in his development – the human being was able to perceive in the sun-sphere. *These* divine-spiritual beings have separated from the sun and have left behind only the part of themselves that has died, so that the

Leiblichkeit durch die Sonne nurmehr die Kraft toter Gedanken aufnehmen kann.

Aber diese Wesenheiten haben den Christus aus der Sonne zur Erde gesandt. Dieser hat *sein* Wesen zum Heile der Menschheit mit der Erstorbenheit des göttlich-geistigen Seins in Ahrimans Reich verbunden. So hat die Menschheit die zweifache Möglichkeit, die die Gewähr ihrer Freiheit ist: zu Christus sich wenden in der Geistgesinnung, die beim Heruntersteigen aus der Anschauung des übersinnlichen Geistdaseins bis zum Gebrauche der Intelligenz unterbewusst vorhanden war, jetzt in bewusster Art; oder sich erfühlen wollen in der Losgelöstheit von diesem Geistdasein und damit verfallen in die Orientierung, die die ahrimanischen Mächte nehmen.

In dieser Situation ist die Menschheit seit dem Beginn des fünfzehnten Jahrhunderts. Vorbereitet ist diese – in der Entwickelung geschieht ja alles allmählich – seit dem Mysterium von Golgatha, das als das größte Erden-Ereignis dazu bestimmt ist, den Menschen vor dem Verderben zu retten, dem er ausgesetzt sein muss, weil er ein freies Wesen sein soll.

Man kann nun sagen: Was von Seite der Menschheit bisher innerhalb dieser Situation geschehen ist, vollzog sich halbunbewusst. Und in dieser Art hat es zu dem Guten der in abstrakten Ideen lebenden Naturanschauung und zu manchen ebenso guten Prinzipien der Lebenshaltung geführt.

human bodily nature can now receive through the sun only the power of dead thoughts.

But these beings have sent Christ from the sun to the earth. For the healing of humanity, Christ united *His* Being with the dying part of divine-spiritual existence in Ahriman's realm. Thus the human being has a twofold possibility, and this possibility guarantees his freedom: to turn to Christ consciously in the spiritual frame of mind that the human being possessed subconsciously during his descent from the beholding of suprasensory spirit-existence to the use of intelligence; or, to wish to feel his having been released from spirit-existence and thus fall into the orientation taken by the ahrimanic powers.

Humanity has been in this situation since the beginning of the fifteenth century. It has been in preparation – for everything takes place gradually in the course of development – since the Mystery of Golgotha, which, as the greatest event of earth development, is destined to rescue the human being from the ruination to which he must be exposed in his process of becoming a free being.

Now one may say that what has hitherto been done by humanity itself within this situation has taken place half-unconsciously. It has led to what is good in the view of nature that lives in abstract ideas, and to many equally good principles of practical life.

Aber dieses Zeitalter, in dem der Mensch unbewusst in der gefährlichen Ahriman-Sphäre sein Dasein entfalten darf, ist vorüber.

Der Erforscher der geistigen Welt *muss* heute die Menschheit auf die geistige Tatsache aufmerksam machen, dass Michael die geistige Führung der Menschheitsangelegenheiten übernommen hat. Michael vollbringt, was er zu vollbringen hat, so, dass er die Menschen nicht dadurch beeinflusst; aber *sie* können in Freiheit *ihm* folgen, um mit der Christus-Kraft den Weg aus der Ahriman-Sphäre wieder herauszufinden, in die sie notwendig kommen mussten.

Wer ehrlich, aus dem tiefsten Wesen seiner Seele, sich mit Anthroposophie eins fühlen kann, der ist ein rechter Versteher dieses Michael-Phänomens. Und Anthroposophie möchte die Botschaft von dieser Michael-Mission sein.

But the age in which the human being could unfold his existence thus unconsciously while dwelling in the dangerous sphere of Ahriman, has come to an end.

In the present time, the investigator into the spiritual world *must* draw the attention of humanity to the spiritual fact that Michael has taken over the spiritual guidance of human affairs. Michael fulfills what he has to do in such a way that he does not thereby wield an influence over human beings; but *they* may follow *him* in freedom, in order with the Christ-force to find the way out of the sphere of Ahriman which they had of necessity to enter.

One who honestly, out of the deepest being of his soul, can feel himself one with Anthroposophy, understands this Michael-phenomenon truly. And Anthroposophy would like to be the message of this mission of Michael.

Leitsätze Nr. 106 bis 108

106. Michael geht die Wege wieder aufwärts, welche die Menschheit abwärts auf den Stufen der Geistesentwickelung bis zur Intelligenzbetätigung gegangen ist. Nur wird Michael den Willen aufwärts die Bahnen führen, welche die Weisheit bis zu ihrer letzten Stufe, der Intelligenz, abwärts gegangen ist.

107. Wie Michael von diesem Zeitpunkte der Weltentwickelung seinen Weg *bloß zeigt*, sodass ihn der Mensch in Freiheit wandeln kann, das unterscheidet *diese* Michael-Führung von allen früheren Erzengel-Führungen, ja, von allen früheren Michael-Führungen selbst. Diese Führungen *wirkten* im Menschen; sie zeigten nicht bloß *ihr* Wirken, sodass der Mensch in dem seinigen damals nicht frei sein konnte.

108. Dieses *einzusehen*, ist des Menschen gegenwärtige Aufgabe, damit er mit seiner ganzen Seele seinen Weg des Geistes innerhalb des Michael-Zeitalters finden könne.

Leading Thoughts 106 to 108

106. Michael goes upward again along the paths by which humanity had once descended, stage by stage in the development of the spirit, down to the active use of intelligence. Michael will lead the will upward, retracing the paths by which the wisdom descended to the final stage of intelligence.

107. The way in which Michael, in this period of world-development, *merely shows* his path, so that the human being is able to follow it in complete freedom – this distinguishes the *present* Michael-leadership from all preceding phases of Archangelic leadership, including even those of Michael himself. For the former phases of leadership *worked themselves out* in the human being; they did not merely reveal *their own* working – thus, the human being could not be free in his own deeds.

108. *To see and comprehend* this is the human being's present task. For then, with all the forces of his soul, he will be able to find his path of spirit within the Michael Age.

Michaels Erfahrungen und Erlebnisse während der Erfüllung seiner kosmischen Mission

Goetheanum, 19. Oktober 1924

Man kann das Fortschreiten der Menschheit von der Bewusstseinsetappe, auf der sich der Mensch als Glied der göttlich-geistigen Ordnung, bis zu der gegenwärtigen, durch die er sich als eine vom Göttlich-Geistigen losgelöste Individualität mit Eigengebrauch der Gedanken erfühlt, vom Gesichtspunkte der Menschheit verfolgen. Das ist im letzten Aufsatz geschehen.

Man kann aber auch durch übersinnliches Schauen ein Bild von dem entwerfen, was Michael und die seinen während dieser Entwickelungsströmung erleben, also dieselbe Tatsachenreihe von dem Gesichtspunkte Michaels schildern. Das soll diesmal versucht werden.

Es gibt zunächst eine älteste Zeit, in der man eigentlich nur von dem sprechen kann, was unter göttlich-geistigen Wesenheiten geschieht. Man hat es mit einem fortlaufenden Götterhandeln zu tun. Götter vollbringen, was ihnen die Impulse ihrer Wesenheiten eingeben; sie sind entsprechend befriedigt in dieser Tätigkeit. Und was *sie* bei alledem erleben, kommt allein in Betracht. Nur in einer Ecke im Felde

Michael's Experiences during the Fulfillment of His Cosmic Mission

Goetheanum, 19 October 1924

It is possible to follow the progress of humanity – from the point of view of the human being himself – from the stage of consciousness in which he felt himself a member of the divine-spiritual order, up to the present time, where he is conscious of himself as an individual freed from the divine-spiritual and able to think autonomously. This has been done in the last essay.

But it is also possible, through suprasensory seeing, to form an image of what Michael and those who belong to him experience during this developmental process – that is, to describe the series of realities as they appear to Michael himself. This will be attempted in the present study.

There is an oldest time in evolution, where it is only possible to speak of what takes place among divine-spiritual beings. Here one has to deal with the actions of the gods alone. The gods carry out what is inspired by the impulses of their natures, and are correspondingly fulfilled in this activity. Only what *they themselves* experience comes into consideration. But in one corner of this field of the gods' activity, something

dieses Götterhandelns ist etwas wie die Menschheit bemerkbar. Sie ist ein Teil in dem Götterhandeln.

Die geistige Wesenheit aber, die von Anfang an ihren Blick auf die Menschheit gelenkt hat, ist Michael. Er gliedert gewissermaßen das Götterhandeln so, dass in einer kosmischen Ecke die Menschheit bestehen kann. Und die Art, wie er sich da betätigt, ist verwandt dem Tun, das später im Menschen als Intellekt zur Offenbarung kommt; nur ist sie als Kraft betätigt, die in Ideenordnung durch den Kosmos strömt, Wirklichkeit verursachend. In dieser Kraft wirkt Michael. Die kosmische Intellektualität zu verwalten, ist sein Amt. Er möchte den weiteren Fortschritt auf seinem Gebiete. Und der kann nur darin bestehen, dass, was als Intelligenz durch den ganzen Kosmos wirkt, später sich konzentriert in der menschlichen Individualität. Was dadurch zustande kommt, ist dieses: Es tritt in der Weltentwickelung eine Zeit ein, in der der Kosmos nicht mehr von seiner gegenwärtigen, sondern von seiner vergangenen Intelligenz lebt. Und die gegenwärtige Intelligenz ist in der menschheitlichen Entwickelungsströmung.

Michael möchte, was sich da innerhalb der Menschheit als Intelligenz entwickelt, fortdauernd im Zusammenhange mit den göttlich-geistigen Wesen erhalten.

Dem aber steht ein Widerstand entgegen. Was die Götter als Entwickelung durchmachen in der Linie von der Ablösung der Intellektualität von ihrem kosmischen Tun bis zur

resembling humanity is to be observed. This is a part of their divine activity.

The spiritual being who from the beginning directed his gaze toward humanity is Michael. He so orders the deeds of the gods that in one part of the cosmos humanity may exist. And the way in which he thus engages himself is related to the action that later comes to expression in the human being as intellect; but this intellect is active as a force which streams through the cosmos in the ordered nature of ideas, giving rise to realities. Michael works in this force. His office is to steward the cosmic intellectuality. He would like to further the progress in his domain. And this can only consist in this: that that which works as intelligence throughout the whole cosmos should later become concentrated within the human individuality. As a result, the following takes place: There comes a time in world-development when the cosmos lives no longer through its own present intelligence, but through the intelligence belonging to its past. And the present intelligence is located in the human stream of development.

Michael would like to keep the intelligence, which is developing within humanity, continuously in connection with the divine-spiritual beings.

But there is a resistance to this. What the gods accomplish in their development, in that they release the intellectuality from their own cosmic deeds so that it may become embodied

Eingliederung in die menschliche Natur hin, das steht offen als Tatsache in der Welt drinnen. Sind Wesen vorhanden, die ein Wahrnehmungsvermögen haben, durch das sie diese Tatsachen schauen können, so können sie sich diese zunutze machen. – Und solche Wesenheiten sind vorhanden. Es sind die ahrimanischen Wesen. Sie sind ganz dazu veranlagt, alles, was sich als Intelligenz von den Göttern loslöst, in sich aufzusaugen. Sie sind dazu veranlagt, die Summe aller Intellektualität mit ihrem eigenen Wesen zu vereinigen. Sie werden damit die größten, die umfassendsten und eindringlichsten Intelligenzen des Kosmos.

Michael sieht voraus, wie der Mensch, indem er immer mehr zum Eigengebrauch der Intelligenz vorrückt, sich mit den ahrimanischen Wesen begegnen muss und wie er dann ihnen verfallen kann, indem er eine Verbindung mit ihnen eingeht. – Deshalb bringt Michael die ahrimanischen Mächte unter seine Füße, er stößt sie fortwährend in ein tieferes Gebiet, als das ist, in dem der Mensch sich entfaltet. Michael, den Drachen zu seinen Füßen, ihn in den Abgrund stoßend: Das ist das im Menschenbewusstsein lebende gewaltige Bild der hier geschilderten übersinnlichen Tatsachen.

Die Entwickelung rückt vorwärts. Die Intellektualität, die zuerst ganz im Bereiche der göttlichen Geistigkeit war, löst sich so weit los, dass sie zur Beseelung des Kosmos wird. Was vorher nur von den Göttern ausstrahlte, das erglänzt jetzt als

in human nature, stands revealed as a fact within the world. If there are beings with power to perceive this fact, then they can take advantage of it. – And such beings do indeed exist. They are the ahrimanic beings. It is entirely within their nature to absorb into themselves all that detaches from the gods as intelligence. They have the capacity to unite with their own being the sum-total of all intellectuality, and thus they become the greatest, the most comprehensive and penetrating intelligences in the cosmos.

Michael foresees how the human being, in progressing more and more toward his own individual use of intelligence, must encounter these ahrimanic beings, and how by entering into connection with them he may then succumb to them. – For this reason Michael brings the ahrimanic powers under his feet; he continually thrusts them into a deeper region than the one in which the human being is evolving. Michael, thrusting the dragon at his feet into the abyss: that is the mighty image, living in human consciousness, of the suprasensory facts here described.

Development progresses. The intellectuality which was at first entirely in the sphere of divine spirituality detaches itself so far that it becomes the element which ensouls the cosmos. That which previously had only radiated from the gods

die Offenbarung des Göttlichen aus der Sternenwelt. Vorher ward die Welt gelenkt durch die *göttliche Wesenheit* selbst, jetzt wird sie gelenkt durch die objektiv gewordene *göttliche Offenbarung*, hinter der die göttliche Wesenheit die nächste Stufe *ihrer* eigenen Entwickelung durchläuft.

Wieder ist Michael der Verwalter der kosmischen Intelligenz, insofern diese durch die Offenbarungen des Kosmos in Ideenordnung strömt.

Die dritte Phase der Entwickelung ist ein weiteres Loslösen der kosmischen Intelligenz von ihrem Ursprunge. In den Sternenwelten waltet nun nicht mehr die gegenwärtige Ideenordnung als göttliche Offenbarung; es laufen die Sterne und ordnen sich nach der in der Vergangenheit ihnen eingepflanzten Ideenordnung. Michael sieht, wie immer mehr, was er im Kosmos verwaltet hat, die kosmische Intellektualität, den Weg zur Erdenmenschheit nimmt.

Michael sieht aber auch, wie die Gefahr, dass die Menschheit den ahrimanischen Mächten verfällt, immer größer wird. Er weiß: *Für sich* wird er Ahriman immer unter seinen Füßen haben; ob aber auch für den Menschen?

Das größte Erden-Ereignis sieht Michael eintreten. Aus dem Reiche, dem Michael selbst diente, steigt die Christus-Wesenheit hinunter in den Erdbereich, um da zu sein, wenn die Intelligenz völlig bei der menschlichen Individualität sein wird. Denn dann wird der Mensch den Drang am stärksten

themselves now shines as the revelation of the divine from the world of the stars. Formerly the world had been guided by the *divine Being* itself; now it is guided by the *divine revelation* that has become objective, behind which the divine Being passes through the next stage of *its* own development.

Michael is again the steward of the cosmic intelligence, in so far as this streams through the revelations of the cosmos in the ordered nature of ideas.

The third phase of development is a further separation of the cosmic intelligence from its origin. In the worlds of the stars, the present order of ideas no longer holds sway as divine revelation; the stars move and are regulated according to the order of ideas implanted in them in the past. Michael sees how the cosmic intellectuality, which he has until now ruled in the cosmos, proceeds on its way to earthly humanity.

But Michael also sees how the danger of humanity succumbing to the ahrimanic powers grows greater and greater. He knows that *as regards himself* he will always have Ahriman under his feet; but will it also be the case with the human being?

Michael beholds the greatest event of earth-development taking place. From the realm served by Michael himself, Christ descends to the sphere of the earth, so as to be there when the intelligence is wholly with the human individuality. For at that point, the human being will feel most strongly the

empfinden, sich an die Macht hinzugeben, die restlos in aller Vollkommenheit sich zum Träger der Intellektualität gemacht hat. Aber Christus wird da sein; er wird in derselben Sphäre durch sein großes Opfer leben, in der auch Ahriman lebt. Der Mensch wird wählen können zwischen Christus und Ahriman. Die Welt wird in der Menschheitsentwickelung den Christus-Weg finden können.

Das ist Michaels kosmische Erfahrung mit dem, was er im Kosmos zu verwalten hat. Er tritt, um bei dem Gegenstande seiner Verwaltung zu bleiben, den Weg vom Kosmos zu der Menschheit an. Er ist auf diesem Wege seit dem achten nachchristlichen Jahrhunderte, ist aber eigentlich angekommen bei seinem Erdenamte, in das sich sein kosmisches Amt verwandelt hat, erst im letzten Drittel des neunzehnten Jahrhunderts.

Zwingen kann Michael die Menschen zu nichts. Denn der Zwang hat ja eben dadurch aufgehört, dass die Intelligenz ganz in den Bereich der menschlichen Individualität getreten ist. – Aber als eine majestätische, vorbildliche Handlung in der an die sichtbare zunächst angrenzenden übersinnlichen Welt kann Michael entfalten, was er entfalten will. Mit einer Licht-Aura, mit einer Geistwesen-Geste kann da Michael sich zeigen, in der sich aller Glanz und alle Herrlichkeit der vergangenen Götter-Intelligenz offenbart. Zur Erscheinung kann er da bringen, wie die Wirkung dieser Vergangenheitsintelligenz in der Gegenwart noch wahrer, schöner und

impulse to devote himself to the power which has made itself fully and completely into the carrier of intellectuality. But Christ will be there; through His great sacrifice, He will live in the same sphere in which Ahriman also lives. The human being will be able to choose between Christ and Ahriman. In the development of humanity, the world will be able to find the Christ-path.

That is Michael's cosmic experience with that which he has to govern in the cosmos. In order to remain connected with the matters of his governance, he enters upon the path that leads from the cosmos to humanity. He has been on this path since the eighth century AD; but he really only took up his earthly office, into which his cosmic office has been transformed, in the last third of the nineteenth century.

Michael cannot compel human beings to do anything. For it is just through intelligence having come entirely into the sphere of the human individuality that compulsion has ceased. – However, in the suprasensory world first bordering on this visible world, Michael can unfold, as a majestic, exemplary gesture, that which he wishes to accomplish. He can show himself there with an aura of light, with the gesture of a spirit being, in which all the splendor and glory of the past intelligence of the gods is revealed. He can there show how the working of this past intelligence in the present is more true, more beautiful, and more virtuous than all that is contained in

tugendhafter ist als alles in unmittelbarer Gegenwartsintelligenz, das in trugvollem, verführerischem Glanz von Ahriman herströmt. Er kann bemerklich machen, wie *für ihn* Ahriman immer der niedrige Geist unter seinen Füßen sein wird.

Diejenigen Menschen, welche die an die sichtbare Welt angrenzende nächste übersinnliche schauen, nehmen so, wie hier geschildert, Michael und die seinen bei dem wahr, was sie für die Menschen tun möchten. Solche Menschen sehen, wie der Mensch in Freiheit durch das Bild Michaels in der Ahriman-Sphäre von Ahriman ab zu Christus geführt werden soll. Wenn es solchen Menschen gelingt, durch ihr Schauen auch Herzen und Sinnen anderer Menschen aufzuschließen, damit ein Kreis von Menschen wisse, wie jetzt Michael unter den Menschen lebt, dann wird die Menschheit beginnen, Michael-Feste mit dem rechten Inhalt zu feiern, auf denen die Seelen werden in sich die Kraft Michaels aufleben lassen. Michael wird dann als eine reale Macht unter den Menschen wirken. Der Mensch aber wird *frei* sein und doch in inniger Gemeinschaft mit Christus seinen Geist-Lebensweg durch den Kosmos gehen.

the immediate intelligence of the present day, which streams from Ahriman in deceptive, tempting splendor. He can make evident how *for him* Ahriman will always be the lower spirit, under his feet.

Those who can see the suprasensory world just bordering on the visible world can perceive Michael and those belonging to him, in the manner here described, engaged in what they would like to do for humanity. Such persons see how – through the image of Michael in Ahriman's sphere – the human being is to be led in freedom away from Ahriman to Christ. When through their vision such persons also succeed in opening the hearts and minds of others, so that there is a circle of people who know how Michael is now living among human beings, humanity will then begin to celebrate Festivals of Michael which will have the right content, and at which souls will allow the force of Michael to come to renewed life in them. Michael will then work as a real power among human beings. The human being will be *free* and yet proceed along his spiritual path of life through the cosmos in intimate companionship with Christ.

Leitsätze Nr. 109 bis 111

109. Sich der Michael-Wirksamkeit im geistigen Weltzusammenhang recht bewusst werden, heißt das Rätsel der menschlichen Freiheit aus den kosmischen Zusammenhängen heraus lösen, soweit die Lösung dem Erdenmenschen notwendig ist.

110. Denn die «Freiheit» ist als Tatsache jedem Menschen, der sich selber im gegenwärtigen Abschnitt der Menschheitsentwickelung versteht, unmittelbar gegeben. Keiner darf sagen, wenn er nicht eine offenbare Tatsache leugnen will, «Freiheit ist nicht». Aber man kann einen Widerspruch finden zwischen dem, was so tatsächlich gegeben ist, und den Vorgängen im Kosmos. In der Betrachtung von Michaels Sendung im Kosmos fällt dieser Widerspruch hinweg.

111. In meiner *Philosophie der Freiheit* findet man die «Freiheit» des Menschenwesens in der gegenwärtigen Weltzeit als Inhalt des Bewusstseins nachgewiesen; in den Darstellungen der Michael-Mission, die hier gegeben werden, findet man das «Werden dieser Freiheit» kosmisch begründet.

Leading Thoughts 109 to 111

109. To become rightly conscious of the working of Michael in the spiritual world-context is to solve the riddle of human freedom in relation to the cosmos, insofar as the solution is necessary for the earthly human being.

110. For "freedom" as a fact is directly given to every human being who understands himself in the present period of humanity's development. No one can say, "freedom is not," unless one wishes to deny an obvious fact. But one can find a certain contradiction between this fact of experience and the processes of the cosmos. In contemplating the mission of Michael within the cosmos, this contradiction falls away.

111. In my *Philosophy of Freedom* (*Philosophy of Spiritual Activity*), the "freedom" of the human being in the present world-epoch is proven as a content of consciousness. In the descriptions here given of the mission of Michael, the cosmic foundations of the "becoming of this freedom" can be found.

Menschheitszukunft und Michael-Tätigkeit

Goetheanum, 25. Oktober 1924

Wie steht heute der Mensch auf seiner Entwickelungsstufe zu Michael und den seinen?

Der Mensch steht einer Welt gegenüber, die einstmals ganz göttlich-geistiger Wesenheit war. Einer solchen göttlich-geistigen Wesenheit, der auch er selbst als ein Glied zugehörte. Damals also war die dem Menschen zugehörige Welt göttlich-geistiger *Wesenheit.* In einer folgenden Entwickelungsetappe war sie es nicht mehr. Da war sie kosmische *Offenbarung des* Göttlich-Geistigen, und dessen Wesenheit schwebte hinter dieser Offenbarung. Aber sie webte und lebte doch eben in der Offenbarung. Eine Sternenwelt war schon da. In ihrem Scheinen und Sich-Bewegen webte und lebte *als Offenbarung* das Göttlich-Geistige. Man kann sagen: Wie damals ein Stern stand oder sich bewegte, darinnen konnte unmittelbar die *Tätigkeit* des Göttlich-Geistigen gesehen werden.

In alledem, wie der göttliche Geist in dem Kosmos wirkte, wie der Mensch in seinem Leben ein Ergebnis war der Tätigkeit des Göttlich-Geistigen im Kosmos, da war Michael widerstandslos noch in seinem Element. Er vermittelte das Verhältnis des Göttlichen zum Menschen.

The Future of Humanity and the Activity of Michael

Goetheanum, 25 October 1924

How does the human being stand today in his present stage of development with respect to Michael and his hosts?

The human being is surrounded today by a world that was once of a wholly divine-spiritual nature – a divine-spiritual Being of which he himself had once been a member. Thus at that time the world belonging to the human being was one of divine-spiritual *Being*. But this was no longer the case in a later stage of development. The world had then become a cosmic *revelation of* the divine-spiritual, while its Being hovered behind this revelation. Nevertheless, the divine-spiritual lived and moved in all that was thus manifested. A world of stars was already there. In the light and movement of this world, the divine-spiritual lived and moved *as revelation*. One may say that at that time, in the position or movement of a star, the *activity* of the divine-spiritual was directly evident.

In all this – in the working of the divine spirit in the cosmos, and in the human life resulting from this divine activity – Michael was still in his own element, unhindered and unresisted. He mediated the relation between the divine and the human being.

Andere Zeiten kamen. Die Sternenwelt hörte auf, unmittelbar gegenwärtig die göttlich-geistige Tätigkeit in sich zu tragen. Sie lebte und regte sich, indem sie beharrend weiter fortsetzte, was solche Tätigkeit früher in ihr war. Das Göttlich-Geistige lebte im Kosmos nicht mehr als Offenbarung, sondern nur noch als *Wirksamkeit*. Es war eine deutliche Zweiheit zwischen dem Göttlich-Geistigen und dem Kosmischen aufgetreten. Michael hielt sich aufgrund seiner eigenen Wesenheit beim Göttlich-Geistigen. Er suchte, den Menschen so nahe als möglich bei diesem zu erhalten. Das tat er immer weiter. Er wollte den Menschen davor bewahren, zu stark in einer Welt zu leben, die nur *Wirksamkeit* des Göttlich-Geistigen ist, nicht Wesenheit und nicht Offenbarung.

Michael rechnet es sich zur tiefsten Befriedigung an, dass es ihm gelungen ist, die Sternenwelt *durch den Menschen* noch unmittelbar mit dem Göttlich-Geistigen auf die folgende Art verbunden zu erhalten. Wenn der Mensch, nachdem er das Leben zwischen dem Tode und einer neuen Geburt vollbracht hat, wieder den Weg zu einem neuen Erdendasein antritt, dann *sucht* er beim Hinabstieg zu diesem Dasein, eine Harmonie zwischen dem Sternengang und seinen Erdenleben herzustellen. Diese Harmonie, die vor Zeiten selbstverständlich da war, weil das Göttlich-Geistige in den Sternen wirkte, in denen auch das Menschenleben seinen Quell hatte: Sie würde heute, wo der Sternengang bloß die *Wirksamkeit* des Göttlich-

Other ages dawned. The world of the stars ceased to be a direct and present revelation of divine-spiritual activity. The constellations lived and moved, maintaining what the divine activity had been in them in the past. The divine-spiritual lived in the cosmos no longer as revelation, but in the manner of its *working* only. There now arose a certain distinct separation between the divine-spiritual and the cosmic. Michael, by virtue of his own nature, adhered to the divine-spiritual, and endeavored to keep human beings as closely as possible in connection with it. This he continued to do. His will was to preserve the human being from living too intensively into a world which represents only the *working* of the divine-spiritual, but not its essential Being, nor its revelation.

It is a deep source of fulfillment for Michael that *through the human being himself* he has succeeded in keeping the world of the stars in direct union with the divine-spiritual. For when the human being, having fulfilled his life between death and a new birth, enters on the way to a new earthly life, in his descent he *seeks* to establish a harmony between the course of the stars and his coming life on earth. In former times this harmony existed as a matter of course, because the divine-spiritual was active in the stars, where human life too had its source. But today, when the course of the stars is a mere continuation of the *working* of the divine-spiritual, this harmony could not exist unless the human being actively sought it. The human

Geistigen fortsetzt, nicht da sein, wenn der Mensch sie nicht suchte. Er bringt sein aus früherer Zeit bewahrtes Göttlich-Geistiges in ein Verhältnis zu den Sternen, die ihr Göttlich-Geistiges nur noch als Nachwirkung einer früheren Zeit in sich haben. Dadurch kommt ein Göttliches in das Verhältnis des Menschen zur Welt, das früheren Zeiten entspricht, doch aber in späteren Zeiten *erscheint*. Dass dies so ist, *das ist die Tat Michaels*. Und diese Tat gibt ihm eine so tiefe Befriedigung, dass er in dieser Befriedigung einen Teil seines Lebenselementes, seiner Lebens-Energie, seines sonnenhaften Lebenswillens hat.

Heute aber sieht er, wenn er das Geistesauge zur Erde richtet, noch einen wesentlich anderen Tatbestand. Der Mensch ist während seines Lebens im Physischen zwischen Geburt und Tod von einer Welt umgeben, die unmittelbar auch nicht mehr die Wirksamkeit des Göttlich-Geistigen zeigt, sondern nur etwas, das von dieser Wirksamkeit geblieben ist; man kann sagen, nur noch das *Werk* des Göttlich-Geistigen. Dieses *Werk* ist in seinen Formen durchaus göttlich-geistiger Art. Für das menschliche Anschauen zeigt sich das Göttliche in den Formen, in dem naturhaften Geschehen; aber es ist *nicht mehr* als Lebendiges darinnen. Die Natur ist dies gottgewirkte Werk des Göttlichen und ist überall Abbild der göttlichen Wirksamkeit.

In dieser sonnenhaft-göttlichen, aber nicht lebendig-göttlichen Welt lebt der Mensch. Er aber hat, als Ergebnis des

being brings his divine-spiritual component, preserved from earlier times, into relation with the stars, which now only bear their divine-spiritual nature within them as an aftereffect from an earlier phase. In this way there comes into the human being's relation to the world a divine element that corresponds to former ages and yet *appears* in these later times. That this is so – *that is the deed of Michael.* And this deed gives him such a deep experience of fulfillment that in it he finds a portion of his life-element, his life-energy, his sun-radiant life-will.

But at the present time, when Michael directs his spiritual eyes to the earth, he sees yet another essential circumstance. During his physical life between birth and death, the human being has a world around him in which even the working of the divine-spiritual no longer appears directly, but only something that has remained over as its result; one may describe it by saying it is only the *accomplished work* of the divine-spiritual. This *accomplished work*, in all its forms, is essentially of a divine-spiritual nature. To human vision, the divine manifests in the forms and processes of nature; but it is *no longer* indwelling them as a living principle. Nature is this divinely accomplished work of the divine, and it is everywhere an image of the divine working.

In this sun-radiant yet no longer living divine world, there lives the human being. Yet as a result of Michael's working

Wirkens Michaels an ihm, als Mensch den Zusammenhang mit dem Wesen des Göttlich-Geistigen bewahrt. Er lebt als Gott-durchdrungenes Wesen in einer nicht Gott-durchdrungenen Welt.

In diese Gott-leergewordene Welt wird der Mensch hineintragen, was in ihm ist, das, zu dem *seine* Wesenheit in diesem Zeitalter geworden ist.

Menschheit wird sich hineinentfalten in eine Welt-Entwickelung. Das Göttlich-Geistige, dem der Mensch entstammt, kann als kosmisch sich ausbreitende Menschenwesenheit durchleuchten den Kosmos, der nur noch in dem Abbild des Göttlich-Geistigen vorhanden ist.

Nicht mehr dieselbe Wesenheit, die einst als Kosmos war, wird da durch die Menschheit aufleuchten. Das Göttlich-Geistige wird im Durchgang durch das Menschentum ein Wesen erleben, das es vorher nicht offenbarte.

Dass die Entwickelung diesen Fortgang nehme, dagegen wenden sich die ahrimanischen Mächte. Sie wollen nicht, dass die ursprünglichen göttlich-geistigen Mächte das Weltall in seinem weiteren Fortgang erleuchten; sie wollen, dass die von ihnen aufgesogene kosmische Intellektualität den ganzen neuen Kosmos durchstrahle und dass der Mensch in diesem intellektualisierten und ahrimanisierten Kosmos weiterlebe.

Bei einem solchen Leben würde der Mensch den Christus verlieren. Denn dieser ist mit einer Intellektualität in die Welt

upon him, the human being has maintained his connection with the essential Being of the divine-spiritual. He lives as a God-permeated being in a world no longer permeated by God.

Into this world that has become empty of God, the human being will carry forth what is in him, what *his* being has become in this present age.

Humanity will unfold its being into a world-development. The divine-spiritual from which the human being originates can, as a cosmically expanding human essence, illuminate the cosmos, which now exists only as image of the divine-spiritual.

That which will thus shine forth through humanity will no longer be the same Being which once was the cosmos. In its passage through humankind, the divine-spiritual will experience a Being which it did not manifest previously.

The ahrimanic powers try to prevent development from taking the course here described. It is not their will that the original divine-spiritual powers should illumine the universe in its further course. They want the cosmic intellectuality that has been absorbed by them to radiate through the whole of the new cosmos, and they want the human being to live on in this intellectualized and ahrimanized cosmos.

Were he to live such a life, the human being would lose Christ. For Christ came into the world with an intellectuality

hereingetreten, die ganz so ist, wie sie einst in dem Göttlich-Geistigen gelebt hat, da dies noch in seiner *Wesenheit* den Kosmos bildete. Sprechen wir heute so, dass unsere Gedanken auch die des Christus sein können, so setzen wir den ahrimanischen Mächten etwas entgegen, das uns behütet, ihnen zu verfallen.

Den Sinn der Michael-Mission im Kosmos verstehen, heißt, so sprechen können. Man muss heute über die Natur so sprechen können, wie es die Entwickelungsetappe der Bewusstheitsseele fordert. Man muss die rein naturwissenschaftliche Denkungsart in sich aufnehmen können. Aber man sollte auch so *über die Natur* sprechen – das heißt *empfinden* – lernen, wie es Christus gemäß ist. Nicht bloß über Erlösung von der Natur, nicht bloß über Seele und Göttliches sollen wir die Christus-Sprache lernen, sondern über den Kosmos.

Dass unser menschlicher Zusammenhang mit dem ursprünglich Göttlich-Geistigen so gewahrt bleibe, dass wir über den Kosmos die Christus-Sprache zu pflegen verstehen, dazu werden wir kommen, wenn wir uns in innerlichem herzlichen Erfühlen ganz in das einleben, was Michael und die seinen mit ihren Taten, mit ihrer Mission unter uns sind. Denn Michael verstehen, heißt heute den Weg finden zu dem Logos, den Christus unter Menschen auf der Erde lebt.

Anthroposophie schätzt in rechter Art, was die naturwissen-

that is still of the very same essence as what once lived in the divine-spiritual when the divine-spiritual in its own *Being* still formed the cosmos. But if at the present time we speak in such a manner that our thoughts can also be the thoughts of Christ, we set over against the ahrimanic powers something which can save us from succumbing to them.

To understand the meaning of Michael's mission in the cosmos is to be able to speak in this way. In the present time, one must be able to speak of nature in the way demanded by the developmental stage of the consciousness soul. One must be able to receive into oneself the purely natural-scientific way of thinking. But one ought also to learn to speak *about nature* – that is, learn *to sense* – in a way that is in accord with Christ. We ought to learn the Christ-language not merely about redemption from nature, not merely about matters of the soul and of the divine, but about the cosmos.

When with inward, heartfelt feeling, we fully live into the mission and the deeds of Michael and those belonging to him – when we enter into the fullness of their presence in our midst – then we shall be able to maintain our human connection with the original divine-spiritual and understand how to cultivate the Christ-language with regard to the cosmos. For to understand Michael is to find the present-day path to the Logos as lived by Christ among human beings on earth.

Anthroposophy rightly values what the natural-scientific

schaftliche Denkweise gelernt hat, seit vier bis fünf Jahrhunderten über die Welt zu sagen. Aber sie spricht außer *dieser* Sprache eben noch eine andere über das Wesen des Menschen, über die Entwickelung des Menschen und über das Werden des Kosmos; sie möchte die Christus-Michael-Sprache sprechen.

Denn werden beide Sprachen gesprochen, dann wird die Entwickelung nicht abreißen und vor dem Finden des ursprünglich Göttlich-Geistigen auf das Ahrimanische übergehen können. Die bloße naturwissenschaftliche Art zu sprechen, entspricht der Loslösung der Intellektualität von dem ursprünglich Göttlich-Geistigen. Sie *kann* ins Ahrimanische übergehen, wenn der Mission Michaels nicht geachtet wird. Sie *wird* es *nicht*, wenn der frei gewordene Intellekt sich durch die Kraft des Michael-Vorbildes wieder findet in der vom Menschen losgelösten, ihm gegenüber objektiv gewordenen ursprünglichen kosmischen Intellektualität, die im Quell des Menschen liegt und die in Christus innerhalb des Menschheitsbereiches wesenhaft erschienen ist, nachdem sie aus dem Menschen zur Entfaltung seiner Freiheit gewichen war.

way of thinking has learned to say about the world over the course of the last four to five centuries. But apart from *this* language it speaks another one about the nature of the human being, about his development and that of the cosmos; for it would like to speak the Christ-Michael language.

If both these languages are spoken, it will not be possible for development to be broken off or to pass over to Ahriman before the original divine-spiritual is rediscovered. To speak only in the natural-scientific way corresponds to the detachment of intellectuality from the original divine-spiritual. This *can* become ahrimanic if the mission of Michael is not heeded. But *it will not do so* if, through the power of Michael's example, the intellect that has become free is able once again to find itself in the original cosmic intellectuality which has detached from the human being and become objective to him – the cosmic intellectuality which lives in the source of the human being and which appeared in Christ in full reality of Being within the sphere of humanity, after having separated from the human being for a time for the unfolding of human freedom.

Leitsätze Nr. 112 bis 114

112. Das Göttlich-Geistige kommt im Kosmos in den folgenden Etappen auf verschiedene Art zur Geltung: 1. durch seine ureigene *Wesenheit*; 2. durch die *Offenbarung* dieser Wesenheit; 3. durch die *Wirksamkeit*, wenn die Wesenheit aus der Offenbarung sich zurückzieht; 4. durch das *Werk*, wenn in dem erscheinenden Weltall das Göttliche nicht mehr ist, sondern nur dessen Formen.

113. Der Mensch hat in der gegenwärtigen Naturanschauung nicht ein Verhältnis zu dem Göttlichen, sondern nur zu dessen Werk. Mit dem, was sich der menschlichen Seelenverfassung durch diese Anschauung mitteilt, kann man sich als Mensch sowohl mit den Christus-Mächten wie mit den ahrimanischen Gewalten zusammenschließen.

114. Michael ist durchdrungen von dem Bestreben, das im Menschen aus den Zeiten der göttlichen Wesensgeltendmachung und der Offenbarung bewahrte Verhältnis zum Kosmos in einer solchen Art durch sein *frei* wirkendes Vorbild der menschlich-kosmischen Entwickelung einzuverleiben, dass, was die rein auf das Bild,

Leading Thoughts 112 to 114

112. The divine-spiritual comes to expression in the cosmos in various ways, in the following succeeding stages: 1. through its own original *Being*; 2. through the *revelation* of this Being; 3. through the *active working*, when the Being withdraws its presence from the revelation; 4. through the *accomplished work*, when in the externally visible universe the divine is no longer present, but only its forms.

113. In the current view of nature, the human being does not have a relation to the divine, but only to its accomplished work. With what is imparted to the human soul-constitution through this view of nature, one can, as human being, unite both with the Christ-powers and with the ahrimanic forces.

114. Michael is permeated with the striving – working through his example *in freedom* – to embody in human-cosmic development the relation to the cosmos which is still preserved in the human being himself from the ages when the divine Being and the divine revelation still held sway. In this way, all that is said by a view of nature

die Form des Göttlichen bezügliche Naturanschauung sagt, einläuft in eine höhere, geistgemäße Naturanschauung. Diese wird zwar im Menschen vorhanden sein; sie wird aber eben ein menschliches Nacherlebnis des göttlichen Verhältnisses zum Kosmos während der zwei ersten Etappen der kosmischen Entwickelung sein. Anthroposophie bejaht in dieser Art die Naturanschauung des Bewusstseinszeitalters; sie ergänzt sie aber auch durch eine solche, die von dem Blick des Geistesauges aus sich ergibt.

that relates purely to the image, purely to the form of the divine will merge into a higher, spiritual view of nature. This higher view will indeed come about in the human being; but it will be an after-experience of the divine relation to the cosmos that prevailed in the first two stages of cosmic development. In this way Anthroposophy confirms the view of nature evolved by the consciousness-soul age, while completing this view with what is revealed to the gaze of the spirit-eye.

Das Michael-Christus-Erlebnis des Menschen

Goetheanum, 2. November 1924

Wer die von gründlicher Empfindung getragene innere Anschauung von Michaels Wesen und Taten in seine Gesinnung aufnehmen wird, dem wird das rechte Verständnis davon aufgehen, wie eine Welt von dem Menschen zu nehmen ist, die nicht göttlicher Wesenheit oder Offenbarung oder Wirksamkeit, sondern der Götter *Werk* ist. In diese Welt erkennend blicken, bedeutet Formen, Gestaltungen vor sich haben, die überall laut von dem Göttlichen sprechen; in denen aber selbstlebendes göttliches Sein nicht gefunden wird, wenn man sich keiner Illusion hingibt. Und man wird nicht bloß auf das Erkennen der Welt blicken dürfen. An diesem offenbart sich wohl die Konfiguration der Welt, die heute den Menschen umgibt, am deutlichsten. Wesentlicher für das alltägliche Leben ist aber das Fühlen, das Wollen, das Arbeiten in einer Welt, die in ihrer Gestaltung wohl als göttlich empfunden, aber nicht als *göttlich belebt* erfahren werden kann. In diese Welt wirkliches sittliches Leben zu bringen, dazu sind die ethischen Impulse notwendig, die ich in der *Philosophie der Freiheit* gezeichnet habe.

In dieser *Werk-Welt* kann für den echt fühlenden Menschen

The Human Being's Michael-Christ Experience

Goetheanum, 2 November 1924

When with deep and earnest feeling, one takes the inner vision of Michael's being and deeds into one's life-outlook, there will dawn upon one the true understanding of the way in which this world is to be engaged by the human being – this world which is neither the divine Being, nor the revelation, nor the active working, but the *accomplished work* of the gods. To look with understanding into this world is to have before one forms, formations, that speak aloud of the divine – in which, however, if one is under no illusion about it, self-existent divine Being cannot be found. And one must not merely consider our knowledge of the world. It is true that with respect to knowledge this configuration of the world, as it surrounds the human being at the present time, is revealed most strikingly. But more essential for everyday life is the feeling, the willing, the work in a world which – though in its formation it may well be felt as divine – cannot really be experienced as *divinely enlivened*. In order to bring real moral life into such a world, the ethical impulses I have described in the *Philosophy of Freedom* (*Philosophy of Spiritual Activity*) are necessary.

For the human being who feels truly, Michael's being and

Michaels Wesen und gegenwärtige Tatenwelt leuchten. Michael kommt als Erscheinung nicht in die physische Welt herein. Er hält sich mit all seinem Wirken innerhalb einer übersinnlichen Region, die aber unmittelbar an die physische Welt der gegenwärtigen Weltentwickelungsphase angrenzt. Dadurch kann nie die Möglichkeit eintreten, dass durch die Eindrücke, die Menschen vom Michaels-Wesen her erhalten, sie die Naturanschauung ins Fantastische führen oder das sittlich-praktische Leben in einer gottgestalteten, aber gottunbelebten Welt so bilden möchten, wie wenn Impulse da sein könnten, die nicht von dem Menschen selbst ethisch-geistig getragen sein müssten. Man wird stets, ob denkend oder wollend, durch ein Sich-Versetzen ins Geistige an Michael herankommen müssen.

Dadurch wird man in der folgenden Art geistig leben. Man wird Erkennen und Leben so hinnehmen, wie sie nun einmal seit dem fünfzehnten Jahrhundert hingenommen werden müssen. – Aber man wird sich an die Michael-Offenbarung halten; man wird diese Offenbarung als ein Licht in die Gedanken leuchten lassen, die man aus der Natur empfängt; man wird sie als Wärme im Herzen tragen, wenn man der göttlichen Werk-Welt gemäß leben muss. – Man wird sich dann *nicht* nur Beobachtung und Erleben der gegenwärtigen Welt, sondern auch dasjenige, was Michael vermittelt, einen

his present world of deeds can shine forth in this *world of accomplished work.* Michael does not enter into the physical world as visible appearance. He keeps himself with all his activity within a suprasensory region – albeit one which borders directly upon the physical world of the present phase of world-development. Thus the possibility can never arise that human beings' view of nature will be led away into the fantastic through the impressions they receive from the being of Michael; nor will they be inclined thereby to shape their ethical and practical life in the physical world – which is divinely formed but void of divine life – as if impulses could be found in it that do not need to be carried in an ethical-spiritual way by the human being himself. If one transfers oneself into the spiritual, whether in thinking or in willing, one will always be obliged to approach Michael.

Thereby, one shall live spiritually in the following way. One shall take both knowledge and life in the manner in which one is obliged to take them since the fifteenth century. – But one shall hold fast to Michael's revelation. One shall let this revelation shine like a light into the thoughts one receives from nature; one shall carry it as warmth in the heart when one has to live in accordance with a world which is the accomplished work of the divine. – One shall then place before oneself *not only* the observation and experience of the present world but also that which Michael makes possible, namely a

vergangenen Weltzustand, vor Augen stellen, einen Weltzustand, den eben Michael durch sein Wesen und seine Taten in die Gegenwart hereinträgt.

Wäre es anders: Wirkte Michael so, dass er seine Taten hereintrüge in die Welt, die der Mensch gegenwärtig als physische erkennen und erleben muss, so erführe der Mensch in der Gegenwart aus der Welt das, was in Wirklichkeit nicht in ihr *ist*, sondern *war*. Geschieht solches, dann führt dies illusorische Erfassen der Welt die Seele des Menschen aus der *ihr* angemessenen Wirklichkeit in eine andere, nämlich in eine luziferische.

Die Art, wie Michael das Vergangene im gegenwärtigen Menschenleben zur Wirksamkeit bringt, ist die im Sinne des rechten geistigen Weltenfortschritts gehaltene, die nichts Luziferisches enthält. Es ist wichtig, dass in der Auffassung der Menschenseele eine rechte Vorstellung davon lebe, wie in Michaels Mission alles Luziferische vermieden wird.

Diese Stellung zu dem in der Menschheitsgeschichte aufgehenden Michaels-Lichte haben, heißt auch, den rechten Weg zu Christus finden können.

Michael wird die rechte Orientierung geben, wenn es sich um die Welt handelt, die den Menschen für sein Erkennen oder für sein Handeln umgibt. Zu Christus wird man im Innern den Weg finden müssen.

Es ist durchaus begreiflich, dass in der Zeit, in der die

past condition of the world – one which Michael, through his being and his deeds, brings into the present.

If it were otherwise – if Michael were to work in such a manner that he carried his deeds into the world which at the present time the human being must know and experience as the physical – then the human being of our time would experience something which actually *is not* in the world, but which *was* in it. If something of this nature comes about, then this illusory grasp of the world leads the human soul away from the reality that is suited to *it* and into another, namely a luciferic reality.

The way in which Michael brings the past to effectiveness in present human life is the way that is in accord with the rightful spiritual progress of the world, that contains nothing luciferic. It is important that in the understanding of the human soul there lives a correct representation of the way in which, in Michael's mission, everything luciferic is avoided.

To have this demeanor toward the light of Michael, as it is presently dawning in human history, also means to be able to find the right path to Christ.

Michael will give the right orientation in matters pertaining to the world that encompasses the human being as his arena of knowing and acting. The way to Christ, on the other hand, will have to be found *within*.

It is quite comprehensible that, during the period in which

Naturerkenntnis die Form hat, die ihr die letzten fünf Jahrhunderte gegeben haben, auch die Erkenntnis der übersinnlichen Welt so geworden ist, wie sie gegenwärtig die Menschheit erlebt.

Die Natur muss erkannt und erlebt werden so, dass alles götterleer ist. Dadurch erlebt sich in seinem so gestalteten Verhältnis zur Welt der Mensch selbst nicht mehr. Insofern der Mensch ein übersinnliches Wesen ist, gibt ihm die dem Zeitalter angemessene Stellung seiner selbst zur Natur *nichts* über sein eigenes Wesen. Er kann auch, wenn er nur diese Stellung im Auge hat, nicht ethisch so leben, wie es seiner Menschheit angemessen ist.

Dadurch wird die Veranlassung dazu gegeben, diese Erkenntnis- und Lebensart in nichts einfließen zu lassen, was sich auf die übersinnliche Menschenwesenheit, ja, auf die übersinnliche Welt überhaupt bezieht. Es wird dieses Gebiet abgesondert von dem der menschlichen Erkenntnis Erreichbaren. Es wird ein außer- oder überwissenschaftliches Gebiet der Glaubensoffenbarung gegenüber dem Erkennbaren in Anspruch genommen.

Aber dem steht das rein geistige Wirken des Christus gegenüber. Der Christus ist seit dem Mysterium von Golgatha der Menschenseele erreichbar. Und deren Beziehung zu ihm braucht nicht eine unbestimmte, dunkel-gefühlsmystische zu bleiben; sie kann eine völlig konkrete, menschlich tief und klar zu erlebende werden.

the knowledge of nature has the form given to it by the last five centuries, the knowledge of the suprasensory world should also have become such as humanity now experiences.

Nature has to be known and experienced in such a manner that everything is empty of divinity. In consequence of this, in his thus-constituted relation to the world the human being no longer experiences himself. Inasmuch as he is a suprasensory being, the contemporary position of his self with respect to nature gives him *nothing* regarding his own being. Nor, if he has this position alone in view, can he live ethically in a manner corresponding to his humanity.

Naturally, this causes people to prevent this modern approach to knowledge and life from entering into anything that relates to the suprasensory nature of the human being – or even to the suprasensory world altogether. They separate this spiritual realm from anything accessible to human knowledge. A sphere of faith-based revelation, held apart from or above science, is set up in contradistinction to the sphere of what is knowable.

But over against this there stands the purely spiritual activity of Christ. Christ is, since the Mystery of Golgotha, reachable by the human soul. The soul's relation to Christ need not remain indefinite or dimly mystical in feeling; it can become one that is fully concrete, humanly deep, and clearly experienced.

Dann aber strömt aus dem Zusammenleben mit Christus in die Menschenseele herüber, was diese wissen soll über ihre eigene übersinnliche Wesenheit. Die Glaubensoffenbarung muss dann so empfunden werden, dass in sie die lebendige Christus-Erfahrung fortwährend einströmt. Es wird das Leben dadurch durchchristet werden können, dass in Christus das Wesen empfunden wird, welches der Menschenseele die Anschauung ihrer eigenen Übersinnlichkeit gibt.

So werden nebeneinander stehen können: Michael-Erlebnis und Christus-Erlebnis. Durch Michael wird der Mensch gegenüber der äußeren Natur in der rechten Art ins Übersinnliche den Weg finden. Naturanschauung wird, ohne in sich selbst verfälscht zu werden, sich neben eine geistgemäße Anschauung von der Welt und vom Menschen, sofern er ein Weltwesen ist, hinstellen können.

Durch die rechte Stellung zu Christus wird der Mensch dasjenige, was er sonst nur als traditionelle Glaubensoffenbarung empfangen könnte, im lebendigen Verkehr der Seele mit Christus erfahren. Die innere Welt des seelischen Erlebens wird als eine geistdurchleuchtete erlebt werden können wie die äußere Welt der Natur als eine geistgetragene.

Würde der Mensch ohne in dem Zusammenleben mit der Christus-Wesenheit den Aufschluss gewinnen wollen über

Then, from the life together with Christ, there flows into the human soul what it ought to know regarding its own suprasensory being. The faith-based revelation must then be felt in such a manner that the living Christ-experience continually streams into it. It will become possible for life to be filled with Christ through the gradual perception of Christ as the Being who gives to the human soul the perception of its own suprasensory nature.

Thus it will become possible for the Michael-experience and the Christ-experience to stand side by side. Through Michael, the human being will find the path into the suprasensory world in the right way with respect to the outer world of nature. Our view of nature, without being falsified in-itself, will then be able to stand alongside a view that accords with the spiritual reality of the world and the human being inasmuch as he is a cosmic being.

Through the right approach to Christ, the human being will be able to experience in the living relation of his soul to Christ what he could otherwise only receive in the form of traditional faith-based revelation. He will be able to experience the inner world of the soul's life as one that is shone through by the spirit; and he will also experience the outer world of nature as one that is spirit-borne.

If the human being were to seek to gain insight about his own suprasensory nature while leaving aside his living together

seine eigene übersinnliche Wesenheit, so würde ihn dies aus seiner eigenen Wirklichkeit heraus- und in die ahrimanische hineinführen. Christus trägt in sich in kosmisch gerechtfertigter Art die Zukunftsimpulse der Menschheit. Sich mit ihm verbinden, heißt für die Menschenseele, ihre eigenen Zukunftskeime kosmisch gerechtfertigt in sich aufnehmen. Andere Wesen, die in der Gegenwart schon Gestaltungen aufweisen, die kosmisch für Menschen erst in der Zukunft gerechtfertigt sind, gehören der ahrimanischen Sphäre an. Sich mit Christus in rechter Art verbinden, heißt, sich auch vor dem Ahrimanischen in der rechten Art bewahren.

Es liegt bei denjenigen, welche die Bewahrung der Glaubensoffenbarungen vor dem Einfließen menschlicher Erkenntnis streng verlangen, die unbewusste Furcht vor, der Mensch könne auf solchen Wegen in ahrimanische Einflüsse hineinkommen. Das muss verstanden werden. Aber verstanden sollte *auch* werden, dass es zur Ehre und wirklichen Anerkenntnis Christi ist, wenn dem Erleben mit Christus das gnadeerfüllte Einfließen des Geistigen in die Menschenseele zugeschrieben wird.

So können in der Zukunft Michael-Erlebnis und Christus-Erlebnis nebeneinander stehen; dadurch wird der Mensch seinen rechten Freiheitsweg finden zwischen der luziferischen Abirrung in Denk- und Lebensillusionen und der ahrimanischen Verlockung in Zukunftgestaltungen, die seinen Hochmut befriedigen, die aber noch nicht *seine* gegenwärtigen sein können.

with the Christ Being, this would lead him out of his own reality and into that of Ahriman. Christ bears within Himself, in a cosmically justified manner, the impulses for the future of humanity. To unite with Christ signifies for the human soul to receive into itself, with cosmic justification, its own germinal seeds for the future. Other beings who already at the present time manifest forms which will be cosmically right for the human being only in the future, belong to the ahrimanic sphere. To unite oneself with Christ in the right way means also to protect oneself in the right way from the ahrimanic.

Those who strictly demand that the faith-based revelations be preserved from the influences of human knowledge are unconsciously afraid that such paths might lead the human being to come under ahrimanic influences. This fact must be understood. But it should *also* be understood that it is to the honor and true recognition of Christ when the gift of grace, which is the inflowing of the spiritual into the human soul, is ascribed to the experience with Christ.

In this way, the Michael-experience and the Christ-experience can stand side by side in the future; the human being will thereby find his right path of freedom between the luciferic deviation into illusions in thought and life, and the ahrimanic allurement into forms of the future which may satisfy his pride but cannot as yet be *his* present forms.

In luziferische Illusionen verfallen, heißt nicht voll Mensch werden, nicht bis zur Freiheitsetappe vorschreiten wollen, sondern auf einer zu frühen Stufe der Entwickelung – als Gott-Mensch – stehenbleiben wollen. In ahrimanische Verlockungen verfallen, heißt nicht warten wollen, bis bei einem bestimmten Grade des Menschtums der rechte kosmische Augenblick gekommen ist, sondern diesen Grad vorausnehmen wollen.

Michael-Christus wird in der Zukunft als das Richtungswort stehen im Beginne des Weges, auf dem der Mensch kosmischgerecht zwischen den luziferischen und den ahrimanischen Mächten zu seinem Welten-Ziele kommen kann.

To fall into luciferic illusions means not to become fully human – not to wish to progress to the stage of spiritual freedom but to wish to halt, as God-human-being, at a premature stage of development. To succumb to ahrimanic temptation means not to be willing to wait until, at a certain stage of human development, the right cosmic moment will have come – but to wish to pre-empt this stage.

In the future, *Michael-Christ* will stand as the guiding Word at the outset of the path by means of which the human being may arrive – cosmically justified, between the luciferic and the ahrimanic powers – at his world-destination.

Leitsätze Nr. 115 bis 117

115. Der Mensch wandelt seinen Weg durch den Kosmos so, dass ihm die Rückschau in die Vorwelt gefälscht werden kann durch luziferische Impulse und das Vorwärtssinnen in die Zukunft getäuscht werden kann durch ahrimanische Verlockungen.

116. Zu den luziferischen Fälschungen findet der Mensch die rechte Stellung durch die Durchdringung seiner Gesinnung für Erkenntnis und Leben mit der Michael-Wesenheit und der Michael-Mission.

117. Dadurch aber bewahrt sich der Mensch auch vor den ahrimanischen Verlockungen, denn der Geist-Weg in die äußere Natur, der durch Michael angeregt wird, führt zu der rechten Stellung zu dem Ahrimanischen, weil das rechte Erleben mit Christus gefunden wird.

Leading Thoughts 115 to 117

115. The human being goes on his way through the cosmos in such manner that his activity of looking back into past ages can be falsified by the impulses of Lucifer, and his thinking into the future deceived by the allurements of Ahriman.

116. He finds the right relation to the falsifying influences of Lucifer when he imbues his attitude to life and knowledge with the being and the mission of Michael.

117. Moreover, in so doing he fortifies himself against the allurements of Ahriman. For the path of the spirit into external nature, which Michael inspires, leads to a right relation to the ahrimanic, because the rightful experience with Christ is also found thereby.

Michaels Mission im Weltenalter der Menschen-Freiheit

Goetheanum, 9. November 1924

Wenn man mit dem geistigen Erleben an Michaels Wirken in der Gegenwart herankommt, so findet man die Möglichkeit, sich geisteswissenschaftlich über das kosmische Wesen der *Freiheit* Licht zu verschaffen.

Dies bezieht sich *nicht* auf meine *Philosophie der Freiheit.* Diese geht aus den rein menschlichen Erkenntniskräften selbst hervor, wenn diese sich auf das Feld des Geistes begeben können. Man braucht dann, um zu erkennen, was hier erkannt wird, noch nicht ein Zusammengehen mit Wesen anderer Welten. Man kann aber sagen, die *Philosophie der Freiheit* bereitet dazu vor, über die Freiheit das zu erkennen, was dann im geistigen Zusammengehen mit Michael erfahren werden kann.

Und das ist das Folgende.

Soll Freiheit wirklich im menschlichen Handeln leben, so darf, was in ihrem Lichte vollzogen wird, in keiner Art von der menschlichen physischen und ätherischen Organisation abhängig sein. Das «Freie» kann sich nur aus dem «Ich» heraus vollziehen; und mit dem freien Wirken des «Ich» muss der Astralleib mitschwingen können, damit er es auf physischen

Michael's Mission in the World-Era of Human Freedom

Goetheanum, 9 November 1924

When the work of Michael at the present time is approached through spiritual experience, it becomes possible, from the spiritual-scientific point of view, to recognize the cosmic nature of *freedom*.

This does *not* refer to my *Philosophy of Freedom* (*Philosophy of Spiritual Activity*), which is based on the purely human forces of knowledge insofar as they can be applied to the field of the spirit. In order to follow the thought of this book, it is not yet necessary to join together with the beings of other worlds. But it may be said that the *Philosophy of Freedom* prepares the way for an understanding of freedom that can then be experienced in the spiritual coming-together with Michael.

And this is as follows.

If freedom is to be a living reality in human action, then what is accomplished in its light must be completely independent of the human physical and etheric organization. There can be no "freedom" except through the 'I'; and the astral body must be able to resonate with the free activity of the 'I' in order to carry it over to the physical and etheric bodies. –

und ätherischen Leib übertragen kann. – Dies ist aber nur die eine Seite der Sache. Die andere wird eben im Zusammenhange mit Michaels Mission durchsichtig. – Es darf, was in Freiheit vom Menschen erlebt wird, auch nicht in irgendeiner Art auf seinen ätherischen oder physischen Leib wirken. Geschähe dieses, so müsste der Mensch völlig aus dem herauskommen, was er in den Etappen seiner Entwickelung unter dem Einfluss der göttlich-geistigen *Wesenheit* und der göttlich-geistigen *Offenbarung* geworden ist.

Was der Mensch durch dasjenige erlebt, was nur göttlich-geistiges *Werk in seiner Umgebung* ist, darf nur auf sein Geistiges (sein Ich) einen Einfluss haben. Auf seine physische und ätherische Organisation kann nur Einfluss haben, was sich in der Entwickelungsströmung nicht in seiner Umgebung, sondern innerhalb seiner Wesenheit selbst von dem fortsetzt, das seinen Anfang in Wesenheit und Offenbarung des Göttlich-Geistigen gehabt hat. Das aber darf in der Menschen-Wesenheit gar nicht zusammenwirken mit dem, was in dem Elemente der Freiheit lebt.

Dies ist nur dadurch möglich, dass Michael aus urferner Vergangenheit der Entwickelung etwas herüberträgt, das den Menschen einen Zusammenhang mit dem Göttlich-Geistigen gibt, das in der Gegenwart nicht mehr in die physische und ätherische Bildung eingreift. Dadurch entwickelt sich innerhalb von Michaels Mission der Boden für einen Verkehr des

But this is only one side of the matter. The other side becomes clear in connection with the mission of Michael. – For it is also true that what the human being experiences in freedom must not in any way work upon his physical or etheric body. Were this to happen, he would have to lose entirely what he has become through the stages of his development under the influence of divine-spiritual *Being* and divine-spiritual *revelation*.

What the human being experiences through that which is merely the divine-spiritual *accomplished work in his environment* is able to have an influence only upon his spiritual nature (his 'I'). His physical and etheric organization must solely be affected by what flows on in the stream of development not in his outer environment, but within his own being, and which has its origin in the Being and revelation of the divine-spiritual. But in the human being, this element must under no circumstances work together with what lives in the element of freedom.

All this is made possible only through the fact that Michael carries over from the far past of development something that brings the human being into connection with that divine-spiritual reality which in the present no longer intervenes in the physical and etheric organization. Through this the foundation is developed, within the mission of Michael, for an

Menschen mit der geistigen Welt, der gar nicht ins Naturhafte hinübergreift.

Es ist erhebend, anzusehen, wie durch Michael des Menschen Wesenheit in die geistige Sphäre hinaufgehoben wird, während das Unbewusste, Unterbewusste, die sich unter der Sphäre der Freiheit entfalten, immer tiefer mit dem Materiellen zusammenwachsen.

Des Menschen Stellung zum Weltwesen wird ihm fernerhin immer unverständlicher werden, wenn er sich nicht darauf einlässt, außer seinen Beziehungen zu Naturwesen und Naturvorgängen auch noch solche anzuerkennen wie die zur Michael-Mission. – Die Beziehungen zur Natur lernt man wie etwas kennen, das man von außen anschaut; diejenigen zur geistigen Welt gehen aus von etwas, das gewissermaßen ein inneres Gespräch mit einem Wesenhaften ist, zu dem man sich den Zugang dadurch eröffnet hat, dass man auf das geistgemäße Anschauen der Welt eingegangen ist.

Der Mensch muss also, um die Impulse der Freiheit darleben zu können, imstande sein, gewisse Naturwirkungen, die aus dem Kosmos herein die Wirkung auf sein Wesen nehmen, von diesem Wesen fernzuhalten. Diese Fernhaltung spielt sich im Unterbewusstsein dann ab, wenn im Bewusstsein die Kräfte walten, die eben das Leben des Ich in Freiheit darstellen. Für das menschliche innere Wahrnehmen ist das Bewusstsein des Wirkens in Freiheit da; für die geistigen Wesen,

interaction between the human being and the spiritual world which does not interfere at all with the element of nature.

It is uplifting to see how the human being is raised by Michael into the spiritual sphere, whereas the unconscious and subconscious elements that develop beneath the sphere of freedom unite ever more deeply with the material element.

The human being's position with respect to the world will, in the course of time, become ever more incomprehensible to him if he is not prepared to recognize, in addition to his relations to the beings and processes of nature, such relations as this to the Michael mission. – One comes to experience one's relations to nature by looking upon it from outside; one's relations to the spiritual world proceed from something that is, so to speak, an inner conversation with an essential being to whom one has opened up the way by entering into a spiritual view of the world.

In order, therefore, for the human being to realize the impulse of freedom, he must be able to hold at a distance from his being certain influences of nature which affect this being from the cosmos. This "holding at a distance" takes place in the sub-conscious realm when, in the conscious realm, the forces representing the life of the 'I' in freedom hold sway. For the inward perception of the human being himself, there is the consciousness of his activity in freedom; but for the spiritual

die aus anderen Weltensphären mit dem Menschen in Verbindung stehen, ist das anders. Dem Wesen aus der Hierarchie der Angeloi, das mit der Fortführung des Menschenseins von Erdenleben zu Erdenleben zu tun hat, wird gegenüber dem menschlichen Handeln in Freiheit sofort dieses anschaulich: Der Mensch stößt von sich kosmische Kräfte hinweg, die ihn weiterbilden wollen, die seiner Ich-Organisation die nötigen physischen Stützen geben wollen, wie sie sie ihr gegeben haben vor dem Michael-Zeitalter.

Michael erhält als Wesen aus der Hierarchie der Archangeloi seine Eindrücke mit Hilfe der Wesen aus der Angeloi-Hierarchie. Er widmet sich der Aufgabe, dem Menschen aus dem geistigen Teil des Kosmos auf die hier geschilderte Art Kräfte zuzuführen, die die aus dem Naturdasein unterdrückten ersetzen können.

Das erreicht er, indem er seine Wirksamkeit in den vollkommensten Einklang mit dem Mysterium von Golgatha bringt.

In der Wirksamkeit des Christus innerhalb der Erdenentwickelung liegen die Kräfte, die der Mensch im Wirken durch Freiheit zum Ausgleich unterdrückter Natur-Impulse braucht. – Nur muss der Mensch dann wirklich seine Seele in das innere Zusammenleben mit Christus bringen, von dem hier in diesen Mitteilungen über die Michael-Mission schon gesprochen ist.

Der Mensch weiß sich in einer Wirklichkeit, wenn er der

beings connected with the human being from other world-spheres, it is different. The being from the hierarchy of the Angeloi, who leads human existence from one earthly life to another, sees at once how the matter stands regarding human action in freedom; he sees how the human being thrusts away from himself cosmic forces which want to form and mold him further – which want to give to his 'I'-organization the necessary physical supports, just as they had done before the Michael Age.

Michael, who is a member of the hierarchy of the Archangeloi, receives his impressions with the aid of the beings of the Angeloi-hierarchy. He devotes himself, in the manner here described, to the task of bringing to the human being forces from the spiritual part of the cosmos which can replace those forces from the realm of nature that have been suppressed.

He accomplishes this in that he brings his activity into the most perfect consonance with the Mystery of Golgotha.

The forces which the human being has need of, when acting in freedom, for the compensation of suppressed impulses of nature, are contained in Christ's activity within earthly development. – But the human being must then really bring his soul into the inner living together with Christ which has already been spoken of in these communications on the mission of Michael.

When a human being faces the physical sun and receives

physischen Sonne gegenübersteht und durch sie Wärme und Licht empfängt.

So muss er der geistigen Sonne, Christus, die ihr Dasein mit dem Erdendasein vereint hat, gegenüber leben und von ihr in der Seele das lebendig empfangen, was in der geistigen Welt der Wärme und dem Licht entspricht.

Er wird sich von der «geistigen Wärme» durchdrungen fühlen, wenn er den «Christus in sich» erlebt. Er wird sich in dieser Durchdringung erfühlend sagen: Diese Wärme löst dein menschliches Wesen aus Banden des Kosmos, in denen es nicht bleiben darf. Das göttlich-geistige Sein der Urzeit musste dich zur Erringung der Freiheit in Regionen führen, in denen es nicht bei dir bleiben konnte, in denen es aber dir den Christus gegeben hat, dass seine Kräfte dir als freiem Menschen verleihen, was das göttlich-geistige Sein der Urzeit dir einstmals auf dem Naturwege gegeben hat, der damals zugleich der Geistesweg war. Zu dem Göttlichen, aus dem du stammest, führt dich diese Wärme wieder zurück.

Und in diesem Erfühlen wird im Menschen in inniger Seelenwärme zusammenwachsen das Erleben in und mit dem Christus und das Erleben echten und wahren Menschentums. «Christus gibt mir mein Menschenwesen», das wird als Grundgefühl die Seele durchwehen und durchwellen. Und ist erst *dieses* Gefühl vorhanden, so kommt auch das andere, in dem der Mensch durch Christus sich hinausgehoben fühlt

from it warmth and light, he knows that he is living in a reality.

In the same way he must live in the presence of Christ, the spiritual sun, who has joined His life to the life of the earth, and actively receive from Him into his soul what in the spiritual world corresponds to warmth and light.

The human being will feel himself permeated by "spiritual warmth" when he experiences the "Christ in me." Feeling himself thus permeated, he will say to himself: This warmth liberates your human being from bonds of the cosmos in which it must not remain. In order for you to gain freedom, the divine-spiritual Being of primeval times had to lead you into regions where it could not remain with you; where, however, it gave you Christ, that His forces might bestow upon you as a free human being what the divine-spiritual primeval Being once gave you by way of nature, which in that time was likewise the spirit-path. This warmth leads you back again to the divine sources from which you have come.

And in this feeling there will grow together in the human being, in inner warmth of soul, the experience in and with Christ and the experience of real and true humanity. "Christ gives me my humanity" – that will be the fundamental feeling which will well up in the soul and pervade it. When *this* feeling is once there, another comes in which the human being feels raised by Christ beyond mere earthly existence, in which he

über das bloße Erdensein, indem er sich mit der Sternen-Umgebung der Erde eins fühlt und mit allem, was in dieser Sternen-Umgebung zu erkennen ist als Göttlich-Geistiges.

Und so mit dem geistigen Lichte. Der Mensch kann sich in seiner Menschenwesenheit voll erfühlen, indem er sich als freie Individualität gewahr wird. Aber eine Verfinsterung ist damit doch verbunden. Das Göttlich-Geistige der Urzeit leuchtet nicht mehr. Im Lichte, das der Christus dem Menschen-Ich bringt, ist das Urlicht wieder da. Es kann in solchem Zusammenleben mit dem Christus der beseligende Gedanke sonnenhaft die ganze Seele durchglänzen: Das uralt-herrliche göttliche Licht ist wieder da; es leuchtet, obwohl sein Leuchten kein naturhaftes ist. Und der Mensch vereinigt sich in der Gegenwart mit den geistigen kosmischen Leuchtekräften der Vergangenheit, in der er noch nicht eine freie Individualität war. Und er kann in *diesem* Lichte die Wege finden, die seine Menschenwesenheit recht führen, wenn er sich verständnisvoll in seiner Seele mit der Michael-Mission verbindet.

Dann wird der Mensch in der Geist-Wärme den Impuls fühlen, der ihn in seine kosmische Zukunft so hinüberträgt, dass er in dieser treu bleiben kann den Ur-Gaben seiner göttlich-geistigen Wesenheiten, trotzdem er sich in deren Welten zur freien Individualität entwickelt hat. Und er wird in dem Geistes-Lichte die Kraft empfinden, die ihn wahrnehmend mit immer höherem und weiterem Bewusstsein der Welt zu-

feels at one with the starry firmament around the earth and with all that can be recognized in this firmament as spiritual and divine.

And so it is with the spiritual light. The human being can feel himself fully in his true human nature by becoming aware of himself as a free individual. However, a certain darkening is connected with this. The divine-spiritual of primeval times no longer shines. The primeval light appears again in the light brought by Christ to the human 'I'. In the life in union with Christ, this blissful thought may shine like a sun through the whole soul: The glorious primal divine light is here again; it shines, although its light does not come from nature. And the human being unites himself, while in the present, with the spiritual cosmic forces of light belonging to that past in which he was not yet a free individuality. And in *this* light he can find the paths which lead him aright as a human being, when in his soul he unites himself, with understanding, with the mission of Michael.

Then, in spirit-warmth, the human being will feel the impulse which carries him into his cosmic future such that in this future he will be able to remain true to the original gifts of the divine-spiritual beings, despite the fact that he has evolved in their worlds to free individuality. And in the spirit-light he will feel the force which leads him with open eyes and ever higher and wider consciousness to the world in which, as a free

führt, in der er sich als freier Mensch mit den Göttern seines Ursprungs wiederfindet.

In dem ursprünglichen Sein verharren, die ursprüngliche naive, im Menschen waltende Götter-Güte beibehalten wollen und vor dem vollen Gebrauche der Freiheit zurückbeben, führt den Menschen in dieser Welt der Gegenwart, in der alles auf die Entwickelung seiner Freiheit veranlagt ist, doch zu Luzifer, der die gegenwärtige Welt verleugnet wissen will.

Sich dem gegenwärtigen Sein übergeben, die jetzt dem Intellekt erreichbare Welten-Natürlichkeit, die gegen Güte sich neutral verhält, allein walten lassen wollen und den Gebrauch der Freiheit nur im Intellekt erleben wollen, das führt den Menschen in dieser Welt der Gegenwart, in der die Entwickelung in tieferen Seelenregionen fortgesetzt werden muss, da in oberen Freiheit waltet, doch zu Ahriman, der die gegenwärtige Welt ganz in einen Kosmos des intellektuellen Wesens umgewandelt wissen will.

In solchen Regionen, in denen der Mensch den Blick nach der Außenwelt geistig auf Michael, den Blick nach dem Inneren der Seele geistig auf Christus fallen fühlt, gedeiht jene Seelen- und Geistessicherheit, durch die er denjenigen kosmischen Weg zu gehen vermögen wird, auf dem er ohne Verlust seines Ursprungs seine rechte Zukunftsvollendung finden wird.

human being, he will find himself again with the gods of his origin.

If the human being wishes to continue in the original state of being, to hold fast to the primal naive divine goodness which once held sway in him, and to shrink from the full use of his freedom – then this leads him, in this present world in which everything is disposed toward the development of human freedom, to Lucifer, who wishes for the present world to be denied.

If the human being devotes himself to the present state of being and wishes for the natural world alone to hold sway (the natural world which is accessible to the present intellect and which is neutral with respect to goodness) – if he wishes to experience the use of freedom in the intellect alone – then in this present world where development must be continued in deeper regions of the soul while freedom rules in the upper regions, he will in the end be led to Ahriman, who wishes to see the present world entirely transformed into a cosmos of intellectuality.

Certainty of soul and spirit flourishes in those regions where the human being feels that when his gaze is directed to the outer world, it rests spiritually on Michael, and when it is directed to the inner being of the soul, it rests on Christ. This certainty will enable him to traverse the cosmic path on which, without losing his origin, he will find his right fulfillment.

Leitsätze Nr. 118 bis 120

118. Eine freie Handlung kann nur diejenige sein, bei der kein Naturgeschehen in oder außer dem Menschen mitwirkt.

119. Dem steht als der polarische Gegensatz gegenüber, dass im freien Wirken der Menschen-Individualität in dieser ein Naturgeschehen unterdrückt wird, das bei unfreiem Handeln da wäre und dem Menschenwesen seine ihm kosmisch vorbestimmte Gestaltung gäbe.

120. Diese Gestaltung, die dem Menschen, der in seinem Wesen mit dem gegenwärtigen und zukünftigen Welten-Entwickelungsstadium mitlebt, *nicht* auf naturgemäßem Wege zukommt, kommt ihm auf geistgemäßem zu durch das Sich-Verbinden mit Michael, wodurch er auch den Weg zu Christus findet.

Leading Thoughts 118 to 120

118. That action alone can be free in which no process of nature, either within the human being or outside him, plays an active part.

119. But there is also the polar opposite aspect of this. Whenever the human individuality works freely, a nature-process is suppressed in him. In an unfree action, this process of nature would indeed be present, thus giving the human being his cosmically predetermined formation.

120. To the human being who in his own essential nature lives in connection with the present and future stage of world-development, the formative effect of these stages is *not* vouchsafed by way of nature. Rather, it comes to him by way of the spirit when he unites himself with Michael, whereby he also finds the way to Christ.

Die Weltgedanken im Wirken Michaels und im Wirken Ahrimans

Goetheanum, 16. November 1924

Der Betrachter des Verhältnisses Michaels zu Ahriman wird wohl zu der Frage gedrängt: Wie verhalten sich in dem kosmischen Zusammenhange diese beiden Geistesmächte, insoferne doch beide in der Entfaltung der intellektuellen Kräfte tätig sind?

Michael entfaltete die Intellektualität durch den Kosmos hindurch in der Vergangenheit. Da tat er dieses als Diener der göttlich-geistigen Mächte, die sowohl ihm selbst wie dem Menschen den Ursprung gegeben haben. Und bei diesem Verhältnis zur Intellektualität will er bleiben. Als diese von den göttlich-geistigen Mächten sich loslöste, um den Weg in das Innere des Menschenwesens zu finden, da beschloss er, fortan sich in rechter Art zur Menschheit zu stellen, um in dieser sein Verhältnis zur Intellektualität zu finden. Aber er wollte all dieses nur im Sinne der göttlich-geistigen Mächte auch weiterhin als deren Diener tun, der Mächte, mit denen er von seinem und der Menschen Ursprunge her verbunden ist. So ist seine Absicht, dass in Zukunft die Intellektualität durch die Herzen der Menschen ströme, aber als dieselbe

The World Thoughts in the Working of Michael and in the Working of Ahriman

Goetheanum, 16 November 1924

One who considers the relation of Michael to Ahriman may well feel impelled to ask: How are these spiritual powers related to one another in the cosmic sense, seeing that both of them are active in the unfolding of the intellectual forces?

In the past, Michael unfolded the intellectuality throughout the cosmos. He did this as the servant of the divine-spiritual powers to whom both he himself and the human being owed their origin. And he wishes to remain within this relationship to intellectuality. When intellectuality was loosened from the divine-spiritual powers in order to find its way into the innermost being of the human being, Michael resolved thenceforth to assume his rightful relation to humanity in order therein to find his relationship to intellectuality. But he wanted to do all this only in the sense of the divine-spiritual powers and continuing as their servant; for he has been united with these powers ever since his own origin and that of human beings. Therefore it is his intention that in the future, intellectuality shall flow through the hearts of human beings – but that it

Kraft, die sie ausströmend aus den göttlich-geistigen Mächten schon im Anfange war.

Ganz anders steht es bei Ahriman. Dieses Wesen hat sich seit Langem aus der Entwickelungsströmung losgelöst, der die gekennzeichneten göttlich-geistigen Mächte angehören. Es hat sich in urferner Vergangenheit als selbstständige kosmische Macht neben diese hingestellt. – Nun steht es in der Gegenwart zwar räumlich in der Welt darinnen, der der Mensch angehört, aber es entwickelt mit den rechtmäßig dieser Welt angehörenden Wesen keinen Kräftezusammenhang. Nur da die Intellektualität, von den göttlich-geistigen Wesen losgelöst, an diese Welt herankommt, findet Ahriman sich mit dieser Intellektualität so verwandt, dass er sich auf seine Art durch sie mit der Menschheit verbinden kann. Denn er hat, was der Mensch in der Gegenwart wie eine Gabe aus dem Kosmos erhält, schon in urferner Zeit mit sich vereinigt. Ahriman würde, wenn ihm gelänge, was in seiner Absicht liegt, den der Menschheit gegebenen Intellekt ähnlich seinem eigenen machen.

Nun hat Ahriman sich die Intellektualität in einer Zeit angeeignet, als er sie nicht in sich verinnerlichen konnte. Sie blieb eine Kraft in seinem Wesen, die mit Herz und Seele nichts zu tun hat. Als kalt-frostiger, seelenloser kosmischer Impuls strömt von Ahriman die Intellektualität aus. Und *die*

shall flow there as the very same force which it was in the beginning when it poured forth from the divine-spiritual powers.

It is altogether different with Ahriman. He is a being who long ago severed himself from the stream of development to which those divine-spiritual powers belong who have been spoken of here. In an age of primal antiquity he set himself up beside them as an independent cosmic power. – This being, though in the present day he is there in the spatial world to which the human being belongs, evolves no relationship of inner forces with the beings rightly belonging to this world. It is only through the intellectuality, which comes into this world upon its loosening from the divine-spiritual beings, that Ahriman – finding himself akin to it – is able in his own way to unite himself with humanity. For in a primordial past, he already united with himself what the human being receives in the present as a gift from the cosmos. Ahriman, were he to succeed in his intentions, would make the intellect given to humanity similar to his own.

Now Ahriman appropriated intellectuality to himself in an age in which he could not internalize it. It has remained in his being as a force, utterly detached from anything of heart or soul. Intellectuality pours forth from Ahriman as a cold and freezing, soulless cosmic impulse. *Those* human beings who

Menschen, die von diesem Impuls ergriffen werden, entwickeln eine Logik, die in erbarmungs- und liebeloser Art für sich selbst zu sprechen scheint – in Wahrheit spricht eben Ahriman in ihr –, bei der sich nichts zeigt, was rechtes, inneres, herzlich-seelisches Verbundensein des Menschen ist mit dem, was er denkt, spricht, tut.

Michael hat *sich* die Intellektualität aber nie angeeignet. Er verwaltet sie als göttlich-geistige Kraft, indem er sich verbunden fühlt mit den göttlich-geistigen Mächten. Dadurch zeigt sich auch, indem er die Intellektualität durchdringt, in dieser die Möglichkeit, ein Ausdruck des Herzens, der Seele ebenso gut zu sein wie ein solcher des Kopfes, des Geistes. Denn Michael trägt in sich alle die Ursprungskräfte seiner Götter und die des Menschen. Dadurch überträgt er auf die Intellektualität nichts Kalt-Frostiges, Seelenloses, sondern er steht bei ihr in warm-inniger, seelenvoller Art.

Und hierinnen liegt auch der Grund, warum Michael mit ernster Miene und Geste durch den Kosmos wallet. Im Innern *so* verbunden sein mit dem intelligenten Inhalte, wie Michael es ist, bedeutet zugleich, die Anforderung erfüllen müssen, nichts von subjektiver Willkür, von Wunsch oder Begehren in diesen Inhalt hineinzubringen. Sonst wird ja Logik Willkür *eines* Wesens statt Ausdruck des Kosmos. Streng sein Wesen als Ausdruck des Weltwesens zu halten; alles, was sich im Innern als Eigenwesen regen will, auch in diesem Innern

are taken hold of by this impulse bring forth a logic which, in a compassionless and loveless way, seems to speak for itself alone – in truth, it is Ahriman who speaks here – a logic which bears no evidence of a rightful, inward, heartfelt relationship of soul between the human being and what he thinks and speaks and does.

But Michael has never appropriated intellectuality *to himself*. He rules it as a divine-spiritual force, while feeling himself united with the divine-spiritual powers. And when he pervades the power of intellectuality, it becomes apparent that intellectuality can equally well be an expression of the heart and soul as of the head and mind. For Michael carries within him all the original forces of his gods as well as those of the human being. Thereby, he does not convey through intellectuality anything that is cold, frosty, or soulless, but he stands by it in a way that is inwardly warm and full of soul.

Herein lies the reason why Michael moves through the cosmos with earnest demeanor and gesture. To be inwardly united *in this way* with the content of intelligence means at the same time to be obliged to fulfill the requirement that into it shall be brought no subjective caprice, wish, or desire. Otherwise logic becomes the arbitrary activity of *one* being, instead of the expression of the cosmos. Michael considers *his* special virtue to consist in strictly maintaining his being as the expression of the world-being, and keeping within himself all that

zu lassen: Das betrachtet Michael als *seine* Tugend. Sein Sinn ist nach den großen Zusammenhängen des Kosmos gerichtet – davon spricht seine Miene; sein Wille, der an den Menschen herantritt, soll widerspiegeln, was er im Kosmos erschaut –, davon spricht seine Haltung, seine Geste. Michael ist in allem *ernst*, denn Ernst als Offenbarung eines Wesens ist der Spiegel des Kosmos aus diesem Wesen; Lächeln ist der Ausdruck dessen, was, von einem Wesen ausgehend, in die Welt hineinstrahlt.

Eine der Imaginationen von *Michael* ist auch diese: Er wallet durch den *Zeitenlauf*, das Licht aus dem Kosmos wesenhaft als sein Wesen tragend; die Wärme aus dem Kosmos als Offenbarer seines eigenen Wesens gestaltend; er wallet als *Wesen wie eine Welt*, sich selber nur bejahend, indem er die Welt bejaht, wie aus allen Weltenstätten Kräfte zur Erde niederführend.

Dagegen eine solche von *Ahriman*: Er möchte in seinem Gange aus der *Zeit den Raum* erobern, er hat Finsternis um sich, in die er die Strahlen des eigenen Lichtes sendet; er hat um so stärkeren Frost um sich, je mehr er von seinen Absichten erreicht; er bewegt sich als Welt, die sich ganz in *ein* Wesen, das eigene, zusammenzieht, in dem er sich selber nur bejaht durch Verneinung der Welt; er bewegt sich, wie wenn er die unheimlichen Kräfte finsterer Höhlen der Erde mit sich führte.

would make itself felt as his own being. His intention is directed toward the great interrelations of the cosmos; this is expressed in his demeanor. His will, as it approaches the human being, must reflect what he sees in the cosmos; and this is shown in his bearing, his gesture. Michael is *earnest* in all things; for earnestness, as the revelation of a being, is a reflection of the cosmos through this being; smiling is the expression of what proceeds and radiates from a being into the world.

One of the imaginations of *Michael* is the following: He surges through the *course of time*, bearing the light from the cosmos in full reality as his own being, giving form to the warmth from the cosmos as the revealer of his own being. As *a being*, he surges *like a world*, affirming himself only by affirming the world, as if leading forces down to the earth from all realms of the universe.

This can be contrasted with an imagination of *Ahriman*: In following his course, he would conquer *space from time*; he has darkness around him into which he sends the rays of his own light; the more he achieves his aims, the more severe is the frost around him. He moves as a world which contracts entirely into *one* being – that is, his own – in which he affirms himself only by denying the world; he moves as if he carried with him the sinister forces of dark caves in the earth.

Wenn der Mensch die Freiheit sucht, ohne Anwandlung zum Egoismus, wenn ihm Freiheit wird reine Liebe zur auszuführenden Handlung, dann hat er die Möglichkeit, sich Michael zu nahen; wenn er in Freiheit wirken will bei Entfaltung des Egoismus, wenn ihm Freiheit wird das *stolze* Gefühl, *sich selber* in der Handlung zu offenbaren, dann steht er vor der Gefahr, in Ahrimans Gebiet zu gelangen.

Die oben geschilderten Imaginationen leuchten auf aus des Menschen Liebe zur Handlung (Michael) oder seiner Eigenliebe zu sich selbst, indem er handelt (Ahriman).

Indem sich der Mensch als freies Wesen in Michaels Nähe fühlt, ist er auf dem Wege, die Kraft der Intellektualität in seinen «ganzen Menschen» zu tragen; er denkt zwar mit dem Kopfe, aber das Herz fühlt des Denkens Hell oder Dunkel; der Wille strahlt des Menschen Wesen aus, indem er die Gedanken als Absichten in sich strömen hat. Der Mensch wird immer mehr Mensch, indem er Ausdruck der Welt wird; er findet sich, indem er sich nicht *sucht*, sondern in Liebe sich wollend der Welt verbindet.

Indem der Mensch seine Freiheit entfaltend in Ahrimans Verlockungen fällt, wird er in die Intellektualität hineingezogen wie in einen geistigen Automatismus, in dem er ein Glied ist, nicht mehr *er* selbst. All sein Denken wird Erlebnis des Kopfes; allein dieser sondert es vom Eigenherzerleben und

When the human being seeks freedom without inclining toward egoism – when freedom becomes for him pure love of the action to be performed – then it is possible for him to approach Michael. But if he wishes to act freely and at the same time develops egoism – if freedom becomes for him the *proud* feeling of manifesting *himself* in the action – then he is in danger of falling into Ahriman's sphere.

The above-described imaginations shine forth from a human being's pure love for the action (Michael), or from his own self-love in acting (Ahriman).

When the human being, as a free being, feels himself close to Michael, he is on the way to carrying the power of intellectuality into his "whole human being"; he thinks indeed with his head, but his heart feels the brightness or darkness of the thoughts; the will radiates forth the human being's essential nature by allowing thoughts to stream into it as intentions and aims. The human being becomes more and more human by becoming the expression of the world; he finds himself not by *seeking* himself, but by uniting himself in love voluntarily with the world.

When, in unfolding his freedom, the human being succumbs to Ahriman's temptations, he is drawn into intellectuality as if into a spiritual automatic process in which he is a part; he is no longer *himself*. All his thinking becomes an experience of the head; but this separates it from the experience of his own heart

eignem Willensleben ab und löscht das Eigensein aus. Der Mensch verliert immer mehr von seinem innerlich wesenhaftmenschlichen Ausdruck, indem er Ausdruck seines Eigenseins wird; er verliert sich, indem er sich *sucht*; er entzieht sich der Welt, der er die Liebe verweigert; aber der Mensch erlebt *sich* nur wahrhaft, wenn er die Welt liebt.

Es ist aus dem Geschilderten wohl anschaulich, wie Michael der Führer zu Christus ist. Michael geht mit allem Ernste seines Wesens, seiner Haltung, seines Handelns in Liebe durch die Welt. Wer sich an ihn hält, der pfleget *im Verhältnis zur Außenwelt der Liebe*. Und Liebe muss im Verhältnis zur Außenwelt sich zunächst entfalten, sonst wird sie Selbstliebe.

Ist dann diese Liebe in der Michael-Gesinnung da, dann wird *Liebe zum anderen* auch zurückstrahlen können ins eigene Selbst. Dieses wird lieben können, ohne sich selbst zu lieben. Und auf den Wegen solcher Liebe ist Christus durch die Menschenseele zu finden.

Wer sich an Michael hält, der pfleget im Verhältnis zur Außenwelt der Liebe, und er findet dadurch *das* Verhältnis zur Innenwelt seiner Seele, das ihn mit Christus zusammenführt.

Das Zeitalter, das jetzt im Anbrechen ist, bedarf des Hinblickes der Menschheit auf eine Welt, die unmittelbar als geistige an die physisch empfundene angrenzt und in der solches zu

and the life of his own will, and blots out his own being. The human being loses more and more of the essential inner human expression by becoming the expression of his own oneness; he loses himself by *seeking* himself – he withdraws himself from the world which he refuses to love. But the human being truly experiences *himself* only when he loves the world.

From the above description, it may be evident that Michael is the guide to Christ. Michael goes in love through the world with all the earnestness of his being, his attitude, his deeds. The human being who joins himself in union with Michael cultivates *love in relation to the outer world.* And love must be unfolded first of all in relation to the outer world, otherwise it becomes self-love.

If this love in the sense of the Michael-disposition is there, then one's *love for other beings* will shine back into one's own self. The self will be able to love without loving itself. And on the paths of this love, Christ can be found by the human soul.

One who joins himself in union with Michael cultivates love in relation to the outer world, and thereby he finds *that* relation to the inner world of his soul which leads him into relation with Christ.

The age now dawning requires that humanity turn its attention to a world immediately bordering upon the world perceived as physical – one in which there can be found what has

finden ist, wie es hier als Michael-Wesenheit und Michael-Mission geschildert ist. Denn *die* Welt, die sich der Mensch im Anblicke *dieser* physischen Welt als die Natur ausmalt, ist auch nicht die, in der er unmittelbar lebt, sondern eine solche, die so weit *unter* der wahrhaft menschlichen liegt wie die michaelische *über* dieser. Nur merkt der Mensch nicht, dass unbewusst, indem er sich ein Bild seiner Welt macht, eigentlich das einer anderen entsteht. Er ist, indem er dieses Bild malt, schon dabei, sich auszuschalten und dem geistigen Automatismus zu verfallen. Der Mensch kann seine Menschheit nur bewahren, wenn er *diesem* Bilde, in dem er sich als in dem Bilde der Naturanschauung verliert, das *andere* gegenüberstellt, in dem Michael waltet, in dem Michael die Wege zum Christus führt.

here been described as the being and the mission of Michael. For *that* world which the human being pictures as nature when he sees *this* physical world is also not the one in which the human being is immediately living, but one which lies as far *below* the truly human world as the world of Michael lies *above* it. It is simply that the human being fails to notice that unconsciously, when he forms an image of his world, what arises is actually the image of quite another world. When he paints this inner image, he is already in the state of excluding himself and succumbing to spiritual automatism. The human being can only preserve his humanity by placing over against *this* image – in which he loses himself as in the image of the view of nature – the *other*, in which Michael rules, in which Michael leads the ways to Christ.

Leitsätze Nr. 121 bis 123

121. Man hat ein in der Welt Wirkendes, zum Beispiel die Weltgedanken, in seiner Bedeutung für die Welt noch nicht durchschaut, wenn man bei diesem Wirkenden an sich stehen bleibt, sondern man muss erkennend auf die Wesen blicken, von denen das Wirkende ausgeht; zum Beispiel für die Weltgedanken, ob sie von Michael oder Ahriman in und durch die Welt getragen werden.

122. Was von dem einen Wesen ausgehend, wegen dessen Verhältnis zur Welt, heilsam und schaffend wirken kann, das kann sich verderblich und zerstörend erweisen, wenn es von einem anderen Wesen ausgeht. Die Weltgedanken tragen den Menschen in die Zukunft, wenn er sie von Michael empfängt; sie führen ihn von der ihm heilsamen Zukunft hinweg, wenn Ahriman sie ihm geben kann.

123. Durch solche Betrachtungen wird man immer mehr dazu gebracht, die Anschauung von einer unbestimmten Geistigkeit, die pantheistisch auf dem Grunde der Dinge walten soll, zu überwinden; und man wird zu einer bestimmten, konkreten geführt, die von den *geistigen Wesen*

Leading Thoughts 121 to 123

121. One has not fully seen through the significance of something working in the world – for instance, the world-thoughts – so long as one stops short at the thing itself; rather, one must look with recognition upon the beings from whom this working proceeds. For example, for the world-thoughts one must perceive whether it is Michael or Ahriman who bears them out into and through the world.

122. What proceeds from the one being, by virtue of his relation to the world, will work healingly and creatively; proceeding from another being, the same thing will prove pernicious and destructive. The world-thoughts carry the human being into the future when he receives them from Michael; they lead him away from the future that is beneficial for him when Ahriman can give them to him.

123. Such reflections lead one ever more to overcome the view of an undefined spirituality, pantheistically conceived as holding sway at the root of all things. One is led to a conception that is definite and concrete, capable of forming representations of the *spiritual beings* of the

der höheren Hierarchien sich Vorstellungen machen kann. Denn die Wirklichkeit besteht ja überall im Wesenhaften; und was in ihr nicht Wesenhaftes ist, das ist die Tätigkeit, die sich im Verhältnisse von Wesen zu Wesen abspielt. Es kann nur begriffen werden, wenn man den Blick auf die tätigen Wesen werfen kann.

hierarchies. For the reality is everywhere a reality of essential Being. And what in reality is not essential Being, is the activity that plays out in the relation of one being to another. This can only be understood if one can turn one's gaze to the active beings.

Erste Betrachtung: Vor den Toren der Bewusstseinsseele. Wie Michael seine Erdenmission durch Besiegung Luzifers überirdisch vorbereitet

Goetheanum, 23. November 1924

Michaels Eingreifen in die Welt- und Menschheitsentwickelung am Ende des neunzehnten Jahrhunderts erscheint in einer besonderen Beleuchtung, wenn man die Geistesgeschichte in den Jahrhunderten betrachtet, die ihm vorangegangen sind.

Im Beginne des fünfzehnten Jahrhunderts liegt der Zeitpunkt, in dem die Epoche der Bewusstseinsseele ihren Anfang nimmt.

Vor diesem Zeitpunkt offenbart sich ein völliger Wandel in dem Geistesleben der Menschheit. Man kann verfolgen, wie vorher in das menschliche Anschauen überall noch Imaginationen hineingespielt haben. Einzelne Persönlichkeiten haben sich allerdings schon früher zu bloßen «Begriffen» in ihrem Seelenleben gefunden; allein die allgemeine Seelenverfassung der Mehrzahl der Menschen lebt in einem Sich-Durchdringen von Imaginationen mit Vorstellungen, die der rein physischen Welt entstammen. So ist es mit den Vorstellungen über Naturgeschehen, so aber auch mit denen über das geschichtliche Werden.

First Consideration: At the Gates of the Consciousness Soul. How Michael Supersensibly Prepares His Earth-Mission through the Overcoming of Lucifer

Goetheanum, 23 November 1924

A clear light is thrown upon the intervention of Michael into the development of the world and humanity at the end of the nineteenth century by a study of the spiritual history of the preceding centuries.

The epoch of the consciousness soul takes its rise at the beginning of the fifteenth century.

Before this time, a complete change takes place in the spiritual life of humanity. It is evident, on looking back, that imaginations still play a large part in human perception. Single individuals have already associated themselves in their soul-life with pure "concepts"; but the soul-disposition of the majority of people consists in the permeation of imaginations with representations derived from the purely physical world. This is the case concerning both representations of natural events and also those of the processes of historical becoming.

Was die geistige Beobachtung nach dieser Richtung finden kann, wird durch die äußeren Zeugnisse durchaus bestätigt. Auf einige der Letzteren sei hier gedeutet.

Was in den vorangegangenen Jahrhunderten über geschichtliche Ereignisse gesonnen und gesprochen worden war, wird gerade vor dem Anbruch des Bewusstseinszeitalters vielfach niedergeschrieben. Und so haben wir aus dieser Zeit «Sagen» und dergleichen aufbewahrt, die ein getreues Bild davon geben, wie man vorher «Geschichte» vorgestellt hat.

Ein schönes Beispiel ist die Erzählung von dem «guten Gerhard», die in einem Gedichte des Rudolf von Ems, der in der ersten Hälfte des dreizehnten Jahrhunderts lebte, erhalten ist. Der «gute Gerhard» ist ein reicher Kaufmann in Köln. Er unternimmt eine Handelsreise nach Russland, Livland und Preußen, um Zobelfelle zu kaufen. Dann geht er nach Damaskus und Ninive, um Seidenstoffe und Ähnliches zu erwerben.

Auf der Heimreise wird er vom Sturm verschlagen. In dem fremden Gebiet, in das er kommt, lernt er einen Mann kennen, in dessen Gefangenschaft sich englische Ritter und auch die Verlobte des englischen Königs befinden. Gerhard gibt alles hin, was er auf der Reise erhandelt hatte, und erhält dafür die Gefangenen. Die nimmt er auf sein Schiff und tritt die Heimreise an. Als die Schiffe dahin kommen, wo die Wege nach der Heimat Gerhards und nach England sich trennen, entlässt Gerhard die männlichen Gefangenen nach ihrer Heimat; die

What spiritual observation is able to discover in this direction is confirmed throughout by external evidence. A few instances of this will now be cited.

The way in which people in previous centuries had thought and spoken about historical events had found its way into writing just before the age of the consciousness soul set in. Thus from this time we have preserved to us "sagas" and the like, in which a true image is given of how "history" was inwardly pictured in past times.

A fine example is the tale of "Gerhard the Good," contained in a poem by Rudolf von Ems, who lived in the first half of the thirteenth century. "Gerhard the Good" is a rich merchant from Cologne. He undertakes a journey to Russia, Livonia, and Prussia, to buy sables, and then travels farther to Damascus and Nineveh to get silk goods and similar merchandise.

On the homeward journey, he is driven off his course by a storm. In the strange country in which he finds himself, he becomes acquainted with a man who is keeping a number of English knights – and the betrothed of the King of England – in captivity. Gerhard sacrifices all that he has acquired on his journey in a trade, and receives the prisoners in exchange. When the ships arrive at the point where the ways of the travelers part, Gerhard sends the knights home, but the King's betrothed he detains in the hope that the bridegroom,

Verlobte des Königs behält er bei sich, in der Hoffnung, dass ihr Bräutigam, der König Wilhelm, sie abholen werde, sobald er von ihrer Befreiung und ihrem Aufenthaltsorte Kunde erhält. In der denkbar besten Art werden die Königsbraut und ihre mitgekommenen Freundinnen von Gerhard gehalten. Sie lebt wie eine vielgeliebte Tochter in dem Hause ihres Erlösers aus der Gefangenschaft. Es vergeht die längste Zeit, ohne dass der König erscheint, sie abzuholen. Da entschließt sich Gerhard, um der Pflegetochter Zukunft zu sichern, sie mit seinem Sohne zu vermählen. Denn es kann geglaubt werden, dass Wilhelm tot sei. Schon ist das Hochzeitsfest für den Sohn Gerhards im Gange; da erscheint auf demselben als unbekannter Pilger – Wilhelm. Er war lange umhergeirrt, um seine Verlobte zu suchen. Ihm wird nach dem selbstlosen Verzicht von Gerhards Sohn seine Braut zurückgegeben. Einige Zeit bleiben beide noch bei Gerhard; dann rüstet dieser ein Schiff aus, um sie nach England zu bringen. Als die wieder zu Würden gekommenen Gefangenen Gerhard zunächst in England begrüßen können, wollen sie *ihn* zum König wählen. Er aber kann erwidern, dass er ihnen ihr rechtmäßiges Königspaar bringe. Auch sie hatten ja Wilhelm für tot gehalten und wollten einen anderen König für das Land wählen, in dem die Zustände während des Umherirrens Wilhelms chaotisch geworden waren. – Der Kölner Kaufmann schlägt alles, was man ihm an Würden und Reichtümern anbietet, aus und kehrt nach

King William, will come to fetch her himself as soon as he receives news of her release and of the place of her abode. The King's bride and the maidens accompanying her are hosted by Gerhard in the best way imaginable. She lives, like a much loved daughter, in the house of her deliverer from captivity. A long time passes without the King coming to take her away. Then, in order to ensure his foster daughter's future, Gerhard decides to marry her to his son. For the supposition is possible that William is dead. The wedding of Gerhard's son is being celebrated, when an unknown pilgrim arrives. It is William. He has wandered about for a long time, searching for his betrothed. Gerhard's son unselfishly resigns her and she is given back to William. Both remain for a time with Gerhard; then the latter fits out a ship to bring them to England. When Gerhard's prisoners – who have been restored to honor – are first able to greet him in England, they wish to make *him* king. But he is able to reply that he is bringing to them their lawful king and queen. They, too, had thought William dead and wished to choose another king to rule their country, which during William's wanderings had fallen into a chaotic state. – The Cologne merchant renounces all the honors and riches offered to him and returns to Cologne, there to be again the simple merchant he had been before. – The story goes on to relate how the Saxon emperor Otto I (Otto the Great) journeys to Cologne to make the

Köln zurück, um dort weiter der einfache Kaufmann zu sein, der er vorher gewesen. – Die Geschichte wird so eingekleidet, dass der sächsische Kaiser, Otto der Erste, nach Köln reist, um den «guten Gerhard» kennen zu lernen. Denn der mächtige Kaiser ist der Versuchung unterlegen, für manches, was er getan hat, auf «irdischen Lohn» zu rechnen. Dadurch, dass er Gerhard kennen lernt, wird ihm an einem Beispiel fühlbar, wie ein einfacher Mann unsägliches Gutes tut – Hingabe aller Waren, die er erstanden, um Gefangene zu befreien; Rückgabe der Braut des Sohnes an Wilhelm; dann alles, was er verrichtet, um diesen wieder nach England zu bringen und so weiter –, ohne irgendwelchen irdischen Lohn dafür zu begehren, sondern alle Belohnung allein von dem Walten der Gottheit zu erwarten. Der Mann heißt im Menschenmunde der «gute Gerhard»; der Kaiser fühlt, dass er einen mächtigen religiös-moralischen Ruck erhält durch die Bekanntschaft mit Gerhards Gesinnung.

Die Erzählung, deren Gerüst ich hier gegeben habe, um nicht über etwas wenig Bekanntes bloß mit Namen zu deuten, zeigt nun *von der einen Seite* ganz deutlich die Seelenverfassung des Zeitalters vor dem Heraufkommen der Bewusstseinsseele in der Entwickelung der Menschheit.

Wer nämlich die Erzählung, wie sie Rudolf von Ems gibt, auf sich wirken lässt, der kann fühlen, wie das Erleben der Erdenwelt seit jener Zeit, in der Kaiser Otto gelebt (im zehnten Jahrhundert), sich gewandelt hat.

acquaintance of "Gerhard the Good." For the powerful king has succumbed to the temptation to count upon "earthly recompense" for much that he has done. Through becoming acquainted with Gerhard, he learns from his example how a simple human being does an unspeakable amount of good – sacrificing all the goods he had acquired in order to liberate captives, restoring to William his son's affianced bride, then taking the trouble to bring William to England again, etc. – without desiring any earthly reward whatsoever for it, but leaving all reward to the ruling of divine providence. The man is universally known as "Gerhard the Good"; the king feels that he himself receives a powerful moral and religious impulse through becoming acquainted with Gerhard's inner attitude.

The story which I have briefly outlined above – in order to do more than merely mention by name something that is not well known – shows quite clearly *from one aspect* the soul-demeanor of the age before the emergence of the consciousness soul in the development of humanity.

Those who enter into the spirit of the tale, as told by Rudolf von Ems, will be able to feel how the experience of the earthly world has changed since the time of Otto the Great (in the tenth century).

Man sehe hin, wie in dem Zeitalter der Bewusstseinsseele die Welt vor dem Seelenblicke des Menschen gewissermaßen «hell» für alles Erfassen des physischen Seins und Werdens geworden ist. Gerhard fährt mit seinen Schiffen gewissermaßen wie im Nebel. Er kennt nur immer ein Stückchen von der Welt, mit der er in Verbindung kommen will. Man erfährt in Köln nichts von dem, was in England vor sich geht, und muss jahrelang suchen nach einem Menschen, der in Köln ist. Man lernt Leben und Besitz eines solchen Menschen, wie der ist, zu dem Gerhard auf der Heimreise verschlagen wird, erst kennen, wenn man durch das Schicksal unmittelbar an den entsprechenden Ort herangebracht wird. Zu dem Durchschauen der Weltverhältnisse von heute verhält sich das damalige wie das Hineinblicken in eine sonnenerhellte weite Landschaft zu dem Sich-Hintasten im dichten Nebel.

Mit dem, was man heute «geschichtlich» gelten lässt, hat das nichts zu tun, was in Verbindung mit dem «guten Gerhard» erzählt wird. Um so mehr aber mit der Gemütsstimmung und der ganzen geistigen Lage des Zeitalters. *Diese*, nicht die einzelnen Ereignisse der physischen Welt, werden in Imaginationen dargestellt.

In dieser Darstellung spiegelt sich, wie der Mensch sich nicht nur als ein Wesen fühlt, das als ein Glied in der Kette der Ereignisse der physischen Welt lebt und tätig ist, sondern wie er in sein irdisches Dasein geistige, übersinnliche Wesen

Notice how, during the age of the consciousness soul, the world has in a certain way become "clear" to human soul-perception as regards the comprehension of physical existence and its development. Gerhard travels with his ships as if in a mist. He only knows the small portion of the world with which he wishes to come in contact. In Cologne one hears nothing of what is taking place in England, and one has to search for years for a person residing in Cologne. One only comes to know about the life and property of another person – such as the one on whose shore Gerhard is cast on his homeward journey – when one has been brought directly to that place by destiny. The present-day grasp of circumstances in the world is related to that of those earlier times as looking into a broad, sunlit landscape is to groping about in a dense fog.

What is related in connection with "Gerhard the Good" has nothing to do with what one calls "historical" nowadays, but it is all the more concerned with the mood of soul and the whole spiritual circumstances of the time. It is *these*, and not the particular events in the physical world, which are depicted in imaginations.

In this narration, one can see a reflection of how the human being not only feels himself as a being who lives and is active as a member in the chain of events in the physical world, but also feels spiritual, suprasensory beings working

hineinwirken und mit ihnen seinen Willen in Zusammenhang fühlt.

Die Erzählung vom «guten Gerhard» zeigt, wie das Dämmerdunkel, das in Bezug auf das Durchschauen der physischen Welt dem Zeitalter der Bewusstseinsseele vorangegangen ist, den Blick in das Erschauen der geistigen Welt gewiesen hat. Man sah nicht *in die Weiten* des physischen Daseins, man sah um so mehr *in die Tiefen* des geistigen.

Aber so, wie einst ein dämmerhaftes (traumhaftes) Hellsehen der Menschheit die geistige Welt gezeigt hatte, war es in dem gekennzeichneten Zeitalter nicht mehr. Die Imaginationen waren da; aber sie traten innerhalb einer Auffassung der Menschenseele auf, die schon stark nach dem Gedanklichen hindrängte. Das bewirkte, dass man nicht mehr wusste, wie die Welt, die sich in Imaginationen offenbarte, sich zu der des physischen Daseins verhält. Deshalb erschienen die Imaginationen Leuten, die schon eindringlicher sich an das Gedankliche hielten, als willkürliche «Erdichtungen» ohne Wirklichkeit.

Man wusste nicht mehr, dass man durch die Imagination in eine Welt blickt, in der man mit einem ganz anderen Teile seines Menschenwesens steht als in der physischen. So standen in der Darstellung beide Welten nebeneinander; und beide trugen durch die Haltung der Erzählung einen Charakter, dass man meinen konnte, die geistigen Geschehnisse, die

into his earthly existence and standing in connection with his will.

The tale of "Gerhard the Good" shows how the twilight dimness, which in respect of seeing through the physical world preceded the period of the consciousness soul, turned the human being's gaze to the vision of the spiritual world. The human being did not see *the breadth* of the physical world, but he saw all the more *into the depths* of the spiritual.

Yet in the period described, it was no longer the same as it had once been when the spiritual world was shown to humanity in a twilight (dream-like) clairvoyance. The imaginations were there; but when they appeared within the human soul, the soul was already strongly disposed in the direction of *thought* in terms of its apprehension of things. The result of this was that human beings no longer knew how the world revealing itself in imaginations was related to the world of physical existence. Hence, to people who were already holding more strongly to the thought element, these imaginations seemed to be arbitrary "fables" having no reality.

Human beings no longer knew that through the imaginations, they saw into a world in which the human being stands with a quite different part of his essential nature than he does in the physical world. Thus, in the picture before us, two worlds stand side by side; and in the way the story is told, both worlds bear a character that would enable one to think that the

man erzählte, hätten sich so wahrnehmbar zwischen den physischen abgespielt, wie diese selbst wahrnehmbar sind.

Dazu kam, dass man die physischen Ereignisse in vielen dieser Erzählungen durcheinander warf. Personen, deren Leben Jahrhunderte voneinander entfernt liegt, treten als Zeitgenossen auf; Geschehnisse werden an unrichtige Orte oder in unrichtige Zeitpunkte versetzt.

Es werden Tatsachen der physischen Welt so von der menschlichen Seele angeschaut, wie man nur das Geistige anschauen kann, für das Zeit und Raum eine andere Bedeutung als für das Physische haben; die physische Welt wird in Imaginationen statt in Gedanken dargestellt; dafür wird die geistige Welt so in die Erzählung verwoben, wie wenn man es nicht mit einer anderen Daseinsform, sondern mit dem Fortgang physischer Tatsachen zu tun hätte.

Eine nur an das Physische sich haltende Geschichtserfassung denkt, man habe die alten Imaginationen des Orients, Griechenlands und so weiter übernommen und dichterisch mit den geschichtlichen Stoffen verwoben, die die Menschen damals beschäftigten. Man hatte ja in den Schriften Isidors von Sevilla aus dem siebenten Jahrhundert eine förmliche Sammlung alter «Sagenmotive».

Doch dies ist eine äußerliche Betrachtungsweise. Sie hat etwas Bedeutsames nur für denjenigen, der keinen Sinn für *die* menschliche Seelenverfassung hat, die sich mit ihrem Dasein

spiritual events have taken place in the midst of the physical events just as perceptibly as these physical events themselves.

In addition to this, the physical events in many of these tales are in utter confusion. People whose lives are centuries apart appear as contemporaries; events are transferred to an incorrect place or to an inaccurate time-period.

In these tales, facts of the physical world are viewed by the human soul in such a manner as one can really only employ in viewing the spiritual, for which time and space have a whole different significance. The physical world is depicted in imaginations instead of in thoughts. On the other hand, the spiritual world is woven into the narrative as if one were dealing not with a different form of existence, but with something that was a continuation of physical facts.

A historical conception that keeps to the physical only, thinks that the old imaginations of the East, of Greece, etc., have been taken over and interwoven poetically with the historical subjects occupying the minds of people at that time. And in the writings of Isidore of Seville of the seventh century, one indeed had a recognized collection of old "saga motifs."

Yet this is merely an external point of view and has significance only for those who have no understanding for *that* particular condition of soul which still knows itself to be in direct

noch im unmittelbaren Anschluss an die geistige Welt weiß und die dieses Wissen in Imaginationen auszudrücken sich gedrängt fühlt. Wird dann statt der eigenen Imagination eine geschichtlich überlieferte verwendet, in die man sich eingelebt hat, so ist das nicht das Wesentliche. Dieses liegt darin, dass die Seele nach der geistigen Welt hin orientiert ist, sodass sie ihr eigenes Tun und das Naturgeschehen in diese Welt eingegliedert sieht.

Doch ist in der Erzählungsart der Zeit vor dem Anbruch des Bewusstseinszeitalters Verirrung zu bemerken.

In dieser Verirrung schaut die geistgemäße Beobachtung das Wirken der luziferischen Macht.

Was die Seele drängt, Imaginationen in ihren Erlebnisgehalt aufzunehmen, das entspricht weniger den Fähigkeiten, die sie in der Vorzeit – durch ein traumhaftes Hellsehen – hatte, sondern schon mehr denjenigen, die im achten bis vierzehnten nachchristlichen Jahrhundert vorhanden waren. *Diese* Fähigkeiten drängten schon mehr nach einer gedanklichen Erfassung des sinnlich Wahrgenommenen hin. Beide Fähigkeiten sind in der Übergangszeit nebeneinander vorhanden. Die Seele ist hineingestellt zwischen die alte Orientierung, welche auf die Geisteswelt geht und die die physische nur wie im Nebel sieht, und die neue, die auf das physische Geschehen geht und in der das geistige Anschauen verblasst.

connection with the spiritual world, and which feels itself impelled to express this insight in imaginations. Whether a writer makes use of his own imagination, or whether he applies, in an authentic and living way, an imagination that has been handed down through history, is not the essential point. The essential point is that the soul is oriented toward the spiritual world and sees both its own actions and the events in the course of nature as forming a part of that world.

It is however true that in the way stories and legends were told in the time before the dawn of the consciousness-soul age, disorientation is noticeable.

In this disorientation, spiritual observation sees the working of the luciferic powers.

That which urges the soul to receive imaginations into its experience is the result not so much of faculties possessed by the soul in ancient times – through a dreamlike clairvoyance – but rather of faculties present in the periods between the eighth and fourteenth centuries AD. *These* faculties were already pressing more strongly toward an understanding, in terms of thought, of what was perceived by the senses. Both faculties were present simultaneously during the transition period. The soul was placed between the old orientation, which goes to the spiritual world and sees the physical only as in a mist, and the new orientation, which is centered on physical happenings and in which the spiritual vision fades.

In dieses schwankende Gleichgewicht der Menschenseele wirkt die luziferische Macht hinein. Sie möchte den Menschen verhindern, die volle Orientierung in der physischen Welt zu finden. Sie möchte ihn in geistigen Regionen, die ihm in der Vorzeit angemessen waren, mit seinem Bewusstsein erhalten. Sie möchte in sein traumhaft-imaginatives Weltanschauen nicht rein Gedankliches, das auf das Erfassen des physischen Daseins gerichtet ist, einfließen lassen. Sie kann sein Anschauungsvermögen in unrechter Art wohl von der physischen Welt zurückhalten. Sie kann aber das Erleben der alten Imaginationen nicht in der rechten Art aufrecht erhalten. So lässt sie ihn in Imaginationen sinnen, ohne ihn seelisch ganz in die Welt versetzen zu können, in der Imaginationen vollgültig sind.

Im Anbruche des Bewusstseinszeitalters waltet Luzifer so, dass durch ihn der Mensch in die an die physische zunächst angrenzende übersinnliche Region auf eine ihm nicht entsprechende Art versetzt wird.

Man sehe dies ganz anschaulich an der «Sage» vom «Herzog Ernst», die zu den beliebtesten des Mittelalters gehörte und die im weiten Umkreise überall erzählt wurde.

Der Herzog Ernst kommt in Zwiespalt mit dem Kaiser, der ihn ungerecht durch Krieg zugrunde richten will. Der Herzog fühlt sich gedrängt, dem unmöglichen Verhältnis mit dem Reichshaupte dadurch zu entgehen, dass er an der

The luciferic power works into this wavering balance of the human soul. It wants to prevent the human being from attaining to complete orientation in the physical world. It wants to keep him, with his consciousness, in spiritual realms that were appropriate for him in ancient times. It wants to prevent pure thinking, directed toward the understanding of physical existence, from flowing into his dreamlike, imaginative conception of the world. It is able to hold back, in a wrongful way, the human being's power of perception from the physical world. It is not, however, able to maintain in the right way the experience of the old imaginations. It allows the human being to reflect in imaginations without being able to transfer his soul completely into the world in which the imaginations are fully valid.

At the dawn of the consciousness-soul epoch, Lucifer is active in such a manner that, through him, the human being is transferred into the suprasensory region immediately bordering on the physical in a way not in keeping with his nature.

One can see this quite clearly in the "Legend" of "Duke Ernst," which was one of the most beloved legends of the Middle Ages and was retold in wide circles.

Duke Ernst has a disagreement with the Emperor, who is determined to make war upon him unjustly and bring him to ruin. The Duke feels impelled to escape from this untenable relation with the head of the state by taking part in the

Kreuzzugsbewegung nach dem Orient teilnimmt. In den Erlebnissen, die er nun durchmacht, bis die Reise ihn nach dem Ziele führt, wird «sagenhaft» das Physische mit dem Geistigen in der angedeuteten Art verwoben. Der Herzog gelangt zum Beispiel auf seinem Wege zu einem Volke, das den Kopf gestaltet hat wie Kraniche; er wird an den «Magnetberg» mit den Schiffen verschlagen, von dem diese magnetisch angezogen werden, sodass Menschen, die in die Nähe des Berges kommen, nicht wieder zurück können, sondern elendig umkommen müssen. Der Herzog Ernst und sein Gefolge machen sich dadurch los, dass sie sich in Häute einnähen, von Greifen, die gewohnt sind, die nach dem Magnetberg verschlagenen Menschen zur Beute sich zu holen, auf einen Berg sich bringen lassen und dort nach dem Durchschneiden der Häute in Abwesenheit der Greife entkommen. Die weitere Wanderung führt dann zu einem Volke, dessen Ohren so lang sind, dass sie wie eine Kleidung um den ganzen Körper geschlagen werden können; zu einem anderen, dessen Füße so groß sind, dass sich die Leute, wenn es regnet, auf den Boden legen können und die Füße als Schirme über sich breiten können. Er kommt zu einem Zwergen-, einem Riesenvolke und so weiter. Dergleichen vieles wird in Verbindung mit der Kreuzzugsreise des Herzogs Ernst erzählt. Die «Sage» lässt nicht in der rechten Art fühlen, wie überall da, wo Imaginationen eintreten, die Hinorientierung auf eine geistige Welt

Crusade to the East. In the experiences he undergoes before he reaches his destination, the physical and spiritual are woven together in "saga-form" in the manner indicated. For instance, the Duke, in the course of his wanderings, encounters a people with heads shaped like those of cranes. He is driven ashore on the "Magnet Mountain," which draws ships with magnetic power, so that people who come into the vicinity of the mountain cannot escape but are doomed to a miserable end. Duke Ernst and his followers effect their escape by sewing themselves up in skins and letting themselves be carried up to a hill by griffins, who are accustomed to capturing those driven onto the Magnet Mountain; thence, after cutting the skins, they escape in the absence of the griffins. The continuation of the journey leads them to a people whose ears are so long that they can fling them round themselves like a cloak; and to yet another people whose feet are so large that when it rains, they can lie on the ground and spread their feet over themselves like umbrellas. He comes to a race of dwarfs, then to a race of giants, and so forth. Many similar things are related in connection with Duke Ernst's journey to the Crusades. The "Legend" does not let one feel in the right way how, whenever imaginations enter into the story, an orientation is set up toward a spiritual world, and how events are then related through images which are enacted in the astral world and which are

stattfindet, wie da Dinge durch Bilder erzählt werden, die in der Astralwelt sich abspielen und die mit Wille und Schicksal der Erdenmenschen zusammenhängen.

Und so ist es mit der schönen «Rolandsage», in der Karls des Großen Zug gegen die Heiden nach Spanien verherrlicht wird. Da wird sogar in Anlehnung an die Bibel gesagt, dass, damit Karl der Große ein von ihm erstrebtes Ziel erreichen könne, die Sonne sich in ihrem Laufe hemme, sodass *ein* Tag so lang werde wie sonst zwei.

Und in der «Nibelungensage» sieht man, wie diejenige Form, die sich in nordischen Ländern erhalten hat, das Anschauen des Geistigen reiner aufrecht erhält, während in Mitteleuropa die Imaginationen an das physische Leben nahe herangebracht werden. An der nordischen Form der Erzählung ist ausgedrückt, dass sich die Imaginationen auf eine «astralische Welt» beziehen; in der mitteleuropäischen Gestalt des Nibelungenliedes gleiten die Imaginationen in das Anschauen der physischen Welt hinein.

Auch die in der Herzog-Ernst-Sage auftretenden Imaginationen beziehen sich ja in Wirklichkeit auf das, was *zwischen* den Erfahrungen in der physischen Sphäre in einer «astralischen Welt» erlebt wird, der der Mensch ebenso angehört wie der physischen.

Wendet man auf all das den Geistesblick, so schaut man, wie das Eintreten in das Bewusstseinszeitalter das Herauswachsen

connected with the will and destiny of the earthly human being.

This is also the case with the beautiful "Song of Roland," in which Charlemagne's crusade against the heathen in Spain is commemorated. It is related there, following the Bible, that in order for Charlemagne to attain the end he was striving for, the sun stopped in its course, so that *one* day became as long as two.

In the "Nibelung Saga," one can see how the form which had been preserved in Nordic lands is one that maintains more purely and directly the perception of the spiritual, whereas in Central Europe the imaginations are brought nearer to physical life. In the Nordic form of the story, the imaginations relate to an "astral world"; in the Central European form of the Song of the Nibelungs, the imaginations glide over into the perception of the physical world.

The imaginations appearing in the Legend of Duke Ernst refer in reality to what is lived through in an "astral world" *between* the experiences in the physical sphere – an "astral world" to which the human being belongs just as much as to the physical.

If one applies spiritual vision to all this, then one sees how the entrance into the age of the consciousness soul signifies the

aus einer Entwickelungsphase bedeutet, in der die luziferischen Mächte über die Menschheit siegen würden, wenn nicht durch die Bewusstseinsseele mit ihrer Kraft der Intellektualität ein neuer Entwickelungseinschlag in das Menschenwesen käme. Die Hinorientierung auf die geistige Welt, die in die Bahnen der Verirrung einlenken will, wird durch die Bewusstseinsseele gehindert; der Menschenblick wird herausgeholt in die physische Welt. Alles, was nach dieser Richtung geschieht, entzieht die Menschheit der sie beirrenden luziferischen Macht.

Da ist Michael schon von der geistigen Welt aus für die Menschheit tätig. Er bereitet vom Übersinnlichen aus sein späteres Werk vor. Er gibt der Menschheit Impulse, die das vorzeitige Verhältnis zur geistig-göttlichen Welt bewahren, ohne dass dieses Bewahren einen luziferischen Charakter annimmt.

Dann, im letzten Drittel des neunzehnten Jahrhunderts, dringt Michael mit der Tätigkeit, die er vom fünfzehnten bis in das neunzehnte Jahrhundert vorbereitend vom Übersinnlichen aus geübt hat, in die physische Erdenwelt selbst vor.

Die Menschheit musste eine Zeitlang die geistige Entwickelung daraufhin durchmachen, dass sie sich von dem Verhältnisse zur geistigen Welt befreit, das ein unmögliches zu werden drohte. Darauf lenkte diese Entwickelung durch die Michael-Mission in Bahnen ein, die den Fortgang der Erdenmenschheit wieder in ein Verhältnis zur geistigen Welt bringen, das ihr heilsam ist.

outgrowing of a phase of development in which the luciferic powers would have prevailed over humanity, had a new developmental impulse not come into the human being through the consciousness soul with its force of intellectuality. That orientation toward the spiritual world which would lead to paths of error is hindered through the consciousness soul; the gaze of human beings is drawn away and turned upon the physical world. Everything that happens in this direction withdraws humanity from the luciferic powers attempting to mislead it.

At this time, Michael is already active for humanity from the spiritual world. He prepares his later work from out of the suprasensory. He gives humanity impulses which preserve the former relation to the divine-spiritual world without this preservation adopting a luciferic character.

Then, in the last third of the nineteenth century, Michael himself comes forward into the physical earthly world with the preparatory activity he had practiced from the suprasensory realm from the fifteenth to the nineteenth century.

Humanity had to undergo a certain period of spiritual development for the purpose of freeing itself from the relation to the spiritual world which threatened to become untenable. Then the development was guided, through the mission of Michael, into paths which brought the progression of earthly humanity once more into a healing relation to the spiritual world.

So steht Michael in seinem Wirken zwischen dem luziferischen *Weltbild* und dem ahrimanischen *Weltverstand.* Das Weltbild wird bei ihm weisheitsvolle *Weltoffenbarung*, die den Weltverstand als göttliches *Weltenwirken* enthüllt. In diesem *Weltenwirken* lebt des Christus Sorge für die Menschheit, das so aus Michaels *Weltoffenbarung* dem Menschenherzen sich enthüllen kann.

(Die zweite und dritte Betrachtung folgen.)

Thus Michael stands in his activity between the luciferic *world-image* and the ahrimanic *world-intellect*. Through him, the world-image becomes a *world-revelation* full of wisdom, which reveals the world-intellect as divine *world-working*. And in this *world-working* lives Christ's concern for humanity, which can thus reveal itself to the human heart out of Michael's *world-revelation*.

(The second and third considerations will follow.)

Leitsätze Nr. 124 bis 126

124. Dem Aufgange des Bewusstseinszeitalters (fünfzehntes Jahrhundert) geht in der Abenddämmerung des Zeitalters der Verstandes- oder Gemütsseele ein erhöhtes luziferisches Wirken voran, das auch noch in der neuen Epoche eine Zeitlang fortdauert.

125. Dieses luziferische Wirken möchte alte Formen des Bild-Vorstellens der Welt unrechtmäßig bewahren und den Menschen davon zurückhalten, das physische Weltdasein durch Intellektualität zu begreifen und sich in dieses hineinzuleben.

126. Michael verbindet sich mit dem Menschheitswirken, damit die selbstständige Intellektualität bei dem angestammten Göttlich-Geistigen verbleibe, doch nicht in luziferischer, sondern in rechtmäßiger Art.

Leading Thoughts 124 to 126

124. The dawn of the consciousness age in the fifteenth century was preceded, in the twilight of the intellectual- or mind-soul age, by a heightened luciferic activity, which continued for a certain time even into the new epoch.

125. This luciferic influence tried to preserve ancient forms of an image-like representation of the world in a wrongful way. Thus it tried to prevent the human being from understanding with intellectuality and entering with fullness of life into the physical existence of the world.

126. Michael connects himself with the activity of humanity so that the independent intellectuality may remain in connection with the divine-spiritual from which it stems – though not in a luciferic, but in a rightful way.

Zweite Betrachtung: Wie die Michael-Kräfte in die erste Entfaltung der Bewusstseinsseele wirken

Goetheanum, 30. November 1924

In der Zeit während des Einschlages der Bewusstseinsseele in die Erdenentwickelung der Menschheit war es für die Wesen der dem Erdendasein nächsten geistigen Welt schwierig, an die Menschheit heranzukommen. Die Erdenereignisse nehmen eine Form an, die zeigt, dass Verhältnisse ganz besonderer Art notwendig sind, um dem Geistigen den Weg in das physische Leben der Menschheit möglich zu machen. Aber es zeigt andererseits diese Form auch wieder in oftmals klärendster Art, wie das eine Geistige da, wo die Mächte der Vergangenheit *noch* wirken und die Mächte der Zukunft *schon* zu wirken beginnen, sich energisch gegen ein anderes Geistiges seinen Weg in das Erdenleben der Menschheit sucht.

Da entwickelt sich zwischen 1339 und 1453 ein mehr als hundertjähriger verwirrender Krieg zwischen Frankreich und England. In dieser von einer gewissen, der Menschenentfaltung ungünstigen geistigen Strömung herrührenden Verwirrung finden Ereignisse ihre Hemmungen, die schneller die Bewusstseinsseele in die Menschheit eingeführt hätten, wenn

Second Consideration: How the Michael Forces Work in the First Unfolding of the Consciousness Soul

Goetheanum, 30 November 1924

At the time when the consciousness soul was entering the earthly development of humanity, it was difficult for the beings of the spiritual world bordering this earthly existence to approach humanity. The form assumed by earthly events at that time proves that conditions of a very special kind were necessary in order to enable the spirit to find its way into the physical life of humanity. But this form shows another thing as well, and in a way that is often most illuminating. It shows how, at a point when the powers of the past are *still* effective and those of the future already *beginning* their activity, one spiritual influence tries to find its way into the earthly life of humanity in vigorous opposition to another.

Between 1339 and 1453 a chaotic war develops between France and England, spanning over a hundred years. In the chaos of this war, which was due to a certain spiritual current unfavorable to the unfolding of humanity, events which would otherwise have brought the consciousness soul into humanity more quickly were decisively hindered. *Chaucer* (who died in

die Hemmungen nicht dagewesen wären. *Chaucer* (der 1400 gestorben ist) hat die englische Literatur begründet. Man braucht nur daran zu denken, was von dieser Literaturbegründung für geistige Folgen in Europa ausgegangen sind, und man wird es bedeutsam finden, dass das Ereignis nicht frei sich gestalten konnte, sondern dass es in eine Kriegsverwirrung hineinfiel. Dazu kommt, dass schon vorher (1215) in England dasjenige politische Denken begonnen hatte, das durch die Bewusstseinsseele seine rechte Ausprägung erhalten kann. Auch die weitere Entwickelung dieses Ereignisses fällt in die Kriegshemmungen hinein.

Man hat es da mit einer Zeit zu tun, in der die geistigen Kräfte, die den Menschen so entwickeln wollen, wie er von ihnen übergeordneten göttlich-geistigen Mächten von Anfang an veranlagt ist, ihre Widersacher finden. Diese Widersacher wollen den Menschen in andere Bahnen einlenken, als die ihm vom Anbeginne gewiesenen sind. Er würde dann die Kräfte seines Anfangs für seine spätere Entwickelung nicht anwenden können. Seine kosmische Kindheit bliebe für ihn unfruchtbar. Sie würde zum verdorrenden Teile seiner Wesenheit. Die Folge davon wäre, dass der Mensch die Beute der luziferischen oder ahrimanischen Mächte werden könnte und ihm seine selbsteigene Entfaltung entfiele. Hätten es die Menschheitswidersacher mit diesen ihren Bestrebungen nicht bloß bis zu Hemmungen, sondern bis zu einem vollen Erfolg

1400) laid the foundations of English literature. One need only remember the spiritual consequences which emanated into Europe from the founding of this literature, and one shall see the importance of the fact that such an event was not able to work itself out freely but fell into the midst of the confusions of a prolonged war. Moreover, as early as 1215, in England, there had begun the stream of political thought which can receive its true stamp and character through the consciousness soul. The further development of this event, too, occurred in the midst of all the hindrances of war.

This was a time when the spiritual forces, seeking to evolve the human being according to the potentialities laid in him from the very beginning by yet loftier divine-spiritual powers, encountered their strong adversaries. These adversaries wish to divert the human being into channels other than those appointed for him from the beginning. If they were to succeed, the human being would not be able to apply the forces of his origin to his further development. His cosmic childhood would remain unfruitful for him. It would become a dying, withering element within his being. The consequence would be that the human being could then fall prey to the luciferic or ahrimanic powers and lose to them his own unfolding. If the adversaries of humanity had succeeded in their efforts – if they had not only put hindrances in the way, but achieved

gebracht, so hätte der Einschlag der Bewusstseinsseele unterbunden werden können.

Ein Ereignis, in dem das Einströmen des Geistigen in die Erdenereignisse besonders hell leuchtend sich offenbart, ist das Auftreten und Schicksal der Jeanne d'Arc, der Jungfrau von Orleans (1412 – 1431). Was sie tut, hat für sie selbst die Impulse tief in den unterbewussten Untergründen der Seele. Sie folgt den dunklen Eingebungen der geistigen Welt. Auf der Erde herrscht Verwirrung, durch die das Bewusstseinszeitalter verhindert werden soll. Michael muss seine spätere Mission von der Geistwelt her vorbereiten. Er kann es da, wo seine Impulse in Menschenseelen aufgenommen werden. Die Jungfrau hat eine solche Seele. Er wirkt, wenn dies auch nur in minderem Grade möglich und für das äußere geschichtliche Leben weniger sichtbar ist, auch durch viele andere Seelen. In solchen Ereignissen, wie in dem Kriege zwischen England und Frankreich, findet er seine ahrimanische Gegnerschaft.

Von dem luziferischen Widersacher, den er in dieser Zeit gefunden hat, ist in der vorigen Betrachtung gesprochen. Aber dieser Widersacher zeigt sich ja auch ganz besonders darinnen, wie die Ereignisse sich abspielten, die dem Auftreten der Jungfrau von Orleans folgten. Man sieht an diesen Ereignissen, dass die Menschen keine Stellung mehr gewinnen konnten gegenüber einem Eingreifen der Geistwelt in die Geschicke der Menschheit, das begriffen und auch von den

complete success – then the entry of the consciousness soul could have been prevented.

An event which reveals the inpouring of the spiritual into the earthly events in a most clear and radiant way is the appearance and subsequent history of Joan of Arc, the Maid of Orleans (1412–1431). The impulses for what she does lie deep in the subconscious foundations of her soul. She follows dim inspirations from the spiritual world. On the earth there is confusion and disorder, through which the age of consciousness is to be hindered. Michael has to prepare from the spiritual world his later mission; this he is able to do where his impulses are received into human souls. Such a soul lives in the Maid of Orleans. And Michael also worked through many other souls, although this was possible only in a minor degree and is less apparent in outer historical life. In events such as the war between England and France, he met with opposition from his ahrimanic opposition.

In the previous consideration, the luciferic adversary was spoken of whom Michael found at the same time. And indeed, this adversary is particularly apparent in the course of events following upon the appearance of the Maid of Orleans. From these events, it may be seen that human beings no longer knew how to deal with an intervention of the spiritual world into the destiny of humanity. Previously, such an intervention could have been understood and also received by human

Menschen in ihren Willen aufgenommen werden konnte, als noch imaginatives Verstehen vorhanden war. Die Stellung zu solchem Eingreifen ist mit dem Aufhören des Wirkens der Verstandes- oder Gemütsseele unmöglich geworden; die Stellung, die der Bewusstseinsseele entspricht, war damals noch nicht gefunden; sie ist auch heute noch nicht errungen.

So ist es denn gekommen, dass damals die Gestaltung Europas von der geistigen Welt aus zustande gekommen ist, ohne dass die Menschen ein Verständnis für das hatten, was geschieht, und ohne dass, was sie vermochten, einen nennenswerten Einfluss auf diese Gestaltung hat haben können.

Man braucht ja nur sich vorzustellen, was im fünfzehnten Jahrhundert geschehen wäre, wenn es keine Jungfrau von Orleans gegeben hätte, und man wird die Bedeutung dieses aus dem Geiste bedingten Ereignisses wohl einsehen. – Es gibt ja auch Persönlichkeiten, die eine solche Erscheinung materialistisch erklären wollen. Mit ihnen ist eine Verständigung deshalb unmöglich, weil sie das offenbar Geistige im materialistischen Sinne willkürlich umprägen.

Deutlich zeigt sich nun auch in gewissen geistigen Bestrebungen der Menschheit, wie diese den Weg zum Göttlich-Geistigen nicht mehr ohne Schwierigkeiten findet, auch wenn sie ihn intensiv sucht. Es sind Schwierigkeiten, die in den Zeitaltern nicht vorhanden waren, in denen noch mit Imaginationen Einsicht geschaffen werden konnte. Man hat, um

beings into the will as long as imaginative understanding existed. The earlier stance toward such intervention became impossible when the intellectual- or mind-soul ceased to be effective; but at that time, the stance corresponding to the consciousness soul had not yet been discovered, nor has it yet been achieved even today.

Thus it came about that Europe was molded from the spiritual world without human beings understanding what was happening, and without what they were able to do having any appreciable influence on this process.

The significance of this event, the determining causes of which lay in the spiritual world, will be perceived if one tries to imagine what would have happened in the fifteenth century had there been no Maid of Orleans. – There are some who wish to explain this phenomenon materialistically. It is impossible to come to an understanding with such people because they arbitrarily interpret in the materialistic sense something that is obviously spiritual.

In certain directions of spiritual striving, too, it is now clearly apparent that humanity can no longer find the way to the divine-spiritual without difficulty, even though human beings search intensively. There are difficulties which did not exist in the age when insight could still be gained with the aid of imaginations. In order to judge correctly what is here meant,

das hier Gemeinte richtig zu beurteilen, nur nötig, die als philosophische Denker auftretenden Persönlichkeiten im klaren Lichte zu sehen. Ein Philosoph kann nicht nach seiner Wirkung auf sein Zeitalter allein betrachtet werden, nicht darnach, wie viele Menschen seine Ideen aufgenommen haben. Er ist vielmehr der *Ausdruck*, die offenbare Wesenheit für sein Zeitalter. Was der große Teil der Menschheit unbewusst als Seelenverfassung, als unbewusste Gefühle und Lebensantriebe in sich trägt, das bringt der Philosoph in seine Ideen. Er zeigt, wie das Thermometer den Wärmezustand seiner Umgebung, so den Seelenzustand seines Zeitalters an. Die Philosophen sind ebenso wenig die Ursachen der Seelenverfassung ihrer Zeitalter wie die Thermometer die der Wärmeverfassung ihrer Umgebung.

Man sehe unter diesen Voraussetzungen auf den Philosophen *René Descartes*, der wirkte, als das Bewusstseinszeitalter schon im Gange war. (Er lebte 1596 bis 1650.) Die schmale Stütze seiner Verbindung mit der Geistwelt (dem wahren Sein) ist das Erlebnis «Ich denke, also bin ich.». Im Zentrum des Selbstbewusstseins, des Ich, sucht er die Realität zu empfinden; und zwar nur so viel, als ihm die Bewusstseinsseele sagen kann.

Und über alles übrige Geistige sucht er auf dem intellektualistischen Wege sich klar zu werden, indem er untersucht, wie viel Bürgschaft die Gewissheit des eigenen Selbstbewusstseins über die Gewissheit von anderem gibt. Er fragt überall

it is only necessary to see in a clear light those individuals who come forward as philosophical thinkers. A philosopher cannot be judged by his effect on his age alone, nor by observing how many people have accepted his ideas. He is rather the *expression*, the revealed essential being of his age. The philosopher presents in his ideas what the greater part of humanity bears within it as its frame of mind, unconscious feelings, and impulses of life. Like a thermometer which registers the degree of the surrounding warmth, he registers the condition of soul of his age. The philosophers are no more the causes of the soul-state of their age than the thermometer is the cause of the surrounding temperature.

Consider, from this point of view, the philosopher *René Descartes*, who worked when the age of consciousness had already begun. (He lived from 1596 to 1650.) The slender support for his connection with the world of spirit (the world of true Being) is the experience "I think, therefore I am." In the center of self-consciousness, in the 'I', he tries to feel reality; and indeed, only so much as the consciousness soul can tell him.

And he endeavors intellectually to understand everything else of the spiritual by inquiring what guarantee the certainty of his own self-consciousness provides for the certainty of anything else. Regarding the truths handed on to him historically,

gegenüber den Wahrheiten, die ihm geschichtlich überliefert sind: Sind sie so klar wie das «Ich denke, also bin ich.»? Und kann er das bejahen, so nimmt er sie an.

Ist bei einem solchen menschlichen Denken nicht aller Anschauung, die auf die Dinge der Welt orientiert ist, der Geist ausgetrieben? Die Offenbarung dieses Geistes hat sich auf die kleinste Stütze im Selbstbewusstsein zurückgezogen; alles andere erweist sich *unmittelbar* ohne Geistesoffenbarung. Es kann auf das außer dem Selbstbewusstsein Liegende nur mittelbar durch den Intellekt in der Bewusstseinsseele ein Licht dieser Geistesoffenbarung geworfen werden.

Der Mensch dieses Zeitalters lässt gewissermaßen den noch fast leeren Inhalt seiner Bewusstseinsseele in intensiver Sehnsucht nach der Geistwelt strömen. Ein dünner Strahl geht dahin.

Die Wesen der an die Erdenwelt unmittelbar angrenzenden Geistwelt und die Menschenseelen auf Erden kommen schwer zueinander. Michaels übersinnliche Vorbereitung seiner späteren Mission wird nur unter den größten Hemmungen von der Menschenseele miterlebt.

Man vergleiche, um das Wesen *der* Seelenstimmung zu erfassen, die in Descartes zum Ausdrucke kommt, diesen Philosophen mit Augustinus, der der äußeren Formulierung nach dieselbe Stütze für das Erleben der geistigen Welt geltend macht wie Descartes. Nur geschieht es bei Augustinus aus der vollen

he always inquires: Are they as clear as the "I think, therefore I am"? And if he can answer this in the affirmative, then he accepts them.

In this attitude of human thinking, is not the spirit eliminated from all observation oriented to the things of the world? The revelation of the spirit has withdrawn into the smallest support in self-consciousness; all else shows itself *immediately* to be void of spirit-revelation. Only indirectly – by the intellect in the consciousness soul – can the light of this spirit-revelation be thrown on what lies outside of self-consciousness.

The human being of this age allows the content of his consciousness soul, which is as yet almost empty, to stream toward the spiritual world with intense longing. A tiny ray goes forth in this direction.

The beings in the world of spirit immediately bordering upon the earthly world, and the human souls on earth, come to one another only with difficulty. Michael's suprasensory preparation for his later mission is experienced by the human soul only in the midst of the greatest hindrances.

In order to grasp the essential nature of *this* mood of soul expressed in Descartes, compare this philosopher with Augustine, who, in his outer formulation, sets up for the experience of the spiritual world the same support as Descartes. It is only that in Augustine, this takes place out of the full force of the

imaginativen Kraft der Verstandes- oder Gemütsseele. (Er lebte 354 bis 430.) Man findet Augustinus mit Descartes mit Recht verwandt. Nur ist der Intellekt des Augustinus noch der Rest des Kosmischen, der bei Descartes der schon in die einzelne Menschenseele einziehende. Gerade an dem Fortgang des Geistesstrebens von Augustinus zu Descartes kann man sehen, wie der kosmische Charakter der Gedankenkräfte sich verliert und wie dieser dann in der Menschenseele wieder auftritt. Man schaut aber zugleich, wie Michael und die Menschenseele unter Schwierigkeiten sich so zusammenfinden, dass Michael im Menschen leiten kann, was er einst im Kosmos geleitet hat.

Es sind gegen dieses Zusammenfinden die luziferischen und ahrimanischen Kräfte am Werke. Die luziferischen wollen am Menschen nur das zur Entfaltung kommen lassen, was ihm in seiner kosmischen Kindheit eigen war; die ahrimanischen als Gegner, und doch mit ihnen zusammenwirkend, möchten die in späteren Weltaltern erlangten Kräfte allein entwickeln und die kosmische Kindheit verdorren lassen.

Unter solchen gesteigerten Widerständen wurde von den Menschenseelen Europas das verarbeitet, was an geistigen Impulsen durch die Kreuzzüge an alten Weltanschauungsideen vom Osten nach dem Westen geströmt war. Die Michael-Kräfte lebten ja ganz stark in diesen Ideen. Die kosmische Intelligenz, deren Verwaltung das alte geistige Erbgut Michaels war, beherrschte diese Weltanschauungen.

intellectual- or mind-soul. Augustine (354–430) is justly found to be related to Descartes, but his intellect is still the remnant of what is cosmic – whereas the intellect of Descartes is already entering the individual human soul. In the progress of spiritual striving from Augustine to Descartes, it may be seen how the cosmic character of the forces of thought is lost, and how it then reappears in the human soul. But it can simultaneously be seen with what difficulty Michael and the human soul come together so that Michael may lead that element within the human being which he once led in the cosmos.

The luciferic and ahrimanic forces are at work to prevent this coming together. The luciferic forces want the human being to unfold only what was proper to him during his cosmic childhood; the ahrimanic forces, which are opposed to the luciferic and yet cooperate with them, would like to develop only those forces which were gained in later ages of the world, and so allow the human being's cosmic childhood to wither away.

Under increased forms of resistance such as these, the human souls in Europe handled the spiritual impulses contained in old world-conceptions which had streamed from the East to the West through the Crusades. The Michael-forces lived very strongly in these conceptions. The cosmic intelligence, the stewardship of which was the ancient spiritual heritage of Michael, was dominant in these old world-conceptions.

Wie konnten sie aufgenommen werden, da eine Kluft lag zwischen den Kräften der Geist-Welt und den Menschenseelen? Sie fielen in die erst leise werdende Bewusstseinsseele. Einerseits begegneten sie dem Hindernis, das in der noch schwach entwickelten Bewusstseinsseele gegeben war. Sie übertönten deren Wirksamkeit, lähmten sie. Aber andererseits auch auf ein noch von Imagination getragenes Bewusstsein stießen sie nicht mehr. Die Menschenseele konnte sie nicht mit voller Einsicht mit sich verbinden. Man nahm sie entweder ganz oberflächlich oder abergläubisch auf.

In diese Geistesverfassung muss geschaut werden, wenn die Gedankenbewegungen, die an Namen von Wicliff, Huß und andere einerseits, an die Bezeichnung «Rosenkreuzerwesen» andererseits sich anschließen, verstanden sein wollen.

Davon soll im Weiteren gesprochen werden.

(Die Fortsetzung dieser zweiten und die dritte Betrachtung folgen.)

How could they be received, seeing that there was a chasm separating the forces of the world of spirit from human souls? These forces entered into the gradually becoming consciousness-soul. On one side, they met with the hindrance given in the as yet weakly developed consciousness soul. They drowned out their effectiveness, paralyzed them. And on the other, they no longer found a consciousness supported by imagination. The human soul could not with full insight unite them with itself. They were accepted either quite superficially or superstitiously.

One must assume this state of mind if one wishes to understand the movements of thought connected on the one hand with the names of Wycliffe, Hus, and others, and on the other with the designation "Rosicrucianism."

This will be spoken of further in what follows.

(The continuation of the second consideration, as well as the third consideration, will follow.)

Leitsätze Nr. 127 bis 130

127. Die Menschenseele entwickelt im Beginne des Bewusstseinszeitalters noch in geringem Maße ihre intellektuellen Kräfte. Es entsteht eine Zusammenhanglosigkeit zwischen dem, was diese Seele in ihren unbewussten Untergründen ersehnt, und dem, was ihr die Kräfte aus der Region, in der Michael ist, geben können.

128. In dieser Zusammenhanglosigkeit besteht eine gesteigerte Möglichkeit für die luziferischen Mächte, den Menschen bei den kosmischen Kindheitskräften zurückzuhalten und ihn zur weiteren Entfaltung *nicht* auf den Wegen der göttlich-geistigen Mächte, mit denen er vom Anfang an verbunden war, sondern auf den luziferischen kommen zu lassen.

129. Es besteht die weitere gesteigerte Möglichkeit für die ahrimanischen Mächte, den Menschen von den kosmischen Kindheitskräften abzuschnüren und ihn für die weitere Entfaltung in ihren eigenen Bereich zu ziehen.

130. Beides ist nicht geschehen, weil die Michael-Kräfte *doch* tätig waren; aber die Geistesentwickelung der

Leading Thoughts 127 to 130

127. At the beginning of the consciousness age, the human being had evolved the intellectual forces of his soul only to a small extent. Hence, there arose a loss of connection between what the human soul longed for in unconscious depths, and what the forces from the region of Michael's abode could give him.

128. Owing to this loss of connection, there was a greater possibility for the luciferic powers to hold the human being back within the forces of cosmic childhood, thus bringing about his further unfolding *not* on the paths of the divine-spiritual powers with whom he was united from the beginning, but on those of Lucifer.

129. There came about the heightened possibility for the ahrimanic powers to wrest the human being away from the forces of his cosmic childhood, thus dragging him down, for his further unfolding, into their own domain.

130. Neither of these dangers was realized, for the forces of Michael were *nevertheless* at work. But the spiritual

Menschheit musste unter den durch diese Möglichkeiten entstandenen Hemmungen geschehen und wurde *dadurch*, was sie bis jetzt geworden ist.

development of humanity would need to take place in the midst of the resulting hindrances, and became *through this* what it has become so far.

Fortsetzung der zweiten Betrachtung: Hemmung und Förderung der Michael-Kräfte im aufkommenden Zeitalter der Bewusstseinsseele

Goetheanum, 6. Dezember 1924

Die Einverleibung der Bewusstseinsseele bewirkte durch ganz Europa hindurch auch eine Störung in den religiösen Bekenntnis- wie in den Kulterlebnissen. Man sieht um die Wende des elften und zwölften Jahrhunderts eine deutliche Ankündigung dieser Störung in dem Auftauchen des «Gottesbeweises» (besonders durch Anselm von Canterbury). Die Existenz Gottes sollte durch Verstandesgründe bewiesen werden. Eine solche Sehnsucht konnte nur eintreten, als die alte Art, «Gott» mit den Kräften seiner Seele zu erleben, im Schwinden war. Denn, was man so erlebt, das beweist man nicht logisch.

Die vorige Art war, die wesenhaften Intelligenzen – bis zur Gottheit hinauf – seelisch wahrzunehmen; die neue Art wurde die, auf intellektuelle Art über die «Urgründe» des Weltalls sich Gedanken auszubilden. Für die erstere Art hatte man in dem an den Erdbereich unmittelbar angrenzenden geistigen Bereich die Kräfte Michaels, welche die Seele hinter den auf das Sinnliche gerichteten Gedankenkräften mit Fähigkeiten ausrüsteten, das wesenhaft Intelligente im Weltall

Continuation of the Second Consideration: Hindrances and Helps to the Michael Forces at the Dawn of the Consciousness-Soul Age

Goetheanum, 6 December 1924

Throughout Europe, the embodiment of the consciousness soul brought about a disturbance in the experiences of religious faith and ritual. A clear sign of the coming disturbance may be seen around the turn of the eleventh and twelfth centuries in the arising of the "Proofs of God" (especially in the work of Anselm of Canterbury). The existence of God was now to be proven by intellectual reasoning. Such a longing could only arise when the old way of experiencing "God" with the forces of the soul was on the wane. For what one experiences in this way does not need to proven logically.

The old way was to perceive the essential intelligences – up to the Godhead – with one's inner soul. The new way, arising at this time, was to evolve intellectual thoughts about the "primal foundations" of the universe. The former way was supported by the forces of Michael in the spiritual realm immediately bordering the earth. Behind the thought-forces directed to the things of outer sense, the forces of Michael equipped the soul with faculties to perceive the essential intelligence in

wahrzunehmen; für die zweite Art musste erst der Zusammenschluss der Seele mit den Michael-Kräften ausgebildet werden.

Im Kultgebiet kam von Wiclif in England (vierzehntes Jahrhundert) bis zu Hus in Böhmen auf weiten Bereichen menschlichen religiösen Erlebens eine solche Mittelpunktslehre wie die Abendmahlslehre ins Wanken. Im Abendmahl konnte der Mensch seine Verbindung mit der Geistwelt finden, die ihm durch Christus eröffnet war, denn er konnte mit dem Christus in seiner Wesenheit sich so vereinigen, dass die Tatsache der sinnlichen Vereinigung zugleich eine geistige war.

Vorstellen konnte das Bewusstsein der Verstandes- oder Gemütsseele diese Vereinigung. Denn diese Seele hatte sowohl von dem Geiste wie von der Materie noch Ideen, die sich nahe standen, sodass die eine (Materie) in den anderen (Geist) im Übergange gedacht werden konnte. Solche Ideen dürfen aber nicht solch intellektualistische sein, die auch Beweise für das Dasein Gottes verlangen; es müssen solche sein, die noch etwas von der Imagination haben. Dadurch wird in der Materie der in ihr tätige Geist, in dem Geiste das Streben nach der Materie empfunden. Ideen *dieser* Art haben hinter sich die kosmischen Kräfte Michaels.

Man bedenke nur, *wie viel* in dieser Zeit für die Menschenseele ins Wanken kam! Wie viel von dem, was mit ihrem

the universe. On the other hand, for the second way to find its fulfillment, the inner union of the soul with the forces of Michael would first need to be developed.

In the realm of religious ritual, even the central doctrine of the Holy Communion began to be shaken. This happened in far-spread regions of the human religious experience, from Wycliffe in England (fourteenth century) to Hus in Bohemia. In Holy Communion, the human being was able to find his connection with the spirit world which was opened up to him through Christ. For he was able to unite with Christ in his being to such an extent that the fact of the outer sensory union was at the same time a spiritual fact.

The consciousness of the intellectual- or mind-soul was able to form a representation of this union. For this soul still possessed ideas of both spirit and matter that stood near to one another – thus it was possible for it to conceive of the one (matter) passing over into the other (spirit). Ideas of this kind, however, cannot possibly be so intellectualistic as to even require proofs of God's existence; these ideas must be such that they still contain something of imagination. Thereby, in matter, the spirit active in it will be felt; and in the spirit, the striving toward matter. Ideas of *this* nature have the cosmic forces of Michael behind them.

Think only *how much* was beginning to totter for the human soul at that time: how much of what was connected with the

innersten heiligsten Erleben zusammenhing! Persönlichkeiten, in denen das Wesen der Bewusstseinsseele am hellsten aufstrahlte, die von einer Seelenverfassung waren, die sie mit den Michael-Kräften in einer Stärke verband, die für die anderen erst nach Jahrhunderten kommen sollte, Huß, Wicliff und andere, traten auf. Sie machten aus der Michael-Stimme in ihrem Herzen heraus das Recht der Bewusstseinsseele geltend, sich aufzuschwingen zum Ergreifen der tiefsten religiösen Geheimnisse. Sie fühlten: Die Intellektualität, die mit der Bewusstseinsseele heraufzog, muss fähig sein, in den Bereich ihrer Ideen das einzubeziehen, was in alten Zeiten durch Imagination zu erreichen war.

Demgegenüber stand, dass die alte, geschichtlich überbrachte Stellung der Menschenseele in den weitesten Kreisen alle innere Kraft verloren hatte. Was man in der Geschichte die Übelstände des Bekenntnislebens nennt, womit sich die großen Reformkonzilien in dem Zeitalter der beginnenden Wirksamkeit der Bewusstseinsseele beschäftigten, das hängt alles mit dem Leben derjenigen Menschenseelen zusammen, die in sich die Bewusstseinsseele noch nicht fühlten, aber die in der überkommenen Verstandes- oder Gemütsseele auch nicht mehr etwas haben konnten, das ihnen innere Kraft und Sicherheit gab.

Man kann wirklich sagen, solche geschichtlichen menschlichen Erlebnisse, wie sie auf den Konzilien zu Konstanz, zu

human being's innermost and holiest experience! Personalities arose – Hus, Wycliffe, and others – in whom the existence of the consciousness soul shone forth most radiantly. Their inner state of soul was such as to unite them with the Michael forces with an intensity that would not come for others until centuries later. From the voice of Michael in their hearts, they proclaimed the worthiness of the consciousness soul to rise to the conception and comprehension of the deepest religious mysteries. They felt that the intellectuality which was coming with the consciousness soul must be able to include in the realm of its ideas what had been attainable, in older times, by imagination.

On the other hand, the historical and traditional stance of the human soul toward these things had in very wide circles lost all its inner force and strength. What history refers to as the evils and abuses of religious life, which were dealt with by the great Councils of the Reformation in the age when the consciousness soul was beginning its activity – all this is connected with the life of those human souls who, not yet feeling the consciousness soul within them, were on the other hand no longer able to find in the old intellectual- or mind-soul a sufficient source of inner strength or certainty.

Historical experiences of human beings, such as were laid bare at the Councils of Constance and Basel, may be said to

Basel zutage traten, zeigen oben in der Geistwelt das Herabströmen der Intellektualität, die zu den Menschen will, und unten den Erdbereich mit der nicht mehr der Zeit entsprechenden Verstandes- oder Gemütsseele. Dazwischen schweben die Michael-Kräfte, zurückblickend auf ihre vergangene Verbindung mit dem Göttlich-Geistigen und hinunterblickend nach dem Menschlichen, das ebenso diese Verbindung hatte, das aber jetzt in eine Sphäre übergehen musste, in der ihm Michael vom Geiste aus helfen soll, das er aber selbst innerlich nicht mit sich vereinigen soll. In diesem Bestreben Michaels, das in der kosmischen Entwickelung *notwendig* ist, das aber zunächst doch eine Störung des Gleichgewichts im Kosmos bedeutet, liegt begründet, was die Menschheit in diesem Zeitalter auch in Bezug auf die heiligsten Wahrheiten erleben musste.

Man schaut tief in das Charakteristische dieser Zeit hinein, wenn man den Kardinal Nicolaus Cusanus ins Auge fasst. (Man lese über ihn in meinem Buche *Die Mystik im Aufgange des neuzeitlichen Geisteslebens.*) Seine Persönlichkeit ist wie eine Merksäule der Zeit. Er möchte Ansichten zur allgemeinen Geltung bringen, die die Missstände der physischen Welt nicht in schwarm-geistigen Tendenzen bekämpfen, sondern durch den gesunden Menschensinn das, was aus dem Geleise gekommen ist, wieder in dieses zurückführen. Man sehe sein Wirken auf dem Basler Konzil und auch sonst

reveal the following: In the spiritual world above, the down-pouring of the intellectuality sought to find its way to human beings; and in the earthly realm below, the working of the intellectual- or mind-soul was no longer in accordance with the time. The Michael forces hover between looking back to their own past union with the divine-spiritual, and looking down upon the human realm. The human realm likewise enjoyed the same union in the past, but it must now pass into a sphere in which Michael will help it from the spirit, though he is not to unite his own inner being with this realm. Absolutely *necessary* as it is in cosmic development – yet signifying, to begin with, a disturbance in the balance of the cosmos – this striving of Michael underlies what humanity had to experience in that age even with respect to the most sacred truths.

One gazes deeply into the characteristic features of that age when one turns one's thoughts to Cardinal Nicholas of Cusa. (One can read about him in my book *Mystics at the Dawn of the Modern Age*.) His personality is like an outstanding monument of time. He wanted to further general acceptance of an outlook which – instead of fighting the deficiencies of the physical world with effusive-spiritual tendencies – would attempt to meet them with healthy common-sense, seeking to restore to the proper track what has been diverted from it. One can see this tendency in the influence he brought to bear

innerhalb seiner kirchlichen Gemeinschaft; und man wird dieses bemerken.

Ist der Cusaner damit dem Umschwung der Entwickelung mit der Entfaltung der Bewusstseinsseele voll zugeneigt, so sieht man ihn andererseits Anschauungen offenbaren, die Michaels Kräfte in leuchtender Art an sich zeigen. Er stellt in seine Zeit die guten alten Ideen hinein, die den Menschenseelensinn zur Entfaltung von Fähigkeiten für das Wahrnehmen der wesenhaften Intelligenzen im Kosmos führten, als Michael noch die Welt-Intellektualität verwaltete. Die «gelehrte Unwissenheit», von der er spricht, ist ein über dem auf die Sinneswelt gerichteten Wahrnehmen gelegenes Begreifen, das das Denken über die Intellektualität – das gewöhnliche Wissen – hinaus in eine Region führt, wo – im Unwissen – dafür aber im erlebenden Schauen das Geistige erfasst wird.

So ist der Cusaner diejenige Persönlichkeit, die in dem eigenen Seelenleben die Störung des kosmischen Gleichgewichtes durch Michael empfindend intuitiv möglichst viel dazu beitragen möchte, dass diese Störung zum Heile der Menschheit hin orientiert werde.

Zwischen dem, was auf diese Art geistig zutage trat, lebte im Verborgenen ein anderes. Einzelne Persönlichkeiten, die Sinn und Verständnis für die Stellung der Michael-Kräfte im

at the Council of Basel and generally within his ecclesiastical community.

Thus, Nicholas of Cusa is fully inclined toward the great change in development which comes with the unfolding of the consciousness soul. On the other hand, he brings forth thoughts and ideas which reveal in a most radiant way the working of Michael's forces within them. Into the midst of his age he places the good ideas of older times which, in the epoch when Michael still ruled the cosmic intellectuality, led the human soul to the unfolding of faculties enabling perception of the essential intelligences in the cosmos. The "learned ignorance" of which he speaks is a perception over and above what is directed to the sensory world – a perception which leads the human being's thinking beyond the intellectuality of ordinary understanding and into a region where, in ignorance or emptiness of knowledge, the spiritual is taken hold of in the experience of seeing.

Thus Nicholas of Cusa is a personality who, feeling in his own soul-life the disturbance of the cosmic balance through Michael, would like intuitively to contribute as much as possible toward the turning of this disturbance to the welfare of humanity.

Among the matters of spiritual life that came to light in this way, there lived something else which remained hidden. Individual personalities who perceived and understood the position

Weltenall hatten, wollten die Kräfte ihrer Seele so zubereiten, dass sie den bewussten Zugang zu dem an den Erdbereich angrenzenden Geistbereich fanden, in dem Michael seine Anstrengungen für die Menschheit macht.

Sie suchten, sich die Berechtigung zu diesem geistigen Unterfangen dadurch zu erwerben, dass sie äußerlich im Leben beruflich und auch sonst sich so verhielten, dass ihr Dasein von dem anderer Menschen nicht zu unterscheiden war. Dadurch, dass sie so gegen das Irdische im ganz gewöhnlichen Sinne ihre Pflichten in Liebe vollführten, konnten sie das Innere ihres Menschentums frei dem gekennzeichneten Geistigen zuwenden. Was sie nach dieser Richtung taten, war ihre und derjenigen Sache, mit denen sie sich «im Geheimen» verbanden. Die Welt wurde mit Bezug auf das, was im Physischen geschah, zunächst scheinbar gar nicht von diesem Geiststreben berührt. Doch war dies alles notwendig, um die Seelen in die nötige Verbindung mit der Michael-Welt zu bringen. Es handelte sich nicht um «Geheimgesellschaften» in irgendeinem schlimmen Sinne, nicht um irgendetwas, das das Verborgene aufsucht, weil es das Licht des Tages scheut. Es handelte sich vielmehr um das Zusammenfinden von Menschen, die in diesem Zusammenfinden sich überzeugen, dass, wer zu ihnen gehört, ein rechtes Bewusstsein der Michael-Mission hat. Die so Zusammenarbeitenden sprechen dann nicht von ihrer Arbeit vor

of the Michael-forces in the universe wished to prepare the forces of their own souls in such a way that they might consciously enter the spirit-realm bordering upon the earthly realm – the realm in which Michael makes his efforts on behalf of humanity.

They sought justification for this spiritual enterprise by conducting themselves outwardly in life, in their calling and in other circumstances, in such a way that their life could not be distinguished from that of other human beings. By lovingly performing their earthly duties in the ordinary sense, they were able to turn their inner humanity freely toward the spiritual which has been described. What they did in this direction was a matter concerning only those thus "secretly" united. As regards what took place in the physical realm, the world was at first apparently quite unaffected by this spiritual striving. And yet all this was needed in order to bring souls into the necessary union with the Michael-world. It was not a question of "secret societies" in any bad sense, or of anything that seeks out concealment because it fears the light of day. Rather, it was a matter of persons coming together and, in so doing, coming to the conviction that those belonging to this circle had a right understanding of the Michael-mission. Those who thus worked together did not speak of their work in the presence of others who, through lack of understanding, could only have disturbed the aims they had set themselves.

denen, die durch Verständnislosigkeit nur ihre Aufgaben stören könnten. Diese Aufgaben lagen ja zunächst in dem Wirken in Geistesströmungen, die nicht innerhalb des irdischen Lebens verlaufen, sondern in der angrenzenden Geist-Welt, die aber in das irdische Leben ihre Impulse hineinwerfen.

Es ist damit auf die Geist-Arbeit von Menschen verwiesen, die innerhalb der physischen Welt stehen; aber die mit Wesen der Geist-Welt zusammenwirken; mit Wesen, die selbst nicht die physische Welt betreten, sich nicht in derselben verkörpern. Was – recht wenig tatsachengemäß – als die «Rosenkreuzer» vor der Welt genannt wird, darauf ist hier verwiesen. Das wahre Rosenkreuzertum liegt durchaus in der Linie der Wirksamkeit der Michael-Mission. Es half Michael, auf der Erde vorzubereiten, was er als seine Geistarbeit für ein späteres Zeitalter vorbereiten wollte.

Was damit geschehen konnte, wird man ermessen, wenn man den Sinn auf das Folgende lenkt.

Die Schwierigkeiten, ja, Unmöglichkeiten Michaels, in Menschenseelen hineinzuwirken, die charakterisiert worden sind, hängen damit zusammen, dass er selbst mit seinem Wesen in keinerlei Berührung mit der physischen Gegenwart des Erdenlebens kommen will. Er will in den Kräftezusammenhängen verbleiben, die für Geister seiner Art und für Menschen *in der Vergangenheit* bestanden haben. Jede Berührung mit dem, womit als im gegenwärtigen physischen Erdenleben

These aims consisted primarily in working in spiritual streams which flow, not within earthly life, but in the world of spirit bordering it, but which nevertheless cast their impulses into earthly life.

This gives an indication of the spirit-work of human beings who, while living in the physical world, cooperate with beings of the world of spirit – beings who do not themselves enter the physical world or incarnate in it. Here reference is being made to those who, with very little reference to the facts, are known to the world as the "Rosicrucians." True Rosicrucianism lies thoroughly in line with the influence and intentions of the Michael mission. It helped Michael to prepare on earth the spirit-work that he wished to arrange for a later age.

One shall be able to estimate just *what* could be achieved thereby if one considers the following.

The above-described difficulties – indeed, impossibilities – for Michael to work into human souls, are connected with the fact that Michael himself, in his essential being, does not wish to come in contact in any way with the physical present of earthly life. He wishes to remain in the nexus of forces which existed for spirits of his kind, and for human beings, *in the past*. Any contact with what, in present earthly life, the human being is *obliged* to come in contact with – this Michael *could only*

der Mensch in Berührung kommen *muss*, *könnte* Michael nur als eine Verunreinigung seiner Wesenheit betrachten. Nun wirkt ja im gewöhnlichen Menschenleben das geistige Erleben der Seele in das physische Erdenleben herein und umgekehrt, dieses wirkt auf jenes zurück. Ein Zurückwirken, das sich namentlich in der Stimmung des Menschen und in der Orientierung auf irgendetwas Irdisches hin zum Ausdruck bringt. Ein derartiges Ineinanderwirken ist in der Regel – nicht immer – insbesondere bei den Persönlichkeiten der Fall, die in der Öffentlichkeit stehen. Daher waren die Hemmungen für Michaels Wirken bei manchen Reformatoren wirklich sehr groß.

Das Schwierige von dieser Seite bezwangen die Rosenkreuzer dadurch, dass sie ihr äußeres Leben im Sinne der Erdenpflichten ganz abseits hielten von ihrem Arbeiten mit Michael. Wenn dieser mit seinen Impulsen auf das aufstieß, was ein Rosenkreuzer in seiner Seele für ihn zubereitete, so fand er sich in keiner Weise der Gefahr ausgesetzt, auf Irdisches aufzutreffen. Denn dies ward ja eben von dem, was den Rosenkreuzer mit Michael verband, durch die besonders hergestellte Seelenverfassung ferngehalten.

Dadurch bildete *für Michael* das echte Rosenkreuzerwollen den auf der Erde befindlichen Weg zu *seiner* kommenden Erden-Mission.

(Die dritte Betrachtung folgt.)

consider as an impurity of his being. Now in ordinary human life, the spiritual experience of the soul works into the physical earthly life; and conversely, the latter works back upon the former. It is a reaction which is expressed in particular in the human being's mood and in his orientation toward this or that earthly thing. An interaction of this kind as a rule comes about – though not invariably – especially in persons engaged in public life. Hence, the hindrances to Michael's work were very great in the case of many of the Reformers.

The Rosicrucians overcame the difficulty in this direction by keeping their external life – which consisted of their earthly duties – quite apart from their work with Michael. When Michael, together with his impulses, came in contact with what a Rosicrucian prepared in his soul for him, Michael found himself in no way exposed to the danger of meeting what was earthly. For through the state of soul which the Rosicrucian intentionally cultivated, anything earthly was kept away from what united him with Michael.

In this way, true Rosicrucian striving formed *for Michael* the path here on the earth toward *his* coming earthly mission.

(The third consideration will follow.)

Leitsätze Nr. 131 bis 133

131. Im beginnenden Zeitalter der Bewusstseinsseele will sich die im Menschen emanzipierte Intellektualität mit den Bekenntnis- und Kultuswahrheiten beschäftigen. Das menschliche Seelenleben muss dadurch ein Schwanken erleben. Man will Wesenhaftes, das vorher seelisch erlebt worden ist, logisch beweisen. Man will Kultusinhalte, die in Imaginationen ergriffen werden müssen, mit der logischen Schlussfolgerung ergreifen; ja, sie nach dieser gestalten.

132. Das alles ist damit zusammenhängend, dass *Michael* unter allen Umständen jede Berührung mit der gegenwärtigen Erdenwelt, die der *Mensch* betreten *muss*, vermeiden will, dass er aber dennoch die kosmische Intellektualität, die er in der Vergangenheit verwaltet hat, weiter im Menschen geleiten soll. Dadurch entsteht durch die Michael-Kräfte eine dem Fortgang der Welt-Entwickelung *notwendige* Störung des kosmischen Gleichgewichtes.

133. Erleichtert wird Michael dadurch seine Mission, dass gewisse Persönlichkeiten – die echten Rosenkreuzer – ihr äußeres Erdenleben so einrichten, dass es mit gar

Leading Thoughts 131 to 133

131. In the beginning of the consciousness-soul age, the now-emancipated human intellectuality wanted to occupy itself with the truths of religious faith and ritual. The life of the human soul was thereby brought into instability. Human beings tried by logic to prove essential realities that were formerly a direct experience within the soul. They tried to grasp, indeed even to fashion by logical deduction, the content of sacred ritual which can only be taken hold of in imaginations.

132. All of this is connected with the fact that *Michael* is determined to avoid any kind of contact with the present earthly world, which *the human being must* enter – but that it is still his task to continue to guide the cosmic intellectuality, which he had ruled in ages past, within the human being. Thus there arises through the Michael-forces a disturbance in the cosmic balance, though one that is *necessary* for the further progress of world-development.

133. Michael's mission is made easier for him by certain personalities – the genuine Rosicrucians – who arranged their outward life on earth so that it in no way interfered

nichts in ihr inneres Seelenleben hineinwirkt. Sie können dadurch in ihrem Innern Kräfte ausbilden, durch die sie im Geistigen mit Michael zusammenwirken, ohne dass dieser in die Gefahr kommt, in das gegenwärtige Erdengeschehen verstrickt zu werden, was ihm unmöglich wäre.

with their inner soul-life. They could thus develop forces within themselves whereby they work together in spiritual realms with Michael without the danger of entangling him in present earthly happenings, which would be impossible for him.

Dritte Betrachtung: Michaels Leid über die Menschheitsentwicklung vor der Zeit seiner Erdenwirksamkeit

Goetheanum, 14. Dezember 1924

Im weiteren Fortschritt des Bewusstseinszeitalters hört immer mehr die Möglichkeit der Verbindung Michaels mit der allgemeinen Menschenwesenheit auf. In dieser hält die vermenschlichte Intellektualität ihren Einzug. Aus dieser schwinden imaginative Vorstellungen, die wesenhafte Intelligenz im Kosmos dem Menschen zeigen können. Für Michael beginnt die Möglichkeit, an den Menschen heranzukommen, erst mit dem letzten Drittel des neunzehnten Jahrhunderts. Vorher kann es nur auf solchen Wegen geschehen, die als die echt rosenkreuzerischen gesucht werden.

Der Mensch sieht mit seinem aufkeimenden Intellekt in die Natur. Er sieht dann eine physische, eine Ätherwelt, in denen er nicht drinnen ist. Er gewinnt durch die großen Ideen der Kopernikus, Galilei ein Bild der außermenschlichen Welt; aber er verliert sein eigenes. Er sieht auf sich selbst und hat keine Möglichkeit, zu einer Einsicht darüber zu kommen, *was* er ist.

In den Tiefen seines Wesens wird das in ihm erweckt, was seine Intelligenz zu tragen bestimmt ist. Mit dem verbindet

Third Consideration: Michael's Suffering over Human Development before the Time of His Earthly Activity

Goetheanum, 14 December 1924

As the new age of the consciousness soul proceeds, it grows less and less possible for Michael to connect himself with the overall being of humanity. In this situation, the humanized intellectuality makes its entrance into the being of humanity. The imaginative representations which could reveal to humanity the essential intelligence of the cosmos are now vanishing. The possibility for Michael himself to approach the human being begins only with the last third of the nineteenth century. Before that time, it was only possible upon those paths which were sought for in the true Rosicrucian sense.

With his own budding intellectuality, the human being looks out into nature. He sees there a physical and etheric world, of which he himself is not a part. Through the great ideas of personalities such as Copernicus and Galileo, he attains an image of the world beyond the human realm; but he loses the image of himself. When he gazes upon himself, he has no possibility of reaching any insight as to *what* he truly is.

In the depths of his being, that which is destined to bear and sustain his intelligence is being awakened in him. His 'I'

sich sein Ich. So trägt jetzt der Mensch ein Dreifaches in sich. Erstens: in seinem Geist-Seelenwesen als physisch-ätherisch erscheinend *das*, was ihn einstmals, schon in Saturn- und Sonnenzeit und dann immer wieder, in das Reich des Göttlich-Geistigen gestellt hat. Es ist dasjenige, wo Menschenwesen und Michaelwesen zusammengehen können. Zweitens trägt der Mensch in sich sein späteres physisches und ätherisches Wesen. Dasjenige, was ihm während Monden- und Erdenzeiten geworden ist. Das ist alles Werk und Wirksamkeit des Göttlich-Geistigen; aber dieses ist selbst darinnen nicht mehr lebendig anwesend.

Es wird erst wieder voll lebendig anwesend, als der Christus durch das Mysterium von Golgatha schreitet. In dem, was geistig in dem physischen und ätherischen Leib des Menschen wirkt, kann der Christus gefunden werden. Drittens hat der Mensch in sich denjenigen Teil seines Geistig-Seelischen, der in Monden- und Erdenzeiten neues Wesen angenommen hat. In diesem ist Michael tätig geblieben, während er in dem Mond und Erde zugewandten immer untätiger geworden ist. In diesem hat *er* dem Menschen sein Menschen-Götterbild erhalten.

Das konnte er bis zum Aufgange des Bewusstseinszeitalters. Dann versank gewissermaßen das gesamte Geistig-Seelische des Menschen in das Physisch-Ätherische, um daraus die Bewusstseinsseele zu holen.

becomes united with this. Thus, the human being now bears a threefold nature within him. First, in his spiritual-soul being, manifesting as the physical-etheric element: *that component* which once originated in the Old Saturn and Old Sun epochs and then ever and again placed him within the realm of the divine-spiritual. It is here that the human being and the Michael being can unite. Secondly, the human being bears within him his later physical and etheric nature: that which evolved in him during the Old Moon and Earth epochs. All this is the accomplished work and active working of the divine-spiritual. But the divine-spiritual itself is no longer livingly present within it.

It only becomes fully livingly present once more when Christ passes through the Mystery of Golgotha. In what is at work spiritually in the human physical and etheric body, Christ can indeed be found. Thirdly, the human being has within him that part of his spiritual-soul element which received new being in the Moon and Earth epochs. In this element Michael has remained active – whereas in that which inclines toward the Moon and Earth epochs, he has become increasingly inactive. In the former, *Michael* has preserved, for the human being, his human-divine image.

He was able to do this until the dawn of the consciousness-soul age. Then the entire spiritual-soul element of the human being sank down, as it were, entirely into the physical-etheric in order from there to draw forth the consciousness soul.

Dem Menschen stieg leuchtend im Bewusstsein auf, was ihm sein physischer Leib und sein ätherischer Leib über Physisches und Ätherisches in der Natur sagen konnten. Es versank vor seinem Schauen, was ihm astralischer Leib und Ich über sich selbst sagen konnten.

Eine Zeit steigt herauf, in der in der Menschheit das Gefühl auflebt, sie komme mit ihrer Einsicht nicht mehr an sich selbst heran. Ein *Suchen* nach der Erkenntnis der Menschenwesenheit beginnt. Man kann dieses nicht befriedigen durch das, was die Gegenwart vermag. Man geht historisch in frühere Zeiten zurück. Der Humanismus steigt in der Geistesentwickelung auf. Humanismus erstrebt man nicht, weil man den Menschen hat, sondern weil man ihn *verloren* hat. Solange man ihn hatte, hätten *Erasmus von Rotterdam* und andere aus einer ganz anderen Seelennuance gewirkt, als aus dem, was ihnen der Humanismus war.

In *Faust* fand später Goethe eine Menschengestalt auf, die ganz und gar den Menschen verloren hatte.

Immer intensiver wird dieses Suchen nach «dem Menschen». Denn man hat nur die Wahl, sich abzustumpfen gegenüber dem Erfühlen des eigenen Wesens; oder die Sehnsucht nach ihm als ein Element der Seele zu entwickeln.

Radiantly there arose in the human being's consciousness what his physical and etheric bodies could tell him about the physical and etheric in the world of nature. And what his astral body and 'I' had been able to tell him about himself vanished away from his vision.

In the age now beginning, there arose in the human being the feeling that with his own insight he could no longer reach *himself*. Thus there began a *search* for knowledge of the human being. The human being could no longer find satisfaction for this quest in what the present was able to provide. He went back to earlier ages of history. Humanism arose in the development of spiritual life. Humanism became the object of human beings' striving, not because they had grasped the human being but because they had *lost* him. As long as they possessed this knowledge, *Erasmus of Rotterdam* and others would have worked from an inclination of soul quite different from anything that Humanism could give them.

At a later time, Goethe discovered in *Faust* a figure representing the human being who had completely lost hold of his humanness.

This search for "the human being" grows ever more intensive as time goes on. For one now has no other alternative: One must either make oneself blunt and insensitive as regards one's own being, or else the longing for it must grow forth as an essential element of one's soul life.

Bis in das neunzehnte Jahrhundert herein entwickeln die besten Menschen auf den verschiedensten Gebieten des europäischen Geisteslebens in verschiedenster Art Ideen – historische, naturwissenschaftliche, philosophische, mystische –, die ein Streben darstellen, in dem, was intellektualistisch gewordene Weltanschauung ist, den *Menschen* zu finden.

Renaissance, geistige Wiedergeburt, Humanismus hasten, ja, stürmen nach einer Geistigkeit in einer Richtung, in der sie *nicht* zu finden ist; Ohnmacht, Illusion, Betäubung – nach der Richtung, in der man sie suchen muss. Dabei überall der Durchbruch der Michael-Kräfte, in der Kunst, in der Erkenntnis, in den Menschen herein, nur noch nicht in die auflebenden Kräfte der Bewusstseinsseele. – Ein Schwanken des geistigen Lebens. Michael, alle Kräfte nach rückwärts in der kosmischen Entwickelung wendend, auf dass ihm Macht werde, den «Drachen» unter seinen Füßen im Gleichgewicht zu erhalten. Gerade unter diesen Machtanstrengungen Michaels entstehen die großen Schöpfungen der Renaissance. Aber sie sind noch eine Erneuerung des Verstandes- oder Gemütsseelenhaften durch Michael, nicht ein Wirken der neuen Seelenkräfte.

Man kann Michael voll Sorge schauen, ob er auch in der Lage sei, den «Drachen» auf die Dauer zu bekämpfen, wenn er wahrnimmt, wie die Menschen auf dem einen Gebiete aus dem neugewonnenen Naturbilde ein solches des Menschen

Right into the nineteenth century, the best minds in the spiritual life of Europe evolve ideas in the most varied fields and in the most unique ways – ideas historical, scientific, philosophical, mystical, all of which represent the striving to find the *human being* in what has now become an intellectualistic world-conception.

Renaissance, spiritual rebirth, Humanism: these are all striving restlessly – even tempestuously – for a spirituality in a direction in which it is *not* to be found. And, in the direction in which it should be sought, there is impotence, illusion, numbness. And yet everywhere – in art, in knowledge, in the human being himself – the Michael-forces are breaking through, though not as yet into the newly-growing forces of the consciousness soul. – It is a wavering of the spiritual life. Michael turns all his forces toward the past in cosmic development so that he may gain the power to hold the "dragon" in equilibrium under his feet. It is under these mighty exertions of Michael that the great creations of the Renaissance are born. Yet they still only represent a renewal, through Michael, of the intellectual- or mind-soul forces. They are not yet a working of the new soul-forces.

One can behold Michael filled with concern as to whether he will really be able to master the "dragon" in the long run, when he perceives human beings, in a particular sphere of thought, trying to gain an image of the human being out of the

gewinnen wollen. Michael sieht, wie die Natur beobachtet wird und wie man aus dem, was man «Naturgesetze» nennt, ein Menschenbild formen will. Er sieht, wie man sich vorstellt, diese Eigenschaft eines Tieres werde vollkommener, jene Organverbindung werde harmonischer, und dadurch «entstehe» der Mensch. Aber vor Michaels Geistesauge entsteht nicht «ein Mensch», weil, was in Vervollkommnung, in Harmonisierung gedacht wird, eben nur «gedacht» wird; niemand kann schauen, dass es auch in Wirklichkeit *wird*, weil das eben nirgends der Fall ist.

Und so leben die Menschen mit solchem Denken vom Menschen in wesenlosen Bildern, in Illusionen; sie jagen einem Menschenbilde nach, das sie nur glauben zu haben; aber in Wahrheit ist nichts in ihrem Gesichtsfelde. «Die Kraft der Geistessonne bescheinet ihre Seelen, Christus wirkt; aber sie können dessen noch nicht achten. Bewusstseinsseelenkraft waltet im Leibe; sie will noch nicht in die Seele.» So etwa kann man die Inspiration hören, die da Michael spricht aus banger Sorge. Ob denn nicht etwa die Illusionskraft in den Menschen dem «Drachen» so viel Macht geben werde, dass ihm – Michael – die Aufrechterhaltung des Gleichgewichts eine Unmöglichkeit sein werde.

Andere Persönlichkeiten suchen mit mehr innerlich-künstlerischer Kraft, die Natur mit dem Menschen in eins zu

newly-acquired image of nature. He sees how nature is observed, and how one then seeks to form an image of the human being from what one calls the "laws of nature." He sees human beings forming their conceptions: This animal quality becomes more perfect, that system of organs more harmonious, and the human being "originates." But before the spirit-gaze of Michael, there does not arise "a human being" – for what is thought out as being in a state of perfection, in a state of harmonization, is after all merely "thought out." No one can see that it also *is so* in reality, for it is precisely nowhere the case.

And so, with such conceptions about the human being, people live in images devoid of being, in illusions. They are forever chasing an image of the human being which they only believe that they have, while in real truth there is nothing in their field of vision. "The power of the spiritual sun shines upon their souls. Christ Himself works; but they are not yet able to perceive His presence. The power of the consciousness soul holds sway in the body; but it still does not want to enter into their souls." That is approximately the inspiration one can hear of what Michael, in great concern, speaks. Is it possible that the forces of illusion in the human being will give the "dragon" so much power that it will be impossible for Michael to maintain the balance?

Other personalities try with more inward artistic power to feel nature at one with the human being. Mighty are the words

empfinden. Gewaltig klingt das Wort, das Goethe gesprochen hat, als er Winckelmanns Wirken in einem schönen Buche charakterisierte: «Wenn die gesunde Natur des Menschen als ein Ganzes wirkt, wenn er sich in der Welt als in einem großen, schönen, würdigen und werten Ganzen fühlt, wenn das harmonische Behagen ihm ein reines, freies Entzücken gewährt, dann würde das Weltall, wenn es sich selbst empfinden könnte, als an sein Ziel gelangt, aufjauchzen und den Gipfel des eigenen Werdens und Wesens bewundern.» Was Lessing mit Feuergeistigkeit anregte, was in Herder den großen Weltblick beseelte: Es klingt in diesem Goethe-Wort. Und Goethes ganzes eigenes Schaffen ist wie allseitige Offenbarung dieses seines Wortes. Schiller hat in den *Ästhetischen Briefen* einen idealen Menschen geschildert, der so, wie es in diesem Worte klingt, das Weltall in sich trägt und es im sozialen Zusammenschluss mit anderen Menschen verwirklicht. Aber woher stammt *dieses* Menschenbild? Es leuchtet wie die Morgensonne über der Frühlingserde. Aber in die Menschenempfindung ist es aus der Betrachtung des griechischen Menschen eingezogen. Menschen hegten es mit starkem inneren Michael-Impuls; aber sie konnten diesen Impuls nur ausgestalten, indem sie den Seelenblick in die Vorzeit versenkten. Goethe empfand ja, indem er den «Menschen» erleben wollte, die stärksten Konflikte mit der Bewusstseinsseele. In Spinozas Philosophie suchte er ihn; während der italienischen Reise, als er in griechisches Wesen

with which Goethe described Winckelmann's work in a beautiful book: "When the healthy nature of the human being acts as a whole, when he feels himself in the world as in a great, beautiful, majestic, and worthy whole, when harmonious ease gives him pure, free delight – then would the universe, if it were conscious of itself, shout joyfully for having reached its goal, and marvel at the high point of its own development and being." What motivated Lessing with fiery spirit and ensouled Herder's wide outlook on the world rings out in these words of Goethe. And the whole of Goethe's own work is like a many-sided revelation of these his own words. In his *Aesthetic Letters*, Schiller has described an ideal human being who, in the sense related in the above words, bears the universe within himself and realizes it in social interaction with other human beings. But whence comes *this* image of the human being? It shines like the morning sun over the earth in spring. But it has entered into human feeling from consideration of the ancient Greeks. It arose in human beings with a strong inner Michael-impulse; but they could give form to this impulse only by turning the mind's eye to earlier times. When Goethe wished to experience the "human being," he felt himself in the greatest conflict with the consciousness soul. He sought for the truly human in Spinoza's philosophy; but only during his tour in Italy, when he studied the Greek character, did he feel that he had a glimpse of the truly human. He went

hineinblickte, glaubte er ihn erst recht zu ahnen. Er eilte von der Bewusstseinsseele, die in Spinoza strebt, doch zuletzt zur verglimmenden Verstandes- oder Gemütsseele. Er kann nur unbegrenzt viel von dieser in die Bewusstseinsseele in seiner umfassenden Naturanschauung herübertragen.

Ernst schaut Michael auch auf dieses Suchen nach dem Menschen. Was nach seinem Sinne ist, kommt ja wohl in die menschliche Geistesentwickelung hinein; es ist *der* Mensch, der einst das wesenhaft Intelligente geschaut hat, als es Michael noch aus dem Kosmos heraus verwaltet hat. Aber das müsste, wenn es nicht von der vergeistigten Kraft der Bewusstseinsseele erfasst würde, zuletzt Michaels Wirken entfallen und unter Luzifers Macht gelangen. Dass Luzifer in dem Schwanken der kosmisch-geistigen Gleichgewichtslage die Obermacht gewinnen könne, das ist die andere bange Sorge in dem Leben Michaels.

Michaels Vorbereitung seiner Mission für das Ende des neunzehnten Jahrhunderts strömt in kosmischer Tragik dahin. Unten auf Erden herrscht oft tiefste Befriedigung über das Wirken des Naturbildes; im Gebiete, da Michael wirkt, waltet Tragik über die Hemmnisse, die sich dem Einleben des Menschenbildes entgegenstellen.

Ehedem lebte in dem Strahlen der Sonne, in dem Schimmern der Morgenröte, in dem Funkeln der Sterne Michaels herbe, vergeistigte Liebe; jetzt hatte diese Liebe am stärksten

away finally from the consciousness soul, which strives upwards in Spinoza, to the intellectual- or mind-soul which was gradually dying out. However, with his far-reaching view of nature he was able to carry over an infinite amount from the mind soul into the consciousness soul.

Michael also looks with earnestness upon this search for the human being. What is in accord with his approach indeed enters here into human spiritual development: It is a search for *that* human being who once beheld the essential intelligence when Michael still ruled it from the cosmos. But if this were not laid hold of by the spiritualized force of the consciousness soul, it would in the end inevitably fall away from Michael's control and come under the sway of Lucifer. The other fearful concern in Michael's life is the possibility of Lucifer gaining the upper hand in the swaying of the cosmic-spiritual equilibrium.

Michael's preparation of his mission for the end of the nineteenth century streams forth in cosmic tragedy. Below, on the earth, there is often the greatest satisfaction in working out the new image of nature; whereas in the region where Michael works, there tragedy reigns regarding the hindrances to the emergence of the image of the human being.

Formerly Michael's austere, spiritualized love lived in the sun's rays, in the shimmering dawn, in the sparkling of the stars; this love had now acquired most strongly the

die Note des leiderweckenden Hinschauens auf die Menschheit angenommen.

Michaels Situation im Kosmos wurde eine tragisch-schwierige, aber auch zu einer Lösung drängende, gerade in dem Zeitabschnitte, der seiner Erdenmission voranging. Die Menschen konnten die Intellektualität nur im Bereich des Leibes und da nur der Sinne halten. Sie nahmen daher auf der einen Seite nichts in ihre Einsicht auf, was ihnen nicht die Sinne sagten; die Natur wurde ein Feld der Sinnesoffenbarung, aber diese Offenbarung ganz materiell gedacht. In den Naturformen vernahm man nicht mehr das Werk des Göttlich-Geistigen, sondern etwas, das geistlos da ist und von dem man doch behauptete, dass es das Geistige, in dem der Mensch lebt, hervorbringt. Auf der anderen Seite wollten von einer Geisteswelt die Menschen nur noch das annehmen, wovon die historischen Nachrichten sprachen. Ein Schauen des Geistes nach der Vergangenheit wurde so streng verpönt wie ein solches in die Gegenwart.

Es lebte nur noch das in des Menschen Seele, das aus dem Gegenwartsgebiete kommt, das Michael nicht betritt. Der Mensch ward froh, auf «sicherem» Boden zu stehen. *Den* glaubte er zu haben, weil er nichts von Gedanken, in denen er sogleich Fantasiewillkür fürchtete, in der «Natur» suchte. Michael aber war nicht froh; er musste jenseits vom Menschen, in seinem eigenen Gebiet, den Kampf gegen Luzifer

note of looking down upon humanity with awakening sorrow.

Michael's situation in the cosmos became tragically difficult, but it also pressed for a solution just at the period of time which preceded his earthly mission. Human beings were able to keep intellectuality only in the sphere of the body, and there only in the sphere of the senses. On one hand, therefore, they received into their views nothing that the senses did not tell them; nature became the field of the revelations of the senses, considered quite materially. The forms of nature were no longer perceived as the work of the divine-spiritual, but as something devoid of spirit – and yet one nevertheless asserted that it brings forth that spiritual element in which the human being lives. On the other hand, as regards a world of spirit, human beings would now accept only what the historical accounts narrated. A seeing of the spirit in accordance with the past was as strictly repudiated as a seeing of the spirit in the present.

In the human soul there now lived only what came from the sphere of the present, which Michael does not enter. The human being was glad to stand on "sure" ground. He believed he possessed *this ground* because in "nature" he sought no thoughts in which he might have had to fear the presence of arbitrary fantasy. But Michael was not glad; in his own sphere, beyond the human being, he had to wage war with Lucifer and

und Ahriman führen. Das ergab die große tragische Schwierigkeit, weil Luzifer um so leichter an den Menschen herankommt, je mehr Michael, der ja auch das Vergangene bewahrt, sich von dem Menschen abhalten muss. Und so spielte sich ein heftiger Kampf Michaels mit Ahriman und Luzifer in der an die Erde unmittelbar angrenzenden geistigen Welt *für* den Menschen ab, während dieser im Erdbereich selbst gegen das Heilsame seiner Entwickelung seine Seele in Tätigkeit hielt.

Alles dieses gilt selbstverständlich für das europäische und amerikanische Geistesleben. Für das asiatische müsste anders gesprochen werden.

Ahriman. This resulted in tragic difficulty, for Lucifer is able to approach the human being the more easily the more Michael – who indeed also preserves the past – is obliged to keep himself away from the human being. And thus a severe battle *for the human being* took place between Michael on one hand and Ahriman and Lucifer on the other, in the spiritual world immediately bordering the earth – while in the earthly realm itself the human being kept his soul actively opposed to what was salutary for his development.

All this applies, of course, to European and American spiritual life. Another way of speaking would be necessary with respect to Asian spiritual life.

Leitsätze Nr. 134 bis 136

134. In der allerersten Zeit der Bewusstseinsseelenentwickelung erfühlt der Mensch, wie ihm das vorher imaginativ gegebene Bild der Menschheit, seiner eigenen Wesenheit, verloren gegangen ist. Ohnmächtig, es in der Bewusstseinsseele schon zu finden, sucht er es auf naturwissenschaftlichem oder historischem Wege. Er möchte in sich das alte Menschheitsbild wieder erstehen lassen.

135. Man gelangt dadurch nicht zu einem wirklichen Erfülltsein mit der menschlichen Wesenheit, sondern nur zu Illusionen. Aber man bemerkt es nicht und sieht darin etwas die Menschheit Tragendes.

136. So muss Michael in der Zeit, die seiner Erdenwirksamkeit vorangeht, mit Sorge und in Leid auf die Menschheitsentwickelung sehen. Denn die Menschheit verpönt jede Geistesbetrachtung und schneidet sich dadurch alles ab, was sie mit Michael verbindet.

Leading Thoughts 134 to 136

134. In the very earliest time of the development of the consciousness soul, the human being began to feel that he had lost the image of humanity – the image of his own being – which had formerly been given to him in imagination. Powerless as yet to find it in the consciousness soul, he sought for it by way of natural science or history. He wanted the ancient image of humanity to arise in him again.

135. One reaches no fulfillment as a human being in this way, but is led only into illusions. Yet one is unaware that this is so, and sees in it something which sustains humanity.

136. Thus, in the time preceding his working upon earth, Michael had to observe the development of humanity with concern and suffering. For in this time, human beings disdained any real consideration of the spirit, and thus they severed all that connected them with Michael.

Weihnachtsbetrachtung: Das Logos-Mysterium

Goetheanum, zu Weihnacht 1924

In die Betrachtung des Michael-Mysteriums strahlte die des Mysteriums von Golgatha herein. Das ist durch die Tatsache gegeben, dass Michael die Macht ist, die den Menschen in der ihm heilsamen Art an den Christus herangeleitet.

Aber die Michael-Mission ist eine solche, die sich im kosmischen Menschheitswerden in rhythmischer Folge wiederholt. Man hatte sie in ihrer wohltätigen Wirkung auf die Erdenmenschheit wiederholt vor dem Mysterium von Golgatha. Da hing sie zusammen mit alledem, was die noch außerirdische Christus-Kraft zur Entfaltung der Menschheit für die Erde tätig zu offenbaren hatte. Nach dem Mysterium von Golgatha wird sie dem dienstbar, was durch Christus der Erdenmenschheit geschehen soll. Sie tritt in abgewandelter und fortschreitender Form in ihren Wiederholungen auf, aber eben in Wiederholungen.

Dem gegenüber ist das Mysterium von Golgatha ein alles übergreifendes kosmisches Ereignis, das nur *einmal* stattfindet im Laufe der ganzen kosmischen Menschheitsentwickelung.

Als die Menschheit bis zur Entfaltung der Verstandes- oder Gemütsseele vorgeschritten ist, da macht sich die fortwirkende

A Christmas Consideration: The Mystery of the Logos

Goetheanum, Christmas 1924

Into our consideration of the Michael Mystery, there rayed forth our consideration of the Mystery of Golgotha. This is so by virtue of the fact that Michael is the power who leads the human being to the Christ in a way that is salutary for him.

But the mission of Michael is one that is repeated in rhythmic succession in the course of humanity's cosmic becoming. In its beneficial influence on earthly humanity, it was repeated before the Mystery of Golgotha. In that time, it was connected with all the active revelations which the Christ-force – as yet external to this world – had to pour down to the earth for the unfolding of humanity. After the Mystery of Golgotha, the mission of Michael enters the service of what must now be achieved in earthly humanity through Christ. In its repetitions, the mission of Michael now appears in a changed and ever-progressing form – but indeed, in repetitions.

The Mystery of Golgotha, on the other hand, is an all-embracing cosmic event that takes place only *once* in the whole course of humanity's cosmic development.

It was only when humanity had reached the unfolding of the intellectual- or mind-soul that the continuous danger present

Gefahr der schon urzeitlich veranlagten Herauslösung des Menschheitswesens aus dem Wesen des Göttlich-Geistigen erst voll geltend.

Und in demselben Maße, in dem die Menschenseele das Mit-Erleben mit den göttlich-geistigen Wesenheiten verliert, taucht um sie herum das auf, was man heute «Natur» nennt.

Der Mensch schaut nicht mehr das Menschenwesenhafte in dem göttlich-geistigen Kosmos; er schaut das Werk des Göttlich-Geistigen im Irdischen. Er schaut es zunächst nicht in der abstrakten Form, in der es heute geschaut wird: sinnlich-physische Wesen und Geschehnisse, die durch diejenigen abstrakten Ideen-Inhalte zusammengehalten werden, die man «Naturgesetze» nennt. Er schaut es als göttlich-geistiges Wesen. Dieses göttlich-geistige Wesen wogt auf und ab in allem, was er als Entstehen und Vergehen der tierischen Lebewesen, im Wachsen und Sprossen der Pflanzenwelt sieht, was er in Quell- und Flusstätigkeit, in Wind- und Wolkenbildung gewahr wird. All diese Wesenhaftigkeiten und Vorgänge um ihn herum sind ihm die Gebärden, die Taten, sind ihm die Sprache des Götterwesens, das der «Natur» zugrunde liegt.

Wie dereinst in den Sternenstellungen und Sternenbewegungen die Taten, Gebärden der Weltengötterwesen von dem Menschen geschaut wurden, wie ihre Worte darinnen gelesen wurden, so wurden nunmehr die «Naturtatsachen»

in potential from the beginning – the danger that humanity's existence might become severed from the existence of the divine-spiritual – made itself fully felt.

And in the same manner in which the human soul loses the conscious experience in and with the divine-spiritual beings, there emerges around him that which one today calls "nature."

The human being no longer sees the essential being of humanity in the divine-spiritual cosmos; he sees the accomplished work of the divine-spiritual in this earthly realm. To begin with, however, he sees it not in the abstract form in which it is seen today – not as physically sensory events and entities held together by that abstract ideal content which one calls "the laws of nature." To begin with, he sees it still as divine-spiritual Being – divine-spiritual Being surging back and forth in all that he perceives around him, in the birth and decay of living animals, in the growing and sprouting of the plant-world, in springs and rivers, in cloud and wind and weather. All these essential beings and processes around him represent to him the gestures, deeds, and speech of the divine Being that underlies "nature."

There was once a time when the human being had seen in the constellations and movements of the stars the deeds and gestures of the divine beings of the cosmos, whose words he was thus able to read in the heavens. In like manner, the "facts

der Ausdruck für die Erdgöttin. Denn das in der Natur wirksame Göttliche wurde weiblich vorgestellt.

Reste dieser Vorstellungsart als imaginative Erfüllung der Verstandes- oder Gemütsseele waren noch bis weit herein ins Mittelalter in den Menschenseelen tätig.

Die Erkennenden sprachen von den Taten der «Göttin», wenn sie das «Naturgeschehen» zum Begreifen bringen wollten. Erst mit dem allmählichen Heraufkommen der Bewusstseinsseele ist diese lebendige, innerlich beseelte Naturbetrachtung für die Menschheit unverständlich geworden.

Und die Art, wie im Zeitalter der Verstandes- oder Gemütsseele nach dieser Richtung hin geschaut wurde, erinnert an den Persephone-Mythos mit dem ihm zugrunde liegenden Mysterium.

Die Tochter der Demeter, Persephone, wird von dem Gotte der Unterwelt gezwungen, ihm in sein Reich zu folgen. Es kommt das schließlich in der Form zustande, dass sie nur die Hälfte des Jahres in der Unterwelt zubringt, die andere auf der Oberwelt verweilt.

Gewaltig groß drückt dieser Mythos noch aus, wie man einst in urferner Vergangenheit in traumhaftem Hellsehen all das Werden des Irdischen erkennend durchschaut hat.

Alles Weltenwirken ging in Urzeiten von der Erden-

of nature" now became for him an expression of the Earth Goddess. For the divine at work in nature was conceived as feminine.

Far down into the Middle Ages, the relics of this mode of representation were still at work in the souls of human beings, filling the intellectual- or mind-soul with an imaginative content.

When those who knew wanted to bring the "processes of nature" to understanding, they spoke of the deeds of the "Goddess." It was only with the gradual dawn of the consciousness soul that this living consideration of nature, filled as it was with inner soul, became incomprehensible to humanity.

The way in which human beings looked in this direction in the age of the intellectual- or mind-soul is reminiscent of the Myth of Persephone and of the Mystery that underlies it.

Persephone, daughter of Demeter, is compelled by the God of the Underworld to follow him into his realm. Eventually it is achieved that she spends one-half of the year confined to the underworld, and dwells for the remainder of the year in the upper-world.

This Myth of Persephone was still a powerful expression of the way in which the human being, in an age of immemorial antiquity, had perceived and known the becoming of the earthly realm in dream-like clairvoyance.

In primeval times, all the world-creative activity had proceeded

Umgebung aus. Die Erde war selber erst im Entstehen. Sie bildete ihr Wesen in der kosmischen Entwickelung aus dem Wirken ihrer Umgebung heraus. Die göttlich-geistigen Wesen des Kosmos waren die an ihrem Wesen Schaffenden. – Als sie weit genug war, ein selbstständiger Weltkörper zu werden, da stieg Göttlich-Geistiges aus dem allgemeinen Kosmos auf sie hernieder und wurde Erdengottheit. Diese kosmische Tatsache hat das traumhafte Hellsehen alter Menschheit erkennend durchschaut; von dieser Erkenntnis ist der Persephone-Mythos geblieben; aber es ist auch geblieben, wie man bis tief ins Mittelalter hinein die «Natur» erkennend zu durchdringen suchte. Denn man schaute da noch nicht wie später nach den Sinnes-Eindrücken, das heißt nach dem, was an der Oberfläche des Irdischen erscheint, sondern nach den Kräften, die aus den Tiefen der Erde zur Oberfläche herauf wirken. – Und diese «Tiefenkräfte», die «Kräfte der Unterwelt», schaute man in Wechselwirkung mit den Sternen- und Elementen-Wirkungen der Erden-Umgebung.

Da wachsen die Pflanzen in ihren mannigfaltigen Formen, da offenbaren sie sich in ihrer bunten Farben-Erscheinung. Darinnen wirken die Sonnen-, Monden- und Sternenkräfte mit den Kräften der Erdentiefe zusammen. Die Grundlage gaben dafür ab die Mineralien, die schon ganz durch das ihr

from the surroundings of the earth. The earth itself was only in a process of becoming, and molded its existence in cosmic development from out of the workings of the surrounding world. The divine-spiritual beings of the cosmos were the creators and molders of the earth's existence. – But when the earth was far enough advanced to become an independent heavenly body, divine-spiritual Being descended from the great cosmos to the earth and became the Earth Divinity. The dream-like clairvoyance of primeval humanity had seen and known this cosmic fact; and from such knowledge the Myth of Persephone is left to us – but the knowledge is also left to us how, deep down into the Middle Ages, human beings sought to penetrate knowingly into "nature." It was not yet as in these later times, during which human beings only see according to their sense impressions, i.e., according to what appears on the surface of the earth. Rather, they still saw according to the forces working upwards to the surface from the depths of the earth. – And they saw these "forces of the depths," the "forces of the underworld," in mutual interplay with the influences of the stars and the elements working from the earth's environment.

The plants grow forth in their varied forms, revealing themselves in many-colored glory. Therein are at work the forces of sun and moon and stars, together with the forces of the earth's depths. The ground and foundation for this is given in the minerals, whose existence is entirely conditioned by that

Wesen haben, was von Weltenwesen irdisch geworden ist. Das Gestein sprießt durch die irdisch gewordenen Himmelskräfte allein aus der «Unterwelt» herauf. Die Tierwelt hat die Kräfte der «Erdentiefe» nicht angenommen. Sie entsteht allein durch die aus der Erden-Umgebung wirksamen Weltenkräfte. Sie verdankt ihr Werden, Wachsen, Sprießen, ihre Ernährungsfähigkeit, ihre Bewegungsmöglichkeiten den auf die Erde einströmenden Sonnenkräften. Sie kann sich fortpflanzen unter dem Einfluss der auf die Erde einströmenden Mondenkräfte. Sie erscheint in vielen Formen und Arten, weil aus dem Weltall herein die Sternenstellungen in der mannigfaltigsten Art gestaltend auf das Tierleben wirken. Aber die Tiere sind vom Weltall auf die Erde nur hereingestellt. Sie nehmen nur mit ihrem dumpfen Bewusstseinsleben an dem Irdischen teil; mit ihrer Entstehung, ihrem Wachsen, mit allem, was sie sind, damit sie wahrnehmen und sich bewegen können, sind sie keine Erdenwesen.

Diese großangelegte Idee von dem Werden der Erde lebte dereinst in der Menschheit. Was davon in das Mittelalter hereinragt, lässt nur in geringem Maße dieses Großangelegte noch erkennen. Man muss, um zu dieser Erkenntnis zu gelangen, mit dem Blick der schauenden Erkenntnis in sehr alte Zeiten zurückgehen. Denn auch aus den vorhandenen physischen Dokumenten ist nur für *den* zu ersehen, was in den

part of the world-being which has become earthly. Through those heavenly forces alone, having become earthly, rock and stone shoot forth out of the "underworld." The animal realm, on the other hand, has not assumed the forces of the "earthly depths." It comes into being solely through those world-forces at work in the surroundings of the earth. It owes its growth, development, and surging life, its powers of nutrition, its possibilities of movement, to the sun-forces streaming down to the earth. And under the influence of the moon-forces streaming down to the earth, it has the power to reproduce itself. It appears in manifold forms and species because the starry constellations are working in manifold ways from the cosmos, shaping and molding this animal life. The animals are, as it were, only placed down here on earth from out of the cosmos. It is only with their dim life of consciousness that they partake in the earthly realm; in terms of their origin, development, and growth, with all that they are which enables them to perceive and move about, they are no earthly creatures.

This mightily conceived idea of the earth's becoming once lived in humanity. The greatness of the conception is scarcely recognizable any longer in the relics of it which came down to the Middle Ages. To attain this knowledge, one must go back, with the gaze of seeing cognition, into very ancient times. For even the extant physical documents do not reveal what was really present there in the souls of human beings, save to

Seelen der Menschen vorhanden war, der dies auf geistgemäße Art durchschauen kann.

Nun ist der Mensch nicht in der Lage, sich der Erde so ferne zu halten wie die Tierheit. Indem man dieses ausspricht, tritt man an das Mysterium der Menschheit ebenso wie an das der Tierheit heran. Diese Mysterien spiegeln sich in dem Tierkult der alten Völker, vor allem der Ägypter. In den Tieren sah man Wesen, die Gäste der Erde sind, an denen man Wesen und Wirksamkeit der geistigen Welt, die an die irdische angrenzt, schauen kann. Und in der Verbindung der Menschengestalt mit der tierischen, die man in Bildern darstellte, vergegenwärtigte man sich die Gestalten derjenigen elementarischen Zwischenwesen, die wohl im Weltenwerden auf dem Wege zur Menschheit sind, aber in das Irdische nicht eintreten, um nicht Menschen zu werden. Solche elementarischen Zwischenwesen sind vorhanden. Die Ägypter gaben nur ihr Schauen wieder, indem sie sie abbildeten. Aber solche Wesen haben nicht das volle Selbstbewusstsein des Menschen. Um das zu erlangen, musste der Mensch die irdische Welt in solch vollständiger Art betreten, dass er vom Erdenwesen in sein Wesen etwas aufnahm.

Er musste dem ausgesetzt werden, dass in dieser irdischen Welt das Werk der ihm verbundenen göttlich-geistigen Wesen vorliegt, *aber eben nur deren Werk*. Und *weil* nur das

those who are able to penetrate to this knowledge in a spiritual way.

The human being is not in a position to hold himself as aloof from the earth as the animals do. In saying this, one is approaching the Mystery of Humanity as well as the Mystery of the Animal Realm. These Mysteries were reflected in the animal cults of the ancient peoples, and above all in that of the Egyptians. They saw the animals as beings who are but guests upon the earth, and in whom one may perceive the nature and activity of the spiritual world immediately adjoining this earthly realm. And when in images they portrayed the human figure in connection with the animal, they were representing to themselves the forms of those elemental, intermediate beings who, though they are indeed in the cosmic process of becoming on the way to humanity, yet purposely refrain from entering the earthly realm in order not to become human. For there do indeed exist such elemental, intermediate beings; and in picturing them, the Egyptians were but reproducing what they saw. Such beings, however, do not have the full human self-consciousness, toward the attainment of which the human being had to enter this earthly world so completely as to receive something of this earthly nature into his own being.

The human being had to be exposed to the fact that in this earthly world, although the work of the divine-spiritual beings with whom he is connected is indeed present here, *it is only*

vom Ursprunge losgelöste *Werk* vorliegt, so haben in dieses Zutritt die luziferischen und ahrimanischen Wesenheiten. Es ergibt sich damit für den Menschen die Notwendigkeit, das von Luzifer und Ahriman durchsetzte Werk zum Orte eines Teiles seiner Lebensgestaltung – der irdischen – zu machen.

Es ist dies so lange ohne die bleibende Loslösung des Menschlichen von seinem ursprünglichen Göttlich-Geistigen möglich, als der Mensch noch nicht zur Entfaltung seiner Verstandes- oder Gemütsseele fortgeschritten ist. Da findet im Menschen eine Korrumpierung seines physischen, seines ätherischen und astralischen Leibes statt. Eine ältere Wissenschaft kennt diese Korrumpierung als etwas, das in der Menschen Wesenheit lebt. Man weiß, dass sie notwendig ist, damit das Bewusstsein zum Selbstbewusstsein im Menschen vorrücken könne. In der Erkenntnispflege, die an den Stätten stattgefunden hat, die von Alexander dem Großen der Wissenschaft gegeben worden sind, lebte ein Aristotelismus, der, richtig verstanden, diese Korrumpierung als ein maßgebendes Element seiner Seelenwissenschaft in sich trägt. Solche Ideen wurden nur später in ihrer inneren Wesenheit nicht mehr durchdrungen.

In den Zeiten vor der Entwickelung der Verstandes- oder Gemütsseele war der Mensch dennoch mit den Kräften seines

their accomplished work. And *just because* only the *accomplished work*, severed from its divine origin, is present here, the luciferic and ahrimanic beings have access to it. Thus it becomes necessary for the human being to make this realm of the divinely accomplished work, permeated as it is by Lucifer and Ahriman, the field of action for one part – the earthly part – of his life's development.

So long as the human being had not progressed to the unfolding of his intellectual- or mind-soul, it was possible to achieve this without human nature becoming permanently severed from its original divine-spiritual foundation. But when this point was reached, a corruption took place in the human being – a corruption of the physical, etheric, and astral bodies. To an ancient science, this corruption was known as something that was living in the human being's nature. It was known as a thing that was necessary in order that consciousness might advance to human self-consciousness. In the culture of cognition practiced in the centers of learning given to science by Alexander the Great, there lived an Aristotelianism which, rightly understood, contained this "corruption" as an essential element in its knowledge of the soul. It was only at a later time that these ideas were no longer comprehended in their inner being.

In the ages before the development of his intellectual- or mind-soul, the human being was, however, still interwoven

göttlich-geistigen Ursprunges so verwoben, dass diese Kräfte von ihrem kosmischen Orte aus die auf Erden an ihn herandringenden luziferischen und ahrimanischen Mächte im Gleichgewichte halten konnten. Da war von menschlicher Seite aus Genüge geschehen zur Mitwirkung an diesem Gleichgewichte, wenn in Kult- und Mysterienhandlung das *Bild* des in Luzifers und Ahrimans Reich untertauchenden und wieder siegreich hervorgehenden göttlich-geistigen Wesens entfaltet wurde. Man sieht daher in den Zeiten, die dem Mysterium von Golgatha vorangingen, in den Völkerkulten bildhafte Darstellungen dessen, was dann im Mysterium von Golgatha eine Wirklichkeit wurde.

Als die Verstandes- oder Gemütsseele entfaltet war, konnte die Menschenwesenheit nur durch die Wirklichkeit vor der Loslösung von ihren göttlich-geistigen Wesenheiten bewahrt bleiben. Es musste in die während des irdischen Daseins vom Irdischen lebende Organisation der Verstandes- oder Gemütsseele auch *im* Irdischen innerlich das Göttliche als Wesenheit eintreten. Das geschah dadurch, dass der göttlich-geistige Logos, Christus, für die Menschheit sein kosmisches Schicksal mit der Erde verband.

Persephone ist in das Irdische untergetaucht, um die Pflanzenwelt davon zu befreien, bloß vom Irdischen sich bilden zu müssen. Das ist der Niederstieg eines göttlich-geistigen Wesens in die Natur der Erde. Auch Persephone

with the forces of his divine-spiritual origin – so much so that from their cosmic field of action, these forces were able to balance and hold in check the luciferic and ahrimanic powers that reach out to the human being on earth. And from the human side, enough was done by way of cooperation to maintain the balance – for instance, in those activities of ritual and of the Mysteries wherein the *image* was unfolded of the divine-spiritual Being diving down into the realm of Lucifer and Ahriman and emerging again triumphant. Hence, in times prior to the Mystery of Golgotha one finds in the religious rites of different peoples image-like representations of what later, in the Mystery of Golgotha, became reality.

Once the intellectual- or mind-soul had unfolded, it was only through reality that the human being could continue to be preserved from release from the divine-spiritual beings belonging to him. The divine had to enter inwardly as Being, even *in* the earthly life, into the organization of the intellectual- or mind-soul which, during earth-existence, receives its life from what is earthly. This took place through the divine-spiritual Logos, Christ, uniting His cosmic destiny with the earth for the sake of humanity.

Persephone came down to the earthly realm in order to save the plant realm from being obliged to form itself merely from what is earthly. That is the descent of a divine-spiritual being into the nature of the earth. Persephone, too, has a kind of

hat ja eine Art «Auferstehung», aber jährlich in rhythmischer Folge.

Diesem Ereignis, das als kosmisches auf Erden geschieht, steht gegenüber der Niederstieg des Logos für die Menschheit. Persephone steigt nieder, um die Natur in ihre ursprüngliche Orientierung zu bringen. Da muss Rhythmus zugrunde liegen; denn das Geschehen der Natur erfolgt im Rhythmus. Der Logos steigt nieder in die Menschheit. Es geschieht das einmal während der Entwickelung der Menschheit. Denn *diese* Entwickelung ist nur *ein* Glied in einem gigantischen Weltenrhythmus, in dem die Menschheit vor ihrem Mensch-Sein etwas ganz anderes als Menschheit war und nach demselben etwas ganz anderes sein wird, während ja das Pflanzenleben in kurzen Rhythmen *als solches* sich wiederholt.

Das Mysterium von Golgatha in diesem Lichte zu sehen, das hat die Menschheit vom Bewusstseinszeitalter an nötig. Denn es wäre schon im Zeitalter der Verstandes- oder Gemütsseele die Loslösung des Menschen als Gefahr vorhanden gewesen, wenn nicht das Mysterium von Golgatha erfolgt wäre. Im Zeitalter der Bewusstseinsseele müsste eine völlige *Verdunkelung* der Geisteswelt für den Menschen in seinem Bewusstsein eintreten, wenn nicht die Bewusstseinsseele sich so weit erkraften könnte, dass sie zu ihrem göttlich-geistigen Ursprung in Einsicht zurückblickte. Kann sie das aber, so findet sie den Weltenlogos als die Wesenheit, die sie zurückführen kann. Sie

"resurrection." But this takes place annually, in rhythmic succession.

This event – a cosmic event occurring on the earth – must be seen alongside the descent of the Logos for the sake of humanity. Persephone descends in order to bring nature into its original orientation. For this, there must be rhythm at the foundation; for the events of nature take place rhythmically. The Logos descends into humanity. This occurs once during the development of humanity. For *this* development is but *one* member of a gigantic cosmic rhythm in which, before the stage of human existence, humanity had been something altogether different, and in which, after this stage has passed, it will be something altogether different again; whereas the realm of plant life repeats itself *as such* in shorter rhythms.

From the age of the consciousness soul onwards, it is necessary for humanity to see the Mystery of Golgotha in this light. For as early as the age of the intellectual- or mind-soul, there would have been a danger that the human being would separate off from evolution had the Mystery of Golgotha not taken place. In the age of the consciousness soul, a complete *darkening* of the world of spirit would necessarily come about for human consciousness if the consciousness soul were unable to strengthen itself sufficiently to look back in insight to its divine-spiritual origin. If, however, it is able to do this, it finds the World Logos as the Being who can lead it back. It fills

durchdringt sich mit dem gewaltigen Bilde, das offenbart, was auf Golgatha geschehen ist.

Und der Beginn dieses Verständnisses ist die liebevolle Erfassung der Welten-Weihe-Nacht, an die jedes Jahr festlich erinnert wird. Denn die Erkraftung der Bewusstseinsseele geschieht ja dadurch, dass sie, die zunächst die Intellektualität aufnimmt, in dieses kälteste Seelen-Element die warme Liebe einziehen lässt. Jene warme Liebe, die am erhabensten strömt, wenn sie dem Jesus-Kinde gilt, das in der Welten-Weihe-Nacht auf Erden erscheint. Damit hat der Mensch die höchste irdische Geistes-Tatsache, die zugleich eine physische war, auf seine Seele wirken lassen; er hat sich auf den Weg begeben, den Christus in sich aufzunehmen.

Die Natur muss so erkannt werden, dass sie in Persephone oder dem Wesen, auf das man noch im frühen Mittelalter geschaut hat, wenn man von «Natur» gesprochen hat, die göttlich-geistige Ursprungs- und ewige Kraft offenbart, aus der sie entstanden ist und fortdauernd entsteht als die Grundlage des irdischen Menschendaseins.

Die Menschenwelt muss so erkannt werden, dass sie in Christus den Ursprungs- und ewigen Logos offenbart, der im Bereich der mit dem Menschen ursprünglich verbundenen göttlich-geistigen Wesenheit zur Entfaltung der Geist-Wesenheit des Menschen wirkt.

itself with the mighty image which reveals what took place on Golgotha.

The beginning of this understanding is the loving comprehension of Christmas, the World Consecration Night, the festive remembrance of which is celebrated each year. For the strengthening of the consciousness soul – that component which first receives the intellectuality – takes place in that the warmth of love is allowed to enter into this coldest element of soul. And the warmth of love is present in its highest form when it goes out to the Jesus child who appears on earth during the World Consecration Night. In this way the human being has allowed the highest earthly spiritual fact, which was at the same time a physical event, to work upon his soul; he has entered upon the path on which he may receive Christ into himself.

Nature must come to be known in such a way that in the figure of Persephone – or the being who was still seen in the early Middle Ages when one spoke of "nature" – one sees the revelation of the divine-spiritual, original, and eternal force out of which nature emerged, and continually emerges, as the foundation of earthly human existence.

The human world must be recognized such that in Christ it reveals the original and eternal Logos, working for the unfolding of the spirit-being of humanity, in the sphere of divine-spiritual Being which was connected with humanity from the beginning.

In Liebe das Menschenherz zu diesen großen kosmischen Zusammenhängen zu lenken, das ist der rechte Inhalt jener Festes-Erinnerung, die im Hinblicken auf die Welten-Weihe-Nacht jedes Jahr an den Menschen herantritt. Lebt *solche* Liebe im Menschenherzen, dann durchfeuert sie das kalte Licht-Element der Bewusstseinsseele. Müsste diese ohne diese Durchfeuerung verbleiben: Der Mensch käme nie zu ihrer Durchgeistigung. Er erstürbe in der Kälte des intellektuellen Bewusstseins, oder er müsste in einem Geistesleben verbleiben, das nicht zur Entfaltung der Bewusstseinsseele fortschreitet. Er würde dann in der Entfaltung der Verstandes- oder Gemütsseele stehen bleiben.

Aber ihrem Wesen nach ist die Bewusstseinsseele nicht kalt. Sie scheint es nur *im Anfange* ihrer Entfaltung, weil sie da erst das Lichtvolle ihres Inhaltes offenbaren kann, noch nicht die Weltenwärme, aus der sie ja doch stammt.

Weihnachten in dieser Art empfinden und erleben, kann in der Seele gegenwärtig machen: *wie die Glorie der in Sternenweiten ihre Abbilder offenbarenden göttlich-geistigen Wesen sich vor dem Menschen verkündiget und wie die Befreiung des Menschen innerhalb der Erdenstätte von den Mächten geschieht, die ihn von seinem Ursprünge entfernen wollen.*

To turn the human heart in love to these great cosmic facts: this is the true content of the festival of remembrance approaching the human being each year when he contemplates the World Consecration Night of Christmas. If such love as *this* lives in human hearts, it permeates the cold light-element of the consciousness soul with fire. Were the consciousness soul obliged to remain without such permeation, the human being would never become spiritualized. He would die in the cold of intellectual consciousness; or he would have to remain in a mental life that did not progress to the unfolding of the consciousness soul. He would then come to a standstill in the unfolding of the intellectual- or mind-soul.

But in its essence, the consciousness soul is not cold. It only appears to be so at the *beginning* of its unfolding, because at that stage it can only reveal the light-element of its nature, and not as yet the cosmic warmth in which it indeed has its origin.

To feel and experience Christmas in this way will enable the soul to realize *how the glory of the divine-spiritual beings – whose images are revealed in the stars – announces itself to the human being, and how the human being's liberation from the powers striving to alienate him from his origin takes place within the precincts of the earth.*

Leitsätze Nr. 137 bis 139

137. Die Tätigkeit in der Welt- und Menschheitsentwickelung, die durch die Michael-Kräfte zustande kommt, *wiederholt* sich *rhythmisch*, wenn auch in abgeänderter und fortschreitender Form vor und nach dem Mysterium von Golgatha.

138. Das Mysterium von Golgatha ist das *einmalige* größte Ereignis innerhalb der Menschheitsentwickelung. Da kann nicht von einer rhythmischen Wiederholung die Rede sein. Denn wenn auch diese Menschheitsentwickelung in einem gewaltigen Weltenrhythmus drinnensteht, so ist sie doch eben das weit ausgedehnte *eine* Glied in diesem Rhythmus. Bevor sie dieses eine Glied wurde, war die Menschheit etwas wesentlich anderes als Menschheit; nachher wird sie wieder etwas anderes sein. Es finden also während der Menschheitsentwickelung viele Michael-Ereignisse, aber nur *ein* Ereignis von Golgatha statt.

139. In der schnellen rhythmischen Wiederholung eines Jahreslaufes vollzieht das göttlich-geistige Wesen, das zur Durchgeistigung des Naturgeschehens in die Erdentiefen niedergestiegen ist, dieses Geschehen. Es

Leading Thoughts 137 to 139

137. The activity in the development of the world and of humanity which comes about through the forces of Michael *repeats* itself *rhythmically* – though in ever-changing and progressing forms – before and after the Mystery of Golgotha.

138. The Mystery of Golgotha is a *one-time* event, as well as the greatest event in all of human development. Here there can be no question of a rhythmic repetition. For while the development of humanity also stands within a mighty cosmic rhythm, still it is only *one* widely extended member in this rhythm. Before it became this one member, humanity was something altogether different from what is now known as humanity; afterwards it will again be altogether different. Thus there are many Michael-events in the development of humanity, but there is only *one* event of Golgotha.

139. In the quick rhythmic repetition of the seasons of the year, the divine-spiritual being which descended into the depths of earth to permeate nature's process with the spirit, accomplishes this process. It is the ensouling of

stellt die Durchseelung der Natur mit den Ursprungs- und ewigen *Kräften* dar, die wirksam bleiben müssen, wie der herabgestiegene Christus die Durchseelung der Menschheit mit dem Ursprungs- und ewigen *Logos* darstellt, der zum Heile der Menschheit mit seiner Wirksamkeit niemals aufhören soll.

nature with the *forces* of the beginning and of eternity, which must remain at work – just as Christ's descent is the ensouling of humanity with the *Logos* of the beginning and of eternity, whose working for the healing of humanity will never cease.

Himmelsgeschichte. Mythologische Geschichte. Erdgeschichte. Mysterium von Golgatha

Goetheanum, um Weihnachten 1924

Im räumlichen Kosmos stehen einander gegenüber: Weltenweite und Erdenzentrum. In der Weltenweite sind die Sterne gewissermaßen «ausgestreut». Vom Erdenzentrum strahlen Kräfte nach allen Richtungen der Weltenweite.

So wie der Mensch in der gegenwärtigen kosmischen Epoche in der Welt darinnen steht, kann ihm das Sternenscheinen und Erdenkräftewirken nur als das Gesamtwerk der göttlich-geistigen Wesen, mit denen er in seinem Innern verbunden ist, erscheinen.

Aber es gab eine kosmische Zeit-Epoche, da waren dieses Scheinen und diese Erdenkräfte noch unmittelbare geistige Offenbarung der göttlich-geistigen Wesen. Der Mensch in seinem dumpfen Bewusstsein fühlte die göttlich-geistigen Wesen wirksam in *seiner* Wesenheit.

Dann kam eine andere Zeit-Epoche. Der Sternenhimmel löste sich als körperliches Wesen aus dem göttlich-geistigen Wirken heraus. Es entstand das, was man Weltengeist und Weltenleib nennen kann. Der Weltengeist ist eine Vielheit göttlich-geistiger Wesenheiten. Sie wirken in der älteren

History of Heaven. Mythological History. Earth History. Mystery of Golgotha

Goetheanum, Christmas 1924

In the spatial cosmos, one has the contrast of the cosmic expanses and the earthly center. In the cosmic expanses, the stars are "scattered wide," so to speak. From the earthly center, forces stream out in all directions into the cosmic expanses.

To the human being as he stands in the world in the present cosmic epoch, it is only as a great totality that the glory of the stars and the working of the earthly forces can represent the finished work of the divine-spiritual beings with whom he is connected in his inner being.

But there was once a cosmic epoch when the glory of the stars and the forces of the earth were still a direct spiritual revelation of the divine-spiritual beings. At that time, the human being in his dim consciousness felt the divine-spiritual beings actively working in *his own* being.

Another epoch of time ensued. The starry heavens became severed, as a corporeal existence, from the divine-spiritual working. There originated what one may call the world-spirit and the world-body. The world-spirit is a multitude of divine-spiritual beings. In the former epoch, these beings had worked

Epoche aus den Sternen-Orten auf die Erde herein. Was da von den Weltenweiten erglänzte, was vom Erdenzentrum als Kräfte erstrahlte, das waren in Wirklichkeit Intelligenz und Wille der göttlich-geistigen Wesenheiten, die an der Erde und ihrer Menschheit schufen.

In der späteren kosmischen Epoche – nach der Saturn- und Sonnenentwickelung – wurde das Wirken von Intelligenz und Wille der göttlich-geistigen Wesen immer geistig innerlicher. Worinnen sie ursprünglich wirksam anwesend waren, das wurde «Weltenleib», harmonische Anordnung der Sterne im Weltenraume. Man kann, wenn man in geistgemäßer Weltanschauung auf diese Dinge zurückblickt, sagen: Aus dem ursprünglichen Geist-Leib der weltschöpferischen Wesen sind Weltengeist und Weltenleib entstanden. Und der Weltenleib zeigt in Sternen-Anordnung und Sternenbewegung, wie einst das intelligente und willensgemäße Götterwirken war. Aber für die kosmische Gegenwart ist, was *einst* frei bewegliche Götterintelligenz und Götterwille in den Sternen war, in diesen gesetzmäßig fest geworden.

Was also heute aus den Sternenwelten zu dem Menschen auf der Erde hereinscheint, ist nicht unmittelbarer Ausdruck von Götterwillen und Götterintelligenz, sondern stehengebliebenes Zeichen für das, was diese *in den Sternen* einst waren. In der Bewunderung aus der Menschenseele lösenden

from the starry worlds inward toward the earth. All that had shone forth from cosmic expanses, all that had radiated by way of forces from the earthly center, was in reality the intelligence and will of divine-spiritual beings working creatively upon the earth and its humanity.

In the later cosmic epochs – after the Saturn and Sun periods of development – the working of the intelligence and will of the divine-spiritual beings became more and more spiritually inward. That in which they had been actively present in the beginning became the "world-body": the harmonious arrangement of stars in universal space. Looking back on these matters with a spiritual world-conception, one may express it thus: From the original spirit-body of the world-creative beings, the world-spirit and the world-body came into being. And in the ordering and movement of the stars, the world-body now shows what the intelligence and will-imbued working of the gods once was like. For the cosmic present, however, what was *once* the divine intelligence and divine will living and moving freely in the stars has become fastened in the fixed laws of the starry universe.

Today, therefore, what shines inward from the starry worlds down to the human being on earth is no longer an immediate expression of divine will and divine intelligence, but rather a sign indicating what this divine will and divine intelligence once were *in the stars*. In the wonder of the human soul

Himmels-Stern-Gestaltung kann man daher eine vergangene, aber nicht die gegenwärtige Götteroffenbarung sehen.

Aber dasjenige, was so im Sternenschein «vergangen» ist, in der Geist-Welt ist es «gegenwärtig». Und der Mensch lebt mit seinem Wesen in diesem «gegenwärtigen» Weltengeist.

Man muss in der Weltgestaltung zurückblicken auf eine *alte* kosmische Epoche, in der Weltengeist und Weltenleib als eine Einheit wirken. Man muss die *mittlere* Epoche ins Auge fassen, in der sie als Zweiheit sich entfalten. Und man muss in die Zukunft, die *dritte* Epoche, denken, in der der Weltengeist den Weltenleib wieder in seine Wirksamkeit übernehmen wird.

Für die *alte* Epoche wären Sternenkonstellation und Sternenlauf nicht zu «berechnen» gewesen, denn sie waren Ausdruck der freien Intelligenz und des freien Willens von göttlich-geistigen Wesen. In der Zukunft werden sie wieder nicht zu berechnen sein.

«Berechnung» hat nur eine Bedeutung für die mittlere kosmische Epoche.

Und wie für Sternenkonstellation und Sternenlauf, so gilt dieses auch für die Wirksamkeit der vom Erdenzentrum in die Weltenweite strahlenden Kräfte. Da wird das, was «aus der Tiefe» wirkt, «berechenbar».

Aber alles strebt aus der älteren kosmischen Epoche der

toward the sublime formation of the starry heavens, one can see a past revelation of the gods – though not their present revelation.

That, however, which in the shining of the stars is "of the past," is "present" in the world of spirit. And the human being lives with his essential being in this "present" world-spirit.

One must look back in the formation of the world to an *ancient* cosmic epoch when the world-spirit and the world-body still worked as an undivided unity. Then one must envision the *middle* epoch, in which they unfold as a duality. And at length one must think into the future – into the *third* epoch, when the world-spirit will once again take up the world-body into its active working.

For the *ancient* epoch, it would have been impossible to "calculate" the constellations and the course of the stars; for at that time these were the expression of the free intelligence and free will of divine-spiritual beings. Moreover, in the future they will once again become "incalculable."

"Calculation" has a meaning only for the middle cosmic epoch.

And this holds good not only for the constellations and the movements of the stars, but also for the working of the forces radiating from the earthly center to the cosmic expanses. Thereby, what works "out of the depths" also becomes "calculable."

Everything strives from the older cosmic epoch toward

mittleren zu, in der das Räumliche und Zeitliche «berechenbar» werden und das Göttlich-Geistige als Intelligenz- und Willens-Offenbarung «hinter» dem «Berechenbaren» gesucht werden muss.

Nur in dieser mittleren Epoche sind die Bedingungen gegeben, in denen die Menschheit von einem dumpfen Bewusstsein zu einem hellen, freien Selbstbewusstsein, zu eigener freier Intelligenz und eigenem freien Willen fortschreiten kann.

Es musste einmal die Zeit kommen, in der Kopernikus und Kepler den Weltenleib «berechneten». Denn aus den kosmischen Kräften, die mit der Herbeiführung dieses Augenblickes zusammenhängen, musste das menschliche Selbstbewusstsein sich gestalten. In älterer Zeit wurde dieses Selbstbewusstsein veranlagt; dann kam die Zeit, wo es so weit war, die Weltenweite zu «berechnen».

Auf der Erde spielt sich die «Geschichte» ab. Die wäre nie gekommen, wenn die Weltenweite nicht zu «festen» Sternkonstellationen und Sternenlaufen geworden wäre. In dem «geschichtlichen Werden» auf Erden ist ein Abbild – aber ein durchaus gewandeltes – dessen vorhanden, was einst «Himmelsgeschichte» war.

Ältere Völker haben in ihrem Bewusstsein noch diese «Himmelsgeschichte», und sie blicken viel mehr auf diese als auf die «Erdengeschichte».

In der «Erdengeschichte» leben Intelligenz und Wille der

the *middle* epoch, when the spatial and temporal become "calculable," and the divine-spiritual as revelation of intelligence and will must be sought for "behind" this "calculable" world.

Only in this middle epoch are the conditions given for the human being to progress from a dim state of consciousness to one of free and bright self-consciousness – to a state of free intelligence and free will.

Thus there had to come the time when Copernicus and Kepler could "calculate" the world-body. For it was through the cosmic forces connected to this moment that the self-consciousness of the human being was able to take shape. The germinal seed of human self-consciousness had been laid in an older time; and now the time had come when it was far enough advanced to "calculate" the cosmic expanses.

On the earth, "history" takes place. What is known as "history" would never have come about if the cosmic expanses had not evolved into the "fixed" constellations and courses of the stars. In "historical becoming" on earth there is given an image – albeit thoroughly transformed – of what was once upon a time the "history of heaven."

Earlier peoples still had this "history of heaven" in their consciousness, and were indeed far more aware of it than of the earthly.

In earth history, there lives the intelligence and will of

Menschen, erst im Zusammenhange mit dem kosmischen Götterwillen und der Götterintelligenz, dann selbstständig.

In der «Himmelsgeschichte» lebten Intelligenz und Wille der mit der Menschheit zusammenhängenden göttlich-geistigen Wesen.

Blickt man zurück auf das geistige Leben der Völker, so ist in urferner Vergangenheit ein Bewusstsein des Zusammenseins und Zusammenwollens mit den göttlich-geistigen Wesenheiten so bei den Menschen vorhanden, dass deren Geschichte Himmelsgeschichte ist. Der Mensch erzählt, indem er über «Ursprünge» spricht, nicht irdische, sondern kosmische Vorgänge. Ja, auch für *seine* Gegenwart erscheint ihm das, was in seiner Erden-Umgebung vorgeht, so unbedeutend gegenüber den kosmischen Vorgängen, dass er nur diese, nicht jenes beachtet.

Es gab eine Epoche, in der die Menschheit das Bewusstsein hatte, die Himmelsgeschichte in mächtigen Eindrücken zu schauen, in denen die göttlich-geistigen Wesen selbst vor der Seele des Menschen standen. Sie sprachen; und der Mensch vernahm die Sprache in Traum-Inspiration; sie offenbarten ihre Gestalten; und der Mensch schaute sie in Traum-Imagination.

Diese «Himmelsgeschichte», die eine lange Zeit die Menschenseelen erfüllte, wurde gefolgt von der mythischen Geschichte, die man heute vielfach für alte Dichtung hält. Sie

human beings – first, in connection with the cosmic will and intelligence of the gods; then, independent of them.

In the "history of heaven," there lived solely the intelligence and will of the divine-spiritual beings who were connected with humanity.

When one looks back into the spiritual life of peoples, one comes to an age of far-distant antiquity when there was present in the human being a consciousness of existing and willing in communion with the divine-spiritual beings – so much so that the history of human beings *was* the history of heaven. The human being, when speaking of "origins," speaks not of earthly but of cosmic events. And even in relation to *his own* present time, what took place in his earthly environment seemed to him so insignificant relative to the cosmic processes that he gave his attention to the latter only, not to the former.

There was an epoch when humanity was conscious of beholding the history of heaven in powerful impressions, wherein the divine-spiritual beings themselves stood before the human soul. They spoke, and in dream-inspiration the human being hearkened to their speech; they revealed their forms, and in dream-imagination the human being saw them.

This "history of heaven," which for a long time filled the souls of human beings, was followed by the mythical history, generally regarded in our time as a poetic creation of the

verbindet Himmelsgeschehen mit Erdgeschehen. Es treten zum Beispiel «Heroen» auf, übermenschliche Wesen. Es sind das Wesen, die in der Entwickelung höher stehen als die Menschen. Diese haben zum Beispiel in einer gewissen Zeit die menschlichen Wesensglieder nur bis zur Empfindungsseele ausgestaltet. Der «Heros» aber hat bereits entwickelt, was im Menschen als Geistselbst einmal auftreten wird. Der «Heros» kann nicht innerhalb der Erdenverhältnisse unmittelbar sich verkörpern; aber er kann es dadurch, dass er in den Körper eines Menschen untertaucht und so sich fähig macht, als Mensch unter Menschen zu wirken. In «Eingeweihten» der älteren Zeit hat man solche Wesen zu sehen.

Die Tatsachen im Weltgeschehen liegen bei alledem so, dass nicht etwa die Menschheit sich in den aufeinanderfolgenden Epochen die Geschehnisse so «vorstellte»; sondern, was sich zwischen der mehr geistigen «unberechenbaren» und der körperlichen «berechenbaren» Welt abspielte, das wandelte sich. Nur das liegt vor, dass lange, nachdem die Weltverhältnisse sich schon gewandelt hatten, das menschliche Bewusstsein dieses oder jenes Volkes noch an einer «Weltanschauung» festhielt, die einer viel früheren Wirklichkeit entsprach. Zuerst geschah das so, dass das menschliche Bewusstsein, das nicht gleichen Schritt hält mit dem kosmischen Geschehen, das Alte wirklich noch schaute. Dann kam eine Zeit, wo das Schauen verblasste und das Alte nur durch Tradition noch

ancients. Mythical history combines heavenly events with earthly events. "Heroes," for instance – superhuman beings – appear on the scene. They are beings at a higher stage of development than the human being. In a given epoch, for example, the human being had developed the members of human nature only as far as the sentient soul, but the "hero" had already evolved what will one day appear in the human being as spirit-self. In the existing conditions of the earth, the "hero" could not incarnate directly, but he could do so indirectly by diving down into the body of a human being, thereby enabling himself to work as a human being among others. Such beings are to be seen in the "initiates" of ancient times.

The facts of the world-process are not such that in the successive epochs humanity "imagined" the events in just this way; rather, what actually took place between the more spiritual "incalculable" world and the corporeal "calculable" world underwent a change. Long after the world-relationships had actually changed, human consciousness in this or that people still held fast to a "world-conception" corresponding to a far earlier reality. To begin with, this was due to the fact that the consciousness of human beings, which does not keep pace exactly with the cosmic process, really continued to behold the old condition. Afterwards there came a time in which the vision faded, but human beings still held fast to the old knowledge through tradition. Thus in the Middle Ages, an in-playing of

festgehalten wurde. So wird im Mittelalter traditionell ein Hereinspielen der Himmelswelt in die irdische noch vorgestellt, das nicht mehr geschaut wird, weil die Kraft des Bildschauens nicht mehr da ist.

Und im Erdbereich entwickeln sich die Völker so, dass sie in verschiedener Zeitenlänge den einen oder anderen Weltanschauungsinhalt festhalten, sodass *neben*einander Weltanschauungen leben, die ihrem Wesen gemäß nacheinander liegen. – Nur rühren die verschiedenen Weltanschauungen der Völker nicht allein von dieser Tatsache her, sondern auch davon, dass nach ihren Anlagen die verschiedenen Völker Verschiedenes schauten. So sahen die Ägypter die Welt, in der Wesen sind, welche auf dem Wege der Menschwerdung vorzeitig stehen geblieben und nicht Erdenmenschen geworden sind; und sie sahen den Menschen nach seinem Erdenleben in alledem, was er mit solchen Wesen zu tun hat. Die chaldäischen Völker sahen mehr, wie außerirdische geistige Wesen – gute und böse – in das Erdenleben eintraten, um da zu wirken.

Auf die alte, einer ganz langen Zeitepoche angehörige eigentliche «Himmelsgeschichte» folgt die «mythologische» Geschichte, die kürzer, aber im Verhältnis zur späteren eigentlichen «Geschichte» doch noch lang ist.

the heavenly world into the earthly was still conceived out of tradition but was no longer seen, for the force of seeing in images was no longer present.

In the earthly realm, the different peoples evolved in such a way as to hold fast to the content of one or other world-conception for varying lengths of time. Thus, world-conceptions which by their nature follow one upon the other are found living *side by side*. – The variety of world-conceptions is due not to this alone, but also to the fact that the different peoples, according to their dispositions, really did see differently in a spiritual sense. Thus the Egyptians beheld the world in which there dwell beings which have come to a premature standstill on the path of human becoming and have not yet become earthly human beings. The Egyptians likewise saw the human being himself, after his earthly life, in the midst of all that he had to do with beings such as these. The Chaldean peoples, on the other hand, saw more the way in which spiritual beings from beyond this world, both good and evil, entered into the life of earth to work there.

The ancient "history of heaven," which belonged to a very long epoch of time, was followed by the epoch of "mythological" history; this epoch was shorter, but in comparison to the subsequent period of "history" in the accepted sense, nonetheless very long.

Die Menschen verlassen – wie ich schon charakterisiert habe – nur schwer in ihrem Bewusstsein die alten Anschauungen, in denen Götter und Menschen zusammenwirkend vorgestellt werden. – So ist «eigentliche Erdgeschichte» längst – seit Entfaltung der Verstandes- oder Gemütsseele – vorhanden. Der Mensch «denkt» noch im Sinne dessen, was gewesen ist. Erst da, wo die ersten Keime der Bewusstseinsseele sich entwickeln, beginnt man damit auf die «eigentliche Geschichte» zu blicken.

Und in dem, was losgelöst vom Göttlich-Geistigen als Menschlich-Geistiges Geschichte wird, kann von den Menschen die freie Intelligenz und der freie Wille erlebt werden.

So verläuft das Weltgeschehen, in das der Mensch einverwoben ist, zwischen dem voll Berechenbaren und dem Wirken der freien Intelligenz und des freien Willens. In allen Zwischennuancen des Zusammenwirkens von beidem offenbart sich das Weltgeschehen.

Der Mensch vollbringt sein Leben zwischen Geburt und Tod so, dass ihm im Berechenbaren die leibliche Grundlage zur Entfaltung des innerlichen geistig-seelischen freien Unberechenbaren geschaffen wird. Sein Leben zwischen Tod und neuer Geburt durchläuft er im Unberechenbaren, doch so, dass ihm da als in dem «Inneren» des geistig-seelischen

As I have characterized, it is only with difficulty that in his consciousness the human being takes leave of the old conceptions wherein the gods and human beings are imagined as working together. – Thus the period of "actual earth history" has long been present; it has in fact been present since the unfolding of the intellectual- or mind-soul. The human being still "thinks" in the sense of what had been before. Only when the first germinal seeds of the consciousness soul evolve does one begin to pay attention to what is known as "actual history."

And in what is loosened from the divine-spiritual as the human-spiritual, thus becoming history, human beings may consciously experience their free intelligence and free will.

Thus the world-process in which the human being is interwoven runs its course between the fully calculable on one hand, and the working of the free intelligence and free will on the other. This world-process manifests itself in all conceivable intermediate shades of cooperation between these two.

The human being lives his life between birth and death in such a manner that in the calculable the bodily foundation is created for the unfolding of his inner spiritual-soul nature, which is free and incalculable. He goes through his life between death and new birth in the incalculable, but in such a way that the calculable unfolds, in thought, "within" his

Seins das Berechenbare sich gedanklich entfaltet. Er wird dadurch – aus diesem Berechenbaren heraus – der Aufbauer seines kommenden Erdenlebens.

In der «Geschichte» lebt sich auf Erden das Unberechenbare aus, in das sich aber das Berechenbare, wenn auch im schwachen Maße, eingliedert.

Gegen die Ordnung, die durch die mit dem Menschen seit Urbeginn verbundenen göttlich-geistigen Wesen zwischen Unberechenbarem und Berechenbarem festgelegt ist – gegen deren Harmonisierung des Kosmos durch «Maß, Zahl und Gewicht» –, stellen sich die luziferischen und ahrimanischen Wesen. Luzifer kann mit der Art, die er seinem Wesen gegeben hat, nichts Berechenbares vereinigen. Sein Ideal ist kosmische unbedingte Intelligenz- und Willenswirkung.

Diese luziferische Tendenz, sie ist angemessen der Weltenordnung in den Gebieten, in denen freies Geschehen herrschen soll. Und da ist Luzifer der berechtigte geistige Helfer der Menschheitsentfaltung. Ohne seine Hilfe könnte in das Geistig-Seelische des Menschen, das sich auf der Grundlage des berechenbaren Leiblichen aufbaut, Freiheit nicht einziehen. Aber Luzifer möchte diese Tendenz auf den ganzen Kosmos ausdehnen. Und da wird seine Tätigkeit zum Kampfe gegen die göttlich-geistige Ordnung, zu der der Mensch ursprünglich gehört.

Da tritt Michael ein. Er steht mit dem eigenen Wesen im

spiritual-soul existence. Out of this calculable element he thereby becomes the builder of his coming life on earth.

That which cannot be calculated lives itself out on earth in "history," but into it the calculable is incorporated, though only to a slight extent.

The luciferic and ahrimanic beings stand opposed to the divine order established between the incalculable and the calculable – i.e., the harmonizing of the cosmos through "measure, number, and weight." This order was established by the divine-spiritual beings who have been united with the human being from the very beginning. Lucifer cannot unite anything calculable with the nature that he has given to his being. His ideal is a cosmically unconditioned activity of intelligence and will.

This luciferic tendency is in keeping with the cosmic order in the realms in which there should reign free actions. And in this realm Lucifer is the competent spiritual helper of the unfolding of humanity. Without his help, freedom could not enter into the human spiritual-soul element which is built on the foundation of the calculable bodily nature. But Lucifer would like to extend this tendency into the whole cosmos. And in this, his activity becomes a battle against the divine-spiritual order to which the human being originally belongs.

Here Michael comes in. With his own being he stands

Unberechenbaren; aber er bewirkt den Ausgleich zwischen dem Unberechenbaren und dem Berechenbaren, das er als Weltgedanke in sich trägt, den er von seinen Göttern empfangen hat.

Anders stehen die ahrimanischen Mächte in der Welt. Sie sind der völlige Gegensatz der göttlich-geistigen Wesen, mit denen der Mensch ursprünglich verbunden ist. Diese sind gegenwärtig rein geistige Mächte, die in sich vollkommene freie Intelligenz und vollkommen freien Willen tragen, die aber in dieser Intelligenz und diesem Willen die weise Einsicht von der Notwendigkeit des Berechenbaren, Unfreien als Weltgedanken schaffen, aus dessen Schoße der Mensch als freies Wesen sich entfalten soll. Und sie sind mit allem Berechenbaren, mit dem Weltgedanken, im Kosmos *in Liebe* verbunden. Diese Liebe strömt von ihnen durch das Weltall.

In vollem Gegensatz dazu lebt in dem gierigen Begehren der ahrimanischen Mächte der *kalte Hass* auf alles in Freiheit sich Entfaltende. Ahrimans Streben geht dahin, aus dem, was er von der Erde in den Weltenraum strömen lässt, eine kosmische Maschine zu machen. Sein Ideal ist «einzig und allein» «Maß, Zahl und Gewicht». Er wurde in den der Menschenentwickelung dienenden Kosmos hereingerufen, weil «Maß, Zahl und Gewicht», sein Gebiet, entfaltet werden mussten.

Nur wer die Welt geistig-körperlich *überall* begreift, der begreift sie wirklich. Das muss bis in die Natur hinein mit

within the incalculable; but he balances the incalculable with the calculable, which he bears within himself as the world-thought received from his gods.

The position of the ahrimanic powers in the world is different. They are the exact opposite of the divine-spiritual beings with whom the human being was originally united. At the present time, the divine-spiritual beings are purely spiritual powers possessing absolutely free intelligence and absolutely free will, but in this intelligence and will they create the wise insight of the necessity of the calculable and the unfree – the world-thought out of whose lap the human being is to unfold as a free being. And in the cosmos these divine-spiritual beings are united *in love* with all that is calculable – with the world-thought. This love streams from them through the universe.

In complete contrast with this, there lives, in the greedy desire of the ahrimanic powers, *cold hatred* toward all that unfolds in freedom. Ahriman's efforts are directed toward making a cosmic machine out of all that he allows to stream forth from the earth into universal space. His ideal is "solely and exclusively" "measure, number, and weight." He was called into the cosmos that serves the development of humanity because "measure, number, and weight," which is his sphere, had to be unfolded.

The world is truly understood only by one who comprehends it *everywhere* in a spiritual-corporeal manner. This must

Bezug auf solche Mächte wie die göttlich-geistigen in Liebe wirkenden und die in Hass wirkenden ahrimanischen beachtet werden. Man muss in der naturhaften Weltenwärme, die mit dem Frühling einsetzt und gegen den Sommer zu wirkt, die naturhafte Liebe der göttlich-geistigen Wesen wahrnehmen; man muss in dem wehenden Froste des Winters die Wirkung Ahrimans gewahr werden.

Im Hochsommer webt sich Luzifers Kraft in die naturhafte Liebe, die Wärme, hinein. In der Weihnachtszeit wendet sich die Kraft der göttlich-geistigen Wesen, denen der Mensch ursprünglich verbunden ist, gegen den Frost-Hass Ahrimans. Und gegen den Frühling zu mildert fortdauernd naturhafte göttliche Liebe naturhaften Ahriman-Hass.

Das Erscheinen dieser alljährlich auftretenden göttlichen Liebe ist die Zeit der Erinnerung, da das freie Gottes-Element in das berechenbare Erd-Element mit dem Christus eingetreten ist. Christus wirkt in völliger Freiheit in dem Berechenbaren; damit macht er unschädlich, was nur das Berechenbare begehrt, das Ahrimanische.

Das Ereignis von Golgatha ist die freie kosmische Tat der Liebe innerhalb der Erdengeschichte; sie ist auch nur erfassbar für die Liebe, die der Mensch zu diesem Erfassen aufbringt.

be carried right into nature with respect to such powers as the divine-spiritual, who work in love, and the ahrimanic, who work in hatred. In nature's cosmic warmth, coming in spring and working more strongly toward summer, one must perceive the love of the divine-spiritual beings working through nature; in the icy blast of winter one must become aware of Ahriman's working.

At midsummer, Lucifer's power weaves itself into the love that works in nature: into the warmth. During Christmas, the power of the divine-spiritual beings with whom the human being is originally united is directed against the frost-hatred of Ahriman. And toward spring, the divine love working in nature continually softens down the Ahriman-hatred there.

The appearance of this divine love, which comes each year, is the time of remembrance for the fact that with Christ, the free element of God entered into the calculable element of earth. Christ works in absolute freedom in the calculable; in this way, He renders innocuous that which craves for the calculable alone: the ahrimanic.

The Event of Golgotha is the free cosmic deed of love within earthly history; and it can only be grasped by the love that the human being brings toward its comprehension.

Leitsätze Nr. 140 bis 143

140. Das kosmische Geschehen, in das die Menschheitsentwickelung einverwoben ist und das sich im Menschenbewusstsein als «Geschichte» im umfassendsten Sinne spiegelt, gliedert sich: in die langdauernde Himmelsgeschichte, die kürzere mythologische Geschichte und in die verhältnismäßig ganz kurze Erdgeschichte.

141. Dieses kosmische Geschehen zerfällt gegenwärtig in das «nicht zu berechnende» Wirken göttlich-geistiger Wesen, die in freier Intelligenz und freiem Willen schaffen, und in das «berechenbare» Geschehen des Weltenleibes.

142. Gegen das Berechenbare des Weltenleibes stellen sich die luziferischen, gegen das in freier Intelligenz und freiem Willen Schaffende die ahrimanischen Mächte.

143. Das Ereignis von Golgatha ist eine freie kosmische Tat, die der Welten-Liebe entstammt und nur durch Menschen-Liebe erfasst werden kann.

Leading Thoughts 140 to 143

140. The cosmic process in which the development of humanity is interwoven – reflected, in human consciousness, as "history" in the widest sense – reveals the following successive epochs: a long epoch of the history of heaven; a shorter epoch of "mythological history"; and the epoch, relatively very short, of earth history.

141. At the present time, this cosmic process is divided into the "incalculable" working of divine-spiritual beings in free intelligence and will, and the "calculable" process of the world-body.

142. Against the calculable order of the world-body, the luciferic powers stand opposed; against all that creates in free intelligence and will, the ahrimanic stand opposed.

143. The Event of Golgotha is a freely enacted cosmic deed stemming from World-Love, and it can be comprehended only through the love of human beings.

Was sich offenbart, wenn man in die wiederholten Erdenleben zurückschaut

Goetheanum, zu Neujahr 1925

Wenn das geistgemäße Erkennen zurückschauen kann in frühere Erdenleben eines Menschen, so zeigt sich, dass es eine Anzahl solcher Erdenleben gibt, in denen der Mensch schon Person war. Sein Äußeres glich dem gegenwärtigen, und er hatte ein Innenleben, das individuelles Gepräge trug. Es treten Erdenleben auf, die offenbaren, wie die Verstandes- oder Gemütsseele da war, noch nicht die Bewusstseinsseele, und solche, in denen erst die Empfindungsseele ausgebildet war und so weiter.

In den erdgeschichtlichen Zeitaltern ist das so; es war auch schon lange vorher so.

Man kommt aber im Anschauen zurück zu Zeitaltern, in denen es noch nicht so war. Da findet man den Menschen noch nach Innenleben und nach der äußeren Bildung mit der Welt der göttlich-geistigen Wesen verwoben. Der Mensch ist als Erdenmensch da, aber nicht losgelöst vom göttlich-geistigen Wesen, Denken und Wollen.

In noch älteren Zeiten verschwindet der losgelöste Mensch ganz; es sind nur göttlich-geistige Wesen vorhanden, die den Menschen in ihrem Schoß tragen.

What Reveals Itself When One Looks Back into Repeated Lives on Earth

Goetheanum, for the New Year 1925

When the capacity of spiritual knowing is able to look back into the former earthly lives of a human being, it is revealed that there are a number of such lives in which the human being was already a "personality." His outward form was similar to what it is today, and he had an inner life colored by his individual character. Earthly lives emerge, revealing that the intellectual- or mind-soul was present in them, but not as yet the consciousness soul; other such lives appear in which only the sentient soul was developed – and so forth.

It is so in the epochs of earthly history; and indeed, it was so long before these epochs.

But as one looks back still farther, one comes into ages of time when it was not yet so – ages in which one finds the human being interwoven still, both in his inner life and in his outer formation, with the world of divine-spiritual beings. The human being is already there as earthly being, but he is not yet detached from divine-spiritual Being, thinking, and willing.

And in yet earlier epochs, the human being as a separate being disappears altogether; there are only the divine-spiritual beings, bearing the human being within them.

Diese drei Stadien seiner Entwickelung hat der Mensch während seiner Erdenzeit durchgemacht. Der Übergang des ersten in das zweite liegt in der spätesten lemurischen, der vom zweiten in das dritte in der atlantischen Zeit.

Wie nun der Mensch im gegenwärtigen Erdenleben seine Erlebnisse als Erinnerung in sich trägt, so trägt er alles, was er in der geschilderten Art durchgemacht hat, als kosmische Erinnerung in sich. Was ist das irdische Seelenleben? Die Welt der Erinnerungen, die bereit ist, in jedem Augenblicke neue Wahrnehmungen zu machen. In diesem Wechselwirken von Erinnerung und neuer Erfahrung lebt der Mensch sein innerliches Erdendasein.

Aber dieses innerliche Erdendasein könnte nicht zur Entfaltung kommen, wenn nicht als kosmische Erinnerung im Menschen gegenwärtig noch vorhanden wäre, was man schaut, wenn man geistig zurückblickt in das erste Stadium seines Erden-Mensch-Werdens, in dem er von dem göttlich-geistigen Wesen noch nicht losgelöst war.

Von dem, was damals in der Welt geschah, ist heute auf Erden nur noch das lebendig vorhanden, was innerhalb der menschlichen Nerven-Sinnesorganisation entwickelt wird. In der äußeren Natur sind alle die Kräfte, die damals wirksam waren, erstorben und nur in toten Formen beobachtbar.

So lebt in der menschlichen Gedankenwelt als gegenwärtige Offenbarung, was, um Erdenexistenz zu haben, zur Grundlage

The human being has undergone these three stages of development during his earthly phase. The transition from the first to the second took place in the latest epoch of Lemuria; that from the second to the third in Atlantean times.

Now just as in his present earthly life the human being bears his experiences within him as memory, so does he bear within him as cosmic memory all that he has undergone in the way described above. What is the earthly soul-life? It is the world of memories, ready at every moment to have fresh perceptions. In this interplay of memory and fresh experience, the human being lives his inner life on earth.

But this inner life on earth could not unfold at all if there were not still present in the human being, as cosmic memory, what one sees when looking back with spiritual vision into the first stage of his becoming as earthly human being – the stage in which he was not yet separated from divine-spiritual Being.

Of all that took place in the world at that time, there is still livingly present on earth today only what has been developed within the human system of nerves and senses. In outer nature, all the forces at work at that time have died and are now perceivable only in their dead forms.

Thus in the human thought-world there lives as a present revelation something that, in order to have earthly existence,

das haben muss, was im Menschen schon entwickelt war, bevor er individuelles Erdendasein erlangte.

In dem Leben zwischen Tod und neuer Geburt erlebt der Mensch jedes Mal aufs Neue dieses Stadium. Nur trägt er in die Welt der göttlich-geistigen Wesen, die ihn wieder aufnimmt, wie sie ihn einst in sich gehabt hat, sein volles in den Erdenleben gebildetes individuelles Dasein hinein. Er ist zwischen Tod und neuer Geburt zugleich in der Gegenwart, aber auch in aller Zeit, die er durch wiederholte Erdenleben und wiederholte Leben zwischen Tod und neuer Geburt durchgemacht hat.

Anders verhält es sich mit dem, was in der Gefühlswelt des Menschen lebt. Sie steht zu den Erlebnissen in Beziehung, die unmittelbar nach denen kamen, die den Menschen noch nicht als solchen offenbaren. Zu den Erlebnissen, die der Mensch schon als Mensch, aber noch nicht losgelöst von göttlich-geistigem Wesen, Denken und Wollen durchmacht. Der Mensch könnte gegenwärtig keine Gefühlswelt entfalten, wenn diese nicht auf der Grundlage seiner rhythmischen Organisation erstehen würde. In dieser ist die kosmische Erinnerung an das geschilderte zweite Stadium der Menschheitsentwickelung vorhanden.

So wirken in der Gefühlswelt zusammen die menschliche seelische Gegenwart und das, was in ihm nachwirkt aus einer alten Zeit.

requires as its basis what had already developed in the human being before he attained individual earthly existence.

Every time he passes through the life between death and a new birth, the human being experiences this stage anew. But into the world of divine-spiritual beings, which receives him again even as it once entirely enveloped him – into this world he now carries his full individual existence that has taken shape during his lives on earth. Between death and a new birth, the human being is indeed in the present, but he likewise lives within all the time of his repeated earthly lives and periods of life between death and a new birth.

It is different with respect to what lives in the human feeling-world. This is related to the experiences of the past which came immediately after the experiences in which the human being was yet unmanifest as such. It is related, that is to say, to experiences which the human being already underwent as human being, but during which he was not yet separated from divine-spiritual Being, thinking, and willing. The human being in the present would be unable to unfold the world of feeling if it had not arisen on the foundation of his rhythmic system. And in his rhythmic system there is the cosmic memory of the above-described second stage of his development.

Thus, in the world of feeling there works the "present" state of the human soul together with what works on in the human being from an ancient time.

In dem Leben zwischen dem Tod und einer neuen Geburt erlebt der Mensch den Inhalt der Zeit, von der hier die Rede ist, wie die Grenze seines Kosmos. Was dem Menschen im physischen Erdenleben der Sternenhimmel ist, das ist geistig in dem Leben zwischen Tod und neuer Geburt sein Dasein, das zwischen seiner völligen Verbundenheit mit der göttlich-geistigen Welt und seinem Losgelöstsein liegt. Da erscheinen an der «Weltengrenze» nicht die physischen Himmelskörper, sondern an jedem Sternenort die Summe der göttlich-geistigen Wesen, die ja in Wirklichkeit der Stern sind.

Mit dem Willen allein, nicht mit Gefühl und Denken verbunden, lebt im Menschen dasjenige, was die Erdenleben aufweisen, die sich beim Beobachten schon als persönlich-individuell offenbaren. Was dem Menschen aus dem Kosmos heraus seine äußere Gestalt gibt, das erhält sich in dieser äußeren Gestalt als kosmische Erinnerung. Diese lebt in der menschlichen Gestalt als Kräfte. Es sind das nicht unmittelbar die Kräfte des Willens, sondern das, was in der menschlichen Organisation die Grundlage der Willenskräfte ist.

In dem Leben zwischen Tod und neuer Geburt liegt *dieses* Gebiet des menschlichen Wesens außerhalb der «Weltengrenze». Der Mensch stellt es da vor als dasjenige, das ihm beim neuen Erdenleben wieder eigen sein wird.

In seiner Nerven-Sinnesorganisation ist der Mensch heute

In the life between death and a new birth, the human being experiences the content of the epoch here under consideration as the boundary of his cosmos. What the starry heavens are to the human being in the physical life on earth, his existence between his full union with the divine-spiritual world and his severance from it is to him spiritually in his life between death and a new birth. In that life, there appear to him at the "boundary of worlds," not the physical heavenly bodies, but in the place of each star the totality of divine-spiritual beings who indeed actually constitute the star.

Connected with the will alone – not with feeling or with thought – there lives in the human being what is manifested by those earthly lives which, when they are looked back upon, reveal already the personal, individual character. That which, from cosmic sources, gives the human being his outer form, is preserved in this outer form as cosmic memory. This cosmic memory lives in the human form as a totality of forces. But these are not the immediate forces of the will; they represent that in the human organism which is the foundation of the will-forces.

In the life between death and a new birth, *this* region of the human being lies beyond the "boundary of worlds." The human being there conceives of it as of something that will belong to him once more in his new life on earth.

In his system of nerves and senses, the human being is today

noch so mit dem Kosmos verbunden, wie er es war, als er noch innerhalb des Göttlich-Geistigen nur keimhaft sich offenbarte.

In seiner rhythmischen Organisation lebt der Mensch heute noch so im Kosmos, wie er lebte, als er als Mensch schon vorhanden, aber noch nicht losgelöst vom Göttlich-Geistigen war.

In seiner Stoffwechsel-Gliedmaßen-Organisation, als der Grundlage der Willensentfaltung, lebt der Mensch so, dass in dieser Organisation alles nachwirkt, was er seit der Zeit der persönlich-individuellen Erdenleben in diesen und in den Leben zwischen Tod und neuer Geburt durchgemacht hat.

Aus den Kräften der Erde hat der Mensch nur dasjenige, was ihm das Selbstbewusstsein verleiht. Auch die physische Leibesgrundlage dieses Selbstbewusstseins stammt aus dem, was die Erde bewirkt. Alles Übrige im Menschenwesen ist außerirdisch-kosmischen Ursprungs. Der empfindende und gedankentragende Astralleib und seine ätherisch-physische Grundlage, alle Lebensregsamkeit im Ätherleib, ja sogar, was im physischen Leib physisch-chemisch wirkt, ist außerirdischen Ursprungs. So befremdend dies auch sein mag: Das innerhalb des Menschen wirksame Physisch-Chemische stammt nicht aus der Erde.

Dass der Mensch dieses außerirdische Kosmische in sich entwickelt, ist Wirkung der *Planeten* und sonstiger *Sterne*. Was er so entwickelt, das trägt die *Sonne* mit ihren Kräften zur Erde. Das Menschlich-Kosmische wird durch die Sonne in

still united with the cosmos in the way he was when he was only germinally manifest within divine-spiritual Being.

In his rhythmic system, the human being is today still living in the cosmos in the way he lived when he was already there as human being but not yet separated from divine-spiritual Being.

In his system of metabolism and limbs – the foundation for the unfolding of his will – the human being lives in such a way that all he has undergone in the period of his personal-individual lives on earth, as well as in his lives between death and a new birth, works on within this system.

From the forces of the earth, the human being receives that alone which grants him self-consciousness. The physical-bodily foundation of self-consciousness also stems from what the earth brings about. But everything else in the human being has an origin that is cosmic and from beyond this world. The sentient and thought-bearing astral body with its etheric-physical foundation, all the life-movement in the etheric body, and even what works in a physical-chemical way in the physical body, has an origin from beyond this world. Strange as this may seem, the physical-chemical at work within the human being does not stem from the earth.

The fact that the human being evolves within himself this cosmic life from beyond this world is due to the working of the *planets* and *stars*. All that he thus unfolds, the *sun* with its forces carries to the earth. By means of the sun, the human-cosmic

den Bereich des Irdischen versetzt. Durch sie lebt der Mensch als Himmelswesen auf der Erde. Nur dasjenige, wodurch er über seine Menschenbildung hinausgeht, die Fähigkeit seinesgleichen hervorzubringen, ist eine Gabe des Mondes.

Selbstverständlich sind dies nicht die einzigen Wirkungen von Sonne und Mond. Von ihnen gehen auch hochgeistige Wirkungen aus.

Wenn die Sonne um die Weihnachtszeit immer mehr an Kräften für die Erde gewinnt, so ist dieses die im Physisch-Irdischen *rhythmisch* sich offenbarende Jahreswirkung, die ein Ausdruck des Geistes in der Natur ist. Die Menschheitsentwickelung ist ein einziges Glied in einem gewissermaßen gigantischen Weltenjahr. Das geht aus den vorangehenden Ausführungen hervor. In diesem Weltenjahr ist Welten-Weihe-Nacht da, wo die Sonne nicht bloß aus dem Geiste der Natur heraus zur Erde wirkt, sondern wo die Seele der Sonne, der Christus-Geist, auf die Erde niedersteigt.

Wie im einzelnen Menschen das individuell Erlebte mit der kosmischen Erinnerung zusammenhängt, so wird die alljährliche Weihnacht von der Menschenseele richtig empfunden, wenn das himmlisch-kosmische Christus-Ereignis als *fortwirkend* gedacht und wie eine nicht bloß menschliche, sondern kosmische Erinnerung aufgefasst wird. Nicht bloß der Mensch gedenkt festlich zu Weihnachten des Christus' Niederstieges, sondern auch der Kosmos.

element is transplanted into the earthly realms. Through the sun, the human being lives as a heavenly being on the earth. However, that power whereby he transcends his own human formation – namely, his power to bring forth his kind – is a gift of the moon.

Needless to say, these are not the only influences of sun and moon. Lofty spiritual influences also proceed from them.

When, around Christmas, the sun achieves ever more power for the earth, this is the seasonal influence manifesting *rhythmically* in the physical-earthly realm, which is an expression of the spirit in nature. The development of humanity is a single member in what may be described as a gigantic cosmic year, as shown before. And within this cosmic year, the Cosmic Christmas stands at the point where the sun not only works toward the earth out of the spirit of nature, but where the soul of the sun, the Christ-spirit, descends to earth.

Just as, in the single human being, what he experiences individually is connected with the cosmic memory, so will the human soul have a right feeling of the yearly Christmas when he conceives of the heavenly and cosmic Christ Event *as working on and on*, comprehending it not merely as a human but as a cosmic memory. For during Christmas it is not merely that the human being remembers in celebration the descent of Christ, but the cosmos does so as well.

Leitsätze Nr. 144 bis 146

144. Schaut man in die wiederholten Erdenleben eines Menschen zurück, so gliedern sich diese in drei verschiedene Stadien: ein ältestes, in dem der Mensch noch nicht individuell-wesenhaft, sondern als Keim in göttlich-geistiger Wesenheit vorhanden ist. Man findet da beim Zurückschauen noch nicht einen Menschen, sondern göttlich-geistige Wesen (die Urkräfte, Archai).

145. Daran schließt sich ein mittleres Stadium, in dem der Mensch zwar schon individuell-wesenhaft vorhanden ist, aber noch nicht losgelöst von Denken und Wollen und Wesen der göttlich-geistigen Welt. Er hat da noch nicht seine gegenwärtige Persönlichkeit, die damit zusammenhängt, dass er ein völlig eigenes Wesen in seiner Erderscheinung, losgelöst von der göttlich-geistigen Welt, ist.

146. Als drittes Stadium tritt erst das gegenwärtige auf. Der Mensch erlebt sich in seiner Menschengestalt, losgelöst von der göttlich-geistigen Welt; und er erlebt die Welt als Umgebung, der er individuell-persönlich gegenübersteht. Dieses Stadium beginnt in der atlantischen Zeit.

Leading Thoughts 144 to 146

144. Looking back into a human being's repeated lives on earth, one finds three distinct stages: In a remote past, the human being did not exist with individuality of being, but as a germ in the divine-spiritual. As one looks back into this stage, one finds not yet a human being but divine-spiritual beings (what are known as the Primal Forces or Archai).

145. This was followed by an intermediate stage in which the human being existed with individuality of being, though he was not yet separated from the thinking and willing and Being of the divine-spiritual world. At this stage, he did not yet have his present personality, with which he appears on earth as a being completely self-possessed and separated from the divine-spiritual world.

146. As the third stage, there emerges for the first time the condition that one experiences in the present time. Here the human being experiences himself in human form and figure, separated from the divine-spiritual world; and he experiences the world as an environment with which he stands face to face in an individual-personal way. This stage begins in the Atlantean epoch.

Erster Teil der Betrachtung: Was offenbart sich, wenn man in die vorigen Leben zwischen Tod und neuer Geburt zurückschaut?

Goetheanum, um die Jahreswende 1925

In der vorigen Betrachtung wurde das Gesamt-Menschenleben so verfolgt, dass der Seelenblick auf die aufeinanderfolgenden Erdenleben gelenkt wurde. Der andere Gesichtspunkt, der in noch helleres Licht rücken kann, was der erste offenbart, ist der, die aufeinanderfolgenden Leben zwischen dem Tod und einer neuen Geburt zu betrachten.

Auch da zeigt sich, dass der Inhalt dieser Leben, wie er in der Gegenwart ist, nur bis zu einem gewissen Zeitpunkte der Erdenentwickelung zurückgeht. *Dieser* Inhalt ist ja dadurch bestimmt, dass der Mensch durch die Todespforte die innerliche Kraft des Selbstbewusstseins hindurchträgt, die im Erdenleben erworben ist. Der Mensch steht dadurch auch den göttlich-geistigen Wesen, in deren Mitte er tritt, als volle Individualität gegenüber.

So war es in einer vorangehenden Periode nicht. Da war der Mensch in der Entfaltung seines Selbstbewusstseins noch nicht weit. Die auf Erden erlangte Kraft reichte nicht hin, die Loslösung von der göttlich-geistigen Welt bis zum individuellen

First Part of the Consideration: What Reveals Itself When One Looks Back into Former Lives between Death and a New Birth?

Goetheanum, at the turn of the year 1925

In our last consideration, human life as a whole was followed by turning soul-perception to the reality of successive lives on earth. The second point of view, which can throw still brighter light upon what was revealed by the first, is given when consideration is given to the successive lives between death and a new birth.

Here it is likewise evident that the content of these lives, such as they are at the present, goes back only to a certain point of time in earthly development. *This* content is determined by the fact that the human being carries with him through the gate of death the inward power of self-consciousness gained in earthly life. This also enables him to confront, as a full individuality, the divine-spiritual beings into whose presence he comes.

This was not the case in a preceding period. At that time, the human being had not yet progressed very far in the unfolding of his self-consciousness. The power gained on earth was insufficient to separate him from the divine-spiritual beings and

Dasein zwischen Tod und neuer Geburt zu bewirken. Der Mensch befand sich da zwar nicht in den göttlich-geistigen Wesen, wohl aber innerhalb deren Wirkungskreis so, dass sein Wollen im Wesentlichen *ihr* Wollen, nicht *seines* war.

Vor dieser Periode liegt eine andere, in der man beim Zurückschauen gar nicht auf den Menschen in seiner gegenwärtigen geistig-seelischen Verfassung trifft, sondern auf die Welt göttlich-geistiger Wesen, *in denen* der Mensch erst keimhaft ist. Es sind die Urkräfte (Archai).

Und zwar trifft man, wenn man *eines* Menschen Leben zurückverfolgt, nicht auf *ein* göttlich-geistiges Wesen, sondern auf alle, die zu dieser Hierarchie gehören.

In diesen göttlich-geistigen Wesen lebt der Wille, dass der Mensch werde. An dem Werden jedes einzelnen Menschen ist der Wille aller beteiligt. In ihrem chormäßigen Zusammenwirken liegt als Weltenziel die Entstehung der menschlichen *Gestalt.* Denn noch ungestaltet lebt der Mensch in der göttlich-geistigen Welt.

Es erscheint vielleicht sonderbar, dass auch schon für *einen* Menschen der ganze Chor göttlich-geistiger Wesen wirkt. Aber schon früher wirkten so die Hierarchien Exusiai, Dynameis, Kyriotetes, Throne, Cherubim, Seraphim durch die Monden-, Sonnen- und Saturnentwickelung, damit der Mensch werde.

Was früher entstand, eine Art Vormensch, auf Saturn, Sonne

thus to give him individual existence between death and a new birth. The human being did not find himself within the divine-spiritual beings, yet he was within their sphere of influence such that his will was essentially *their* will, not *his own*.

Before this period lies another in which, as one looks back, one does not meet with the human being in his present spiritual-soul constitution at all, but rather finds a world of divine-spiritual beings *within whom* the human being only exists in germinal form. These beings are the Primal Forces (Archai).

And indeed, if one traces back the life of *one* human being, one finds not *one* divine-spiritual being, but all the beings belonging to this hierarchy.

In these divine-spiritual beings lives the intention that the human being shall become. The will of all these beings plays a part in the "becoming" of each individual human being. The cosmic aim of their choir-like cooperation is the emergence of the human *form*; for the human being is still without form in the divine-spiritual world.

It may seem strange that the whole choir of divine-spiritual beings works for *a single* human being. But the hierarchies of the Exusiai, Dynamis, Kyriotetes, Thrones, Cherubim, and Seraphim also worked in this way at a still earlier stage throughout the Moon, Sun, and Saturn phases of development, in order that the human being might come into being.

What had previously originated as a kind of pre-human

und Mond, hatte nicht einheitliche Gestalt. Es gab solche Vormenschen, die mehr nach dem Gliedmaßensystem, andere, die mehr nach dem Brustsystem, wieder andere, die nach dem Kopfsystem organisiert waren. Es waren das doch wirkliche Menschen; sie werden hier nur Vormenschen genannt, um sie zu unterscheiden von dem späteren Stadium, wo der ausgeglichene Zusammenfluss aller Systeme in der menschlichen Gestalt erscheint. Die Differenzierung bei diesen Vormenschen geht noch viel weiter. Man kann von Herzmenschen, Lungenmenschen und so weiter sprechen.

Die Hierarchie der Urkräfte betrachtet es als ihre Aufgabe, alle diese Vormenschen, deren Seelenleben ja auch ihrer einseitigen Gestaltung entsprochen hat, in die allgemeine menschliche Gestalt hineinzuführen.

Aus der Hand der Exusiai übernehmen sie den Menschen. Diese hatten schon *in Gedanken* aus der menschlichen Vielheit eine Einheit geschaffen. Allein bei den Exusiai war diese Einheit noch eine Idealgestalt, eine Weltgedankengestalt. Die Archai formten die Äthergestalt daraus, aber so, dass diese Äthergestalt schon die Kräfte zur Entstehung der physischen Gestalt enthielt.

Es offenbart sich ein Gewaltiges beim Hinblicken auf diese Tatbestände. Der Mensch ist Götter-Ideal und Götter-Ziel. Aber dieses Hinblicken kann nicht der Quell von Überhebung und Hochmut beim Menschen sein. Denn *er* darf sich ja

being on Saturn, Sun, and Moon, had no uniform shape. Some of these pre-human beings were principally organized with respect to the limb-system, others with respect to the chest-system, others again with respect to the head-system. These were actual human beings; they have been described here as pre-human only in order to distinguish them from the later stage, when the union of all these systems appears in the human form. The differentiation among them goes even further, for one may speak of heart human beings, lung human beings, and so on.

The hierarchy of the Primal Forces considered it their task to lead into the general human form all these pre-human beings, whose soul-life also corresponded to their one-sided formation.

The Primal Forces overtook the human being from the hands of the Exusiai. The latter had already *in thought* created unity out of the human multiplicity; but among the Exusiai this unity was still an ideal form, a world-thought-form. Out of this the Archai molded the etheric form, and this etheric form already contained the forces which made it possible for the physical form to originate.

When these things are observed, a profound fact is revealed: namely, that the human being is the ideal and aim of the gods. But the perception of this fact cannot be a source of vanity and pride for the human being; for *he* may only deem as his own

nur, als von ihm kommend, zurechnen, was er in den Erdenleben mit Selbstbewusstsein aus sich gemacht hat. Und dies ist, in kosmischen Verhältnissen ausgedrückt, wenig gegenüber dem, was als die Grundlage seines Eigenwesens die Götter aus dem Makrokosmos, der sie selber sind, heraus als Mikrokosmos, der *er* ist, geschaffen haben. Die göttlich-geistigen Wesen stehen im Kosmos einander gegenüber. Der sichtbare Ausdruck dieses Gegenüberstehens ist die Gestalt des gestirnten Himmels. Sie wollten, was sie so zusammen sind, in einer Einheit als Mensch schaffen.

Um recht zu verstehen, was die Hierarchie der Archai vollbrachte, als sie in ihrem Chor die menschliche Gestalt schuf, muss man bedenken, dass ein gewaltiger Unterschied ist zwischen dieser Gestalt und dem physischen Leib des Menschen. Physischer Leib ist, was sich physisch-chemisch im Menschenwesen abspielt. Das geschieht bei dem gegenwärtigen Menschen innerhalb der menschlichen Gestalt. Diese selbst aber ist ein durch und durch Geistiges. Feierlich sollte es stimmen, ein Geistiges mit physischen Sinnen in der physischen Welt als Menschengestalt wahrzunehmen. Für den, der geistig schauen kann, liegt dieses so, dass er in der Menschengestalt eine wirkliche Imagination sieht, die in die physische Welt heruntergestiegen ist. Will man Imaginationen schauen, muss man aus der physischen Welt in die nächste geistige übertreten. Dann aber wird man gewahr,

achievement what he has with full self-consciousness made of himself during earthly life. And, expressed in cosmic proportions, this – the microcosm which he is – is little as compared with the foundation for his individual being that the gods have created out of the macrocosm which they themselves are. The divine-spiritual beings stand over against one another in the cosmos. The visible expression of this standing over against one another is the form of the starry heavens. They wished to create in a unity – as the human being – all that they themselves are together.

In order really to understand what the whole choir of the hierarchy of the Archai accomplished when they created the human form, one must remember that there is a very great difference between this form and the human physical body. The physical body is made up of the physical and chemical processes that play out in the human being. These processes take place in the present human being within the human form. But this form itself is something altogether spiritual. To perceive with physical senses the human form as a spiritual reality in the physical world should evoke solemnity. For one who is able to see spiritually, it is really the case that in the human form one sees a true imagination which has descended into the physical world. If one wishes to perceive imaginations, one must pass from the physical world to the neighboring spiritual world. Then, however, one will become

wie die menschliche Gestalt diesen Imaginationen verwandt ist.

Das Entstehen dieser Menschengestalt findet der rückschauende Seelenblick des Menschen als erste Periode, wenn er die Leben zwischen Tod und neuer Geburt beobachtet. Es offenbart sich dabei zugleich, welches tiefere Verhältnis besteht zwischen dem Menschen und der Hierarchie der Archai.

Man kann in dieser Periode schon von einer *Andeutung* des Unterschiedes zwischen Erdenleben und Leben zwischen Tod und neuer Geburt sprechen. Die Hierarchie der Archai schafft nämlich in rhythmischen Epochen an dem Werden der Menschengestalt. Einmal richtet sie dabei die Gedanken, die den Willen der Einzelnen lenken, mehr nach dem außerirdischen Kosmos. Das andere Mal schaut sie auf die Erde herab. Und aus dem Zusammenwirken dessen, was vom außerirdischen Kosmos und von der Erde angeregt ist, wird die menschliche Gestalt gebildet, die so der Ausdruck dafür ist, dass der Mensch zugleich Erden- und außerirdisches Kosmos-Wesen ist.

Die menschliche Gestalt, wie sie hier als Schöpfung der Hierarchie der Archai geschildert ist, umfasst aber nicht bloß die äußeren Umrisse des Menschen und die Flächengestaltung, wie sie in der Hautbegrenzung gegeben ist, sondern auch die Kräftegestaltung, die in seiner Haltung, in seiner den Erdenverhältnissen angepassten Bewegungsfähigkeit und in

aware of how the human form is related to these imaginations.

When with inner vision of soul, the human being looks back over the lives between death and a new birth, he finds a first period during which this human form came into being. And at the same time the deeper relation that exists between the human being and the hierarchy of the Archai is revealed.

In this period, one can already speak of an *indication* of the difference between earthly life and the life between death and a new birth. For the hierarchy of the Archai works toward the development of the human form in rhythmical epochs. In one period of their work, the Archai direct the thoughts which guide their various will-impulses more toward the cosmos beyond this world; at another time, they look down to the earth. And out of the cooperation of what is aroused from the cosmos and from the earth, the human form is developed, which is thus the expression of the fact that the human being is an earth-being and at the same time a cosmos-being from beyond this world.

But the human form – here described as the creation of the hierarchy of the Archai – comprises not merely the external outline of the human being and the formation of the surface as it is determined by the limit of the skin. It also comprises the formation of the forces contained in his way of carrying himself, in his capacity of movement – which is adapted to the

der Fähigkeit liegt, seinen Körper als Ausdrucksmittel für sein Inneres zu gebrauchen.

Dass sich der Mensch in die Schwereverhältnisse der Erde in aufrechter Stellung hineinfügen kann, dass er innerhalb dieser Schwereverhältnisse das Gleichgewicht in freier Bewegung bewahren kann, dass er Arme und Hände der Schwere entreißen und in Freiheit gebrauchen kann, das und noch manches andere, das zwar im Innern liegt, aber doch Gestaltung ist: All das verdankt der Mensch dieser Schöpfung der Archai-Hierarchie. All das wird da vorbereitet in dem Leben, das man auch für diese Periode das zwischen Tod und neuer Geburt nennen kann. Es wird hier so vorbereitet, dass der Mensch dann in der dritten Periode, in unserer Gegenwart, während seines Lebens zwischen Tod und neuer Geburt die Fähigkeit hat, selbst an dieser Gestaltung für sein Erdendasein zu arbeiten.

conditions on earth – and the capacity to use his body as a means of expressing his inner being.

It is owing to this creative work of the hierarchy of the Archai that the human being is able to assume his upright position within the earthly conditions of gravity, and that within these conditions he can maintain his balance while moving freely – likewise, that he can liberate his arms and hands from the force of gravity and use them freely – and still more that lies in his inner being and yet has form: All this he owes to the creation of the Archai hierarchy. All this is prepared during the life which, for this period, may also be called the life between death and a new birth. It is here prepared in such a manner that, in the third period – at the present time – the human being is himself able, during his life between death and a new birth, to work upon this form for his earthly existence.

Leitsätze Nr. 147 bis 149

147. Auch die Leben zwischen Tod und neuer Geburt zeigen drei Perioden. In einer ersten lebt der Mensch ganz in der Hierarchie der Archai. Von ihnen wird seine spätere Menschengestalt für die physische Welt vorbereitet.

148. Die Archai bereiten damit das Menschenwesen dazu vor, später das freie Selbstbewusstsein zu entfalten; denn dieses kann nur in Wesen sich entwickeln, die es durch die Gestalt, die hier geschaffen wird, aus einem inneren Impuls der Seele zur Darstellung bringen können.

149. Damit zeigt sich, wie die Keime der Menschheitseigenschaften und Menschheitskräfte, die in unserem Weltenalter zur Offenbarung kommen, in längst vergangenen Weitenaltern veranlagt werden und wie der Mikrokosmos aus dem Makrokosmos herauswächst.

Leading Thoughts 147 to 149

147. The human being's periods of life between death and a new birth also show three distinct periods. In the first of these, he lived entirely within the hierarchy of the Archai; they prepared the human form and figure which he would later bear in the physical world.

148. Thus the Archai prepared the human being subsequently to unfold the capacity of free self-consciousness. For this self-consciousness can only evolve in beings who can bring it forth, in the form and figure which was here created, out of an inner impulse of the soul.

149. In this it is shown how qualities and powers of humanity revealed in the present cosmic age were laid down in germinal form in ages long past. It is shown how the microcosm grows forth from the macrocosm.

Zweiter Teil der Betrachtung: Was offenbart sich, wenn man in die vorigen Leben zwischen Tod und neuer Geburt zurückschaut?

Goetheanum, Jahreswende 1925

In einer zweiten Periode gelangt der Mensch aus dem Gebiet der Archai in das der Archangeloi. Mit diesen ist er aber nicht so körperlich-geistig verbunden wie vorher mit den Archai. Seine Verbindung mit der Archangeloi-Hierarchie ist eine mehr geistige. Aber sie ist doch so innig, dass man für diese Zeit von einem Losgelöstsein des Menschen von der göttlich-geistigen Welt noch nicht sprechen kann.

Die Erzengel-Hierarchie gibt dem Menschen das für seinen Ätherleib, was in diesem entsprechend ist der Gestalt im physischen Leib, die er den Archai verdankt. Wie der physische Leib durch die Gestalt der Erde angepasst ist, um auf dieser Träger des Selbstbewusstseins zu sein, so der Ätherleib den außerirdischen kosmischen Kräfteverhältnissen. Im physischen Leib lebt die Erde, und im Ätherleib lebt die Sternenwelt. Was der Mensch an inneren Kräften in sich trägt, um auf der Erde so zu sein, dass er sich zugleich mit Haltung, Bewegung, Gebärde der Erde entreißt, das verdankt er der Schöpfung der Erzengel in seinem Ätherleib.

Second Part of the Consideration: What Reveals Itself When One Looks Back into Former Lives between Death and a New Birth?

Goetheanum, at the turn of the year 1925

In a second period, the human being passes from the realm of the Archai to that of the Archangeloi. With these beings, however, he is no longer united in such a corporeal-spiritual way as he was with the Archai. His union with the hierarchy of the Archangeloi is more spiritual. But it is still so intimate that in this period he cannot yet be said to have been severed from the divine-spiritual world.

The Archangel hierarchy gives to the human being for his etheric body that in it which corresponds to the form in the physical, which he owes to the Archai. The physical body, through its form, is adapted to the earth in such a way as to become on earth the vehicle of self-consciousness. In like manner, the etheric body is adapted to the extra-earthly cosmic forces. In the physical body lives the earth; in the etheric, the world of the stars. All the inner forces which the human being bears within him in such a way that while on earth – in his posture, movement, and gesture – he is able to emancipate himself from the earth, he owes to the creation of the

Wie im physischen Leib die Erdenkräfte durch die Gestaltung leben können, so leben im Ätherleib die Kräfte, die aus dem Umkreis des Kosmos von allen Seiten auf die Erde zuströmen. Es sind die in der physisch erscheinenden Gestaltung lebenden Erdkräfte solche, die die Gestalt zu einer verhältnismäßig abgeschlossen-festen machen. Die Umrisse des Menschen bleiben mit untergeordneter Metamorphose für das Erdenleben fest; die Bewegungsfähigkeiten verfestigen sich in Gewohnheiten und so weiter. – Im Ätherleib herrscht fortwährende Beweglichkeit, die ein Spiegelbild ist der sich während des menschlichen Erdenlebens ändernden Sternenkonstellationen. Schon den Veränderungen des Himmels von Tag und Nacht entsprechend, gestaltet sich der Ätherleib; aber auch den Veränderungen, die zwischen der Geburt und dem Tode des Menschen vor sich gehen.

Diese Anpassung des Ätherleibes an die Himmelskräfte widerspricht nicht der allmählichen Loslösung des Sternenhimmels von den göttlich-geistigen Mächten, von der in anderen Betrachtungen gesprochen worden ist. Es ist richtig, in ganz alten Zeiten lebte in den Sternen Götterwille und Götterintelligenz. In den späteren Zeiten sind diese in das «Berechenbare» übergegangen. Die Götter wirken nicht mehr durch das, was ihr Werk geworden ist, auf den Menschen. Aber der Mensch gerät allmählich durch seinen Ätherleib in ein eigenes

Archangels in his etheric body. Just as the earth-forces are able to live in the physical body through its formation, so in the etheric body there live the forces which stream down on all sides from the encircling cosmos to the earth. The earth-forces living in the physically visible formation of the body are those which make the human form relatively complete, securely established within itself. Subject to a certain metamorphosis, the main outlines of the human being remain established throughout his earthly life. His faculties of movement, too, have hardened into permanent habits, and so forth. – In the etheric body, there is perpetual mobility, mirroring the constellations of the stars as they change during the earthly life of the human being. The etheric body forms itself even in accordance with the changes in the heavens from day to night; and it does so also with the changes that take place between the birth and death of the human being concerned.

This adaptation of the etheric body to the heavenly forces is not in contradiction to the gradual severance of the starry heavens from the divine-spiritual powers, mentioned in earlier considerations. It is true to say that in very ancient times divine will and divine intelligence were living in the stars, and that in later times the stars passed over into the "calculable." Through what has now become their finished work, the gods no longer work upon the human being. Nevertheless, through his etheric body the human being gradually achieves a

Verhältnis zu den Sternen, wie er durch seinen physischen Leib in ein solches zur Erdenschwere gelangt.

Was der Mensch sich einfügt, wenn er zur Geburt auf Erden aus der Geistwelt herabsteigt, seinen Ätherleib, der in sich die außerirdischen kosmischen Kräfte aufnimmt, das wird in dieser zweiten Periode durch die Hierarchie der Archangeloi geschaffen.

Ein Wesentliches, das da der Mensch durch diese Hierarchie bekommt, ist die Zugehörigkeit zu einer Gruppe von Menschen auf Erden. Die Menschen sind über die Erde hin differenziert. Man hat, indem man in diese zweite Periode zurückschaut, nicht die heutige Rassen- und Völkerdifferenzierung vor sich, sondern eine etwas andere, eine mehr geistige. Eine solche, die davon herrührt, dass auf die verschiedenen Orte der Erde die Sternenkräfte in verschiedenen Konstellationen auftreffen. Auf der Erde, in Land- und Wasserverteilung, in Klima, in Pflanzenwuchs und so weiter lebt ja der Sternenhimmel. Insoferne sich der Mensch an *diese* Verhältnisse, die auf der Erde als Himmelsverhältnisse sind, anpassen muss, gehört diese Anpassung in den Ätherleib, und dessen Gestaltung ist eine Schöpfung des Chores der Archangeloi.

Nun aber treten gerade während dieser zweiten Periode die luziferischen und ahrimanischen Mächte in einer besonderen Art in das Menschenleben herein. Dieses Hereintreten ist

relationship of his own to the stars, just as he does through his physical body to earthly gravity.

What the human being incorporates into his nature when at birth he descends from the world of spirit to the earth – namely the etheric body which absorbs the cosmic forces from beyond this world – is created in this second period by the hierarchy of the Archangeloi.

An essential element that the human being receives through this hierarchy is his membership in a group of human beings on the earth. Humanity is differentiated over the face of the earth. Looking back into this second period, it is not, however, the present differentiation of races and peoples that one finds, but a somewhat altered, more spiritual differentiation. This is due to the fact that the starry forces strike the different places of the earth in varying constellations. For on the earth itself – in the distribution of land and water, in climate, vegetation, and the like – the starry heavens are indeed active. Inasmuch as the human being must adapt himself to *these* conditions, which are really there as heavenly conditions on the earth, such adaptation belongs to his etheric body; and the forming of the latter is a creative work of the choir of Archangeloi.

But now it is just in this second period that the luciferic and ahrimanic powers enter the life of the human being to a special degree. Their entry is necessary, although to begin with it

notwendig, trotzdem es zunächst so erscheint, als ob es den Menschen *unter* seine Wesenheit herabdrücken würde.

Der Mensch muss, wenn er im Erdenleben Selbstbewusstsein entwickeln soll, von der göttlich-geistigen Welt, aus der er ursprünglich hervorgegangen ist, in einem stärkeren Maße loskommen, als dies durch *diese* Welt selbst geschehen kann. Es geschieht in der Zeit, da die Erzengel an ihm wirken, weil da die Verbindung mit der Geistwelt nicht mehr eine so feste ist, wie sie während des Wirkens der Archai an ihm war. Den mehr geistigen Kräften, die von den Erzengeln ausgehen, sind Luzifer und Ahriman mehr gewachsen als den stärkeren der Archai.

Es wird von den luziferischen Mächten die Äthergestaltung mit einer stärkeren Neigung für die Sternenwelt durchsetzt, als sie haben würde, wenn nur die ursprünglich mit dem Menschen verbundenen göttlich-geistigen Mächte wirken würden. Und es wird durch die ahrimanischen Mächte die physische Gestaltung stärker in die Erdenschwere verstrickt, als es geschehen würde, wenn diese Mächte nicht wirken könnten.

Dadurch wird in den Menschen der Keim des vollen Selbstbewusstseins und des freien Willens gelegt. Wenn auch die ahrimanischen Mächte den freien Willen hassen: *Im Menschen* bewirken sie, da sie ihn losreißen von *seiner* göttlich-geistigen Welt, die Keimanlage dieses freien Willens.

Zunächst aber, in dieser zweiten Periode, wird, was die

may seem to be driving the human being *beneath* the level of his true nature.

If the human being is to develop self-consciousness in his earthly life, he must loosen himself from the divine-spiritual world from which he originally proceeded, in greater measure than *that* world itself can bring about. This is what takes place during the time when the Archangels are at work upon him. For his union with the world of spirit is no longer as strong as it was when the Archai were at work upon him. Lucifer and Ahriman are more able to grapple with the spiritual forces proceeding from the Archangels, than with the stronger forces of the Archai.

The luciferic powers permeate the human etheric formation with a more intense inclination toward the starry world than it would have if the divine-spiritual powers originally united with the human being were alone at work. The ahrimanic powers entwine his physical formation more tightly in the realm of earthly gravity than would have been the case if they were unable to exert their influence.

By this means, the germ of full self-consciousness and free will is planted into the human being. Much as the ahrimanic powers hate free will, *in the human being* they actually bring about the germinal beginnings of this free will by tearing him loose from *his* divine-spiritual world.

To begin with, however, during the second period itself,

verschiedenen Hierarchien von den Seraphim bis zu den Erzengeln in dem Menschen bewirkt haben, *mehr* in den physischen und Ätherleib hineingedrückt, als es ohne luziferischen und ahrimanischen Einfluss geschehen könnte. Ohne diesen Einfluss bliebe die Wirkung der Hierarchien mehr im Astralleib und im Ich.

Dadurch entsteht nicht jene mehr geistige, von den Erzengeln angestrebte Gruppierung der Menschheit über die Erde hin.

In seinem Eingedrücktsein in den physischen und Ätherleib werden die geistigen Kräfte in ihr Gegenteil gewandelt. Es entsteht statt der mehr geistigen Differenzierung die nach Rassen und Völkern.

Ohne den luziferischen und ahrimanischen Einfluss sähen sich die Menschen auf Erden vom Himmel herunter differenziert. Die Gruppen verhielten sich zueinander in ihrem Leben wie Wesen, die Geistiges willig in Liebe einander geben und voneinander nehmen. In Rassen und Völkern erscheint die Erdenschwere durch den Leib des Menschen; in der geistigen Gruppierung wäre ein Spiegelbild der göttlich-geistigen Welt erschienen.

Mit alledem musste die spätere volle Selbstbewusstheit in der menschlichen Entwickelung schon vorher veranlagt werden. Das bedingte wieder, dass zwar gemildert, aber doch in

what the various hierarchies – from the Seraphim down to the Archangels – have brought about in the human being is impressed into his physical and etheric bodies *more* deeply than would have been possible without the luciferic and ahrimanic influence. For without this influence, the working of the hierarchies would remain more in the astral body and the 'I'.

Thus it happened that the more spiritually oriented process of grouping humanity over the face of the earth, which the Archangels were striving for, did not come about.

When pressed down into the physical and etheric body, the spiritual forces are transformed into their opposite. In place of a more spiritually oriented grouping, the differentiation of races and peoples comes about.

Without the luciferic and ahrimanic influences, human beings on earth would see themselves differentiated by forces working downwards from the heavens. The different groups would be to one another in their life like beings who, willingly and with love, give to one another of the spiritual and receive in turn. In races and peoples, it is earthly gravity which appears through the human body; in the spiritual groupings, a mirrored image of the divine-spiritual world would have appeared.

With all this, the beginnings of what would later become full self-consciousness had to be implanted in human development already at that time. And this meant that – in a milder

einer gewissen Form die uralte Menschendifferenzierung erhalten blieb, die bestand, als der Mensch einst überging von der Hierarchie der Exusiai an diejenige der Archai.

Der Mensch hat wie in einer kosmischen Schule dieses Entwickelungsstadium empfindend-anschauend erlebt. Er hat zwar noch nicht ein Wissen davon entwickelt, dass dies eine wesentliche Vorbereitung für seine spätere Selbstbewusstheit sei. Aber das empfindende Anschauen seiner Entwickelungskräfte damals war doch wichtig für die Eingliederung der Selbstbewusstheit in Astralleib und Ich.

In Bezug auf das Denken ist damals dies geschehen, dass der Mensch durch die luziferischen Mächte mit der Neigung ausgestattet wurde, sich in die alten Formen des Geistigen auch weiter zu versenken und sich den neuen Formen nicht anzupassen. Denn Luzifer hat ja stets das Bestreben, für den Menschen die früheren Formen des Lebens zu bewahren.

Und dadurch bildete sich das Denken des Menschen so aus, dass er allmählich in den Leben zwischen Tod und neuer Geburt diejenige Fähigkeit ausgestaltete, die in uralten Zeiten Gedanken in ihm bildete. *Damals* konnte diese Fähigkeit das Geistige schauen, trotzdem sie so war wie gegenwärtig die bloße Sinnesauffassung. Denn das Physische trug damals das Geistige an seiner Oberfläche. Jetzt aber kann die

sense, yet with a certain form – the primeval differentiation of humanity, which existed when the human being passed over from the hierarchy of the Exusiai to that of the Archai, remained preserved.

The human being – as it were in a cosmic school – experienced this stage in his development, contemplating it with inner feeling. True, he did not yet develop a knowledge of the fact that this was an essential preparation for his subsequent self-consciousness. But his feeling-vision of the forces of his development at that time was nonetheless important for the incorporation of self-consciousness into his astral body and his 'I'.

With respect to thought, the following took place. Through the luciferic powers, the human being was instilled with the tendency to continue immersing himself in the old forms of the spiritual instead of adapting himself to the new. Lucifer indeed always has the striving to conserve for the human being the earlier forms of his life.

By this means, human thinking was evolved: In the life between death and a new birth, the human being gradually developed that faculty which in primeval times had formed the thoughts in him. It was a faculty which *at that time* could behold the spiritual, though it was similar to what is now the mere faculty of sense perception. For at that time, the physical still carried the spiritual upon its surface. Today, however,

von damals bewahrte Denkfähigkeit nurmehr als Sinneswahrnehmung wirken. Allmählich nahm die Fähigkeit, denkend sich zum Geistigen zu erheben, ab. Und voll trat dies erst zutage, als im Zeitalter der Bewusstseinsseele die geistige Welt für den Menschen in gänzliche Dunkelheit gehüllt wurde. Da kam es, dass im neunzehnten Jahrhundert die besten Naturforscher, die nicht Materialisten werden konnten, sagten: Uns bleibt nichts übrig, als *bloß* die Welt zu erforschen, die sich nach Maß, Zahl und Gewicht und durch die Sinne erforschen lässt; aber wir haben kein Recht, eine geistige Welt zu leugnen, die sich hinter dieser sinnlichen verbirgt. Also der Hinweis darauf, dass eine dem Menschen *unbekannte* helle Welt sein könne, wo er nur in die Finsternis starrt.

Wie durch Luzifer das Denken im Menschen verschoben wurde, so durch Ahriman der Wille. Der wurde mit einer Tendenz zu einer Art von Freiheit begabt, in die er erst später hätte eintreten sollen. Diese Freiheit ist keine *wirkliche*, sondern die *Illusion* der Freiheit. In dieser Freiheitsillusion lebte die Menschheit lange. Das gab ihr keine Möglichkeit, geistgemäß die Idee der Freiheit zu entwickeln. Man pendelte hin und her zwischen den Meinungen, der Mensch sei frei, oder auch, er sei in eine starre Notwendigkeit eingesponnen. Und als dann mit dem heraufziehenden Bewusstseinszeitalter die

the faculty of thought preserved from that time can only work as restricted sense-perception. The human being's power to lift himself in thought to the spiritual world gradually declined. This became fully evident at length when, in the age of the consciousness soul, the spiritual world was veiled in complete darkness for the human being. Thus in the nineteenth century it came about that the best scientific minds, unable to become materialists, declared: We have no alternative but to limit our research *merely* to that world which can be investigated by measure, number, and weight and by the senses. We have, however, no right to deny a spiritual world concealed behind this world of nature. In such words they indicated that there might be a world full of light, *unknown* to the human being, where the human being can only stare into an empty darkness.

And just as thought in the human being was misdirected by Lucifer, so was will misdirected by Ahriman. The human being's will was endowed with a tendency to a kind of freedom which he should have entered only at a later stage. This freedom is not *real*; it is but the *illusion* of freedom. Human beings lived in this illusion of freedom for a long time, and thereby became unable to evolve the idea of freedom in a truly spiritual way. They vacillated back and forth, between the one opinion and the other: that the human being is free, or that he is entangled in a world of rigid necessity. And when with the

wirkliche Freiheit kam, da konnte man sie nicht erkennen, weil man das Erkennen allzu lange in die Illusion der Freiheit eingesponnen hatte.

Alles, was sich in diesem zweiten Stadium der Entwickelung der Leben zwischen dem Tode und einer neuen Geburt in das Wesen des Menschen eingesenkt hat, das trug er als kosmische Erinnerung in das dritte Stadium hinein, in dem er noch gegenwärtig lebt. Er steht in diesem Stadium zu der Hierarchie der Angeloi in einem ähnlichen Verhältnis, wie er während des zweiten zu derjenigen der Archangeloi gestanden hat. Nur ist das Verhältnis zu den Angeloi so, dass durch sie die volle selbstständige Individualität zustande kommt. Denn die Angeloi – jetzt nicht der Chor, sondern *einer* für *einen* Menschen – beschränken sich darauf, das rechte Verhältnis der Leben zwischen Tod und neuer Geburt und der Erdenleben zu bewirken.

Eine zunächst merkwürdige Tatsache ist diese, dass für den *einzelnen* Menschen im zweiten Stadium seiner Entwickelung der Leben zwischen Tod und neuer Geburt die ganze Hierarchie der Archangeloi wirkt. Später fällt dieser Hierarchie die Lenkung der Volksstämme zu. Und da ist für ein Volk *ein* Erzengel als Volksgeist. In den Rassen bleiben die Urkräfte tätig. Und wieder wirkt für *eine* Rasse ein Wesen aus der Hierarchie der Urkräfte als Rassengeist.

age of the consciousness soul true freedom came, they were unable to recognize it because their powers of perception had too long been entangled in the illusion of freedom.

All that had sunk into the essential nature of the human being during this second stage in the development of his lives between death and a new birth, he carried as a cosmic memory into the third stage, in which he still lives today. In this third stage, he is related to the hierarchy of the Angeloi in like manner as he was related in the second to that of the Archangeloi. However, this relationship to the Angeloi is such that through it, the full independent individuality comes into being. For the Angeloi – not the entire choir this time, but *one* Angel for *one* human being – restrict themselves to the task of bringing about the right relation between the life between death and a new birth and the life on earth.

A fact that may seem remarkable to begin with is the following. The whole hierarchy of Archangeloi was working for the *individual* human being in the second stage in the development of his lives between death and a new birth. Afterwards, the guidance of peoples and tribes becomes the task of this hierarchy, and there is then *one* Archangel as the Folk-Spirit for one people. In the races, the Primal Forces or Archai remain at work. Here again, for *one* race, one being of the hierarchy of the Primal Forces works as the Race-Spirit.

So enthält der gegenwärtige Mensch auch in dem Leben zwischen Tod und neuer Geburt die kosmische Erinnerung an vorangehende Stadien dieses Erlebens. Und auch da, wo in der physischen Welt Geistgeleitetes in der Art auftritt, wie in Rassen und Völkern, ist diese kosmische Erinnerung deutlich da.

Thus the human being of the present time contains, also in his condition of life between death and a new birth, the cosmic memory of earlier stages of this experience. And likewise there, where in the physical world something of spiritual guidance appears in the manner it does with the formation of races and peoples, this cosmic memory is most distinctly present.

Leitsätze Nr. 150 bis 152

150. In einer zweiten Periode der Entwickelung der Leben zwischen Tod und neuer Geburt tritt der Mensch in den Bereich der Archangeloi. Während derselben wird der Keim zur späteren Selbstbewusstheit in das Seelische gelegt, nachdem er in der Formung der Menschengestalt in der ersten Periode veranlagt worden ist.

151. Der Mensch wird während dieser zweiten Periode durch die luziferischen und ahrimanischen Einflüsse tiefer in das Physische gedrängt, als es ohne diese Einflüsse geschehen würde.

152. In der dritten Periode gelangt der Mensch in den Bereich der Angeloi, die aber nur in Astralleib und Ich ihren Einfluss geltend machen. Diese Periode ist die gegenwärtige. Was in den beiden ersten Perioden geschehen ist, lebt in der Menschenentwickelung fort und erklärt die Tatsache, dass innerhalb des Zeitalters der Bewusstseinsseele (im neunzehnten Jahrhundert) der Mensch in die geistige Welt wie in eine völlige Finsternis hineinstarrt.

Leading Thoughts 150 to 152

150. In a second period of the development of the condition of life between death and a new birth, the human being entered the domain of the Archangeloi. The germ of his later self-conscious disposition – prepared for, in the first period, in the shaping of the human form – was now laid into his soul-element.

151. During this second period, he was driven by luciferic and ahrimanic influences more deeply into the physical than would have happened without their intervention.

152. In the third period, the human being enters the domain of the Angeloi, who only wield their influence, however, in the astral body and the 'I'. This third period is the present period of evolution. What took place in the two former periods still lives on in human development and explains the fact that within the age of the consciousness soul (in the nineteenth century), the human being stared into the spiritual world as into total darkness.

Was ist die Erde in Wirklichkeit im Makrokosmos?

Goetheanum, Januar 1925

Das Werden des Kosmos und der Menschheit ist in diesen Betrachtungen von den verschiedensten Gesichtspunkten aus angeschaut worden. Gezeigt hat sich, wie der Mensch die Kräfte seines Wesens vom außerirdischen Kosmos hat, außer denen, die ihm sein Selbstbewusstsein geben. Diese kommen ihm von der Erde.

Damit ist die Bedeutung des Irdischen für den Menschen dargelegt. Es muss sich daran die Frage knüpfen: Welche Bedeutung hat das Irdische für den Makrokosmos?

Um der Antwort auf diese Frage näher zu kommen, muss man den Blick auf das hier schon Dargestellte werfen.

Der Makrokosmos wird von dem schauenden Bewusstsein in immer größerer Lebendigkeit gefunden, je weiter der Blick in die Vergangenheit zurückdringt. Er lebt in ferner Vergangenheit so, dass jede Berechnung seiner Lebensoffenbarungen da aufhört. Aus dieser Lebendigkeit heraus wird der Mensch abgesondert. Der Makrokosmos tritt immer mehr in die Sphäre des Berechenbaren ein.

What Is the Earth in Reality within the Macrocosm?

Goetheanum, January 1925

In these considerations, the evolution of the cosmos and humanity have been looked at from the most varied points of view. It has been shown how the human being has been given the forces of his being from the cosmos beyond this world, with the exception of those forces that give him self-consciousness. The latter have come to him from the earth.

With this, the significance of the earthly realm for the human being is set forth. But in this connection the question must arise: What is the significance of the earthly realm for the macrocosm?

In order to approach the answer to this question, one must turn one's attention once more to what has been described in previous studies.

The more seeing consciousness penetrates into the past, the more this vision finds the macrocosm to be living and vital. In the far-distant past, the macrocosm lives in such a way that there ceases to be any calculation of its life-revelations. Out of this living vitality, the human being is then brought forth as a separate entity, while the macrocosm enters more and more into the sphere of what is calculable.

Damit aber erstirbt er allmählich. In dem Maße, in dem der Mensch – der Mikrokosmos – als selbstständige Wesenheit aus dem Makrokosmos ersteht, erstirbt dieser.

In der kosmischen Gegenwart besteht ein erstorbener Makrokosmos. Aber im Werden desselben ist nicht nur der Mensch entstanden. Es ist aus dem Makrokosmos auch die Erde erstanden.

Der Mensch, der von der Erde die Kräfte für sein Selbstbewusstsein hat, steht dieser innerlich viel zu nahe, um ihr Wesen zu durchschauen. In der vollen Entfaltung des Selbstbewusstseins im Zeitalter der Bewusstseinsseele hat man sich gewöhnt, den Blick auf die *räumliche* Größe des Weltenalls zu wenden und die Erde wie ein Staubkorn, unbedeutend gegenüber dem physisch-räumlichen Weltall, anzusehen.

Daher wird es zunächst absonderlich erscheinen, wenn ein geistiges Anschauen die wahre kosmische Bedeutung dieses angeblichen «Staubkorns» enthüllt.

In die mineralische Grundlage der Erde sind die anderen Reiche, das Pflanzen- und das Tierreich, eingebettet.

In alledem leben die Kräfte, die sich im Jahreslauf in ihren verschiedenen Erscheinungsformen zeigen. Man sehe auf die Pflanzenwelt. Im Herbst und Winter zeigt sie physisch ersterbende Kräfte. Das schauende Bewusstsein nimmt in dieser Erscheinungsform das Wesen derjenigen Kräfte wahr, die den Makrokosmos zum Ersterben gebracht haben. Im Frühling

But in this it undergoes a gradual process of death. In the same measure in which the human being – the microcosm – arises as a being independent from the macrocosm, the latter dies away.

In the cosmic present, there exists a dead macrocosm. But it was not only the human being who arose in the process of its becoming. The earth too came forth out of the macrocosm.

Because he derives the forces for his self-consciousness from the earth, the human being is far too close to it in his inner life to perceive its nature clearly. In the age of the consciousness soul, with the full unfolding of self-consciousness, one has grown accustomed to focusing one's attention on the *spatial* magnitude of the universe, and to looking upon the earth as a particle of dust, insignificant compared to the great universe of physical space.

Hence it will seem strange, to begin with, when spiritual vision unfolds the true cosmic significance of this alleged "particle of dust."

In the mineral ground of the earth are imbedded the other realms of nature – the animal and plant realms.

In all of this, there live the forces which manifest themselves in varied forms of appearance through the seasons. Consider the world of plants. In autumn and winter it manifests the physically dying forces. In this form of appearance, seeing consciousness perceives the nature of those forces which have brought about the gradual death of the macrocosm. In spring

und Sommer zeigen sich im Pflanzenleben wachsende, sprossende Kräfte. Das schauende Bewusstsein nimmt in diesem Wachsen und Sprossen nicht nur das wahr, was den Pflanzensegen für das Jahr erstehen lässt, sondern einen *Überschuss*. Dieser Überschuss ist ein solcher der *Keimkraft*. Die Pflanzen enthalten *mehr* Keimkraft, als sie für Blätter-, Blüten- und Fruchtwachstum verbrauchen. Dieser Überschuss an Keimkraft strömt vor dem schauenden Bewusstsein hinaus in den außerirdischen Makrokosmos.

Ebenso strömt aber auch überschüssige Kraft vom Mineralreich in den außerirdischen Kosmos. *Diese* Kraft hat die Aufgabe, die von den Pflanzen kommenden Kräfte an die rechten Orte im Makrokosmos zu bringen. Es wird unter dem Einfluss der Mineralkräfte aus den Pflanzenkräften ein neugestaltetes Bild eines Makrokosmos.

Ebenso gibt es vom Tierischen ausgehende Kräfte. Diese wirken aber *nicht* in dem Sinne, wie die mineralischen und pflanzlichen, von der Erde ausstrahlend, sondern so, dass sich, was in Gestaltung durch die mineralischen Kräfte an Pflanzlichem ins Weltall getragen wird, zur Sphäre (Kugel) zusammenhält und dadurch das Bild eines allseitig geschlossenen Makrokosmos ersteht.

So schaut das geist-erkennende Bewusstsein das Wesen des Irdischen. *Dieses steht neu belebend innerhalb des erstorbenen Makrokosmos drinnen.*

and summer, forces of growth, springing and blossoming forces, show themselves in the plant life. In this growing and blossoming process, seeing consciousness perceives not only what brings forth the abundant blessing of the plant life for the given year, but a *surplus*. This surplus is one of *germinating force*. The plants contain *more* germinating force than they expend in the growth of foliage, flower, and fruit. For seeing consciousness, this excess of germinating force flows out into the macrocosm beyond this world.

In the same manner, a surplus of force streams out from the mineral realm to the cosmos beyond this world. *This* force has the task of carrying the forces from the plant-world to the right places in the macrocosm. Under the influence of the mineral forces, the plant-forces become a newly fashioned image of a macrocosm.

Likewise, there are forces proceeding from what is of an animal nature. These however *do not* work in the sense of radiating from the earth, as do the plant and mineral forces; rather, they work in such a way that the plant-nature, which the mineral forces carry in clear formation into the great universe, is gathered into a sphere (ball), so that the image arises of a macrocosm compact and self-contained on all sides.

In this way spirit-seeing consciousness beholds the being of the earthly realm, *which stands as a new, life-enkindling element within the dying macrocosm.*

Wie aus dem Pflanzenkeim, der räumlich so unbedeutend klein ist, die ganze große Pflanze sich wieder bildet, wenn die alte ersterbend zerfällt, so wird aus dem «Staubkorn» Erde ein neuer Makroskosmos, indem der alte erstorbene zerfällt.

Das ist ein wahres Anschauen des Erdenwesens, das überall in ihm eine keimende Welt schaut. Man lernt nur *dadurch* die Naturreiche verstehen, dass man in ihnen dieses Keimende empfindet.

Inmitten dieses keimenden Lebens vollbringt der Mensch sein Erdendasein. – Er nimmt an diesem Keimenden sowohl wie an dem erstorbenen Leben teil. Aus dem erstorbenen hat er seine Denkkräfte. Solange diese Denkkräfte in der Vergangenheit aus dem noch lebenden Makrokosmos kamen, waren sie nicht Grundlage des selbstbewussten Menschen. Sie lebten als Wachstumskräfte in dem Menschen, der noch kein Selbstbewusstsein hatte. Die Denkkräfte dürfen *für sich* kein Eigenleben haben, wenn sie die Grundlage bilden sollen für das freie menschliche Selbstbewusstsein. Sie müssen für sich mit dem erstorbenen Makrokosmos die toten *Schatten* von Lebendigem der kosmischen Vorzeit sein.

Auf der anderen Seite nimmt der Mensch teil an dem Keimenden der Erde. Aus ihm sind seine Willenskräfte. Sie sind Leben, aber dafür nimmt der Mensch mit seinem Selbstbewusstsein nicht an ihrem Wesen teil. Sie strahlen innerhalb

Just as when the old plant has died and fallen away, the new plant, however large, is formed again from the germinal seed in a space so modestly small – so while the old dying macrocosm falls away, a new macrocosm comes forth from this "particle of dust," the earth.

It is a true beholding of the being of the earth which sees in it everywhere a germinating world. One only learns to understand the realms of nature when one feels in them the presence of this germinating life.

The human being fulfills his earth-existence in the midst of this germinating life. – He partakes in the germinating life as well as in the dying processes. From the dying processes he derives the forces of his thought. In the past, when the forces of his thought were coming forth from the still-living macrocosm, they did not provide the foundation for self-conscious humanity. They lived, as forces of growth, in the human being who did not yet have self-consciousness. If they are to provide a basis for free human self-consciousness, the forces of thought may not have a life of their own *for themselves*. With the dying macrocosm, these forces of thought must be, for themselves, the dead *shadows* of what once was living in the primeval cosmos.

On the other side, the human being shares in the germinating life of the earth, from which he has the forces of his will. These forces are indeed life itself, but with his self-consciousness the human being does not take part in their real nature.

des Menschenwesens in die Gedankenschatten herein. Sie werden von diesen Schatten durchströmt, und im Durchströmen des im keimenden Erdenwesen sich entfaltenden freien Gedankens lebt das volle, freie menschliche Selbstbewusstsein sich im Zeitalter der Bewusstseinsseele in den Menschen hinein.

Die Vergangenheit Schatten werfend, die Zukunft Wirklichkeitskeime enthaltend, begegnen sich in der menschlichen Wesenheit. Und die Begegnung ist das Menschenleben der Gegenwart.

Dass sich das so verhält, wird dem schauenden Bewusstsein sofort klar, wenn es sich in diejenige Geist-Region begibt, die sich an die physische unmittelbar anschließt und in der man auch die Betätigung Michaels findet.

Das Leben alles Irdischen wird durchsichtig, wenn man auf seinem Grunde den Weltenkeim empfindet. Jede Pflanzenform, jeder Stein, sie erscheinen der Menschenseele in einem neuen Lichte, wenn diese gewahr wird, wie jedes dieser Wesen durch sein Leben, durch seine Gestalt beiträgt, dass die Erde als Einheit der Embryonal-Keim eines neu auflebenden Makrokosmos ist.

Man versuche nur einmal, den Gedanken an diese Tatsachen in sich ganz lebendig zu machen, und man wird fühlen, was er innerhalb des Menschengemütes bedeuten kann.

They radiate deep down within the human being, into the thought-shadows. They are permeated by these thought-shadows, and in the flowing of free thought as it unfolds within the germinating earthly nature, the full and free human self-consciousness enters into the human being during this age of the consciousness soul.

The past throwing its shadows, and the future filled with the germinal seeds of a new reality, encounter each other in the human being. And their encounter is the human life of the present time.

This is inherently clear to the seeing consciousness as it enters the spirit-region directly bordering the physical realm, in which the active presence of Michael is to be found.

The life of everything earthly becomes transparent when one feels at its foundation the cosmic germ. Every single plant and stone appears in a new light to the human soul when it becomes aware that each of these beings is contributing, by its life or by its form, to the fact that the earth in its unity is an embryonic germ of a macrocosm newly rising into life.

One should but try to make the thought of these matters fully living in oneself, and one will feel what meaning it can hold for the human heart and mind.

Leitsätze Nr. 153 bis 155

153. Man hat sich im Beginne des Zeitalters der Bewusstseinsseele gewöhnt, den Blick auf die räumlich-physische Größe des Weltenalls zu lenken, und vor allem *diese* zu empfinden. Deshalb nennt man die Erde ein Staubkorn innerhalb dieses physisch mächtig erscheinenden Weltenalls.

154. Vor dem schauenden Bewusstsein offenbart sich dieses «Staubkorn» als die Keimanlage eines neu entstehenden Makrokosmos, während der alte sich als erstorben erweist. Er musste ersterben, damit der Mensch mit vollem Selbstbewusstsein sich von ihm absondern konnte.

155. In der kosmischen Gegenwart nimmt der Mensch mit seinen ihn befreienden Gedankenkräften an dem erstorbenen, mit seinen ihm ihrem Wesen nach verborgenen Willenskräften an dem als Erdenwesen keimenden, neu auflebenden Makrokosmos teil.

Leading Thoughts 153 to 155

153. In the beginning of the age of the consciousness soul, it became the custom to turn attention to the spatial-physical vastness of the universe and above all to feel *this*. Therefore, the earth is called a particle of dust within this physically mighty appearance of the universe.

154. To seeing consciousness, this "particle of dust" reveals itself as the creative germ and beginning of a newly arising macrocosm, while the old macrocosm shows itself to be dying away. For the old macrocosm had to die in order that the human being might sever himself from it with full self-consciousness.

155. In the cosmic present, the human being partakes in the dead macrocosm with the thought-forces which enable his freedom; and with the will-forces, whose being is concealed from him, he partakes in the aspect of this earth-being that is newly germinating into life as macrocosm.

Schlaf und Wachen im Lichte der vorangegangenen Betrachtungen

Goetheanum, Januar 1925

Schlaf und Wachen wurde innerhalb der anthroposophischen Auseinandersetzungen oftmals von den verschiedensten Gesichtspunkten aus betrachtet. Aber das Verständnis solcher Lebenstatsachen muss immer von Neuem vertieft werden, wenn anderes aus dem Weltbestande betrachtet worden ist. Die Auseinandersetzungen darüber, dass die Erde ein Keim für den neu erstehenden Makrokosmos ist, ergeben für die Anschauungen von Schlafen und Wachen solche Möglichkeiten eines vertieften Verständnisses.

Im Wachzustande lebt der Mensch in den Gedankenschatten, die von einer erstorbenen Welt geworfen werden, und in den Willensimpulsen, in deren inneres Wesen er mit dem gewöhnlichen Bewusstsein ebenso wenig hineinsieht wie in die Vorgänge des tiefen, traumlosen Schlafes.

In dem Einströmen dieser unterbewussten Willensimpulse in die Gedankenschatten ersteht das freiwaltende Selbstbewusstsein. In diesem Selbstbewusstsein lebt das «Ich».

Indem der Mensch in diesem Zustande die Umwelt erlebt, ist sein inneres Erfühlen durchdrungen von außerirdischen, von kosmischen Impulsen, die aus urferner kosmischer

Sleep and Waking in the Light of Recent Considerations

Goetheanum, January 1925

In the study of Anthroposophy, sleep and waking have been dealt with often and from various points of view. But our understanding of these facts of life must be deepened ever anew whenever other aspects in the constitution of the world come into consideration. Our previous discussion on the theme of the earth as the germ of a newly arising macrocosm provides such possibilities for a deeper understanding of sleep and waking.

In the waking state, the human being lives in the thought-shadows cast by a dying world; and he likewise lives in will-impulses, the inner nature of which he can no more penetrate with ordinary consciousness than he can the processes of deep, dreamless sleep.

Where subconscious impulses of will flow into the thought-shadows, the free sovereignty of self-consciousness arises. In this self-consciousness lives the human 'I'.

While the human being experiences his environment in this condition, his inner feeling is permeated by impulses from beyond this world, by cosmic impulses, which enter into the

Vergangenheit in die Gegenwart hereinragen. Er wird sich dessen nicht bewusst. Ein Wesen kann sich nur dessen bewusst werden, an dem es mit eigenen ersterbenden Kräften teilnimmt, nicht mit wachsenden Kräften, die das Wesen selbst beleben. So erlebt sich der Mensch, indem er das seinem inneren Wesen zugrunde Liegende aus dem Geistesauge verliert. Gerade dadurch aber ist er in der Lage, während des Wachzustandes ganz in den Gedankenschatten sich zu fühlen. Kein Aufleben hindert das innere Dasein an der Teilnahme am Erstorbenen. Aber diesem «Leben in dem Erstorbenen» verschließt sich das Wesenhafte des Irdischen, dass es Keim eines neuen Weltalls ist. Der Mensch nimmt im Wachzustande die Erde nicht wahr, wie sie ist; es entgeht ihm ihr beginnendes kosmisches Leben.

So lebt der Mensch in dem, was ihm als Grundlage seines Selbstbewusstseins die Erde gibt. Er verliert im Zeitalter der selbstbewussten Ich-Entfaltung die wahre Gestalt seiner inneren Impulse wie auch diejenige seiner Umgebung aus dem Geistesauge. Aber gerade in diesem Schweben über dem Sein der Welt erlebt der Mensch das Sein des Ich, erlebt er sich als selbstbewusstes Wesen. Über ihm der außerirdische Kosmos, unter ihm im Irdischen eine Welt, deren Wesenhaftigkeit verborgen bleibt; dazwischen die Offenbarung des freien «Ich»,

present time from a remote and cosmic past. He does not become conscious of this fact. For a being can only become conscious of processes in which it partakes with its own dying forces, and not with the growing forces that are the creative enkindlers of its life. Thus the human being experiences himself in consciousness while what lies at the basis of his inner being is lost to the mind's eye. And by this very fact he is able, during the waking state, to feel himself so entirely within his thought-shadows. There is no glimmer of life to hinder the full absorption of his inner being into the dead and dying element. But from this "life in the dead and dying element," the essential being of the earthly sphere conceals the fact that it is in reality the germ of a new universe. In his waking state, the human being does not perceive the earth in its true nature. The cosmic life germinating within the earth escapes his awareness.

Thus the human being lives in what the earth gives to him as the basis of his self-consciousness. In the age of the unfolding of the self-conscious 'I', the true form both of his inner impulses and of his outer environment is lost to his mind's eye. But it is precisely in this hovering above the being of the world that the human being experiences the being of the 'I', that he experiences himself as a self-conscious essence. Above him the extra-earthly cosmos, below him in the earthly a world whose essential being remains hidden;

dessen Wesenhaftigkeit in vollem Glanze der Erkenntnis und des freien Wollens erstrahlt.

Anders im Schlafzustande. Da lebt der Mensch in seinem Astralleibe und in seinem Ich im Keimesleben der Erde. Intensivstes «Ins-Leben-Wollen» wirkt in des Menschen Umgebung, wenn er im traumlosen Schlafe ist. Und die Träume sind durchsetzt von diesem Leben, aber nicht so stark, dass der Mensch sie nicht in einer Art Halbbewusstheit erleben könnte. In diesem halbbewussten Hinschauen auf die Träume sieht man die Kräfte, durch die die menschliche Wesenheit aus dem Kosmos heraus gewoben wird. Im Aufleuchten des Traumes wird sichtbar, wie das Astralische menschenbelebend in den Ätherleib einströmt. In diesem Aufleuchten *lebt* der Gedanke noch. Nach dem Aufwachen wird er erst umfangen von denjenigen Kräften, durch die er erstirbt, zum Schatten wird.

Bedeutsam ist dieser Zusammenhang zwischen Traumvorstellung und Wachgedanken. Der Mensch *denkt* in denselben Kräften, durch die er wächst und lebt. Nur müssen diese Kräfte, damit der Mensch zum Denker wird, ersterben.

Da ist der Punkt, wo ein rechtes Verständnis darüber aufgehen kann, warum der Mensch denkend die Wirklichkeit erfasst. Er hat in seinen Gedanken das tote Bild dessen,

in between, the revelation of the free 'I' whose essential being shines forth in the full splendor of knowledge and free will.

It is different in the sleeping state. In sleep, the human being lives in his astral body and 'I' in the germinating life of the earth. The strongest "will for life" is there in the human being's environment during dreamless sleep. His dreams too are permeated by this life, though not so intensely as to prevent him from experiencing them only in a kind of semi-consciousness. Gazing half-consciously upon his dreams, the human being witnesses the creative forces whereby he himself is woven out of the cosmos. While the dream lights up, the astral element – enkindling the human being to life – becomes visible as it flows into the etheric body. In this lighting-up of dreams, thought is still *alive*. It is only after the human being awakens that thought is encompassed by the forces through which it dies and becomes shadow.

This connection between dream-representations and waking thoughts is of the greatest significance. The human being *thinks* within the sphere of those very forces whereby he grows and lives. Yet in order that he may become a thinker, these forces must die.

At this point there dawns a true understanding of why it is that the human being takes hold of reality by means of thought. For in his thoughts he possesses the dead image of what,

was ihn aus der lebensvollen Wirklichkeit heraus selber bildet.

Das tote Bild: Dieses tote Bild ist aber das Ergebnis der Tätigkeit des größten Malers, des Kosmos selbst. Aus dem Bilde bleibt zwar das Leben weg. Bliebe es nicht weg, so könnte das Ich sich nicht entfalten. Aber es ist in ihm aller Inhalt des Weltenalls in seiner Herrlichkeit.

So weit als es damals im Zusammenhange der Darstellung möglich war, wies ich schon in meiner *Philosophie der Freiheit* auf dieses innere Verhältnis zwischen Denken und Weltwirklichkeit hin. Es ist an der Stelle geschehen, wo ich davon spreche, dass von den Tiefen des denkenden Ich zu den Tiefen der Natur-Wirklichkeit eine Brücke führt.

Für das gewöhnliche Bewusstsein wirkt der Schlaf deshalb auslöschend, weil er in das in den werdenden Makrokosmos hineinsprießende, keimende Leben der Erde führt. Wird dieses Auslöschen behoben durch das imaginative Bewusstsein, so steht vor der menschlichen Seele nicht eine Erde mit scharfen Konturen im Mineral-, Pflanzen- und Tierreiche. Es steht vielmehr da ein lebendiger Vorgang, der sich innerhalb der Erde entzündet und der in den Makrokosmos hinausflammt.

Es ist so, dass sich der Mensch mit dem eigenen Ich-Sein aus dem Sein der Welt im Wachzustande herausheben muss,

working out of the fully living reality of the world, builds and creates him.

The dead image: But this dead image proceeds from the work of the greatest painter – from the cosmos itself. It is true that the life remains outside of the image. If it did not, then the human 'I' could not unfold. Nevertheless, the full content of the universe, in all its greatness, is contained within this image.

So far as was possible at that time and in that context, I indicated this inner relation between thought and world-reality in my *Philosophy of Freedom* (*Philosophy of Spiritual Activity*). It is in the section where I speak of the fact that there is indeed a bridge leading from the depths of the thinking 'I' to the depths of nature's reality.

Sleep has an extinguishing effect on ordinary consciousness because it carries us into the germinating life of the earth, springing forth into the becoming macrocosm. When the extinction is overcome by imaginative consciousness, there stands before the human soul not a sharply outlined earth in the mineral, plant, and animal realms of nature – but a vital process enkindled to life within this earth and flaming forth into the macrocosm.

It is the case that in the waking state, the human being must lift himself, with his own 'I'-being, out of the being of the

um zum freien Selbstbewusstsein zu kommen. Im Schlafzustande vereinigt er sich dann wieder mit dem Welt-Sein.

Das ist im gegenwärtigen kosmischen Weltenaugenblicke der Rhythmus des irdischen Menschen-Daseins außer dem «Innern» der Welt mit Erleben des Eigenwesens; und des Daseins in dem «Innern» der Welt mit Auslöschung des Bewusstseins vom Eigenwesen.

In dem Zustande zwischen dem Tode und einer neuen Geburt lebt das Menschen-Ich innerhalb der Wesen der Geist-Welt. Da tritt in das Bewusstsein alles, was sich während des irdischen Wachlebens diesem entzieht. Es treten die makrokosmischen Kräfte auf von ihrem Voll-Leben in urferner Vergangenheit bis zu dem Erstorben-Sein in der Gegenwart. Es treten aber auch die irdischen Kräfte auf, die der Keim sind des werdenden Makrokosmos. Und in seine Schlafzustände sieht der Mensch hinein, wie er während des Erdenlebens auf die in der Sonne erglänzende Erde sieht.

Nur dadurch, dass der Makrokosmos, so wie er gegenwärtig ist, ein Erstorbenes wurde, kann das Menschenwesen in dem Leben zwischen Tod und neuer Geburt ein Leben durchmachen, das gegenüber dem wachen Erdenleben ein höheres Aufwachen bedeutet. Ein Aufwachen, durch das der Mensch fähig wird, *die* Kräfte voll zu meistern, die im Traume ein flüchtiges Aufflackern zeigen. *Diese* Kräfte erfüllen den ganzen Kosmos. Sie sind alles durchdringend. Ihnen entnimmt

world in order to attain to free self-consciousness. And in sleep, he unites once more with the being of the world.

Such is the rhythm in the present moment of cosmic time: It is the rhythm of the human being's earthly existence outside the "inner being" of the world in experiencing his own being – and of his existence within the "inner being" of the world in extinguishing the consciousness of his own being.

In the condition between death and a new birth, the human 'I' lives within the being of the world of spirit. There, everything that was withdrawn from the human being's consciousness during his waking life on earth comes into it again. The macrocosmic forces emerge from their full life in a far-distant past to their dead and dying nature of the present. And there likewise emerge the earthly forces – the germ of the becoming macrocosm. Then the human being looks into his sleeping states as clearly as in his earthly life he looks forth upon the earth that glistens in the sun.

The macrocosm, as it is today, has indeed become a thing of death. Yet it is through this alone that between death and a new birth the human being can undergo a life which, compared to the waking life on earth, signifies a loftier awakening. For it is indeed an awakening whereby one becomes fully able to master *those* forces that light up so dimly and fleetingly in dreams. *These* forces fill the whole cosmos; they are all-pervading. From them the human being derives the impulses

das Menschenwesen die Impulse, aus denen es sich beim Heruntersteigen auf die Erde seinen Leib, das große Kunstwerk des Makrokosmos, formt.

Was im Traume wie sonnenverlassen aufdämmert, das lebt in der Geistwelt geistes-sonnenhaft durchströmt, wartend, bis die Wesenheiten der höheren Hierarchien oder der Mensch es wesenbildend im Schaffen aufrufen.

through which, as he descends to earth, he forms his body – the greatest work of art of the macrocosm.

That which lights up so dimly in the dream – abandoned by the sun – lives in the world of spirit, permeated by the spiritual sun, waiting until the beings of the higher hierarchies, or the human being himself, will call it forth as essential substance in the act of creating.

Leitsätze Nr. 156 bis 158

156. Im Wachzustande muss der Mensch, um *sich* im vollen, freien Selbstbewusstsein zu erleben, auf das Erleben der wahren Gestalt der Wirklichkeit im eigenen und im Naturdasein verzichten. Er erhebt sich aus dem Meere dieser Wirklichkeit, um in den Gedankenschatten das *eigene Ich* zum wirklich *eigenen* Erleben zu machen.

157. Im Schlafzustande lebt der Mensch mit dem Leben der Erden-Umgebung; aber dieses Leben löscht sein Selbstbewusstsein aus.

158. Im Träumen flackert im Halbbewusstsein das kraftvolle Weltensein auf, aus dem des Menschen Wesen gewoben ist und aus dem er beim Niedersteigen aus der Geistwelt seinen Leib bildet. Im Erdenleben wird dieses kraftvolle Weltensein im Menschen bis in die Gedankenschatten zum Ersterben gebracht, da es nur so dem selbstbewussten Menschen die Grundlage sein kann.

Leading Thoughts 156 to 158

156. In waking life, to experience *himself* in full and free self-consciousness, the human being must forego the conscious experience of reality in its true form, both in relation to his own existence and to that of nature. He lifts himself out of the ocean of reality, so that in his thought-shadows he may make *his own 'I'* into *his own* actual experience.

157. In sleep, the human being lives with the life of the earth-environment, but this very life extinguishes his self-consciousness.

158. In dreaming, there flickers up into half-consciousness the potent world-being from which the essential nature of the human being is woven and from which, in his descent from the world of spirit, he builds his body. In earthly life, this powerful world-being is brought, in the human being, to the point of death, dying into the thought-shadows. For only in this way can it become the basis of the self-conscious human being.

Gnosis und Anthroposophie

Goetheanum, Januar 1925

Als das Mysterium von Golgatha sich vollzog, war die «Gnosis» die Denkart des Teiles der Menschheit, der zunächst ein erkenntnismäßiges, nicht bloß ein empfindendes Verständnis dem größten Einschlag in die Erdenentwickelung der Menschen entgegenbringen konnte.

Will man die Seelenverfassung verstehen, in der die Gnosis innerhalb des Menschen lebte, so muss man ins Auge fassen, dass das Zeitalter dieser Gnosis dasjenige der Entfaltung der Verstandes- oder Gemütsseele ist.

In dieser Tatsache kann man auch die Ursache für das fast völlige Verschwinden der Gnosis aus der Menschheitsgeschichte finden. Dieses Verschwinden ist wohl, solange es nicht begriffen ist, eines der erstaunlichsten Vorkommnisse im Werdegang der Menschheit.

Der Entfaltung der Verstandes- oder Gemütsseele ging diejenige der Empfindungsseele und dieser die des Empfindungsleibes voraus. Werden die Tatsachen der Welt durch den Empfindungsleib wahrgenommen, so lebt alle Erkenntnis des Menschen in den Sinnen. Die Welt wird farbig, tönend und so weiter wahrgenommen; aber in den Farben, Tönen, in den Wärmezuständen wird eine Welt von geistigen Wesenheiten

Gnosis and Anthroposophy

Goetheanum, January 1925

When the Mystery of Golgotha took place, "Gnosis" was the mode of thought of those among humanity who were able, already at that time, to approach this event – the most momentous event in the earthly development of humanity – with an understanding rooted not only in feeling but in knowledge.

To comprehend the mood of soul whereby Gnosis lived in the human being, one must bear in mind that its age is the age of the unfolding of the intellectual- or mind-soul.

In this same fact one can discover the cause of the almost complete disappearance of Gnosis from human history. The disappearance of Gnosis – so long as it is not fully understood – is one of the most astonishing occurrences in human evolution.

The unfolding of the intellectual- or mind-soul was preceded by that of the sentient soul, and this in turn by that of the sentient body. When the facts of the world are perceived through the sentient body, the whole of the human being's experience of knowledge lives in his senses. He perceives the world as colored, resonant, and so forth; but within the colors and sounds, within the states of warmth, he becomes aware of

gewusst. Von «Stoff», an dem Farben, Wärmezustände und so weiter erscheinen, redet man nicht; man redet von geistigen Wesenheiten, die sich durch das offenbaren, was die Sinne wahrnehmen.

Eine besondere Entfaltung eines «Verstandes», der neben der Sinneswahrnehmung im Menschen lebte, gibt es in diesem Zeitalter noch nicht. Der Mensch gibt sich entweder mit seinem Wesen an die Außenwelt hin, dann offenbaren sich ihm durch die Sinne die Götter. Oder er zieht sich in seinem Seelenleben von der Außenwelt zurück, dann fühlt er in seinem Innern ein dumpfes Lebensgefühl.

Ein bedeutsamer Umschwung tritt ein, wenn sich die Empfindungsseele entfaltet. Die Offenbarung des Göttlichen durch die Sinne dämmert ab. An die Stelle tritt das Wahrnehmen der gewissermaßen entgöttlichten Sinneseindrücke, der Farben, Wärmezustände und so weiter. Im Innern offenbart sich das Göttliche in geistiger Form, in Bild-Ideen. Und der Mensch nimmt die Welt von zwei Seiten her wahr: von außen durch die Sinnes-Eindrücke, von innen durch die ideenhaften Geist-Eindrücke.

Der Mensch muss nun dazu kommen, die Geist-Eindrücke so bestimmt, so gestaltet wahrzunehmen, wie er vorher die durchgöttlichten Sinnes-Eindrücke wahrgenommen hat. – Solange das Zeitalter der Empfindungsseele waltet, kann er das. Denn aus seinem inneren Wesen steigen ihm die Ideenbilder

the presence of a world of spiritual beings. It is not about "matter" to which the phenomena of color, warmth, and so forth are supposed to adhere, but about spiritual beings who manifest themselves through the perceptions of the senses.

In this age there is as yet no special development of an "intellect" – there is no intellect in the human being aside from the faculty of sense perception. The human being either gives himself up with his own being to the outer world, in which case the gods reveal themselves to him through the senses; or else in his soul-life he withdraws from the outer world and is then aware of a dim sense of life within.

But a far-reaching change takes place with the unfolding of the sentient soul. The revelation of the divine through the senses grows dim and fades away. In place of it, the human being begins to perceive the mere sense impressions – colors, states of warmth, and so forth – as being empty, as it were, of the divine. And within him the divine now manifests itself in a spiritual form, in image-like ideas. He now perceives the world from two sides: through sense impressions from without, and from within through ideational spirit-impressions.

At this stage, the human being must come to perceive the spirit impressions in as definite a shape and as clear a form as he had earlier perceived the divinely permeated sense impressions. – And indeed, as long as the age of the sentient soul holds sway, he is still able to do this. For from his inner being,

in vollgestalteter Art auf. Er ist von innen erfüllt mit einem sinnlichkeitsfreien Geist-Inhalt, der ein Abbild des Welt-Inhaltes ist. Haben sich ihm früher die Götter im sinnlichen Kleide geoffenbart; sie offenbaren sich ihm jetzt im Geist-Kleide.

Das ist das Zeitalter der eigentlichen Entstehung und des Lebens der Gnosis. Eine wunderbare Erkenntnis lebt, der sich der Mensch teilhaftig weiß, wenn er sein inneres Wesen in Reinheit entfaltet, sodass der göttliche Inhalt durch dasselbe sich offenbaren kann. Vom vierten bis ins erste Jahrtausend vor dem Eintritte des Mysteriums von Golgatha herrscht bei dem in der Erkenntnis vorgeschrittensten Teile der Menschheit diese Gnosis.

Dann beginnt das Zeitalter der Verstandes- oder Gemütsseele. Von selbst steigen jetzt aus dem Innern des Menschenwesens die Welt-Götter-Bilder nicht mehr auf. Der Mensch muss innerlich Kraft anwenden, um sie aus seiner Seele zu holen. Die Außenwelt mit ihren Sinneseindrücken wird zur Frage. Indem der Mensch die innerliche Kraft anwendet, die Welt-Götter-Bilder aus sich zu holen, erhält er Antworten.

Aber die Bilder sind blass im Verhältnis zu ihrer früheren Gestalt. Es ist dies die Seelenverfassung der Menschheit, die in Griechenland sich in wunderbarer Art entfaltet hat. Der Grieche fühlte sich in der sinnenfälligen Außenwelt,

the idea-images rise before him in a fully concrete shape. He is filled from within with a sense-free spirit-content – itself an image of the content of the world. The gods, who had previously revealed themselves to him in a garment of sense, reveal themselves now in the garment of the spirit.

This was the age when Gnosis really originated and had its life. A wonderful knowledge lived here, of which the human being knew himself to be a part when he unfolded his inner being in purity and thus enabled the divine content to reveal itself through this inner being. From the fourth to the first millennium before the Mystery of Golgotha, this Gnosis held sway in those portions of humanity most advanced in knowledge.

Then begins the age of the intellectual- or mind-soul. The world-images of the gods no longer rise of their own accord out of the inner nature of the human being. Now the human being must apply an inner force to draw them forth from his own soul. The outer world with all its sense impressions becomes a question – a question to which he obtains the answers by enkindling the inner force to draw forth the world-images of the gods from within him.

But in contrast to their earlier configuration, these images are now pale. Such is the soul-condition of the portion of humanity that evolved in such a wonderful way in ancient Greece. The Greek felt himself intensely in the outer world of

und er fühlte in dieser die Zaubergewalt, die die innere Kraft zum Entfalten der Weltbilder anregte. Auf philosophischem Felde entfaltete sich diese Seelenverfassung im Platonismus.

Aber hinter alledem stand die Mysterienwelt. In ihr wurde treu aufbewahrt, was von Gnosis aus dem Zeitalter der Empfindungsseele vorhanden war. Die Seelen wurden für dieses treuliche Aufbewahren geschult. Auf dem Wege der gewöhnlichen Entwickelung erstand die Verstandes- oder Gemütsseele. Durch besondere Schulung wurde die Empfindungsseele belebt. So gab es hinter dem gewöhnlichen Kulturleben gerade im Zeitalter der Verstandes- oder Gemütsseele ein reich entwickeltes Mysterienwesen.

In diesem lebten die Welt-Götter-Bilder auch insofern, als sie zum Inhalte eines Kultus gemacht wurden. Man schaut in das Innere dieser Mysterien und erblickt die Welt im Abbilde der wunderbarsten Kultusverrichtungen.

Die Menschen, die *das* erlebten, sie waren diejenigen, die auch das Mysterium von Golgatha, als es sich vollzog, in seinem tiefen kosmischen Zusammenhange durchschauten. Aber es war ein Mysterienleben, das sich ganz abseits hielt von dem Weltgetriebe, um in Reinheit die Geist-Bilder-Welt zu entfalten. Und für Menschenseelen wurde diese Entfaltung immer schwieriger.

the senses, wherein he also felt the presence of a magic power summoning his own inner force to unfold the world-images. In the field of philosophy, this mood of soul came forth in Platonism.

But behind all this there stood the world of the Mysteries. In the Mysteries, such Gnosis as still remained from the age of the sentient soul was faithfully preserved. Human souls were schooled for this task of diligent preservation. In the time when the intellectual- or mind-soul arose by way of ordinary development, the sentient soul was enkindled into life by special training. Thus it was most especially in the age of the intellectual- or mind-soul that, behind the ordinary life of culture, there was a richly developed being of the Mysteries.

In this being, the world-images of the gods also lived in this way, such that they were made the content of a cult. One gazes into the core of those Mysteries and beholds the world in the image of the most wonderful acts of ritual ceremony.

The human beings who experienced *these things* were also those who, when the Mystery of Golgotha took place, perceived and penetrated it in its deep cosmic significance. But this life of the Mysteries was kept entirely separate from worldly affairs in order to unfold in purity the world of spirit-images. And it became increasingly difficult for the souls of human beings to accomplish this unfolding.

Da stiegen in den höchsten Mysterienstätten Geist-Wesen aus dem geistigen Kosmos, die den Anstrengungen der um Erkenntnis ringenden Menschen zu Hilfe kamen. So entfalteten sich die Impulse des Zeitalters der Empfindungsseele unter dem Einfluss der «Götter» selbst weiter. Es entstand eine Mysterien-Gnosis, von der die wenigsten auch nur etwas ahnten. Neben ihr war das vorhanden, was von den Menschen mit der Verstandes- oder Gemütsseele aufgenommen werden konnte. Es war die exoterische Gnosis, von der Bruchstücke auf die Nachwelt gekommen sind.

In der esoterischen Mysteriengnosis wurden die Menschen immer unfähiger, sich zur Entfaltung der Empfindungsseele zu erheben. Es ging diese esoterische Weisheit immer mehr an die bloße Pflege der «Götter» über. Und *das* ist ein Geheimnis der geschichtlichen Entwickelung der Menschheit, dass in ihr gewissermaßen «göttliche Mysterien» von den ersten christlichen Jahrhunderten an bis ins Mittelalter wirkten.

In diesen «göttlichen Mysterien» bewahrten Engelwesen im irdischen Dasein, was Menschen nicht mehr bewahren konnten. So waltete die Mysterien-Gnosis, während man an der Ausrottung der exoterischen Gnosis arbeitete.

Der *Welt-Bild-Inhalt*, der in der Mysterien-Gnosis auf geistige Art von geistigen Wesen bewahrt wurde, solange er im Werdegang der Menschheit wirken sollte: Er konnte dem

Then it happened that in the highest places of the Mysteries, spirit-beings descended from the spiritual cosmos, coming to help the human beings in their intense strivings after knowledge. Thus under the influence of the "gods" themselves, the impulses of the age of the sentient soul continued to unfold. There arose a Mystery Gnosis of which only very few had any notion. And alongside this was present what human beings were able to receive with the intellectual- or mind-soul. It was the exoteric Gnosis whose fragments have come down to posterity.

In the esoteric Mystery Gnosis, human beings became increasingly incapable of rising to the unfolding of the sentient soul. The esoteric wisdom passed over more and more into the keeping of the "gods" alone. And *this* is a secret of the historical development of humanity: that "divine Mysteries" – for as such they may indeed be described – were at work in this development from the first Christian centuries on into the Middle Ages.

In these "divine Mysteries," Angel-beings preserved in earth-existence what human beings were no longer able to preserve. Thus did the Mystery Gnosis hold sway while human beings were diligently wiping out the exoteric Gnosis.

The influence of *world-image-content*, guarded as it was in the Mystery Gnosis by spirit-beings in a spiritual way, was still required for the becoming of humanity; however, it could not

bewussten Begreifen der Menschenseele nicht erhalten werden. Aber der Gefühlsgehalt sollte bewahrt werden. Und dieser sollte im rechten kosmischen Augenblicke der dazu vorbereiteten Menschheit gegeben werden, damit unter seiner Seelenwärme die Bewusstseinsseele später auf neue Art in das Geistesreich eindringen könne. Geisteswesen haben so die Brücke gebaut zwischen dem alten Welt-Inhalt und dem neuen.

In Andeutungen ist dieses Geheimnis der Menschheitsentwickelung vorhanden. Die heilige Jaspisschale des Grales, derer sich Christus bediente, als er das Brot brach, in die Joseph von Arimathia das Blut aus der Jesuswunde aufgefangen hat, die also das Geheimnis von Golgatha barg, wurde – so lautet die Legende – von Engeln in Verwahrung genommen, bis sie sie nach Erbauung der Gralsburg durch Titurel auf die vorbereiteten Menschen niedersenken konnten.

Geistwesen bargen die Welt-Bilder, in denen die Geheimnisse von Golgatha lebten. Sie senkten, weil das nicht möglich war, nicht den Bild-Inhalt, wohl aber den Gefühlsgehalt in Menschengemüter, als die Zeit dazu gekommen war.

Nur Anregung, aber eben kräftigste Anregung, kann dieses Einpflanzen des Gefühlsinhaltes alter Erkenntnis sein, dass in unserem Zeitalter sich aus der Bewusstseinsseele im Lichte

be preserved for the conscious understanding of the human soul. But its deep feeling-content had to be preserved. For in the right cosmic moment this was to be given to a humanity duly prepared to receive it, so that at a later stage the consciousness soul – fired by the inner warmth of it – might newly penetrate into the spirit-realm. Thus, spirit-beings built the bridge from the old world-content to the new.

Indications of this secret of human development do indeed exist. The sacred jasper cup of the Holy Grail which Christ made use of when He broke the bread, and in which Joseph of Arimathea gathered the blood from the wound of Jesus – which contained therefore the secret of Golgotha – was received into safekeeping, according to the legend, by Angels until Titurel was to build the Castle of the Grail, at which time they could allow this secret to descend to the human beings who were prepared to receive it.

Spiritual beings protected the world-images in which the secrets of Golgotha were living. And when the time had come, they let down, not the image-content – for this was not possible – but the full feeling-content, into the hearts and minds of human beings.

This implanting of the feeling-content of an ancient knowledge can serve only as an incentive – but a powerful incentive – toward the development of a new and full understanding in

von Michaels Wirksamkeit ein neues volles Verständnis des Mysteriums von Golgatha entwickele.

Anthroposophie strebt dieses neue Verständnis an. Aus der gegebenen Schilderung ersieht man, dass sie keine Erneuerung der Gnosis sein kann, die zu ihrem Inhalt die Erkenntnisart der Empfindungsseele hatte, dass sie aber einen ebenso reichen Inhalt aus der Bewusstseinsseele auf völlig neue Art holen muss.

our age, out of the consciousness soul and in the light of Michael's activity, of the Mystery of Golgotha.

Anthroposophy strives for this new understanding, which – as one may see from the above description – cannot be a renewal of Gnosis. For the content of Gnosis was the path of knowledge of the sentient soul, whereas Anthroposophy – in a completely new way – must draw forth a content just as rich from the consciousness soul.

Leitsätze Nr. 159 bis 161

159. Gnosis entfaltet sich in ihrer eigentlichen Gestalt im Zeitalter der Empfindungsseele (viertes bis erstes Jahrtausend vor dem Eintritte des Mysteriums von Golgatha). Das «Göttliche» offenbart sich dem Menschen in diesem Zeitalter im Innern als Geist-Inhalt, wogegen es sich im vorangehenden Zeitalter des Empfindungsleibes an den Sinneseindrücken der Außenwelt geoffenbart hat.

160. Im Zeitalter der Verstandes- oder Gemütsseele kann der Geist-Inhalt des «Göttlichen» nur in verblasster Art erlebt werden. Es wird die Gnosis in strengen Mysterien bewahrt, und als Menschen dies nicht mehr können, weil sie die Empfindungsseele zu beleben nicht mehr imstande sind, da wird in das Mittelalter hinüber durch Geistwesen zwar nicht der Erkenntnis-Inhalt, aber der Gefühlsgehalt getragen. (Die Gral-Legende enthält die Andeutung davon.) Daneben wird die exoterische Gnosis, die in die Verstandes- oder Gemütsseele eindringt, ausgerottet.

161. Die Anthroposophie kann nicht eine Erneuerung der Gnosis sein, denn diese hing an der Entfaltung der

Leading Thoughts 159 to 161

159. Gnosis in its true form evolved in the age of the sentient soul (from the fourth to the first millennium before the Mystery of Golgotha). It was an age in which the "divine" was made manifest to the human being as a spiritual content in his inner being; whereas in the preceding age, the age of the sentient body, it had revealed itself directly in his sense impressions of the outer world.

160. In the age of the intellectual- or mind-soul, the human being could only experience in paler cast the spiritual content of the "divine." Gnosis was preserved in strictly hidden Mysteries. And when human beings could no longer preserve it, because they could no longer enkindle the sentient soul to life, spiritual beings carried over, not the knowledge-content, but the feeling-content of Gnosis into the Middle Ages. (The Legend of the Holy Grail contains an indication of this fact.) Meanwhile the exoteric Gnosis, which penetrated into the intellectual- or mind-soul, was exterminated.

161. Anthroposophy cannot be a revival of Gnosis, for the latter depended on the development of the sentient

Empfindungsseele. Anthroposophie muss im Lichte der Michael-Tätigkeit aus der Bewusstseinsseele heraus ein Welt- und Christus-Verständnis auf neue Art entwickeln. Die Gnosis war die aus alter Zeit bewahrte Erkenntnisart, die das Mysterium von Golgatha bei seinem Eintritte am besten zum Menschenverständnisse bringen konnte.

soul. Anthroposophy must evolve a new understanding of Christ and of the world out of the consciousness soul and in the light of Michael's activity. Gnosis was the mode of knowledge preserved from ancient times which, at the time of the Mystery of Golgotha, was best able to bring this Mystery to human understanding.

Die Freiheit des Menschen und das Michael-Zeitalter

Goetheanum, Januar 1925

In der Erinnerungsfähigkeit des Menschen lebt das persönliche Abbild einer kosmischen Kraft, die in der Art am menschlichen Wesen gewirkt hat, wie das die letzten Betrachtungen gezeigt haben. Diese kosmische Kraft ist aber auch gegenwärtig noch tätig. Sie wirkt als Wachstumskraft, als belebender Impuls im Hintergrunde des Menschenlebens. Da wirkt sie mit ihrem größeren Anteile. Sie sondert nur einen kleinen Teil von sich ab, der als Tätigkeit in die Bewusstseinsseele eintritt. Da wirkt er als Erinnerungskraft.

Man muss diese Erinnerungskraft im rechten Lichte sehen. – Wenn der Mensch in der gegenwärtigen Epoche des kosmischen Werdens mit den Sinnen wahrnimmt, so ist dies Wahrnehmen ein augenblickliches Aufleuchten von Welt*bildern* im Bewusstsein. Das Aufleuchten kommt, wenn der Sinn auf die Außenwelt gerichtet ist; es durchhellt das Bewusstsein; es verschwindet, wenn der Sinn sich nicht mehr an die Außenwelt richtet. – Was da in der Menschenseele aufleuchtet: Es darf nicht Dauer haben. Denn brächte der Mensch es nicht rechtzeitig aus seinem Bewusstsein heraus, er verlöre sich an den Bewusstseinsinhalt. Er wäre nicht mehr *er* selbst. Nur kurze

Human Freedom and the Age of Michael

Goetheanum, January 1925

In the human faculty of memory, there lives the personal image of a cosmic force which worked upon the human being in the past, in the way revealed through our previous considerations. This cosmic force is still active at the present time. It works as the force of growth, as the life-giving impulse in the background of human life. The main portion of it works in this way: Only a small part is separated off as an activity that enters into the consciousness soul, where it works as the force of memory.

One must learn to see this force of memory in its true light. – When in the present epoch of cosmic evolution a human being perceives with his senses, his perception is a momentary lighting-up of world-*images* in consciousness. This lighting-up takes place when the senses are directed to the outer world; it illumines the consciousness and vanishes when the senses are no longer directed outward. – What lights up in the human soul in this way must not have duration. For if the human being were not to eliminate it from his consciousness quickly enough, he would lose himself in this content of consciousness. He would no longer be *himself*. For a short time only – in

Zeit, in den sogenannten Nachbildern, die Goethe so sehr interessierten, darf im Bewusstsein das «Leuchten» durch die Wahrnehmung leben. Es darf dieser Bewusstseinsinhalt auch nicht zum Sein erstarren; er muss *Bild* bleiben. Er darf ebenso wenig real werden, wie das *Bild* im Spiegel real werden kann.

An etwas, das sich als Realität im Bewusstsein auslebte, würde sich der Mensch ebenso verlieren wie an das, was durch sich selbst Dauer hätte. Auch da könnte er nicht mehr *er* selbst sein.

So ist das sinnenfällige Wahrnehmen der Außenwelt ein innerliches Malen der Menschenseele. Ein Malen ohne Malsubstanz. Ein Malen im Geistwerden und Geistvergehen. Wie der Regenbogen in der Natur ersteht und dahingeht, ohne eine Spur zu hinterlassen, so ersteht die Wahrnehmung und geht dahin, ohne dass *sie* Erinnerung durch ihr eigenes Wesen zurücklässt.

Aber gleichzeitig mit *jeder* Wahrnehmung verläuft zwischen der Menschenseele und der Außenwelt ein anderer Vorgang. Ein solcher, der im mehr zurückliegenden Teile des Seelenlebens liegt. Da, wo die Wachstumskräfte, wo die Lebensimpulse wirken. In *diesem* Teile des Seelenlebens prägt sich beim Wahrnehmen nicht nur ein vorübergehendes Bild, sondern ein dauerndes, reales Abbild ein. Das kann der Mensch ertragen, denn das hängt mit dem Sein des Menschen als Weltinhalt

the so-called afterimages which were the source of such interest for Goethe – the inner "illumination" of a sense perception may live on in consciousness. Nor must this content of consciousness solidify into Being. It must remain an *image*. It must on no account become real, any more than the *image* in a mirror can become real.

The human being would lose himself in anything that lives and works itself out as a reality in his consciousness, just as he would lose himself in something which through its own nature possesses duration. In this case, too, he could no longer be *himself*.

Thus, sensory perception of the outer world is an inner act of painting by the human soul; a painting without the substance of paint; a painting in the spirit becoming and in the spirit vanishing. Just as in nature a rainbow arises and passes away, leaving no trace behind, so does a perception arise and pass away, without *itself* leaving any memory behind through its own inherent nature.

But simultaneous to *every* perception, another process takes its course between the human soul and the outer world – a process lying in the more hidden portions of the soul-life, where the forces of growth, the life-impulses, are at work. In *this* part of the soul's life, not only a fleeting image but a permanent and real image is impressed into every act of perception. The human being can endure this, for this is a part of the content of the world, connected with his being. He cannot

zusammen. Indem dies sich vollzieht, kann er ebenso wenig sich verlieren, wie er sich verliert, da er ohne sein volles Bewusstsein wächst, sich ernährt.

Wenn nun der Mensch seine Erinnerungen aus seinem Innern holt, dann ist das ein inneres Wahrnehmen dessen, was geblieben ist in dem zweiten Vorgang, der sich beim äußeren Wahrnehmen abspielt.

Wieder malt die Seele, jetzt aber das im eigenen menschlichen Innern lebende Vergangene. Wieder darf *im Bewusstsein* bei diesem Malen kein dauerndes Reales, sondern nur ein erstehendes und vergehendes Bild sich formen.

So hängen in der Menschenseele wahrnehmendes Vorstellen und Erinnern zusammen.

Aber die Erinnerungskräfte haben das fortwährende Bestreben, mehr zu sein, als sie sein können, wenn der Mensch als selbstbewusstes Wesen *sich* nicht verlieren soll.

Denn die Erinnerungskräfte sind Reste der Vergangenheit im Menschenwerden und kommen als solche in das Machtgebiet Luzifers. Dieser hat das Bestreben, im Menschenwesen die Eindrücke der Außenwelt so zu verdichten, dass sie fortwährend als Vorstellen im Bewusstsein leuchten.

Dieses luziferische Bestreben würde von Erfolg gekrönt sein, wenn die Michael-Kraft ihm nicht entgegenwirkte. Sie

lose himself while this process is taking place any more than he loses himself through the fact that he grows and is nourished without his own full consciousness.

This second process takes place in every act of outward perception. And when the human being now draws forth his memories from within himself, this is an inward perception of what has remained permanent through the second process.

Once again the soul paints, but now it paints the past that lives in the human being's own inner nature. And once again, while the soul is thus painting, no lasting reality may form itself *in consciousness*, but only an image that arises and vanishes again.

Such is the relation in the human soul between the forming of a representation in the act of perception and the remembering of it.

But the forces of memory are perpetually striving to be more than they can be if the human being is not to lose *himself* as a self-conscious being.

For the forces of memory are relics of the past in human evolution, and as such they come within the realm of Lucifer's power. Lucifer strives so to condense the impressions of the outer world in the human being that they may continuously shine as representation in his consciousness.

This luciferic striving would be crowned with success if it were not for the force of Michael which counteracts it.

lässt das im inneren Lichte Gemalte nicht zum Sein erstarren, sondern erhält es im erstehenden und vergehenden Bilde.

Die überschüssige Kraft, die da aber durch Luzifer heraufdrängt aus dem menschlichen Innern, sie wird im Michael-Zeitalter umgewandelt werden in imaginierende Kraft. Denn allmählich wird in das allgemeine intellektuelle Menschheitsbewusstsein die Kraft der Imagination einziehen. – Damit aber wird der Mensch sein Gegenwartsbewusstsein nicht mit dauerndem Realen belasten; das bleibt in erstehenden und vergehenden Bildern wirksam. Mit seinen Imaginationen aber ragt der Mensch in eine höhere Geistwelt hinauf, wie er mit seinen Erinnerungen in seine eigene Menschenwesenheit hineinragt. Der Mensch behält die Imaginationen nicht in sich; sie sind in das kosmische Sein eingezeichnet; und aus diesem kann er sie immer wieder in dem Bild-Vorstellungsleben abmalen.

So wird, was Michael bewahrt vor dem Erstarren im Menschen-Innern, von der geistigen Welt aufgenommen. Was der Mensch von der Kraft des bewussten Imaginierens erlebt, das wird zugleich Welt-Inhalt. Dass dies so sein kann, ist ein Ergebnis des Mysteriums von Golgatha. Die Christuskraft prägt die Menschen-Imagination dem Kosmos ein. Die Christuskraft, die mit der Erde verbunden ist. Solange sie nicht mit der Erde verbunden war, sondern von außen auf die

Michael's force does not allow what is painted in the inner light to solidify into Being, but keeps it in the state of an emerging and fading image.

But the surplus force, which presses upward from within the human being through Lucifer's activity, will be transformed in this Age of Michael into the force of spiritual imagination. For the force of imagination will gradually enter into the common intellectual consciousness of humanity. – But this does not mean that the human being will burden his present consciousness with lasting realities; his present consciousness will still work in the arising and vanishing images. With his imaginations, however, he reaches up into a higher world of spirit, just as with his memories he reaches down into his own human nature. The human being does not keep the imaginations within himself; they are inscribed into cosmic Being, and from there he is able to paint them again and again in his own life of image-representation.

Thus what Michael withholds from crystallization in the inner nature of the human being is received by the spiritual world. What the human being experiences of the force of conscious imagination becomes at once a part of the world-content. That this can be so is an outcome of the Mystery of Golgotha. The Christ-force impresses the spiritual imagination of the human being into the cosmos. It is the Christ-force, united with the earth. So long as it was not united with the

Erde als Sonnenkraft wirkte, gingen alle Wachstums- und Lebensimpulse in das Menschen-Innere. Der Mensch wurde durch sie aus dem Kosmos heraus gebildet und erhalten. Seit der Christus-Impuls mit der Erde lebt, wird der Mensch in seiner selbstbewussten Wesenheit dem Kosmos wieder zurückgegeben.

Der Mensch ist aus einem Weltenwesen ein Erdenwesen geworden; er ist dazu veranlagt, wieder ein Weltenwesen zu werden, nachdem er als Erdenwesen *er selbst* geworden ist.

In dieser Tatsache, dass der Mensch in seinem augenblicklichen *Vorstellen* nicht im Sein, sondern nur in einer Spiegelung des Seins, in einem Bild-Sein lebt, liegt die Möglichkeit der Entfaltung der Freiheit. Alles Sein im Bewusstsein ist ein zwingendes. Allein das *Bild* kann nicht zwingen. Soll durch seinen Eindruck etwas geschehen, so muss es ganz unabhängig *von ihm* geschehen. – Der Mensch wird dadurch frei, dass er mit seiner Bewusstseinsseele aus dem Sein sich erhebt und in dem *nicht-seienden* Bildwesen auftaucht.

Da entsteht die bedeutsame Frage: Verliert denn der Mensch das Sein nicht, indem er es mit einem Teile seines Wesens verlässt und sich in das Nicht-Sein stürzt?

Hier ist wieder einer der Punkte, wo man mit der Betrachtung der Welt vor einem der großen Rätsel steht.

earth but instead worked upon the earth as the sun-force from without, all the impulses of life and growth went into the inner nature of the human being. The human being was formed and maintained by them, out of the cosmos. Since the Christ-impulse has begun to live with the earth, the human being in his self-conscious being is given back again to the cosmos.

From his origin as a cosmic being, the human being has become an earthly being. He has the potential to become a cosmic being once again, when as earthly being he has become *himself*.

Thus in his momentary *living in representations*, the human being is not in real Being, but only in a mirroring of Being – in an image-Being; inherent in this fact lies the possibility of developing freedom. All that is *Being* in consciousness has power to compel. But an *image* alone cannot compel. If anything is to be brought about through the impression that the image makes, it must happen quite *independently of the image*. – The human being becomes free whenever he rises with his consciousness soul out of Being and emerges in the image-existence *which has no Being*.

Here the weighty question arises: Does not the human being lose hold of Being altogether, inasmuch as he leaves it and plunges into non-Being with a portion of his nature?

This is another point where, in consideration of the world, one finds oneself face to face with one of the great riddles.

Was im Bewusstsein als Vorstellen erlebt wird, ist aus dem Kosmos heraus entstanden. Dem Kosmos gegenüber stürzt sich der Mensch in das Nicht-Sein. Er *befreit* sich im Vorstellen von allen Kräften des Kosmos. Er malt den Kosmos, außerhalb dessen er ist.

Wäre es *nur* so, so leuchtete im Menschenwesen für einen kosmischen Augenblick die Freiheit auf; aber in demselben Augenblick löste sich auch die Menschenwesenheit auf. – Aber, indem im Vorstellen der Mensch frei wird vom Kosmos, ist er doch in seinem nicht-bewussten Seelenleben an seine vorigen Erdenleben und Leben zwischen Tod und neuer Geburt angegliedert. Er ist als bewusster Mensch im Bild-Sein, und er hält sich mit seinem Unbewussten in der geistigen Realität. Während er im *gegenwärtigen* Ich die Freiheit erlebt, hält ihn sein *vergangenes* Ich in dem Sein.

In Bezug auf das Sein ist im Vorstellen der Mensch ganz dem hingegeben, das er durch die kosmische und irdische Vergangenheit hindurch geworden ist.

Es ist in der Menschen-Entwickelung hier auf den Abgrund des Nichts gedeutet, über den der Mensch springt, indem er ein freies Wesen wird. Michaels Wirken und der Christus-Impuls machen den Sprung möglich.

What is experienced in consciousness as representation has come into being from the cosmos. In relation to the cosmos, the human being plunges into non-Being. In representation, he *frees* himself from all the forces of the cosmos. He "paints" the cosmos while he himself is outside it.

If this were the *whole* reality, freedom would light up in the human being for a single cosmic moment – but in the very same moment, the human being would dissolve away. – But while the human being becomes free from the cosmos in representation, in his unconscious life of soul he is still connected with his former earthly lives as well as his lives between death and a new birth. As a conscious human being he is in the sphere of image-Being, while with his unconscious life he maintains himself within the spiritual reality. He experiences freedom in the *present* 'I', while his *past* 'I' preserves him in the element of real Being.

With respect to real Being, the human being in his life of representation is completely given to what he has become through the whole course of the cosmic and earthly past.

What is here being pointed to is the abyss of nothingness in human development which the human being must cross to the extent that he becomes a free being. It is Michael's working and the Christ-impulse which make it possible for him to leap across this abyss.

Leitsätze Nr. 162 bis 164

162. Im Vorstellen lebt der Mensch mit seiner Bewusstseinsseele nicht im Sein, sondern im Bild-Sein, im Nicht-Sein. Dadurch ist er vom Mit-Erleben mit dem Kosmos *befreit*. Bilder zwingen nicht. Nur das Sein zwingt. Richtet sich der Mensch doch nach Bildern, so ist das von den Bildern ganz unabhängig, das heißt in Freiheit von der Welt.

163. In dem Augenblicke eines solchen Vorstellens hängt der Mensch mit dem Sein der Welt nur durch das zusammen, das er aus der Vergangenheit seiner früheren Erdenleben und seiner Leben zwischen Tod und Geburt geworden ist.

164. Diesen Sprung über das Nicht-Sein gegenüber dem Kosmos kann der Mensch nur durch die Tätigkeit Michaels und den Christus-Impuls machen.

Leading Thoughts 162 to 164

162. In representation the human being lives, with his consciousness soul, not in Being but in image-Being – in a realm of non-Being. Thus is he *freed* from living and experiencing in union with the cosmos. Images do not compel; Being alone has power to compel. And if the human being does direct himself according to the images, his decision to do so is completely independent of them – that is to say, in freedom from the world.

163. In the moment of such representation, the human being is joined to the Being of the world by that alone which he has become through his own past: through his former lives on earth as well as his lives between death and a new birth.

164. It is only through Michael's activity and the Christ-impulse that the human being can achieve this leap across the abyss of non-Being in relation to the cosmos.

Wo ist der Mensch als denkendes und sich erinnerndes Wesen?

Goetheanum, Januar 1925

Mit dem Vorstellen (Denken) und dem Erleben von Erinnerungen befindet sich der Mensch innerhalb der physischen Welt. Aber, wo immer er den Blick in dieser physischen Welt hinrichtet: Mit seinen Sinnen wird er nirgends etwas finden, das ihm die Kräfte zum Vorstellen und Erinnern geben könnte.

Im Vorstellen erscheint das Selbstbewusstsein. Dieses ist – im Sinne der vorangehenden Betrachtungen – ein Erwerb, den der Mensch von den Kräften des Irdischen hat. Aber *diese* irdischen Kräfte sind solche, die dem sinnlichen Anschauen verborgen bleiben. Der Mensch denkt zwar im Erdenleben nur das, was ihm seine Sinne vermitteln; aber die Kraft zum Denken gibt ihm nichts von alledem, was er so denkt.

Wo findet man diese Kraft, die aus dem Irdischen heraus das Vorstellen (Denken) und die Erinnerungsbilder formt?

Man findet sie, wenn man den Geistesblick auf das richtet, was sich der Mensch aus den vorigen Erdenleben mitbringt. Das gewöhnliche Bewusstsein kennt dieses nicht. Es lebt im Menschen zunächst unbewusst. Aber es erweist sich, indem der Mensch nach dem geistigen Sein die Erde betritt, so-

Where Is the Human Being in Thinking and Remembering?

Goetheanum, January 1925

With his power to form representations (thinking) and his experience of memories, the human being finds himself within the physical world. But wherever he may turn his gaze in this physical world, he will nowhere find with his senses anything that could give him the power to form representations and to remember.

Self-consciousness appears in the act of forming representations. This is, in accordance with our previous considerations, an acquisition that the human being has from the forces of the earth. But *these* earthly forces are such as remain concealed from the vision of the senses. During earthly life the human being thinks only what his senses impart to him, but the power to think gives him nothing of all that he thus thinks.

Where does one find this force, which out of the earthly element forms both representations (thinking) and memory-images?

One finds it when spiritual vision is directed to what the human being brings with him from previous lives on earth. Ordinary consciousness knows nothing of this element, for to begin with it lives in the human being unconsciously. But when, after his purely spiritual existence, the human being enters into

gleich als verwandt mit *den* irdischen Kräften, die nicht in den Bereich von Sinnesbeobachten und Sinnesdenken fallen.

Nicht mit dem Vorstellen (Denken) ist der Mensch in diesem Bereich, sondern mit dem Wollen, das sich im Sinne des Schicksals abspielt.

Man kann in Anbetracht dessen, dass die Erde Kräfte enthält, die außerhalb des Sinnenbereiches fallen, von der «geistigen Erde» als Gegenpol der physischen sprechen. Dann ergibt sich, dass der Mensch als Willenswesen in und mit der «geistigen Erde» lebt, dass er aber als vorstellendes (denkendes) Wesen zwar innerhalb der physischen Erde ist, dass er aber als solches nicht *mit* ihr lebt.

Der Mensch als denkendes Wesen trägt aus der Geist-Welt Kräfte in die physische; aber er bleibt mit diesen Kräften Geistwesen, das in der physischen Welt nur *erscheint*, aber keine Gemeinsamkeit mit ihr eingeht.

Eine Gemeinsamkeit geht der vorstellende (denkende) Mensch während des Erdendaseins nur mit der «geistigen Erde» ein. Und aus *dieser* Gemeinsamkeit erwächst ihm sein Selbstbewusstsein. – Dessen Entstehung ist also verdankt solchen Vorgängen, die sich im Erdenleben mit dem Menschen als geistige abspielen.

Umfasst man mit der Geistesschau, was da beschrieben ist, so hat man das «menschliche Ich» vor dieser Schau.

earthly existence, this element immediately shows itself to be related to *those* earthly forces which do not come into the sphere of sensory observation and sense-related thought.

The human being dwells in the sphere of these forces not with his capacity to form representations (thinking), but with his will, which works in accordance with destiny.

When one considers that the earth contains forces outside the sphere of the senses, one may then speak of the "spiritual earth" as the opposite pole of the physical. It then follows that as a willing being, the human being lives in and with the "spiritual earth," while in forming representations (thinking) he is indeed within the physical earth – though, as such, he does not live *with it*.

As a thinking being, the human being carries forces from the world of spirit into the physical realm; however, with these forces he remains a spirit-being who only *appears* in the physical world, though he still does not enter into communion with it.

During earthly existence, the representing (thinking) human being enters into communion with the "spiritual earth" only. And out of *this* mutual relationship his self-consciousness develops. – The development of self-consciousness is therefore a result of spiritual processes which take place in the human being during earthly life.

If with spiritual seeing one grasps what is here described, one has before oneself the "human I."

Mit den Erinnerungserlebnissen kommt man in das Gebiet des menschlichen Astralleibes. Im Erinnern strömen nicht bloß wie beim Vorstellen (Denken) die Ergebnisse voriger Erdenleben in das gegenwärtige Ich, sondern es strömen die Kräfte der Geist-Welt, die der Mensch zwischen Tod und neuer Geburt erlebt, in sein Inneres ein. Dieses Einströmen geschieht in den Astralleib.

Nun gibt es innerhalb der physischen Erde auch für die unmittelbare Aufnahme der so einströmenden Kräfte kein Gebiet. Der Mensch kann als sich erinnerndes Wesen noch ebenso wenig mit den Dingen und Vorgängen, die seine Sinne wahrnehmen, sich verbinden, wie er sich als vorstellendes Wesen mit diesen verbinden kann.

Aber er geht Gemeinsamkeit ein mit dem, was zwar nicht physisch ist, was aber das Physische in Vorgänge, in Geschehnisse umsetzt. Es sind dies die rhythmischen Vorgänge in Natur- und Menschenleben. In der Natur wechseln rhythmisch Tag und Nacht, folgen rhythmisch Jahreszeiten und so weiter. Im Menschen erfolgt das Atmen und die Blutzirkulation im Rhythmus. Es geht so der Wechsel von Schlafen und Wachen vor sich und so weiter.

Rhythmische Vorgänge sind weder in der Natur noch im Menschen etwas Physisches. Man könnte sie halbgeistig nennen. Das Physische als Ding verschwindet im rhythmischen

With the experience of memory, one comes into the sphere of the human astral body. In the act of remembering, there stream into the present 'I' not merely the results of former earthly lives, as is the case in representation (thinking) – rather, into the human being's innermost being there stream the forces of the world of spirit which he experiences between death and new birth. This in-streaming takes place in the astral body.

Now, there is no sphere within the physical earth for the immediate reception of the forces thus streaming in. As a being who remembers, the human being cannot unite with the objects and processes perceived through his senses any more than he can unite with them as a being who forms representations.

But he enters into communion with that which is not indeed physical but which transposes the physical into processes, into events. These are the rhythmical processes in nature and in human life. In the natural world, day and night alternate rhythmically, the seasons of the year follow in rhythmic succession, and so forth. In the human being, the processes of respiration and the circulation of the blood take place rhythmically; so do the alternating states of waking and sleeping, and so forth.

Rhythmical processes are not at all something physical, neither in nature nor in the human being. One could call them half-spiritual. The physical as object vanishes in the rhythmic

Vorgang. Im Erinnern ist der Mensch mit seinem Wesen in *seinen* und in den Naturrhythmus versetzt. Er lebt in seinem Astralleib.

Indischer Yoga will ganz in dem Erleben des Rhythmus aufgehen. Er will das Gebiet des Vorstellens, des Ich verlassen und in einem inneren Erleben, das dem Erinnern ähnlich ist, in die Welt schauen, die hinter dem liegt, was das gewöhnliche Bewusstsein kennen kann.

Das westliche Geistesleben darf zum Erkennen das Ich nicht unterdrücken. Es muss das Ich an die Wahrnehmung des Geistigen heranbringen.

Es kann das *nicht* geschehen, wenn man von der sinnenfälligen in die rhythmische Welt so vordringt, dass man im Rhythmus nur das Halbgeistig-Werden des Physischen erlebt. Man muss vielmehr *die* Sphäre der Geistwelt finden, die im Rhythmus sich offenbart.

Zweierlei ist also möglich. Erstens: Erleben des Physischen im Rhythmischen, wie dieses Physische halbgeistig wird. Es ist dies ein älterer, heute nicht mehr zu betretender Weg. Zweitens: Erleben der Geist-Welt, die den Weltenrhythmus *in* und außerhalb des Menschen so zu ihrer Sphäre hat, wie der Mensch die Erdenwelt mit ihren physischen Wesen und Vorgängen.

Zu *dieser* Geist-Welt nun gehört alles, was im gegenwärtigen kosmischen Augenblicke durch Michael geschieht. Ein

process. In the act of remembering, the human being's inner being is transposed into *his own* rhythm as well as into that of nature. He lives in his astral body.

Indian Yoga seeks full submergence into the experience of rhythm. It wishes to leave the sphere of forming representations, the sphere of the 'I', and in an inward experience similar to memory, to look into the world that lies behind the one which it is possible for ordinary consciousness to know.

It is not permissible for the spiritual life of the West to suppress the 'I' in order to "know." This spiritual life must bring the 'I' to the perception of the spiritual.

This *cannot* take place if one penetrates from the world of the senses into the world of rhythm, and so experiences in the rhythm only the process in which the physical becomes half-spiritual. Rather, one must find *that* sphere of the world of spirit which reveals itself in rhythm.

Two things are therefore possible. First, the experience of the physical in the rhythmic, as the physical becomes half-spiritual. This is an older path, one not to be followed any longer at the present time. Second, the experience of the world of spirit, which has as its sphere the cosmic rhythm *within* the human being and outside of him, just as the human being's sphere is the earthly world with its physical beings and processes.

Now to *this* world of spirit belongs everything that takes place at the present cosmic moment through Michael. A

Geist wie Michael bringt dasjenige, was sonst im luziferischen Gebiet liegen würde, dadurch in das der rein menschlichen Entwickelung – die von Luzifer nicht beeinflusst ist –, dass er die rhythmische Welt zu seinem Wohnplatz erwählt.

Angeschaut kann das alles werden, indem der Mensch in die Imagination eintritt. Denn die Seele lebt mit der Imagination im Rhythmus; und Michaels Welt ist diejenige, die im Rhythmus sich offenbart.

Erinnerung, Gedächtnis steht schon in dieser Welt darinnen, aber noch nicht tief. Das gewöhnliche Bewusstsein erlebt davon nichts. Tritt man aber in die Imagination ein, dann taucht aus der Rhythmus-Welt zunächst die Welt der subjektiven Erinnerungen auf; diese geht aber sogleich über in die im Ätherischen lebenden, von der göttlich-geistigen Welt geschaffenen Urbilder für die physische Welt. Den in kosmischen Bildern aufleuchtenden, das Weltenschaffen in sich bergenden Äther erlebt man. Und die in diesem Äther webenden Sonnenkräfte: Die sind da nicht bloß strahlend, die zaubern Welten-Urbilder aus dem Lichte heraus. Die Sonne erscheint als der kosmische Weltenmaler. Sie ist das kosmische Gegenbild der Impulse, die im Menschen die Vorstellungs-(Denk-) Bilder malen.

spirit such as Michael brings what would otherwise lie in the luciferic sphere into the purely human development not influenced by Lucifer, by choosing the world of rhythm for his dwelling-place.

All this can be seen when the human being enters into imagination. For with imagination the soul lives in rhythm, and Michael's world is the one which reveals itself in rhythm.

Memory, recollection, stands already in this world, but not very deeply. Ordinary consciousness experiences nothing of it. But if one enters into imagination, there emerges first of all, out of the world of rhythm, the world of subjective memories; and this passes over at once into the archetypal images for the physical world which are created by the divine-spiritual world and which live in the etheric. One experiences the ether which lights up in cosmic images and conceals within it the creative activity of the universe. And the sun-forces weaving in this ether are there not merely radiant, but they conjure up the archetypal world-images out of the light. The sun appears as the cosmic world-painter. It is the cosmic counterimage of the impulses which in the human being paint the representational (thought-) images.

Leitsätze Nr. 165 bis 167

165. Der Mensch lebt zwar als denkendes Wesen in dem Bereich der physischen Erde; aber er geht mit dieser keine Gemeinsamkeit ein. Er lebt als Geist-Wesen so, dass er das Physische wahrnimmt; die Kräfte zum Denken empfängt er aber von der «geistigen Erde» auf demselben Wege, auf dem er das Schicksal im Ergebnis voriger Erdenleben erlebt.

166. Was in der Erinnerung (im Gedächtnisse) erlebt wird, das ist schon in der Welt, wo im Rhythmus das Physische halbgeistig wird und wo solche Geist-Vorgänge sich abspielen, wie diejenigen sind, die im gegenwärtigen kosmischen Augenblicke durch Michael geschehen.

167. Wer Denken und Erinnerung richtig kennen lernt, dem geht das Verständnis dafür auf, wie der Mensch als Erdenwesen zugleich innerhalb des Erdgebietes lebt, aber doch nicht völlig in dieses Gebiet mit seinem Wesen eintaucht, sondern als außerirdisches Wesen durch die Gemeinsamkeit mit der «geistigen Erde» sein Selbstbewusstsein als die Vollendung des Ich sucht.

Leading Thoughts 165 to 167

165. The human being indeed lives as a thinking being in the realm of the physical earth, though he does not enter into communion with it. He lives, as a spiritual being, in such a way as to perceive the physical; but he receives the forces for his thinking from the "spiritual earth" in the same way he receives his destiny as the outcome of his former lives on earth.

166. What he experiences in remembrance (memory) is already within that world where in rhythm the physical becomes half-spiritual, and where such spirit-processes take place as are brought about in the present cosmic moment by Michael.

167. He who learns to know thinking and memory in their true nature will also begin to understand how the human being as an earthly being, though he lives within the earthly realm, does not fully submerge himself into it with his being. For as a being from beyond this world, through communion with the "spiritual earth" he seeks for his self-consciousness, for the fulfillment of his 'I'.

Der Mensch in seiner makrokosmischen Wesenheit

Goetheanum, Januar 1925

Der Kosmos offenbart sich dem Menschen zunächst von Seiten der Erde und von der Seite des Außerirdischen, der Sternenwelt.

Mit der Erde und ihren Kräften fühlt sich der Mensch verwandt. Das Leben belehrt ihn über *diese* Verwandtschaft mit großer Deutlichkeit.

Nicht so fühlt er sich *im gegenwärtigen Zeitalter* verwandt mit der Sternenumgebung. Aber dies dauert nur so lange, als er sich seines Ätherleibes nicht bewusst ist. Den Ätherleib in Imaginationen erfassen, heißt ein Zusammengehörigkeitsgefühl mit der Sternenwelt so entwickeln, wie man dies durch das Bewusstsein vom physischen Leibe von der Erde hat.

Die Kräfte, die den Ätherleib in die Welt hineinstellen, kommen aus dem *Umkreis* der Welt, wie die für den physischen Leib aus dem *Mittelpunkt* der Erde strahlen.

Aber mit den Ätherkräften, die aus dem Umkreis des Kosmos auf die Erde einströmen, kommen auch diejenigen Weltimpulse, die im astralischen Leibe des Menschen wirken.

Der Äther ist wie ein Meer, in dem sich schwimmend aus den allseitigen Weltenfernen die Astralkräfte der Erde nähern.

The Human Being in His Macrocosmic Nature

Goetheanum, January 1925

The cosmos reveals itself to the human being initially from the side of the earth and from the side of what is beyond the earth, the world of the stars.

The human being feels himself related to the earth and its forces. Life gives him very clear instruction regarding *this* relationship.

In the present age, he does not feel himself related in the same way to the stars surrounding him. But this lasts only so long as he is not conscious of his etheric body. To grasp the etheric body in imaginations means to develop a feeling of belonging to the world of the stars, just as one has this feeling regarding the earth through the consciousness of the physical body.

The forces which place the etheric body in the world come from the *circumference* of the world; those for the physical body radiate from the *center* of the earth.

But together with the etheric forces streaming to the earth from the cosmic circumference, there come also the world-impulses working in the human astral body.

The ether is like an ocean in which the astral forces swim from all directions of the cosmos, approaching the earth.

Im gegenwärtigen kosmischen Zeitalter können aber nur das Mineral- und das Pflanzenreich in ein unmittelbares Verhältnis zu dem Astralen kommen, das auf den Wogen des Äthers auf die Erde hereinströmt. Nicht das Tierreich und nicht das Menschenreich.

Beim Tierreich zeigt das geistige Schauen, wie im Embryonalen nicht das gegenwärtig auf die Erde einströmende Astrale lebt, sondern dasjenige, das noch zur alten Mondenzeit eingeströmt ist.

Bei dem Pflanzenreich schaut man, wie die mannigfaltigen wunderbaren Formen gebildet werden, indem aus dem Äther das Astrale sich löst und über die Pflanzenwelt hin wirkt.

Bei der Tierwelt schaut man, wie aus dem Geistigen heraus das vorzeitlich – während der Mondenentwickelung – wirksame Astrale aufbewahrt worden ist und als solches Aufbewahrtes wirkt, das gegenwärtig in der Geistwelt verbleibt und nicht in die Ätherwelt heraustritt.

Die Wirksamkeit *dieses* Astralen wird auch durch die Mondenkräfte vermittelt, die ja ebenfalls aus dem vorigen Erdenstadium verblieben sind.

Man hat also im Tierreich das Ergebnis von Impulsen, die im vorigen Erdenstadium sich äußerlich-naturhaft offenbarten, während sie im gegenwärtigen kosmischen Zeitalter sich in die Geistwelt zurückgezogen haben, die wirksam die Erde durchströmt.

But in the present cosmic age, only the mineral and plant realms come into a direct relation to the astral, which streams down to the earth on the waves of the ether. Neither the animal realm nor the human realm enters such a relation.

Spiritual vision shows that in the animal embryo, there lives not the astral that is now streaming to the earth, but what streamed in during the Old Moon period.

In the case of the plant realm, one sees how its manifold and wonderful forms are developed through the astral loosening itself from the ether and working over to the world of plants.

In the animal realm one sees how, from out of the spiritual, the astral which was active in very ancient times – during the Moon development – has been preserved and works as something stored up and retained, remaining on at the present time in the world of spirit and not coming forth into the etheric world.

The activity of *this* astral element is also mediated by the moon-forces, which have likewise remained in the same condition from the previous stage of the earth.

In the animal realm one has, therefore, the result of impulses which manifested themselves externally in nature in a previous stage of earth-existence, whereas in the present cosmic age they have withdrawn into the world of spirit actively penetrating the earth.

Nun zeigt sich dem geistigen Schauen, dass innerhalb des Tierreiches für die Durchdringung des physischen und des Ätherleibes mit dem Astralleib lediglich die im gegenwärtigen Irdischen aus der Vorzeit bewahrten Astralkräfte bedeutsam sind. Hat aber das Tier einmal seinen Astralleib, dann treten in demselben die Sonnen-Impulse wirksam auf. Die Sonnenkräfte können dem Tiere nichts von Astralischem geben; wohl aber müssen sie, wenn dieses einmal im Tiere ist, für Wachstum, Ernährung und so weiter eintreten.

Anders ist dies für das Menschenreich. Auch dieses erhält zunächst sein Astrales von den bewahrten Mondenkräften. Aber die Sonnenkräfte enthalten Astralimpulse, die für das Tierreich unwirksam bleiben, die aber im menschlichen Astralen so fortwirken, wie die Mondenkräfte beim ersten Durchdringen des Menschen mit Astralität gewirkt haben.

Im tierischen Astralleib schaut man die Mondenwelt; im menschlichen den harmonischen Zusammenklang von Sonnen- und Mondenwelt.

Auf diesem Sonnenhaften im menschlichen Astralleib beruht es, dass der Mensch das im Irdischen ausstrahlende Geistige zur Heranbildung des Selbstbewusstseins aufnehmen kann. Das Astralische strömt aus dem *Umkreis* des Weltenalls. Es wirkt entweder als solches, das gegenwärtig einströmt,

Now it is manifest to spiritual vision that, within the animal realm, only the astral forces which have been preserved in the present earth from the former period are of significance for the permeation of the physical and etheric bodies with the astral body. But once the animal is in possession of its astral body, the sun-impulses become effective within this astral body. The sun-forces cannot give the animal anything of the astral element; but once this element is in the animal, the sun-forces must set to work and foster growth, nutrition, and so forth.

It is different for the human realm. This, too, receives its astrality to begin with from the moon-forces that have been preserved. But the sun-forces contain astral impulses which, while they remain inactive for the animal realm, continue to act in the human astral element in the same way in which the moon-forces worked when the human being was first permeated with astrality.

In the animal astral body one sees the world of the moon; in the human astral body, the harmonious accord of the worlds of sun and moon.

The fact that the human being is able to receive, for the development of self-consciousness, the spiritual which rays forth in what is of the earth, depends upon what belongs to the sun in the human astral body. The astral streams in from the *circumference* of the universe. It acts either as astrality pouring

oder als solches, das in der Vorzeit eingeströmt und bewahrt worden ist. – Alles aber, was sich auf Gestaltung des Ich als Träger des Selbstbewusstseins bezieht, muss von einem *Sternmittelpunkt* ausstrahlen. Das Astralische wirkt aus dem Umkreis, das Ichmäßige aus einem Mittelpunkt. Die Erde als Stern impulsiert von ihrem Mittelpunkte aus das menschliche Ich. Jeder Stern strahlt von seinem Mittelpunkte aus Kräfte, von denen das Ich irgendeiner Wesenheit gestaltet ist.

So stellt sich die Polarität von *Sternmittelpunkt* und *kosmischem Umkreis* dar.

Man sieht aus dieser Darstellung zugleich, wie das Tierreich als ein Ergebnis früherer Entwickelungskräfte des Erdenwesens heute noch dasteht, wie es die bewahrten Astralkräfte verbraucht, wie es aber verschwinden muss, wenn diese verbraucht sind. Beim Menschen werden dagegen vom Sonnenhaften aus neue Astralkräfte erworben. Diese machen es ihm möglich, seine Entwickelung in die Zukunft zu tragen.

Man kann, wie man aus alledem ersieht, den Menschen in seiner Wesenheit nicht verstehen, wenn man sich seines Zusammenhangs mit dem Sternensein nicht ebenso bewusst wird wie desjenigen mit der Erde.

Und was der Mensch von der Erde für die Entfaltung seines Selbstbewusstseins empfängt, rührt ja auch von der innerhalb des Irdischen wirksamen Geist-Welt her. – Dass das Sonnenhafte dem Menschen gibt, was er für sein Astralisches braucht,

in at the present time or as astrality which had streamed in during ancient times and has been preserved. – But everything connected with the shaping of the 'I' as the vehicle of self-consciousness must radiate from the *center of a star*. The astral works from the circumference; what belongs to the 'I' works from a center. From its center, the earth as a star gives the impulse for the human 'I'. Every star radiates, from its center, forces which mold or shape the 'I' of some being.

In this way, a polarity exists between *the center of a star* and *the cosmic circumference*.

From the above, it may also be seen how the animal realm still stands there today as the result of former developmental forces of the earth's being, how it uses up the astral forces which have been preserved, and how it must disappear when these have been consumed. The human being, however, acquires new astral forces from what belongs to the sun. These enable him to carry on his development into the future.

From all this, it may be seen that the nature of the human being cannot be understood unless one is just as conscious of his connection with the stars as of his connection with the earth.

And what the human being receives from the earth for the unfolding of his self-consciousness also depends on the world of spirit active within all that is of the earth. – The fact that the sun gives to the human being what he needs for his astral

das rührt von den Wirkungen her, die sich während der alten Sonnenzeit abgespielt haben. Da hat die Erde die Fähigkeit empfangen, die Ich-Impulse der Menschheit zu entfalten. Es ist das Geistige aus dieser Zeit, das sich die Erde aus dem Sonnenhaften bewahrt hat, das aber durch die gegenwärtige Sonnenwirkung vor dem Ersterben bewahrt wird.

Die Erde war einst selbst Sonne. Da hat sie sich vergeistigt. Im gegenwärtigen kosmischen Zeitalter wirkt das Sonnenhafte von außen. Dieses verjüngt fortdauernd das alt werdende, aus der Vorzeit stammende Geistige. Zugleich bewahrt dieses gegenwärtig wirkende Sonnenhafte das Vorzeitliche vor dem Hineinfallen in das Luziferische. Denn was, ohne in die Kräfte der Gegenwart aufgenommen zu werden, fortwirkt, verfällt dem Luziferischen.

Man kann sagen, des Menschen Zusammengehörigkeitsgefühl mit dem außerirdischen Kosmos sei in dieser kosmischen Epoche so abgedämpft, dass er es nicht innerhalb seines Bewusstseins bemerkt. Und es ist nicht nur abgedämpft, es wird übertönt von dem Zusammengehörigkeitsgefühl mit dem Irdischen. Weil der Mensch sein Selbstbewusstsein im Irdischen finden muss, wächst er mit diesem während des Anfangs des Bewusstseinsseelen-Zeitalters so zusammen, dass es viel stärker auf ihn wirkt, als dies mit dem rechten Verlauf seines Seelenlebens vereinbar ist. – Der Mensch ist gewissermaßen

element depends upon the activities which took place during the Old Sun period. At that time, the earth received the capacity to unfold the 'I'-impulses of humanity. What the earth has preserved for itself of the sun-nature is the spiritual element from that period; and it is preserved from dying out through the present activity of the sun.

The earth was itself sun at one time. Then it passed into a spiritualized state. In the present cosmic age, what is of the sun works from outside. This continually rejuvenates the spiritual element which originated in ancient times and is now growing old. At the same time, what is of the sun and acts in the present restrains what belongs to a former period from falling into the luciferic. For what continues to work without being received into the forces of the present succumbs to the luciferic.

One may say that the human being's feeling of belonging to the cosmos beyond this world is so dim in this cosmic epoch that he does not notice it within his consciousness. And it is not only dim – it is drowned by his feeling of belonging to the earth. As the human being is obliged to find his self-consciousness in the elements of the earth, he so grows together with them during the early part of the consciousness-soul age that they act upon him much more strongly than is compatible with the true course of his soul-life. – The human being is in a way *numbed* by the impressions of the sensory

von den Eindrücken der Sinnenwelt *betäubt*. Er kommt innerhalb dieser Betäubung mit dem freien, in sich selbst lebenden Denken nicht auf.

Die ganze Zeitepoche von der Mitte des neunzehnten Jahrhunderts an war eine solche der Betäubung durch die Sinneseindrücke. Das ist die große Illusion dieser Zeitepoche, dass man in ihr das zu starke Sinnesleben für das rechte genommen hat. Jenes Sinnesleben, das das Leben im außerirdischen Kosmos ganz auszulöschen bestrebt war.

In diese Betäubung hinein konnten die ahrimanischen Mächte ihr Wesen entfalten. Luzifer war durch das Sonnenhafte mehr zurückgewiesen als Ahriman, der in der Lage war, die gefährliche Empfindung gerade in den wissenschaftlichen Menschen hervorzurufen, dass die Ideen nur auf die Sinneseindrücke anwendbar seien. So kann gerade in diesen Kreisen Anthroposophie wenig Verständnis finden. Man steht den Ergebnissen der Geist-Erkenntnis gegenüber. Man sucht, sie mit den Ideen zu verstehen. Doch diese Ideen fassen das Geistige nicht, weil ihr Erleben von der ahrimanisierten Sinneserkenntnis übertäubt ist. Und so kommt man in die Furcht hinein, man verfalle blindem Autoritätsglauben, wenn man sich auf die Ergebnisse des geistig Schauenden einlässt.

Immer finsterer wurde in der zweiten Hälfte des neunzehnten Jahrhunderts für das menschliche Bewusstsein der außerirdische Kosmos.

world. Within this condition of numbness, he is not able to break through to free and self-enlivening thought.

The whole of the period since the middle of the nineteenth century has been one of becoming numb through sensory impressions. It is the great illusion of this age that the overly powerful life of the senses has been considered to be the right one – that life of the senses whose aim was to obliterate completely the life in the cosmos beyond this world.

In this numbed condition, the ahrimanic powers were able to unfold their being. Lucifer was repulsed by the sun-forces more than was Ahriman, who was able to evoke, especially in scientifically minded people, the dangerous feeling that ideas are applicable only to the impressions of the senses. Thus it is precisely in these circles that one can find so little understanding for Anthroposophy. Such people stand face to face with the results of spirit-knowing and try to understand them with their ideas. But these ideas do not grasp the spiritual because the experience of the ideas is drowned out by the ahrimanic sensory knowledge. And so they begin to fear that they may fall into a blind belief in authority if they have anything to do with the results of spiritual seeing.

In the second half of the nineteenth century, the cosmos beyond this world became ever darker for human consciousness.

Wenn der Mensch in sich die Ideen zu erleben wieder fähig wird, auch dann, wenn er sich mit ihnen nicht an die Sinneswelt anlehnt, dann wird dem Blick in den außerirdischen Kosmos wieder Helligkeit entgegenströmen. Das aber heißt, Michael in seinem Reiche kennenlernen.

Wenn einmal das Michael-Fest im Herbste wahr und innig sein wird, dann wird in der Empfindung der das Fest begehenden Menschen mit innerster Ehrlichkeit sich das Leitmotiv loslösen und im Bewusstsein leben: *Ideen-erfüllt erlebt die Seele Geisteslicht, wenn der Sinnenschein nur wie Erinnerung in dem Menschen nachklingt.*

Wenn der Mensch solches wird empfinden können, dann wird er nach der Festesstimmung auch wieder richtig in die Sinneswelt untertauchen können. Und Ahriman wird ihm nicht schaden können.

When the human being is able once more to experience ideas within himself, then, even when he does not support his ideas upon the world of the senses, light will again stream toward his gaze from the cosmos beyond this world. This is what it means to become acquainted with Michael in Michael's own realm.

Once the Festival of Michael in autumn becomes true and inward, the following thought will arise in all sincerity in the feelings, and will live in the consciousness, of one who celebrates this festival: *Suffused with ideas, the soul experiences spirit-light when sense-appearance only echoes in the human being like a memory.*

A person who is able to feel this will also be able, after the festive mood, to dive again into the world of the senses in the right way. And Ahriman will not be able to harm him.

Leitsätze Nr. 168 bis 170

168. Im Beginne des Bewusstseinszeitalters trat eine Abdämpfung des Zusammengehörigkeitsgefühles des Menschen mit dem außerirdischen Kosmos auf. Im Gegensatz hierzu wurde das Zusammengehörigkeitsgefühl mit dem Irdischen im Erleben der Sinneseindrücke gerade bei den wissenschaftlichen Menschen so stark, dass es eine Betäubung darstellt.

169. Innerhalb dieser Betäubung wirken die ahrimanischen Mächte besonders gefährlich, weil der Mensch in der Illusion lebt, das zu starke, betäubende Erleben der Sinneseindrücke sei das Rechte und ein wahrer Fortschritt in der Entwickelung.

170. Der Mensch muss die Kraft finden, seine Ideenwelt zu durchleuchten und durchleuchtet zu erleben, auch wenn er sich mit ihr nicht an die betäubende Sinneswelt anlehnt. An diesem Erleben der selbstständigen, in ihrer Selbstständigkeit durchleuchteten Ideenwelt wird das Zusammengehörigkeitsgefühl mit dem außerirdischen Kosmos erwachen. Die Grundlage für Michael-Feste wird daraus erstehen.

Leading Thoughts 168 to 170

168. In the beginning of the age of the consciousness soul, the human being's sense of togetherness with the cosmos beyond this world grew dim. On the other hand – and this was so especially in scientific minds – his sense of belonging to the earthly realm grew so intense, via the experience of sense impressions, as to amount to a numbing.

169. Within this condition of numbness, the ahrimanic powers work upon the human being most dangerously. For he lives in the illusion that the overly intense, numbing experience of sense impressions is the right thing and represents a true progression in development.

170. The human being must find the strength to fill his world of ideas with light and to experience it as light-permeated, even when this experience is unsupported by the numbing world of the senses. In this experience of the independent world of ideas – which, in its independence, is permeated with light – his sense of togetherness with the cosmos beyond this world will reawaken. In this way, there will arise the true foundation for Michael-festivals.

Des Menschen Sinnes- und Denkorganisation im Verhältnis zur Welt

Goetheanum, Februar 1925

Wenn der Mensch, das eigene Menschenwesen betrachtend, zunächst das imaginative Erkennen auf sich anwendet, so streift er in der Anschauung sein Sinnessystem ab. Er wird für seine Selbstanschauung ein Wesen ohne dieses System. Er hört nicht auf, Bilder vor seiner Seele zu haben, die vorher von den Sinnesorganen getragen waren; aber er hört auf, sich durch diese Organe mit der physischen Außenwelt verbunden zu fühlen. Die Bilder, die er von der physischen Außenwelt vor der Seele hat, sind jetzt nicht von den Sinnesorganen getragen: Sie sind für die unmittelbare Anschauung ein Beweis dafür, dass der Mensch durch die Sinnesverbindung hindurch mit der natürlichen Umwelt noch in einer anderen Verbindung steht, die nicht von den Sinnen getragen ist. Es ist die Verbindung mit dem Geiste, der in der natürlichen Außenwelt verkörpert ist.

In solcher Anschauung fällt also die physische Welt von dem Menschen ab. Es ist das Irdische, das abfällt. Der Mensch fühlt dieses Irdische nicht mehr an sich.

Man könnte glauben, dass ihm damit das Selbstbewusstsein schwindet. Das scheint aus den bisherigen Betrachtungen zu

The Human Sensory and Thought Organization in Relation to the World

Goetheanum, February 1925

When the human being first applies imaginative cognition to the consideration of his own human being, he begins by eliminating his own sensory system from the field of vision. As he now observes himself, he becomes a being without this system. Not that he ceases to have before his soul images such as were previously conveyed by the sense organs; but he ceases to feel himself connected with the outer physical world through these organs. The images of the outer physical world which he now has before his soul are no longer conveyed by the sense organs. His very vision of these images is proof of the fact that even through the sensory connection with the outer world of nature, he has yet another connection with this world – one that does not depend on the senses. It is a connection with the spirit embodied in the world of nature.

In such vision, therefore, the physical world falls away from the human being. It is the earthly element that falls away. The human being no longer feels this earthly element upon him.

It might be imagined that he would in the same moment lose self-consciousness. For this would seem to follow from

folgen, die das Selbstbewusstsein als ein Ergebnis des Zusammenhanges des Menschen mit der Erden-Wesenheit aufgezeigt haben. Es ist aber nicht so. Was der Mensch durch das Irdische erworben hat, das bleibt ihm, auch wenn er *nach der Erwerbung* im erlebenden Erkennen das Irdische von sich abstreift.

Durch die geschilderte geistig-imaginative Anschauung zeigt sich, dass der Mensch im Grunde sein Sinnessystem gar nicht intensiv mit sich verbunden hat. Es lebt eigentlich nicht *er* in diesem Sinnessystem, sondern die Umwelt. Diese hat *sich* mit ihrem Wesen in die Sinnesorganisation hineingebaut.

Und der imaginativ-schauende Mensch betrachtet deshalb auch die Sinnesorganisation als ein Stück Außenwelt. Ein Stück Außenwelt, das ihm allerdings nähersteht als die natürliche Umwelt, das aber doch Außenwelt ist. Es unterscheidet sich von der übrigen Außenwelt nur dadurch, dass der Mensch in diese nicht anders als durch die Sinneswahrnehmung erkennend untertauchen kann. In seine Sinnesorganisation taucht er aber erlebend unter. Die Sinnesorganisation ist Außenwelt, aber der Mensch streckt in diese Außenwelt sein geistig-seelisches Wesen hinein, das er beim Betreten des Erdendaseins aus der Geist-Welt mitbringt.

our previous considerations, which showed self-consciousness to be an outcome of the connection of the human being with the being of the earth. But it is not so. The human being preserves what he has acquired through the earthly element, even when, *after having acquired it*, he divests himself of it in the enlivened experience of knowing.

Through the above-described spiritually imaginative vision, the fact is revealed that the human being's sensory system is, fundamentally speaking, not at all intensively connected with his being. It is not really *he* who lives in this sensory system, but his environment. It is the outer world with *its* nature which has built itself into the human sensory organization.

Therefore, the person with the capacity of imaginative seeing really regards his sensory organization as a part of the outer world. It is of course closer to his being than the world of nature around him; but still, it belongs to the outer world. It is only distinguished from the remaining outer world in this: that the human being can dive down into the latter with knowing activity through sense perception and in no other way. Into his own sensory organization, on the other hand, he dives down with inner experience. The sensory organization is a part of the outer world; but into this outer world the human being extends his own spiritual-soul being, which he brings with him from the world of spirit as he enters earth-existence.

Mit Ausnahme der Tatsache, dass der Mensch seine Sinnesorganisation mit seinem geistig-seelischen Wesen erfüllt, ist diese Organisation Außenwelt, wie es die um ihn sich ausbreitende Pflanzenwelt ist. Das Auge gehört letzten Endes der Welt, nicht dem Menschen, wie die Rose, die der Mensch wahrnimmt, nicht ihm, sondern der Welt gehört.

In dem Zeitalter, das der Mensch in der kosmischen Entwickelung eben durchgemacht hat, traten Erkennende auf, die da sagten: Farbe, Ton, Wärme-Eindrücke seien eigentlich nicht in der Welt, sondern im Menschen. Die «rote Farbe», so sagen sie, sei nichts da draußen in der menschlichen Weltumgebung, sondern nur die Wirkung von etwas Unbekanntem auf den Menschen. – Aber die Wahrheit ist das gerade Gegenteil von dieser Anschauung. Nicht die Farbe gehört mit dem Auge dem Menschenwesen an, sondern das Auge gehört mit der Farbe der Welt an. Der Mensch lässt während seines Erdenlebens nicht die irdische Umgebung in sich hereinströmen, sondern *er wächst* zwischen Geburt und Tod in diese Außenwelt *hinaus*.

Es ist bedeutsam, dass sich am Ende *des finsteren Zeitalters*, in dem der Mensch in die Welt starrt, ohne das Licht des Geistes auch nur ahnend zu erleben, die wahre Ansicht von dem Verhältnis des Menschen zur Umwelt geradezu in das Gegenbild des Wahren verkehrt.

With the exception of the fact that the human being fills his sensory organization with his own spiritual-soul being, this organization is actually part of the outer world, just as is the plant realm spread around him. The eye belongs, in the last resort, to the world and not to the human being – just as the rose that the human being perceives belongs not to him but to the world.

In the age of cosmic development that humanity has just undergone, thinkers arose who declared that color, sound, and warmth-impressions are not really in the world but in the human being. The "red color," they say, is not at all anything out there in the human being's world-environment; it is but the effect of an unknown reality upon him. – But the very opposite of this conception is the truth. It is not the color that, with the eye, belongs to the human being; it is the eye that, with the color, belongs to the world. During his life on earth, the human being does not let the earth-environment pour in upon him, but *grows outward* – from birth to death – *into* this outer world.

It is significant that at the end of *the age of darkness*, when human beings stared out into the world without even dimly experiencing the light of the spirit, the true conception of the human being's relationship to his environment was replaced by its counterimage.

Hat der imaginativ Erkennende *diejenige* Umwelt abgestreift, in der er mit seiner Sinnesorganisation lebt, so tritt in das Erleben eine Organisation ein, von der das *Denken* so getragen ist wie das sinnliche Bild-Wahrnehmen durch die Sinnesorganisation.

Und jetzt weiß sich der Mensch durch diese Denkorganisation mit der kosmischen Sternen-Umgebung so in Zusammenhang, wie er sich vorher durch die Sinnesorganisation mit der Erden-Umgebung in Zusammenhang gewusst hat. Er erkennt sich als kosmisches Wesen. Die Gedanken sind nicht mehr Schattenbilder; sie sind von Wirklichkeit durchtränkt wie die Sinnesbilder in der sinnlichen Wahrnehmung.

Steigt nun der Erkennende zur Inspiration auf, so wird er gewahr, dass er diese Welt, die sich auf die Denkorganisation stützt, ebenso abstreifen kann wie die irdische. Er durchschaut, wie er auch mit dieser Denkorganisation nicht dem eigenen Wesen, sondern der Welt angehört. Er durchschaut, wie die Weltgedanken durch seine eigene Denkorganisation in ihm walten. Er wird wieder gewahr, wie er denkt, indem er nicht Abbilder der Welt in sich hereinnimmt, sondern wie er mit der Denkorganisation in das Weltdenken *hinauswächst*.

Sowohl in Bezug auf die Sinnesorganisation wie auf das Denksystem ist der Mensch *Welt*. Die Welt baut sich in ihn

When, in imaginative cognition, the human being has eliminated *that* environment in which he lives by means of his sensory organization, there enters into the sphere of conscious experience another organization: one which bears his *thinking capacity* in the same way that the sensory organization bears his image-world of sense perception.

And now the human being knows himself to be connected through his thinking organization with the cosmic environment of the stars, just as he previously knew himself to be connected through his sensory organization with the earth-environment. He now recognizes himself as a cosmic being. His thoughts are no longer shadow-images; they are saturated with reality, just as are the sensory images attained through sense perception.

And if at this stage the knower progresses further to inspiration, he becomes aware that he can cast aside this world supported by the thinking organization, just as he can cast aside the earthly. He sees that with his thinking organization, too, he belongs, not to his own being, but to the world. He realizes how the world-thoughts hold sway in him by means of his own thinking organization. Here again he becomes aware that he thinks not by receiving images of the world into himself, but by *growing outward* with his own thinking organization into the thinking of the world.

Both with respect to his sensory organization and his thinking system, the human being is *world*. The world builds itself

hinein. Dadurch ist er im Sinneswahrnehmen und im Denken nicht *er* selbst, sondern er ist da Welt-Inhalt.

In die Denkorganisation streckt nun der Mensch das Geistig-Seelische seines Wesens hinein, das weder der Erden- noch der Sternen-Welt angehört, das ganz geistiger Art ist und von Erdenleben zu Erdenleben in dem Menschen west. *Dieses* Geistig-Seelische ist nur der Inspiration zugänglich.

So tritt der Mensch aus seiner irdisch-kosmischen Organisation heraus, um durch seine Inspiration als rein geistig-seelisches Wesen vor sich zu stehen.

In dieser rein geistig-seelischen Wesenheit trifft der Mensch auf das Walten seines Schicksals auf.

Mit der Sinnesorganisation lebt der Mensch in seinem physischen Leib, mit der Denkorganisation in seinem ätherischen Leib. Nach Abstreifung beider Organisationen durch das erlebende Erkennen ist er in seinem astralischen Leib.

Jedes Mal, wenn der Mensch von seinem angenommenen Wesen etwas abstreift, wird zwar auf der *einen* Seite sein Seelen-Inhalt ärmer; aber er wird auf der anderen Seite zugleich reicher. Hat der Mensch nach der Abstreifung des physischen Leibes die Schönheit der sinnenfälligen Pflanzenwelt nur noch abgeblasst vor sich, so tritt dafür vor seine Seele die ganze Welt der Elementarwesen, die in dem Pflanzenreiche leben.

into him. In sense perception and in thought, he is not *he* himself, but part of the content of the world.

Now the human being penetrates into his thinking organization with the spiritual-soul element of his being – which belongs neither to the earthly world nor to the world of the stars, but is of a wholly spiritual nature and thrives in the human being from one earth life to another. *This* spiritual-soul element is accessible only to inspiration.

Thus the human being steps out of the earthly-cosmic organization, to stand before himself as a pure spiritual-soul being through inspiration.

And in this pure spiritual-soul being he comes to meet the holding sway of his own destiny.

With the sensory organization the human being lives in his physical body; with the thinking organization, in his etheric body. When both organizations have been cast aside in the living activity of knowing, he finds himself in his astral body.

Every time the human being casts aside a portion of the nature which he has assumed, the content of his soul is indeed impoverished on the *one* hand; and yet on the other hand it is enriched. When the physical body has been cast aside, the beauty of the plant world as perceived by the senses is only accessible to him in a far paler form; but on the other hand, the whole world of elemental beings dwelling in the plant realm rises up before his soul.

Weil es so ist, herrscht aber bei dem wirklich geistig Erkennenden nicht eine asketische Stimmung gegenüber dem, was die Sinne wahrnehmen. *Im geistigen Erleben* bleibt ihm vollebendig das Bedürfnis, das Geistig-Erlebte auch wieder durch die Sinne wahrzunehmen. Und wie bei dem Vollmenschen, der nach Erleben der ganzen Wirklichkeit strebt, die Sinneswahrnehmung die Sehnsucht nach dem Gegenpol, nach der Welt der Elementarwesen, weckt, so weckt das Anschauen der Elementarwesen wieder die Sehnsucht nach dem Inhalt der Sinneswahrnehmung.

Im Gesamt-Menschenleben verlangt der Geist nach dem Sinne, und der Sinn nach dem Geiste. – Im geistigen Dasein wäre Leerheit, wenn nicht als Erinnerung die Erlebnisse des Sinnenerlebens darinnen wären; im Sinneserleben wäre Finsternis, wenn nicht leuchtend, obwohl zunächst unterbewusst, die Kraft des Geistigen hereinwirkte.

Es wird daher, wenn sich der Mensch reif gemacht haben wird, die Betätigung des Michael mitzuerleben, nicht etwa ein Verarmen der Seelen an Natur-Erlebnissen eintreten, sondern im Gegenteil eine Bereicherung. Und auch das Gefühlsleben wird nicht dazu neigen, sich von dem Sinneserleben abzuziehen, sondern es wird freudige Neigung da sein, um die Wunder der Sinnenwelt voll in die Seele aufzunehmen.

Because this is so, the true spiritual knower has no ascetic demeanor toward what the senses perceive. *In the spiritual experience*, there remains alive in him the inner need to perceive once more through the senses what he now experiences in the spirit. In the full human being, seeking as he does to experience the whole reality, sense perception awakens the longing for its counterpart – the world of elemental beings. Likewise, the vision of the elemental beings enkindles the longing for the content of sense perception once again.

Thus, in the entirety of human life, spirit longs for sense and sense for spirit. – There would be emptiness in spiritual existence if the experiences of the conscious life in the senses were not there as a memory. There would be darkness in the life of sense-experience if it were not for the active force of the spirit which lights into it, although subconsciously at first.

Hence, when the human being will have made himself ripe to experience the activity of Michael, it will not mean that souls become impoverished in their experience of nature. On the contrary, they will be enriched in this respect. And in the life of feeling, too, the human being will not tend to withdraw from sense experience, but will rather be joyously inclined to receive the wonders of this world of the senses ever more fully into his soul.

Leitsätze Nr. 171 bis 173

171. Die menschliche Sinnesorganisation gehört nicht der Menschen-Wesenheit an, sondern ist von der Umwelt während des Erdenlebens in diese hineingebaut. Das wahrnehmende Auge ist räumlich im Menschen, wesenhaft ist es *in der Welt*. Und der Mensch streckt sein geistig-seelisches Wesen in dasjenige hinein, was die Welt durch seine Sinne in ihm erlebt. Der Mensch nimmt die physische Umgebung während seines Erdenlebens nicht in sich auf, sondern er wächst mit seinem geistig-seelischen Wesen in diese Umgebung hinein.

172. Ähnlich ist es mit der Denkorganisation. Der Mensch wächst durch sie in das Sternendasein hinein. Er erkennt sich selbst als Sternenwelt. In den Weltgedanken webt und lebt der Mensch, wenn er im erlebenden Erkennen die Sinnesorganisation abgestreift hat.

173. Nach Abstreifung von beidem, der Erdenwelt und der Sternenwelt, steht der Mensch als geistig-seelisches Wesen vor sich. Da ist er dann nicht mehr *Welt*, da ist er im wahren Sinne Mensch. Und gewahr werden, was

Leading Thoughts 171 to 173

171. The organization of the human senses belongs not to the human being's own nature, but is built into it by the outer world during his earthly life. Though it is spatially within the human being, in its essential being the perceiving eye is *in the world*. With his spiritual-soul being, the human being reaches out into what the world is experiencing in him through his senses. He does not receive the physical environment into himself during his life on earth, but grows out into it with his own spiritual-soul being.

172. This is likewise so of his thinking organization: Through it, he grows out into the existence of the stars. He comes to know himself as a world of stars. He lives and moves in the world-thoughts when, in the living experience of knowing, he has stripped away the sensory organization.

173. When both have been stripped away – the earthly world as well as the world of the stars – the human being stands before himself as a spiritual-soul being. At this point he is no longer *of the world*; here he is human being

er da erlebt, heißt *Sich-Erkennen*, wie Gewahr-Werden in der Sinnes- und Denkorganisation *Welt-Erkennen* heißt.

in the true sense. To become aware of what he experiences here is *self-knowing*, just as becoming aware within the sensory and thought-organization is *world-knowing*.

Gedächtnis und Gewissen

Goetheanum, Februar 1925

In dem schlafenden Zustande ist der Mensch an den Kosmos hingegeben. Er trägt dem Kosmos entgegen, was er beim Heruntersteigen aus der geistig-seelischen Welt in die irdische als Ergebnis voriger Erdenleben hat. Er entzieht diesen Inhalt seines Menschenwesens dem Kosmos während des Wachens.

In diesem Rhythmus: Hingabe an den Kosmos und Sich-dem-Kosmos-Entziehen verläuft das Leben zwischen Geburt und Tod.

Das Entziehen gegenüber dem Kosmos ist zugleich ein Aufnehmen des geistig-seelischen Menschen durch die Sinnes-Nervenorganisation. Was in dieser als physische und Lebensvorgänge sich abspielt, mit dem vereinigt sich im Wachen das Geistig-Seelische des Menschen zu einer einheitlichen Wirkungsweise. In dieser Wirkungsweise ist Sinneswahrnehmung, Formung der Erinnerungsbilder, Fantasie-Leben enthalten. Diese Betätigungen sind an den physischen Leib gebunden. Die Vorstellungen, das Denk-Erleben, in denen dem Menschen *bewusst* wird, was halbbewusst in Wahrnehmung, Fantasie, Erinnerung sich abspielt, sind an die Denkorganisation gebunden.

In dieser eigentlichen Denkorganisation liegt auch das

Memory and Conscience

Goetheanum, February 1925

In sleep, the human being is given up to the cosmos. He carries out into the cosmos what he has gained as a result of descending from the spiritual-soul world into the earthly world in his former earthly lives. During his waking life he withdraws this content of his human being from the cosmos.

In this rhythm of giving himself up to the cosmos and withdrawing from it, the human being's life between birth and death takes its course.

While he withdraws from the cosmos, the human being's spiritual-soul element is received by the sensory-nervous system. In waking life, the human being's spiritual-soul element combines with the physical- and life-processes taking place in the sensory-nervous system, so that they work together in union. This united action encompasses sense perception, the forming of memory-images, and the life of fantasy. All these activities are bound to the physical body. The forming of representations, the thinking experience – in which the human being becomes *conscious* of what takes place half-consciously in perception, fantasy, and memory – these are bound to the thinking organization.

In this actual thinking organization, there is also the realm

Gebiet, durch das der Mensch sein Selbstbewusstsein erlebt. Die Denkorganisation ist eine Sternen-Organisation. Lebte sie sich einzig *als solche* aus, dann trüge der Mensch in sich nicht ein Selbstbewusstsein, sondern ein Götterbewusstsein. Aber die Denkorganisation ist Sternen-Organisation, herausgehoben aus dem Sternen-Kosmos und versetzt in das irdische Geschehen. Indem der Mensch die Sternenwelt im Irdischen erlebt, wird er ein selbstbewusstes Wesen.

Da hat man also das Gebiet des inneren Menschenlebens vor sich, in dem die göttlich-geistige Welt, die mit dem Menschen verbunden ist, ihn entlässt, damit er in vollem Sinne Mensch werden kann.

Aber gleich unterhalb der Denkorganisation, da wo Sinneswahrnehmung, Fantasie, Erinnerungsbildung sich vollziehen, *lebt* die göttlich-geistige Welt im Menschenleben *mit*. Man kann sagen, in der Gedächtnisentfaltung lebt das Göttlich-Geistige in dem wachenden Zustande des Menschen. Denn die beiden anderen Betätigungen, Sinneswahrnehmung und Fantasie, sind nur Modifikationen der Formung der Erinnerungsbilder. In der Sinneswahrnehmung ist die Bildung des Erinnerungsinhaltes in seiner Entstehung; in dem Inhalte der Fantasie leuchtet in der Seele auf, was sich von diesem Inhalte im Seelen-Dasein erhält.

Der Schlafzustand trägt das Geistig-Seelische des Menschen

in which the human being experiences his self-consciousness. The thinking organization is an organization of the stars. If it lived and expressed itself solely *as such*, the human being would bear within himself not a consciousness of self but a consciousness of the gods. The thinking organization is, however, lifted out of the cosmos of the stars and transferred into the realm of earthly processes. When the human being experiences the world of stars within the earthly realm, he becomes a self-conscious being.

Here, therefore, one has the region of the human being's inner life where the divine-spiritual world – united with the human being – sets him free in order that he may become "human" in the fullest sense.

But directly beneath the thinking organization – namely, where sense perception, fantasy, and the forming of memory take place – the divine-spiritual world *lives on* within the life of the human being. One may say: It is in the unfolding of memory that the divine-spiritual lives in the human waking state. For the other two activities – sense perception and fantasy – are only modifications of the process that occurs in the forming of memory-images. In sense perception, the forming of memory-content is at the moment of its origin; in the content of fantasy, there lights up in the soul that portion of memory-content which is preserved within the soul's existence.

Sleep carries the human being's spiritual-soul element over

in das Kosmische hinüber. Er ist da mit der Betätigung seines Astralleibes und seines Ich in den göttlich-geistigen Kosmos eingetaucht. Er ist nicht nur außerhalb der physischen, sondern auch außerhalb der Sternenwelt. Aber er ist innerhalb der göttlich-geistigen Wesen, durch die sein Dasein den Ursprung hat.

In dem gegenwärtigen Zeitpunkt der kosmischen Entwickelung wirken diese göttlich-geistigen Wesen so, dass sie den moralischen Weltinhalt während des Schlafzustandes in Astralleib und Ich einprägen. Alles Weltgeschehen im schlafenden Menschen ist reales moralisches Geschehen, kein Geschehen, das der Naturwirkung auch nur ähnlich genannt werden könnte.

Dieses Geschehen in seiner Nachwirkung trägt der Mensch aus dem schlafenden in den Wachzustand herüber. Diese Nachwirkung bleibt im schlafenden Zustande. Denn der Mensch wacht nur in dem Leben, das dem Denkgebiete zugeneigt ist. Was in seiner Willenssphäre eigentlich vorgeht, das ist auch während des Wachens in solche Dumpfheit gehüllt wie während des Schlafens das *ganze* Seelenleben. Aber in diesem schlafenden Willensleben webt das Göttlich-Geistige im wachenden Zustande weiter. Der Mensch ist moralisch so gut oder so schlecht, als er es sein kann, je nach der Nähe, in die er schlafend zu den göttlich-geistigen Wesen kommen kann. Und er kommt näher oder bleibt ferner, je nachdem seine früheren Erdenleben in moralischer Richtung waren.

into the cosmic realm. Through the activity of his astral body and his 'I', the sleeping human being is steeped in the divine-spiritual cosmos. He is not only outside the physical, but also outside the world of stars. However, he is within the divine-spiritual beings through whom his own existence has its origin.

In the present moment of cosmic development, these divine-spiritual beings work in such a way as to impress the moral content of the universe into the human astral body and 'I' during sleep. All the world-processes in the sleeping human being are real moral events; these processes cannot be spoken of as even remotely similar to the activities of nature.

The human being carries the aftereffects of these processes over from sleep into the waking state. But the aftereffects remain in a state of sleep. For the human being is awake only in that part of his life which inclines to the sphere of thought. What actually takes place in his sphere of will is wrapped in darkness even in the waking state, just as *the whole* life of the soul is wrapped in darkness during sleep. But in this sleeping life of the will, the divine-spiritual works on in the human being's waking life. Morally, the human being is as good or as bad as he may be according to how near he can approach to the divine-spiritual beings when asleep. And he comes nearer to them, or remains farther away from them, according to the moral quality of his former lives on earth.

Aus den Tiefen des wachenden Seelenwesens tönt herauf, was sich während des Schlafens in Gemeinschaft mit der göttlich-geistigen Welt in dieses Seelenwesen hat einpflanzen können. *Was herauf klingt, ist die Stimme des Gewissens.*

So zeigt sich, wie dasjenige, was eine materialistische Weltansicht am meisten geneigt ist, bloß nach der Naturseite hin zu erklären, für die Geist-Erkenntnis auf der moralischen Seite gelegen ist.

Im *Gedächtnis* wirkt im wachenden Menschen unmittelbar das göttlich-geistige Wesen; im *Gewissen* wirkt im wachenden Menschen mittelbar – als Nachwirkung – dieses göttlich-geistige Wesen.

Gedächtnisbildung spielt sich in der Nerven-Sinnesorganisation ab; Gewissensbildung spielt sich als rein seelisch-geistiger Vorgang ab, aber in der Stoffwechsel-Gliedmaßenorganisation.

Zwischen beiden liegt die rhythmische Organisation. Diese ist nach zwei Seiten hin polarisch in ihrer Wirksamkeit ausgebildet. Sie ist als Atmungsrhythmus in inniger Beziehung zur Sinneswahrnehmung und zum Denken. In dem Lungen-Atmen ist der Vorgang am gröbsten; er verfeinert sich und wird als verfeinertes Atmen sinnliches Wahrnehmen und Denken. Was noch dem Atmen ganz nahesteht, aber ein Atmen durch die Sinnesorgane, nicht durch die Lungen ist, das ist das sinnliche Wahrnehmen. Was dem Lungen-Atmen schon ferner ist

From the depths of the awake soul-being, there *sounds forth* what was able to implant itself in the soul's existence in community with the divine-spiritual world during sleep. *This is the voice of conscience.*

It becomes apparent how the very things which a materialistic view of the world is most inclined to explain merely from the natural side, are found to lie on the moral side of things when seen in the light of spirit-knowledge.

In *memory*, divine-spiritual Being works directly within the waking human being. In *conscience*, the same divine-spiritual Being works in the waking human being indirectly, as an after-effect.

The forming of memory takes place in the nerve-sense organization. The forming of conscience takes place – though only as a pure soul-spiritual process – in the metabolic and limb-system.

Between the two there lies the rhythmic organization. This is built in such a way that its activity is polarized in two directions. In the breathing rhythm, the rhythmic organization stands in intimate relation to sense perception and thought. In the breathing of the lung, the process is at its coarsest; from there it grows finer and finer until, as a highly refined breathing process, it becomes sense perception and thought. Sense perception is still very near to breathing; it is simply a breathing through the sensory organs, as opposed to through the lungs. Forming representations,

und durch die Denkorganisation gestützt wird, das ist Vorstellen, Denken; und was schon nach dem Rhythmus der Blutzirkulation hinübergrenzt, schon ein innerliches Atmen ist, das mit der Gliedmaßen-Stoffwechselorganisation sich verbindet, das offenbart sich in der Fantasie-Tätigkeit.

Diese reicht dann seelisch in die Willenssphäre, wie der Zirkulationsrhythmus in die Stoffwechsel-Gliedmaßenorganisation reicht.

In der Fantasiebetätigung strebt die Denkorganisation an die Willensorganisation nahe heran. Es ist ein Untertauchen des Menschen in seine wachende Schlafsphäre des Willens. Es erscheinen daher bei Menschen, die in dieser Art organisiert sind, die Seelen-Inhalte wie Träume im Wachzustande. In Goethe lebte eine solche Menschen-Organisation. Daher spricht er davon, dass ihm Schiller seine dichterischen Träume deuten müsse.

In Schiller selbst war die andere Organisation wirksam. Er lebte aus dem heraus, was er sich aus den vorigen Erdenleben mitbrachte. Er musste zu einem starken Wollen den Fantasie-Inhalt suchen.

Auf Menschen, die nach der Fantasiesphäre hin veranlagt sind, sodass sich ihnen wie von selbst die Anschauung der sinnlichen Wirklichkeit in Fantasiebilder wandelt, zählt bei ihren Weltenabsichten die ahrimanische Macht. Sie meint, mit Hilfe solcher Menschen die Entwickelung der Menschheit von der

thinking, is farther removed from the lung-breathing, and is upheld by the human thinking-organization. And what reveals itself in the activity of fantasy is already very close to the rhythm of blood-circulation – it is a very inward breathing which comes into connection with the system of metabolism and the limbs.

In a soul sense, too, the activity of fantasy reaches down into the sphere of will, just as the circulatory system reaches down into the system of metabolism and limbs.

In the activity of fantasy, the thinking system comes close to the system of the will. The human being dives down into that sphere of his waking life which is asleep – the sphere of will. Hence, in human beings who are especially developed in this direction, the content of the soul appears like a dream in the waking state. Such a human organization was present in Goethe. Goethe once said that Schiller must interpret for him his own poetic dreams.

In Schiller himself, a different human system was at work. He lived on the strength of what he brought with him from former lives on earth. He had a strong life of will, and had to seek actively for the corresponding wealth of fantasy content.

The ahrimanic powers, in their world-intentions, count on those human beings who are so disposed to the sphere of fantasy that their perceptions of sensory reality transform as if by themselves into fantasy images. With the help of such human beings, the ahrimanic powers hope to be able to cut off the

Vergangenheit ganz abschneiden zu können, um sie in eine Richtung zu bringen, die *sie* will.

Auf Menschen, die nach der Willenssphäre hin organisiert sind, die aber die sinnliche Anschauung in Fantasiebilder aus innerer Liebe zur idealen Weltanschauung kräftig gestalten, zählt die luziferische Macht. Sie möchte die Menschheitsentwickelung durch solche Menschen ganz in den Impulsen der Vergangenheit erhalten. Sie könnte dann die Menschheit vor dem Untertauchen in die Sphäre bewahren, in der die ahrimanische Macht überwunden werden muss.

Man steht im Erdendasein in zwei polarischen Gegensätzen. Oben breiten sich die Sterne. Von da strahlen die Kräfte, die mit allem errechenbaren Regelmäßigen im Erdendasein zusammenhängen. Regelmäßiger Tag- und Nachtwechsel, Jahreszeiten, längere Weltperioden, sie sind die irdische Spiegelung dessen, was Sternen-Geschehen ist.

Der andere Pol strahlt vom Innern der Erde her. Unregelmäßiges lebt in ihm. Wind und Wetter, Donner und Blitz, Erdbeben, Vulkanausbrüche spiegeln dieses innere Erden-Geschehen.

Der Mensch ist ein Abbild dieses Sternen-Erdeseins. In seiner Denkorganisation lebt die Sternen-Ordnung, in seiner Gliedmaßen-Willensorganisation lebt das Erden-Chaos. In der rhythmischen Organisation wird in freiem Ausgleich das irdische Menschenwesen erlebt.

development of humanity from the past, and to bring it into a direction in accord with *their own* objective.

The luciferic power counts on those human beings who, while naturally more oriented toward the sphere of will, are inspired by an inner love for the ideal world-conception to powerfully shape their vision of sensory reality into fantasy images. Through such human beings, the luciferic power would like to keep human development entirely within the impulses of the past. It would thus be able to preserve humanity from diving down into the sphere where the ahrimanic power must be overcome.

In earthly existence, one stands between two opposite poles. Above are spread the stars. From the stars there radiate the forces connected with all things calculable and regular in earth-existence. The regular alternation of day and night, the seasons, and the longer cosmic periods are the earthly reflection of real stellar events.

The other pole radiates out from the interior of the earth. Irregular activities are at work in it. Wind and weather, thunder and lightning, earthquakes, and volcanic eruptions are reflections of these inner earthly events.

The human being himself is an image of this existence of the stars and earth. In his thinking system lives the order of the stars; in the willing system of his limbs lives the chaos of the earth. In the rhythmic system, he experiences his own earthly being in free balance and interplay between the two.

Leitsätze Nr. 174 bis 176

174. Der Mensch ist von zwei Seiten her geistig-leiblich organisiert. Erstens aus dem physisch-ätherischen Kosmos. Was in *diese* Organisation von göttlich-geistiger Wesenheit in die Menschenwesenheit hineinstrahlt, das lebt in dieser als Kraft der Sinneswahrnehmung, der Gedächtnisfähigkeit und der Fantasiebetätigung.

175. Zweitens ist der Mensch organisiert aus seinen vorangegangenen Erdenleben heraus. Diese Organisation ist ganz geistig-seelisch und lebt im Menschen durch Astralleib und Ich. Was sich an göttlich-geistigen Wesenheiten in diese Menschenwesenheit hineinlebt, dessen Wirkung leuchtet als Gewissensstimme und alles, was damit verwandt ist, im Menschen auf.

176. In seiner rhythmischen Organisation hat der Mensch die fortdauernde Verbindung der beiden Seiten göttlich-geistiger Impulse. Im Erleben des Rhythmus wird die Gedächtniskraft in das Willenssein und die Gewissensmacht in das Ideensein getragen.

Leading Thoughts 174 to 176

174. The human being is organized in spirit and in body from two different sides. First, from the physical-etheric cosmos. Whatever radiates from divine-spiritual Being into *this* organization in the human being's nature lives in it as the power of sense perception, the faculty of memory, and the activity of fantasy.

175. Secondly, the human being is organized out of his own past lives on earth. This organization is entirely spiritual-soul in nature, and lives in him through the astral body and the 'I'. Whatever elements of the divine-spiritual beings are able to live into this human nature – their influence lights up within the human being as the voice of conscience and all that is akin to this.

176. In his rhythmic organization, the human being has the constant union of the divine-spiritual impulses from these two sides. In the experience of rhythm, the force of memory is carried into the life of will and the power of conscience into the life of ideas.

Das scheinbare Erlöschen der Geist-Erkenntnis in der Neuzeit

Goetheanum, März 1925

Wer die Anthroposophie in ihrem Verhältnis zur Entwickelung der Bewusstseinsseele richtig beurteilen will, der muss immer von Neuem den Blick auf diejenige Geistesverfassung der Kulturmenschheit lenken, die mit dem Aufblühen der Naturwissenschaften beginnt und die im neunzehnten Jahrhundert ihren Höhepunkt erreicht.

Man stelle sich doch den Charakter dieses Zeitalters vor das Seelenauge hin und vergleiche ihn mit dem früherer Zeitalter. In aller Zeit der bewussten Menschheitsentwickelung war die Erkenntnis als das angesehen, was den Menschen mit der Geistwelt zusammenbringt. Was man im Verhältnis zum Geiste war, das schrieb man der Erkenntnis zu. In Kunst, in Religion *lebte* die Erkenntnis.

Das wurde anders, als die Morgendämmerung des Bewusstseinszeitalters begann. Da fing die Erkenntnis an, sich um einen großen Teil des menschlichen Seelenlebens nicht mehr zu kümmern. Sie wollte erforschen, was der Mensch als Verhältnis zum Dasein entwickelt, wenn er seine Sinne und seinen beurteilenden Verstand nach der «Natur» richtet. Aber sie wollte sich nicht mehr mit dem beschäftigen, was der

The Apparent Extinction of Spirit-Knowledge in Modern Times

Goetheanum, March 1925

To gain a correct judgment of Anthroposophy in relation to the development of the consciousness soul, one must turn one's gaze again and again to the particular mental outlook of civilized humanity which began with the blossoming forth of the science of nature and reached its high point in the nineteenth century.

One should place the character of this age vividly before the soul's eye, comparing it with that of preceding ages. In all ages of the conscious development of humanity, the pursuit of knowledge was regarded as that which brings the human being together with the world of spirit. What the human being had achieved as a relationship with spirit – this he ascribed to knowledge. In art, in religion, there *lived* knowledge.

All this changed when the age of the consciousness soul began to dawn. The pursuit of knowledge now gradually ceased to concern itself with a very great part of the human soul-life. Henceforth, it sought to investigate that relation to existence which the human being unfolds when he directs his senses and his intellectual powers of judgment to the world of "nature." But it no longer wanted to concern itself with what

Mensch als Verhältnis zur Geist-Welt entwickelt, wenn er sein inneres Wahrnehmungsvermögen so gebraucht wie die Sinne.

So entstand die Notwendigkeit, das geistige Leben des Menschen nicht an das Erkennen der Gegenwart anzuschließen, sondern an Erkenntnisse der Vergangenheit, an Traditionen.

Entzwei gespalten wurde das menschliche Seelenleben. Vor dem Menschen stand die Natur-Erkenntnis, immer weiter strebend auf der einen Seite, in lebendiger Gegenwart sich entfaltend. Auf der anderen Seite war das Erleben eines Verhältnisses zur geistigen Welt, für das die entsprechende Erkenntnis in älteren Zeiten erflossen war. Für *dieses* Erleben verlor sich allmählich alles Verständnis, wie die entsprechende Erkenntnis in der Vorzeit zustande gekommen ist. Man hatte die Überlieferung, aber nicht mehr den Weg, auf dem die überlieferten Wahrheiten *erkannt* worden sind. Man konnte nur an die Überlieferung *glauben.*

Der Mensch, der sich in voller Besonnenheit etwa um die Mitte des neunzehnten Jahrhunderts die geistige Situation überlegte, hätte sich sagen müssen: Die Menschheit ist dazu gekommen, sich nur noch für fähig zu halten, eine Erkenntnis zu entfalten, die mit dem Geiste nichts zu tun hat. Was über den Geist gewusst werden kann, hat eine frühere Menschheit erforschen können; die Fähigkeit zu dieser Erforschung ist aber der menschlichen Seele verlorengegangen.

the human being unfolds as a relation to the world of spirit when he makes use of his inner capacity of perception in the way he otherwise makes use of his outer senses.

Thus there arose the necessity to connect human spiritual life not with any living present knowledge, but with knowledge gained in the past – with tradition.

The life of the human soul was divided in two. On the one hand, there stood before the human being the new science of nature, striving ever onward and unfolding in the living present. On the other side, there was the experience of a relation to the spiritual world for which the corresponding knowledge had arisen in ages past. All understanding of how the knowledge corresponding to *this* side of human experience had been gained in ages past was gradually lost. Human beings possessed the tradition, but they had lost the path by which the truths of tradition had been *known* and discovered. All they could do was to *believe* in the tradition.

A human being who had reflected in full consideration on the spiritual situation in approximately the middle of the nineteenth century would have been bound to admit: Humanity has come to a point where it no longer feels itself capable of evolving any knowledge beyond a science that does not concern itself with the spirit. Whatever can be known about the spirit, a humanity of earlier ages was able to investigate – but the human soul has now lost the faculty for such investigation.

In der ganzen Tragweite stellte man sich nicht vor das Seelenauge, was da eigentlich vorlag. – Man beschränkte sich darauf, zu sagen: Erkenntnis reicht eben nicht bis zur geistigen Welt; diese *kann* nur Gegenstand des Glaubens sein.

Man blicke, um etwas Licht für diese Tatsache zu bekommen, in die Zeiten, in denen die griechische Weisheit vor dem christlich gewordenen Römertum zurückweichen musste. Als die letzten griechischen Philosophenschulen durch den Kaiser Justinian geschlossen wurden, wanderten auch die letzten Bewahrer alten Wissens aus dem Gebiete fort, auf dem nun das europäische Geisteswesen sich entwickelte. Sie fanden Anschluss bei der Akademie von Gondischapur in Asien. Sie war eine der Stätten, wo im Osten durch die Taten Alexanders die Überlieferung von dem alten Wissen sich erhalten hatte. In der Form, die Aristoteles diesem alten Wissen hat geben können, lebte es da.

Aber es wurde ergriffen von derjenigen orientalischen Strömung, die man als Arabismus bezeichnen kann. Der Arabismus ist nach der einen Seite seines Wesens eine verfrühte Entfaltung der Bewusstseinsseele. Er bot durch das in der Richtung der Bewusstseinsseele zu früh wirkende Seelenleben die Möglichkeit, dass sich in ihm von Asien aus über Afrika, Südeuropa, Westeuropa eine geistige Welle ergoss, die gewisse europäische Menschen mit einem Intellektualismus erfüllte,

But human beings did not place before themselves the full implication of what was taking place. – They were content to say: The forces of knowledge simply do not reach out into the spiritual world. The spiritual world *can only* be an object of faith.

To help shed some light on these facts of modern history, let us look back into the time when the old Grecian wisdom had to retreat before Christianized Rome. When the last Greek Schools of the Philosophers were closed by the Roman Emperor, the last custodians of the ancient knowledge likewise departed from the regions in which European spiritual life was henceforth to evolve. They found a connection to the Academy of Gondishapur in Asia, to which they now connected themselves. This was one of the places in the East where through the deeds of Alexander, the traditions of ancient knowledge had been preserved. The ancient knowledge continued to live on there in the form Aristotle had been able to give to it.

But in the Academy of Gondishapur, this knowledge was also taken hold of by that Eastern spiritual stream which one may designate as Arabism. Arabism, in one aspect of its nature, is a premature unfolding of the consciousness soul. Through the soul-life working prematurely in the direction of the consciousness soul, the possibility was given in Arabism for a spiritual wave to go forth, extending over Africa to southern and western Europe, and filling certain of the thinkers in Europe

der erst später kommen durfte; Süd- und Westeuropa bekamen im siebenten, achten Jahrhundert geistige Impulse, die erst im Zeitalter der Bewusstseinsseele hätten kommen dürfen.

Diese geistige Welle konnte das Intellektuelle im Menschen wecken, nicht aber das tiefere Erleben, durch das die Seele in die Geist-Welt taucht.

Wenn nun der Mensch im fünfzehnten bis zum neunzehnten Jahrhundert sein Erkenntnisvermögen in Tätigkeit brachte, so konnte er nur bis zu einer Seelentiefe untertauchen, in der er noch nicht auf die geistige Welt stieß.

Der in das europäische Geistesleben einziehende Arabismus hielt die erkennenden Seelen von der Geist-Welt zurück. Er brachte – verfrüht – den Intellekt zur Wirksamkeit, der nur die äußere Natur fassen konnte.

Und dieser Arabismus erwies sich als sehr mächtig. Wer von ihm erfasst wurde, in dem begann ein innerer – zum großen Teile ganz unbewusster – Hochmut, die Seele zu ergreifen. Er empfand die Macht des Intellektualismus; aber er empfand nicht das Unvermögen des *bloßen* Intellektes, in die Wirklichkeit einzudringen. So überließ er sich denn der äußeren sinnenfälligen Wirklichkeit, die sich durch sich selbst vor den Menschen hinstellte; aber er kam gar nicht darauf, an die geistige Wirklichkeit heranzutreten.

Dieser Lage sah sich das mittelalterliche Geistesleben

with an intellectualism that was not intended to come until a later stage. In the seventh and eighth centuries, southern and western Europe received spiritual impulses which ought to have emerged only in the age of the consciousness soul.

This spiritual wave was able to awaken an intellectual life in the human being, but not the deeper founts of experience whereby the soul penetrates into the world of spirit.

And now, when in the fifteenth to nineteenth centuries the human being exercised his capacity of knowledge, he could only reach down to those levels of the soul where he did not yet impinge upon the spiritual world.

Arabism, entering into the spiritual life of Europe, held back the knowing capacity of human souls from the world of spirit. It prematurely brought into activity that intellect which was only able to apprehend the outer world of nature.

This Arabism proved very powerful indeed. One who was taken hold of by it was seized by an inward – though for the most part quite unconscious – arrogance. He felt the power of intellectualism, but not the impotence of the *mere* intellect by itself when it comes to penetrating into reality. Thus he gave himself up to the externally given reality of the senses, which places itself before the human being of its own accord; and it did not even occur to him to approach the spiritual reality.

The spiritual life of the Middle Ages found itself face to

gegenüber. Es hatte die gewaltigen Überlieferungen von der Geist-Welt; aber sein Seelenleben war durch den – man möchte sagen: im geheimen – wirkenden Arabismus intellektualisch so imprägniert, dass sich der Erkenntnis kein Zugang bot zu den Quellen, aus denen der Inhalt dieser Überlieferung doch zuletzt stammte.

Es kämpfte nun vom frühen Mittelalter an das, was instinktiv in den Menschen als geistiger Zusammenhang gefühlt wurde, mit der Gestalt, die das Denken durch den Arabismus angenommen hatte.

Man fühlte die Ideenwelt in sich. Man erlebte sie als etwas Reales. Aber man fand in der Seele nicht die Kraft, in den Ideen den Geist zu erleben. So entstand der *Realismus*, der die Realität in den Ideen empfand, aber diese Realität nicht finden konnte. Der Realismus hörte in der Ideenwelt das Sprechen des Weltenwortes, er war aber nicht fähig, die Sprache zu verstehen.

Der *Nominalismus*, der sich ihm entgegenstellte, leugnete, weil das Sprechen nicht verstanden werden konnte, dass es überhaupt vorhanden sei. Für ihn war die Ideenwelt nur eine Summe von Formeln in der menschlichen Seele ohne eine Wurzelung in einer geistigen Realität.

Was in diesen Strömungen wogte, es lebte fort bis in das neunzehnte Jahrhundert. Der *Nominalismus* wurde die Denkungsart der Natur-Erkenntnis. Sie baute ein großartiges

face with this situation. It had the sublime traditions regarding the spiritual world. But the soul-life was intellectually so imbued with the hidden influence of Arabism that – one can say – medieval knowledge found no access to the sources from which the content of this great tradition had after all proceeded.

Thus, from the early Middle Ages onwards, what human beings felt instinctively within them as a connection with the spirit was battling with thought in the form that this had assumed under Arabism.

The human being felt the world of ideas within him; he experienced it as something real. But he could not find the power in his soul to experience the spirit within the ideas. Thus arose *Realism*, feeling the reality in the ideas and yet unable to discover it. In the world of the ideas, Realism heard the speaking of the Cosmic Word, but it could not understand the speech.

And *Nominalism*, arising in opposition to it and seeing that the sounding of the Word could not be understood, denied that there was any sounding at all. For Nominalism, the world of ideas was but a multitude of formulae within the human soul, without any rootedness in the reality of spirit.

What surged in these currents worked on into the nineteenth century. *Nominalism* became the mode of thought of the science of nature, which built up an imposing conceptual

System von Anschauungen der sinnenfälligen Welt auf, aber sie vernichtete die Einsicht in das Wesen der Ideenwelt. – Der *Realismus* lebte ein totes Dasein. Er wusste von der Realität der Ideenwelt; aber er konnte im lebendigen Erkennen nicht zu ihr gelangen.

Man wird zu ihr gelangen, wenn Anthroposophie den Weg finden wird von den Ideen zu dem Geist-Erleben *in den Ideen.* In dem wahrhaft fortgebildeten Realismus muss dem naturwissenschaftlichen Nominalismus ein Erkenntnisweg zur Seite treten, der zeigt, dass die Erkenntnis des Geistigen in der Menschheit nicht erloschen ist, sondern in einem neuen Aufstieg aus neu eröffneten menschlichen Seelenquellen in die menschliche Entwickelung wieder eintreten kann.

system of the outer world of sense, but destroyed the last relics of insight into the nature of the world of ideas. – *Realism* lived a dead existence. It still knew of the reality of the world of ideas, but was unable to reach it by means of an enlivened capacity of knowledge.

But one will reach it when Anthroposophy finds the way from the ideas to the living experience of spirit *in the ideas*. In Realism truly carried forward, there will arise – alongside the natural-scientific Nominalism – a path of knowledge which will prove that knowledge of the spiritual is not extinguished in humanity but can enter into human development once again, springing forth from newly-opened sources in the human soul.

Leitsätze Nr. 177 bis 179

177. Wer den Seelenblick auf die Entwickelung der Menschheit im naturwissenschaftlichen Zeitalter wirft, dem bietet sich zunächst eine traurige Perspektive. Glänzend wird die Erkenntnis des Menschen in Bezug auf alles, was Außenwelt ist. Dagegen tritt eine Art Bewusstsein ein, als ob eine Erkenntnis der Geist-Welt überhaupt nicht mehr möglich sei.

178. Es *scheint*, als ob eine *solche* Erkenntnis die Menschen nur in alten Zeiten gehabt hätten und als ob man mit Bezug auf die geistige Welt sich eben damit begnügen müsse, die alten Traditionen aufzunehmen und zu einem Gegenstande des Glaubens zu machen.

179. Aus der Unsicherheit, die aus diesem gegenüber dem Verhältnis des Menschen zur geistigen Welt im Mittelalter hervorgeht, entsteht der Unglaube an den Geist-Inhalt der Ideen im *Nominalismus*, dessen Fortsetzung die moderne Naturanschauung ist, und als Wissen von der Realität der Ideen ein *Realismus*, der aber erst durch die Anthroposophie seine Erfüllung finden kann.

Leading Thoughts 177 to 179

177. One who looks through the eye of the soul upon the development of humanity in the age of the science of nature will initially meet with a sorrowful perspective. The knowledge of human beings with respect to all that constitutes the outer world grew ever more brilliant. On the other hand, there arose a feeling as though knowledge of the spiritual world were no longer possible at all.

178. It *seems* as though *such* knowledge had only been the possession of human beings of ancient times, and that one must now rest content – in all that concerns the spiritual world – simply to receive the old traditions, making these an object of faith.

179. From the resulting uncertainty which arose in the Middle Ages as to the human being's relation to the spiritual world, there emerged the non-belief in the real spirit-content of ideas in *Nominalism*, whose continuation is the modern view of nature, and the awareness of the reality of ideas in *Realism*, which, however, can only find its fulfillment through Anthroposophy.

Die geschichtlichen Erschütterungen beim Heraufkommen der Bewusstseinsseele

Goetheanum, März 1925

Der Untergang des Römischen Reiches im Zusammenhang mit dem Auftreten von Völkern, die von Osten herankommen – der sogenannten Völkerwanderung –, ist eine geschichtliche Erscheinung, auf die der Blick des forschenden Menschen immer wieder sich richten muss. Denn die Gegenwart enthält noch vieles von Nachwirkungen dieser erschütternden Geschehnisse.

Aber das Verständnis gerade dieser Ereignisse ist einer äußerlichen geschichtlichen Betrachtung nicht möglich. Man muss auf die Seelen der Menschen blicken, die in «Völkerwanderung» und Untergang des römischen Kaiserreiches gestellt sind.

Griechentum und Römertum blühen in der Zeit, als sich in der Menschheit die Verstandes- oder Gemütsseele entfaltet. Ja, Griechen und Römer sind die eigentlichen Träger dieser Entfaltung. Aber die Entwickelung dieser Seelen-Etappe trägt bei diesen Völkern nicht einen Keim in sich, der in rechter Art die Bewusstseinsseele *aus sich* entwickeln könnte. Alles, was an Geist- und Seelen-Inhalt in der Verstandes- oder Gemütsseele steckt, tritt in reichem Leben in dem Dasein des Griechen- und Römertums zutage. Mit Eigenkraft hinüberströmen in die Bewusstseinsseele kann es nicht.

Historic Upheavals at the Dawn of the Consciousness Soul

Goetheanum, March 1925

The downfall of the Roman Empire and the appearance on the scene of peoples from the East – the great migrations – are a phenomenon of history to which researchers must ever and again turn their attention. For the present time still contains many aftereffects of these stirring events.

An understanding of these events is impossible for the considerations of merely exoteric history. For one must look into the souls of the human beings who were part of these "migrations" and witnessed the downfall of the Roman Empire.

Ancient Greece and Rome flourished in the time when the intellectual- or mind-soul was unfolding in humanity. Indeed, the Greeks and Romans were the actual bearers of this unfolding process. But in the Greek and Roman peoples, the development of this stage of the soul did not contain the germ *from out of which* the consciousness soul could truly have developed. All the content of soul and spirit latent in the intellectual- or mind-soul becomes visible in the rich life of ancient Greece and Rome. It is unable, out of its intrinsic force, to flow into the consciousness soul.

Trotzdem tritt natürlich das Stadium der Bewusstseinsseele auf. Aber es ist, als ob die Bewusstseinsseele nicht etwas aus der Persönlichkeit des Griechen und Römers Hervorgehendes wäre, sondern etwas *von außen* seinem Wesen Eingepflanztes.

Das Verbunden- und Losgelöst-Sein von den göttlich-geistigen Wesenheiten, von dem in diesen Betrachtungen so viel die Rede war, vollzieht sich im Laufe der Zeiten mit verschiedener Intensität. In alten Zeiten war es eine mit starkem Geschehen in die Menschheitsentwickelung eingreifende Macht. Im griechischen und römischen Erleben der ersten christlichen Jahrhunderte ist es eine schwächere Macht. Aber es ist vorhanden. Solange er voll in sich die Verstandes- oder Gemütsseele entfaltete, fühlte der Grieche und Römer – unbewusst, aber für die Seele bedeutsam – ein Losgelöst-Werden von der göttlich-geistigen Wesenhaftigkeit, ein Selbstständig-Werden des Menschhaften. Das hörte in den ersten christlichen Jahrhunderten auf. Das Hereindämmern der Bewusstseinsseele wurde als ein Verbundensein mit dem Göttlich-Geistigen empfunden. Man entwickelte sich wieder zurück von einer größeren zu einer geringeren Selbstständigkeit der Seele. Man konnte den christlichen Inhalt nicht in die menschliche Bewusstseinsseele aufnehmen, weil man diese selbst nicht in die menschliche Wesenheit hereinnehmen konnte.

So empfand man diesen christlichen Inhalt als etwas von

The stage of the consciousness soul did, of course, appear nonetheless. But the consciousness soul was something as if implanted *from outside* into the character of the Greek or Roman – something that really did not proceed out of the personality.

The connection with and severance from the divine-spiritual beings, which has been spoken of so much in these considerations, takes place with varying intensity in the course of succeeding ages. In olden times, it was a power entering into human development with the impulse of a mighty living process. In the Greek and Roman experience of the first Christian centuries, it was a weaker power – but it still existed. While he was unfolding the fullness of the intellectual- or mind-soul within himself, the Greek or Roman felt – unconsciously, but with no less deep a meaning for his soul – a loosening from the divine-spiritual essentiality and a growing independence of the human element. But this ceased in the first Christian centuries. The early dawn of the consciousness soul was felt as a state of connectedness with the divine-spiritual. Human beings evolved back again from a greater to a lesser degree of independence of soul. They could not receive the Christian content into the human consciousness-soul, for they were unable to receive the consciousness soul itself into their human being.

Thus they came to regard the Christian content as

außen – von der geistigen Außenwelt – Gegebenes, nicht aber als etwas, mit dem man durch seine Erkenntniskräfte zusammenwuchs.

Anders war es bei den in die Geschichte eintretenden, von Nordosten kommenden Völkern. Sie hatten das Stadium der Verstandes- oder Gemütsseele in einem Zustande durchgemacht, der sich für sie als Abhängigkeit von der Geistwelt empfinden ließ. Sie fingen erst an, etwas von der menschlichen Selbstständigkeit zu empfinden, als die ersten Kräfte der Bewusstseinsseele in den christlichen Anfängen heraufdämmerten. Bei ihnen trat die Bewusstseinsseele als etwas der Menschenwesenheit Verbundenes auf. Sie empfanden sich in froher innerer Kraftentfaltung, indem die Bewusstseinsseele in ihnen auflebte.

In dieses sprießende Leben der heraufdämmernden Bewusstseinsseele fiel bei diesen Völkern der christliche Inhalt. Sie fühlten ihn als etwas in der Seele Auflebendes, nicht als etwas von außen Gegebenes.

Das war die Stimmung, in der diese Völkerschaften an das Römische Reich und alles, was damit zusammenhing, herankamen. Das war die Stimmung des Arianismus gegenüber dem Athanasianismus. Ein tiefer innerer Gegensatz war in der weltgeschichtlichen Entwickelung da.

In der dem Menschen äußerlichen Bewusstseinsseele des

something given to them from outside – from the outer spiritual world – not as something with which they could become united through their own forces of knowledge.

But it was different with the peoples coming from the north-east, who now entered on the scene of history. They had passed through the stage of the intellectual- or mind-soul in a condition which, to them, conveyed a feeling of dependence on the spiritual world. They only began to feel something of human independence when, with the beginnings of Christianity, the earliest forces of the consciousness soul were dawning. In them the consciousness soul appeared as something deeply bound up with the human being. They felt a joyful sense of unfolding force within them when the consciousness soul was stirring into life.

It was into this new-springing life of the dawning consciousness soul that the Christian content entered in the case of these peoples. They felt the Christian content as something springing to life within their souls – not as something given from outside.

Such was the mood in which these peoples approached the Roman Empire and all that was connected with it. Such was the mood of Arianism in contrast to Athanasianism. It was a deep inner contrast in world-historical development.

In the consciousness soul of the Greek and Roman, external

Römers und Griechen wirkte zunächst die nicht völlig mit dem Erdenleben sich vereinende, sondern nur hereinstrahlende göttlich-geistige Wesenheit. In der erst aufdämmernden Bewusstseinsseele der Franken, Germanen und so weiter wirkte nur noch *schwach*, was von Göttlich-Geistigem mit der Menschheit sich verbinden konnte.

Das Nächste war, dass der christliche Inhalt, der in der über dem Menschen schwebenden Bewusstseinsseele lebte, sich im Leben ausbreitete; der mit der Seele vereinigt etwas blieb, das als Antrieb, Impuls in dem Innern der Menschen verblieb und auf seine Entfaltung wartete, die erst eintreten kann, wenn ein gewisses Stadium in der Entfaltung der Bewusstseinsseele erreicht ist.

Es ist die Zeit, von den ersten christlichen Jahrhunderten angefangen bis in das Zeitalter der Bewusstseinsseelenentwickelung hinein, eine solche, in der als maßgebliches Geistesleben über der Menschheit ein geistiger Inhalt waltet, mit dem sich der Mensch erkennend nicht verbinden kann. Er verbindet sich deshalb äußerlich; er «erklärt» ihn, und er denkt darüber nach, inwiefern die Seelenkräfte nicht ausreichend sind, um die erkennende Verbindung herbeizuführen. Er unterscheidet zwischen dem Gebiete, in das die Erkenntnis reicht, und dem, wohin sie nicht reicht. Es macht sich der Verzicht geltend, Seelenkräfte zu betätigen, die sich erkennend in die

as it was to the human being, there worked, to begin with, the divine-spiritual Being, not uniting fully with the earthly life, but raying into it from without. And in the consciousness soul of the Franks, the Germanic peoples, etc., which was only just dawning into life, such of the divine-spiritual as was able to unite with humanity worked as yet but *weakly*.

To begin with, the Christian content that came to life in the consciousness soul, which hovered over the human being, grew and expanded in outer life. On the other hand, that Christian content which united with the ordinary soul remained as an inner drive, an impulse within the human being waiting for a future development that would become possible only once a certain stage has been attained in the unfolding of the consciousness soul.

In the time from the first Christian centuries until the developmental epoch of the consciousness soul, the dominant spiritual life was a spirit-content hovering above humanity – a content with which the human being was quite unable to unite himself in knowledge. He therefore united with it in an outward way. He "explained" it, and he pondered over the question of how, and why, and to what degree the forces of the soul were insufficient to bring about the full union with this spirit-content in knowing. Thus he distinguished the realm into which the capacity of knowledge can penetrate from that into which it cannot. It became common to renounce the exercise

Geistwelt erheben. Und so kommt die Zeit heran, Wende des siebzehnten und achtzehnten Jahrhunderts, in der man sich mit den auf das Geistige gerichteten Seelenkräften von dem Geistigen überhaupt erkennend abwendet. – Man beginnt, nur in den Seelenkräften zu leben, die auf das sinnlich Wahrnehmbare gerichtet sind.

Stumpf werden die Erkenntniskräfte für das Geistige besonders im achtzehnten Jahrhundert.

Die Denker verlieren aus ihren Ideen den geistigen Inhalt. Sie machen im Idealismus von der ersten Hälfte des neunzehnten Jahrhunderts die geistleeren Ideen selbst als schaffenden Welt-Inhalt geltend. So Fichte, Schelling, Hegel; oder sie weisen auf ein Übersinnliches, das sich verflüchtigt, weil es entgeistigt ist. So Spencer, John Stuart Mill und andere. Die Ideen sind tot, wenn sie den lebendigen Geist nicht suchen.

Der geistige Blick für das Geistige geht nun einmal verloren.

Eine «Fortsetzung» des alten Geist-Erkennens ist nicht möglich. Es müssen die Seelenkräfte, indem die Bewusstseinsseele sich in ihnen entfaltet, ihre erneuerte elementare, unmittelbar lebendige Verbindung mit der Geist-Welt erstreben. Anthroposophie will dieses Erstreben sein.

of those faculties of soul which raise themselves with knowing insight into the spiritual world. And at length the time approached – the turn of the seventeenth and eighteenth centuries – in which the forces of the soul inclining toward the spirit were diverted from the spiritual altogether, as far as the active experience of knowing was concerned. – The human being began to live his conscious life exclusively in those forces of the soul directed to the sense-perceptible.

Blunt indeed became the forces of knowledge for the spiritual – especially in the eighteenth century.

The thinkers now lost the spiritual content from their ideas. In the Idealism of the first half of the nineteenth century, the spirit-empty ideas themselves are represented as the creative substance of the world. Thus Fichte, Schelling, Hegel. Or again, they point to a suprasensory element which vanishes into thin air because it is bereft of spirit. Thus Spencer, John Stuart Mill, and others. The ideas are dead when they no longer seek the living spirit.

The sense of spiritual vision for matters of the spirit is now lost.

A "continuation" of the old life of knowledge of the spirit is impossible. With the consciousness soul unfolding within him, the human being's powers of soul must strive onward to reach their renewed, elemental, and immediately living union with the world of spirit. Anthroposophy wishes to be this striving.

Im geistigen Leben des Zeitalters wissen gerade die führenden Persönlichkeiten zunächst nicht, was sie will. Und damit werden weite Kreise, die diesen Führern folgen, auch abgehalten. Die Führer leben in einem Seelen-Inhalt, der sich allmählich ganz entwöhnt hat, die geistigen Kräfte zu gebrauchen. Für sie ist es, als ob man einen Menschen, der ein gelähmtes Organ hat, veranlassen wollte, dieses zu gebrauchen. Denn gelähmt waren in der Zeit vom sechzehnten bis in die zweite Hälfte des neunzehnten Jahrhunderts die höheren Erkenntniskräfte. Und die Menschheit blieb darüber ganz unbewusst; sie betrachtete das einseitige Gebrauchen der auf die Sinnenwelt gerichteten Erkenntnis als einen besonderen Fortschritt.

In the spiritual life of this age, it is precisely the leading personalities who, to begin with, do not know what Anthroposophy intends. Wide circles of people who follow in their wake are thereby kept away from Anthroposophy. The leading personalities of our time live in a soul-content which, in the course of time, has grown altogether unaccustomed to the use of spiritual capacities. For them, it is as though one would call upon a human being who has a paralyzed organ, to use that organ. For the higher forces of knowledge were paralyzed from the sixteenth into the latter half of the nineteenth century. And humanity remained utterly unconscious of the fact; indeed, the one-sided application of the forces of knowledge directed to the outer sense-world was regarded as a particular step forward.

Leitsätze Nr. 180 bis 182

180. Die Griechen und Römer sind die für die Entfaltung der Verstandes- oder Gemütsseele besonders veranlagten Völker. Sie entwickeln dieses Seelenstadium zur Vollendung. Aber sie tragen nicht die Keime in sich, um in geradliniger Art fortzuschreiten zur Bewusstseinsseele. Ihr Seelenleben geht in die Verstandes- oder Gemütsseele hinein unter.

181. Aber es waltet nun in der Zeit von der Entstehung des Christentums bis in das Zeitalter der Bewusstseinsseelen-Entwickelung eine Geistwelt, die sich nicht mit den menschlichen Seelenkräften vereinigt. Diese «erklären» die Geistwelt, aber sie erleben sie nicht.

182. In den Völkern, die mit der sogenannten «Völkerwanderung» von Nordosten gegen das Römerreich vorrücken, lebt ein gefühlsmäßiges Erfassen der Verstandes- oder Gemütsseele. Dagegen bildet sich in ihren Seelen die in dieses Gefühlsmäßige eingebettete Bewusstseinsseele aus. Das innere Leben dieser Völker wartet auf die Zeit, in der wieder ein Vereinigt-Sein der Seele mit der Geist-Welt voll möglich ist.

Leading Thoughts 180 to 182

180. The Greeks and Romans were the peoples predisposed by their very nature for the unfolding of the intellectual- or mind-soul. They developed this stage of soul to perfection. But they did not bear within them the germinal seeds of a direct, unbroken progress to the consciousness soul. Their soul-life went under in the intellectual- or mind-soul.

181. In the time from the origin of Christianity until the age of the development of the consciousness soul, a world of spirit held sway which did not unite with the forces of the human soul. The latter attempted to "explain" the world of spirit, but they could not experience it.

182. The peoples advancing from the northeast in the so-called "migrations," encroaching on the Roman Empire, took hold of the intellectual- or mind-soul more in the inner life of feeling. Meanwhile, embedded in this element of feeling, the consciousness soul was evolving within their souls. The inner life of these peoples was waiting for the present time, when the reunion of the soul with the world of the spirit is fully possible once more.

Von der Natur zur Unter-Natur

Goetheanum, März 1925

Man spricht davon, dass mit der Überwindung des philosophischen Zeitalters das *naturwissenschaftliche* in der Mitte des neunzehnten Jahrhunderts heraufgezogen ist. Und man spricht auch so, dass dieses naturwissenschaftliche Zeitalter heute noch andauert, indem zugleich viele betonen, man habe sich zu gewissen philosophischen Intentionen wieder zurückgefunden.

Das alles entspricht den Erkenntniswegen, die die neuere Zeit eingeschlagen hat, nicht aber den *Lebenswegen*. Mit seinen Vorstellungen lebt der Mensch noch in der Natur, wenn er auch das mechanische Denken in die Naturauffassung hineinträgt. Mit seinem Willensleben aber lebt er in so weitem Umfange in einer Mechanik des technischen Geschehens, dass dies dem naturwissenschaftlichen Zeitalter seit Langem eine ganz neue Nuance gegeben hat.

Will man das menschliche Leben verstehen, so muss man es zunächst von zwei Seiten her betrachten. Aus den vorigen Erdenleben bringt sich der Mensch die Fähigkeit mit, das Kosmische aus dem Erden-Umkreis und das im Erdenbereich wirkende vorzustellen. Er nimmt durch die Sinne das auf der Erde wirksame Kosmische wahr, und er denkt durch seine

From Nature to Sub-Nature

Goetheanum, March 1925

The age of philosophy is often said to have been superseded, at about the middle of the nineteenth century, by the rising age of *the science of nature*. And it is said that the age of the science of nature still continues into our time, although many people are likewise at pains to emphasize that one has found one's way once more to certain philosophic tendencies.

All this is true of the paths of knowledge that the modern age has taken, but not of its *paths of life*. With his representations, the human being still lives in nature, even if he carries the mechanical habit of thought into his concept of nature. But with his life of will he lives in the mechanical processes of technology to such a far-reaching an extent that it has long imbued this age of science with an entirely new nuance.

To understand human life, one must initially consider it from two sides. From his former lives on earth, the human being brings with him the faculty to inwardly represent the cosmic element which works inward from the earth's circumference and within the earthly realm itself. Through his senses, he perceives the cosmic element at work upon the earth;

Denkorganisation das aus dem Erden-Umkreis auf die Erde hereinwirkende Kosmische.

So lebt er durch seinen physischen Leib im Wahrnehmen, durch seinen Ätherleib im Denken.

Das, was in seinem astralischen Leib und in seinem Ich vor sich geht, waltet in verborgeneren Regionen der Seele. Es waltet zum Beispiel im Schicksal. Aber man muss es zunächst nicht in den komplizierten Schicksalszusammenhängen, sondern in den elementarischen, einfachen Lebensvorgängen aufsuchen.

Der Mensch verbindet sich mit gewissen Erdenkräften, indem er seinen Organismus in diese Kräfte hineinorientiert. Er lernt aufrecht stehen und gehen, er lernt mit seinen Armen und Händen sich in das Gleichgewicht der irdischen Kräfte hineinstellen.

Nun sind *diese* Kräfte keine solchen, die vom Kosmos hereinwirken, sondern die *bloß* irdisch sind.

In Wirklichkeit ist nichts eine Abstraktion, das der Mensch erlebt. Er durchschaut nur nicht, woher das Erlebnis kommt, und so bildet er aus Ideen über Wirklichkeiten Abstraktionen. Der Mensch redet von der mechanischen Gesetzmäßigkeit. Er glaubt, sie aus den Naturzusammenhängen heraus abstrahiert zu haben. Das ist aber nicht der Fall, sondern alles, was der Mensch an rein mechanischen Gesetzen in der Seele

through his thinking organization, he conceives and thinks the cosmic influences working downward to the earth from the earth-circumference.

Thus the human being lives through his physical body in perception, and through his etheric body in thought.

What takes place in his astral body and his 'I' holds sway in the more hidden regions of the soul. It holds sway, for example, in his destiny. One must, however, look for it, to begin with, not in the complicated relationships of destiny, but in the simple and elemental processes of life.

The human being connects himself with certain earthly forces in that he gives his body its right orientation within them. He learns to stand and walk upright; he learns to place himself, with arms and hands, into the equilibrium of earthly forces.

Now *these* are not forces working inward from the cosmos. They are *merely* earthly forces.

In reality, nothing that the human being experiences is an abstraction. He only fails to perceive from where it is that an experience comes to him; and thus he turns ideas about realities into abstractions. He speaks of the laws of mechanics. He thinks he has abstracted them from the connections and relationships of nature. But this is not the case. All that the human being experiences in his soul by way of purely mechanical laws has

erlebt, ist an seinem Orientierungsverhältnis zur Erdenwelt (an seinem Stehen, Gehen usw.) innerlich erfahren.

Damit aber kennzeichnet sich das Mechanische als das rein Irdische. Denn das Naturgesetzmäßige, in Farbe, Ton und so weiter, ist im Irdischen aus dem Kosmos zugeflossen. Erst im Erdenbereich wird auch dem Naturgesetzmäßigen das Mechanische eingepflanzt, wie ihm der Mensch mit seinem eigenen Erleben erst im Erdenbereich gegenübersteht.

Das weitaus meiste dessen, was heute durch die Technik in der Kultur wirkt und in das er mit seinem Leben im höchsten Grade versponnen ist, das ist *nicht Natur*, sondern *Unter-Natur*. Es ist eine Welt, die sich nach unten hin von der Natur emanzipiert.

Man sehe, wie der Orientale, wenn er nach dem Geiste strebt, herauszukommen sucht aus den Gleichgewichtszuständen, die bloß vom Irdischen kommen. Er nimmt eine Meditationsstellung an, die ihn in das bloße kosmische Gleichgewicht hineinbringt. Die Erde wirkt dann nicht mehr auf die Orientierung seines Organismus. (Dies sei nicht zur Nachahmung, sondern nur zur Verdeutlichung des hier Vorgebrachten gesagt. Wer meine Schriften kennt, weiß, wie sich in dieser Richtung östliches und westliches Geistesleben unterscheiden.)

been experienced inwardly through his own orientation in relation to the earthly world (in standing, walking, and so forth).

The mechanical is thus characterized as that which is of a purely earthly nature. For the laws and processes of nature, as they hold sway in color, sound, etc., have entered into the earthly realm from the cosmos. It is only within the earthly realm that these laws too become imbued with the mechanical element, just as is the case with the human being himself, who does not confront the mechanical in his conscious experience until he comes within the earthly realm.

By far the greater part of what works into modern civilization through technology – in which the life of the human being is so intensely interwoven – is *not nature*, but *sub-nature*. It is a world which emancipates itself from nature – emancipates itself in a downward direction.

Look how the person of the East, when striving toward the spirit, seeks to get out of the conditions of equilibrium whose origin is in the merely earthly realm. He assumes a demeanor of meditation which brings him again into the purely cosmic balance. In this demeanor, the earth no longer influences the inner orientation of his body. (This is not being recommended for imitation; it is mentioned merely to clarify what was presented before. Anyone familiar with my writings will know how the Eastern and Western forms of spiritual life are differentiated in this sense.)

Der Mensch brauchte die Beziehung zu dem bloß Irdischen für seine Bewusstseinsseelenentwickelung. Da kam denn in der neuesten Zeit die Tendenz zustande, überall auch im Tun das zu verwirklichen, in das sich der Mensch einleben muss. Er trifft, indem er sich in das bloß Irdische einlebt, das Ahrimanische. Er muss sich mit seinem eigenen Wesen in das rechte Verhältnis zu diesem Ahrimanischen bringen.

Aber es entzieht sich ihm in dem bisherigen Verlauf des technischen Zeitalters noch die Möglichkeit, auch gegenüber der ahrimanischen Kultur das rechte Verhältnis zu finden. Der Mensch muss die Stärke, die innere Erkenntniskraft finden, um von Ahriman in der technischen Kultur nicht überwältigt zu werden. Die Unter-Natur muss als solche begriffen werden. Sie kann es nur, wenn der Mensch in der geistigen Erkenntnis mindestens gerade so weit hinaufsteigt zur außerirdischen Über-Natur, wie er in der Technik in die Unter-Natur heruntergestiegen ist. Das Zeitalter braucht eine *über* die Natur gehende Erkenntnis, weil es innerlich mit einem gefährlich wirkenden Lebensinhalt fertig werden muss, der unter die Natur heruntergesunken ist. Es soll hier natürlich nicht etwa davon gesprochen werden, dass man zu früheren Kulturzuständen wieder zurückkehren soll, sondern davon, dass der Mensch den Weg finde, die neuen Kulturverhältnisse in ein rechtes Verhältnis zu sich und zum Kosmos zu bringen.

The human being needed this relation to the purely earthly for the development of his consciousness soul. Thus in recent times there has arisen a strong tendency to bring to realization everywhere, also in active doing, this element into which the human being had to enter. Insofar as he enters into the merely earthly element, he meets with the ahrimanic. With his own being he must now bring himself into a right relation to the ahrimanic.

But in the age of technology thus far, the possibility of finding a right relationship to the ahrimanic civilization has escaped the human being. He must find the strength, the inner force of knowledge, that will allow him not to be overcome by Ahriman in this technological civilization. He must understand sub-nature for what it really is. This he can do only if he rises, in the capacity of knowledge of the spirit, at least as far into supra-nature beyond this world as he has descended, in technology, into sub-nature. This age requires a capacity of knowledge that *transcends* nature, because in its inner life it must come to grips with a life-content which has sunk far beneath nature – a life-content whose influence is perilous. Needless to say, there can be no question here of advocating a return to earlier states of civilization; rather, the point is that the human being shall find the way to bring the new conditions of modern culture into a right relation both to himself and to the cosmos.

Heute fühlen noch die wenigsten, welche bedeutsamen geistigen Aufgaben sich da für den Menschen herausbilden. Die Elektrizität, die nach ihrer Entdeckung als die Seele des natürlichen Daseins gepriesen wurde, sie muss erkannt werden in *ihrer* Kraft, von der Natur in die Unter-Natur hinabzuleiten. Es darf der Mensch nur nicht mitgleiten.

In der Zeit, in der es eine von der eigentlichen Natur unabhängige Technik noch nicht gab, fand der Mensch den Geist *in* der Naturanschauung. Die sich unabhängig machende Technik ließ den Menschen auf das Mechanistisch-Materielle als das für ihn nun Wissenschaftlich-Werdende hinstarren. In diesem ist nun alles Göttlich-Geistige, das mit dem Ursprunge der Menschheitsentwickelung zusammenhängt, abwesend. Das rein Ahrimanische beherrscht die Sphäre.

In einer Geistwissenschaft wird nun die andere Sphäre geschaffen, in der ein Ahrimanisches gar nicht vorhanden ist. Und gerade durch das erkennende Aufnehmen derjenigen Geistigkeit, zu der die ahrimanischen Mächte keinen Zutritt haben, wird der Mensch gestärkt, um *in der Welt* Ahriman gegenüberzutreten.

There are very few as yet who even feel the greatness of the spiritual tasks approaching the human being in this direction. Electricity, for instance, celebrated since its discovery as the very soul of nature's existence, must be recognized in *its* power of leading down from nature to sub-nature. But the human being should not glide along with it.

In the age when there was not yet a technology independent of true nature, the human being found the spirit *within* his view of nature. But the technology which emancipates itself has caused him to stare more and more fixedly at the mechanical-material aspect of life, as what he now considers the scientific realm. In this, the entirety of the divine-spiritual connected with the origin of human development is completely absent. The purely ahrimanic dominates this sphere.

Through a science of the spirit, another sphere will now be created in which there is no ahrimanic element. It is precisely through the knowing reception of this spirituality to which the ahrimanic powers have no access, that the human being is strengthened to confront Ahriman *within the world*.

Leitsätze Nr. 183 bis 185

183. Im naturwissenschaftlichen Zeitalter, das um die Mitte des neunzehnten Jahrhunderts beginnt, gleitet die Kulturbetätigung der Menschen allmählich nicht nur in die untersten Gebiete der Natur, sondern *unter* die Natur hinunter. Die Technik wird Unter-Natur.

184. Das erfordert, dass der Mensch erlebend eine Geist-Erkenntnis finde, in der er sich eben so hoch in die Über-Natur erhebt, wie er mit der unternatürlichen technischen Betätigung unter die Natur hinuntersinkt. Er schafft dadurch in seinem Innern die Kraft, *nicht* unterzusinken.

185. Eine frühere Naturanschauung barg noch den Geist in sich, mit dem der Ursprung der menschlichen Entwickelung verbunden ist; allmählich ist dieser Geist aus der Naturanschauung geschwunden und der rein ahrimanische ist in sie eingezogen und von ihr in die technische Kultur übergeflossen.

Leading Thoughts 183 to 185

183. In the age of natural science, since about the middle of the nineteenth century, the cultural endeavors of human beings are gradually sliding downward, not only into the lowest regions of nature, but even *beneath* nature. Technology becomes sub-nature.

184. This requires that the human being find, in conscious experience, a form of spirit-knowing wherein he will rise as high into supra-nature as in his sub-natural technological activities he sinks beneath her. Thereby he creates within himself the inner strength *not* to go under.

185. A past conception of nature still bore within it the spirit connected with the source of all human development; gradually, this spirit vanished altogether from humanity's view of nature. The purely ahrimanic element has entered in its place, and has flowed from the view of nature into the reality of technological culture.

ITA WEGMAN INSTITUTE FOR BASIC RESEARCH INTO ANTHROPOSOPHY

At the Ita Wegman Institute for Basic Research into Anthroposophy, the study led by Dr. phil. Rudolf Steiner (1861 – 1925) developed anthroposophical spiritual science in the form of writings and lectures in the history of ideas, with a biographical emphasis on his work and in the context of the scientific and social history of the 19th and 20th centuries.

The Institute maintains several publicly accessible working archives based on the estates of pioneering collaborators of Rudolf Steiner, especially in the fields of medicine, curative education and pedagogy.

The work of the Ita Wegman Institute is supported by various foundations – primarily the Software AG Foundation (Darmstadt) – as well as an international circle of friends and supporters.

Pfeffinger Weg 1A · CH 4144 Arlesheim · Switzerland
Head: Prof. Dr. P. Selg
www.wegmaninstitut.ch · E-mail: sekretariat@wegmaninstitut.ch